KV-638-661

NOVELL'S

LDAP Developer's Guide

ROGER G. HARRISON, JIM SERMERSHEIM, STEVE TROTTIER

Novell.
PRESS

Novell Press
Provo, UT

Novell's LDAP Developer's Guide

Published by
Novell Press
1800 S. Novell Place
Provo, UT 84606

Copyright © 2000 Novell, Inc. All rights reserved. No part of this book, including interior design, cover design, and icons, may be reproduced or transmitted in any form, by any means (electronic, photocopying, recording, or otherwise) without the prior written permission of the publisher.

ISBN: 0-7645-4720-8

Printed in the United States of America

10 9 8 7 6 5 4 3 2 1

1B/QR/QZ/QQ/FC

Distributed in the United States by IDG Books Worldwide, Inc.

Distributed by CDG Books Canada Inc. for Canada; by Transworld Publishers Limited in the United Kingdom; by IDG Norge Books for Norway; by IDG Sweden Books for Sweden; by IDG Books Australia Publishing Corporation Pty. Ltd. for Australia and New Zealand; by TransQuest Publishers Pte Ltd. for Singapore, Malaysia, Thailand, Indonesia, and Hong Kong; by Gotop Information Inc. for Taiwan; by ICG Muse, Inc. for Japan; by Intersoft for South Africa; by Eyrolles for France; by International Thomson Publishing for Germany, Austria, and Switzerland; by Distribuidora Cuspide for Argentina; by LR International for Brazil; by Galileo Libros for Chile; by Ediciones ZETA S.C.R. Ltda. for Peru; by WS Computer Publishing Corporation, Inc., for the Philippines; by Contemporanea de Ediciones for Venezuela; by Express Computer Distributors for the Caribbean and West Indies; by Micronesia Media Distributor, Inc. for Micronesia; by Chips Computadoras S.A. de C.V. for Mexico; by Editorial Norma de Panama S.A. for Panama; by American Bookshops for Finland.

For general information on IDG Books Worldwide's books in the U.S., please call our Consumer Customer Service department at 800-762-2974. For reseller information, including discounts and premium sales, please call our Reseller Customer Service department at 800-434-3422.

For information on where to purchase IDG Books Worldwide's books outside the U.S., please contact our International Sales department at 317-572-3993 or fax 317-572-4002.

For consumer information on foreign language translations, please contact our Customer Service department at 800-434-3422, fax 317-572-4002, or e-mail rights@idgbooks.com.

For information on licensing foreign or domestic rights, please phone +1-650-653-7098.

For sales inquiries and special prices for bulk quantities, please contact our Order Services department at 800-434-3422 or write to IDG Books Worldwide, 919 E. Hillsdale Blvd., Suite 400, Foster City, CA 94404.

For information on using IDG Books Worldwide's books in the classroom or for ordering examination copies, please contact our Educational Sales department at 800-434-2086 or fax 317-572-4005.

For press review copies, author interviews, or other publicity information, please contact our Public Relations department at 650-653-7000 or fax 650-653-7500.

For authorization to photocopy items for corporate, personal, or educational use, please contact Novell, Inc., Copyright Permission, 1800 S. Novell Place, Mail Stop PRV-A231, Provo, UT 84606 or fax 801-228-7077.

For general information on Novell Press books in the U.S., including information on discounts and premiums, contact IDG Books Worldwide at 800-434-3422 or 650 655-3200. For information on where to purchase Novell Press books outside the U.S., contact IDG Books International at 317-572-3993 or fax 317-572-4002.

Library of Congress Cataloging-in-Publication Data

Harrison, Roger
    Novell's LDAP developer's guide / Roger Harrison, Jim Sermersheim, Steve Trottier.
       p. cm.
    ISBN 0-7645-4720-8 (alk. paper)
    1. Application software--Development. 2. Computer network protocols. I. Title: LDAP developer's guide. II. Sermersheim, Jim. III. Trottier, Steve. IV. Title.
QA76.76.A65 H365 2000
005.7'13769--dc21   00-059785

LIMIT OF LIABILITY/DISCLAIMER OF WARRANTY: THE PUBLISHER AND AUTHOR HAVE USED THEIR BEST EFFORTS IN PREPARING THIS BOOK. THE PUBLISHER AND AUTHOR MAKE NO REPRESENTATIONS OR WARRANTIES WITH RESPECT TO THE ACCURACY OR COMPLETENESS OF THE CONTENTS OF THIS BOOK AND SPECIFICALLY DISCLAIM ANY IMPLIED WARRANTIES OF MERCHANTABILITY OR FITNESS FOR A PARTICULAR PURPOSE. THERE ARE NO WARRANTIES WHICH EXTEND BEYOND THE DESCRIPTIONS CONTAINED IN THIS PARAGRAPH. NO WARRANTY MAY BE CREATED OR EXTENDED BY SALES REPRESENTATIVES OR WRITTEN SALES MATERIALS. THE ACCURACY AND COMPLETENESS OF THE INFORMATION PROVIDED HEREIN AND THE OPINIONS STATED HEREIN ARE NOT GUARANTEED OR WARRANTED TO PRODUCE ANY PARTICULAR RESULTS, AND THE ADVICE AND STRATEGIES CONTAINED HEREIN MAY NOT BE SUITABLE FOR EVERY INDIVIDUAL. NEITHER THE PUBLISHER NOR AUTHOR SHALL BE LIABLE FOR ANY LOSS OF PROFIT OR ANY OTHER COMMERCIAL DAMAGES, INCLUDING BUT NOT LIMITED TO SPECIAL, INCIDENTAL, CONSEQUENTIAL, OR OTHER DAMAGES.

Trademarks: Novell, NetWare, the Novell Press logo, GroupWise, ManageWise, Novell Directory Services, and NDPS are registered trademarks; Novell Press, NDS eDirectory, Novell BorderManager, ZENworks, and Novell Distributed Print Services are trademarks; CNE is a registered service mark; and CNI and CNA are service marks of Novell, Inc. in the United States and other countries. All brand names and product names used in this book are trade names, service marks, trademarks, or registered trademarks of their respective owners. IDG Books Worldwide is not associated with any product or vendor mentioned in this book.

John Kilcullen, *CEO, IDG Books Worldwide, Inc.*
Richard K. Swadley, *Senior Vice President, Technology Publishing*

The IDG Books Worldwide logo is a registered trademark or trademark under exclusive license to IDG Books Worldwide, Inc. from International Data Group, Inc. in the United States and/or other countries.

Novell.
PRESS

Phil Richardson, *Publisher, Novell Press, Novell, Inc.*

Novell Press and the Novell Press logo are registered trademarks of Novell, Inc.

Welcome to Novell Press

Novell Press, the world's leading provider of networking books, is the premier source for the most timely and useful information in the networking industry. Novell Press books cover fundamental networking issues as they emerge — from today's Novell and third-party products to the concepts and strategies that will guide the industry's future. The result is a broad spectrum of titles for the benefit of those involved in networking at any level: end user, department administrator, developer, systems manager, or network architect.

Novell Press books are written by experts with the full participation of Novell's technical, managerial, and marketing staff. The books are exhaustively reviewed by Novell's own technicians and are published only on the basis of final released software, never on prereleased versions.

Novell Press at IDG Books Worldwide is an exciting partnership between two companies at the forefront of the knowledge and communications revolution. The Press is implementing an ambitious publishing program to develop new networking titles centered on the current versions of NetWare, GroupWise, BorderManager, ManageWise, and networking integration products.

Novell Press books are translated into several languages and sold throughout the world.

Phil Richardson
Publisher
Novell Press, Novell, Inc.

Novell Press

Publisher
Phil Richardson

IDG Books Worldwide

Acquisitions Editors
Jim Sumser
Ed Adams

Project Editor
Chandani Thapa

Development Editor
Alex Miloradovich

Technical Editors
Steve Merrill
Renea Campbell
Russ Weiser
Pat Felsted

Copy Editor
Cindy Lai

Proof Editor
Patsy Owens

Project Coordinators
Danette Nurse
Joe Shines

Permissions Editor
Carmen Krikorian

Graphics and Production Specialists
Robert Bihlmayer
Darren Cutlip
Jude Levinson
Michael Lewis
Victor Pérez-Varela
Ramses Ramirez

Quality Control Technician
Dina F Quan

Media Development Manager
Laura Carpenter

Media Development Specialist
Travis Silvers

Media Development Coordinator
Marisa Pearman

Illustrators
Brian Drumm
Rashell Smith
Gabriele McCann

Proofreading and Indexing
York Production Services

About the Authors

Roger G. Harrison has been an employee of Novell since 1994 and is currently a team leader for NDS eDirectory management tools and utilities. He received his B.S. degree in Electrical Engineering from Brigham Young University in 1990 and was employed at 3M Health Information Systems in Murray, Utah from 1990 to 1994.

During his career, he has worked on a variety of software projects including clinical information systems, user interface research and development, e-mail servers, portable networking services platforms, and directory services. He actively participates in LDAP-related working groups of the IETF and has authored or co-authored several Internet-Drafts. He has presented papers on user interface design methodologies, networking services, and directory services at several conferences.

Roger is married to Julie Ann Ellsworth and has two daughters, Rachelle and Megan, and two sons, Tanner and Spencer. In quieter moments, Roger enjoys cooking — especially Mexican food, rollerblading, and running a shelter and out-placement service for homeless hi-fi equipment.

During his eleven year stay at Novell Inc. and WordPerfect Corporation, **Jim Sermersheim** has developed and tested various aspects of WordPerfect, helped architect, create, document, and support several Automated Test Application Programming Interfaces. He contributed to the design of various aspects of JNDI and has written several JNDI providers which expose NDS eDirectory and NetWare through Java.

Jim is an active participant in IETF working groups, which concentrate on LDAP and has authored and co-authored a number of IETF Internet-Drafts on the subject of LDAP. He currently works on the NDS eDirectory LDAP server team at Novell where he serves as part-time standards guru, part-time architect, and full-time debugger.

Jim lives in Utah with his wife Roni and three children, Stephen, Matthew, and Hailey. Now that the Grateful Dead has stopped touring, Jim spends his leisure time dawdling in his yard and backyard mountains.

Steve Trottier has worked for Novell since 1991 and has focused on NDS eDirectory related technologies since 1995. He received his B.S. degree in computer science from Utah Valley State College in 1998. His senior project there involved researching and comparing the use of DCOM and CORBA with Java.

Steve married Allison Sampson in 1990 and they have three children: Sarah, Jonathan, and David. He enjoys reading, skiing, amateur astronomy, and exploring the mountains of Utah.

To Julie, for believing in me. — RH

For my family, who encouraged and supported me. — JS

To Allison, for her patience and love. — ST

Foreword

The Internet is quickly becoming an ocean of information and valuable services that is difficult to navigate or control without some kind of structure. Moreover, with bandwidth and access speeds increasing, and storage becoming nearly limitless, the number of devices and services are being added at a phenomenal rate.

It makes perfect sense, therefore, that individuals and institutions are embracing Novell Directory Services (NDS eDirectory) because it brings order to this chaos. It gives an identity to every user, device, service, and each object on the Internet and it provides a single point of network management that makes secure Internet transactions possible.

There is no other directory that provides the power or the scalability of NDS eDirectory. Novell has had NDS eDirectory functioning and operating on NetWare for years and has made this technology available on other platforms as well (UNIX, Linux, and NT). It should come as no surprise that NDS eDirectory is recognized worldwide for its security, performance, and accessibility.

As NDS eDirectory becomes more and more universal, there is a clear need for access to NDS eDirectory from all platforms, applications, and services. The easier it is for software engineers to access and interface with NDS eDirectory, the better. After all, what good is information if it just sits in a repository or is used only by a select few? By the same token, what good is a directory if the information in it is not secure?

The Lightweight Directory Access Protocol (LDAP) has become the standard for directory access. LDAP is a protocol that is backed by the Internet Engineering Task Force (IETF) — the same organization that brought the world TCP/IP, SMTP, HTTP, FTP, and other widely used Internet protocols. Perhaps even more important, LDAP is the directory access protocol being adopted by virtually every directory vendor on the planet.

Software developers can now write directory-enabled applications that leverage the power of the Internet to store information that's accessible anytime from anyplace. They can also personalize your content based on who's using the application. Instead of reinventing the wheel, users can leverage the data already stored in network directories for a particular application. And developers can write their application using one directory protocol — LDAP — that will work with any LDAP server.

Novell understands the power of directory-enabled network computing, and Novell is actively committed to LDAP. We have spent several years creating and enhancing our LDAP implementation and we're actively involved in the IETF to shape LDAP's future and ensure that developers have the tools they need to deliver on the promises of the Internet to their customers.

Ultimately, as important as directory and directory access protocols are to the future of the industry, it is the applications and services written for the Internet that will determine how truly valuable the Internet will be to our future. *Novell's LDAP Developer's Guide* takes you into the world of directory-enabled computing and shows you how to harness the power of LDAP and NDS eDirectory to make it happen.

Dr. Eric Schmidt
Chairman and CEO
Novell, Inc.

Preface

If you've ever written a sizeable application, you've probably discovered that you needed a place to store information for it. Like many developers, you may have written a small database program or used an existing database to store that information. A network directory is a specialized database that allows you to store such information in a centrally accessible location so that it is available to your application from anywhere that network connectivity is available. Access to the information stored in a directory can be securely controlled, and if your application uses data about people or organizations, it may be able to leverage data that already exists in a network directory rather than having to recreate some or all of it.

As the Internet molds the environment in which we do computing, the ability to store and retrieve information from network directories has changed from an esoteric feature into a required commodity for many computing applications. Although Novell Directory Services (NDS eDirectory) has been used by millions of customers for nearly a decade, it has traditionally used a proprietary directory access protocol called Novell Directory Access Protocol (NDAP). The Lightweight Directory Access Protocol (LDAP) is an open, Internet directory access protocol that has been embraced by many vendors and holds the promise of allowing application developers to write directory-enabled applications that can interoperate with any vendor's LDAP directory without rewriting.

Novell's LDAP Developer's Guide was written by Novell software engineers who develop and test Novell's LDAP implementation. Unlike other LDAP books that focus primarily on a set of client APIs, *Novell's LDAP Developer's Guide* takes a holistic view of LDAP that extends from the client APIs through the wire protocol and on to the server implementation. It explains LDAP from bottom to top and Novell's LDAP implementation from the inside out so that you can immediately begin to leverage the full power of LDAP directories for your application's information.

► . . . . ◄

Introduction

In designing a book that discusses LDAP in general and Novell's LDAP implementation in particular, we wanted to achieve four goals.

First, we wanted to provide you, the reader, with a solid foundation of information you can fall back on when you need to solve a tough coding problem or debug a program that isn't working the way you expect it to. While it is certainly possible to write working programs with nothing more than an SDK and some documentation about the APIs it implements, we have always believed that it is far easier for developers to achieve the results they desire if they possess a thorough understanding of what is occurring behind the scenes.

Rather than present an API set and a description of what those APIs do, we have chosen to take a more in-depth approach that will provide you with the ability to see *through* the APIs and visualize what *really* happens when your LDAP application makes calls to those APIs. As we present each topic, we work from the theoretical to the practical. First, we explain the relevant LDAP and directory concepts and give examples. Next, we present useful information on how these features are implemented in Novell's Directory Service. Finally, we give code examples that demonstrate how to elicit the behavior we have described.

We feel that this approach will prove to be an invaluable aid in debugging your applications or when you encounter other unexpected behavior.

Second, we recognize that some mistakes are more common than others. We want you to be able to concentrate on bringing your directory-enabled application to life, not on dealing with mundane configuration and coding issues. We have included advice and tips based on our own experience writing applications for Novell's LDAP server as well as insight from answering hundreds of customer questions about Novell's LDAP server to steer you past problems and on to your destination.

Third, as a developer, you need a broad range of information to successfully design, write, and deploy your application. We make sure you understand the basics of LDAP, and we also cover advanced topics such as schema management, referrals, and LDAP utilities that you'll find very useful as you design and package your application.

Finally, while the promise of LDAP is to provide a standard Internet directory access protocol where applications and servers from many vendors can be freely intermixed and are completely interoperable, that promise is still being fulfilled. Although there are currently several good LDAP server implementations commercially available, there are also still some quirks and interoperability issues between various vendors' versions of LDAP. Novell, like other vendors, is actively perform-ing interoperability testing of its LDAP client and server with other LDAP implementations and resolving the issues that it finds. With this in mind, we have highlighted areas where you may find that Novell's Directory Service behaves dif-ferently from other implementations.

Audience

Novell's LDAP Developer's Guide is written for several audiences.

Novell developers currently using traditional NDS Directory APIs who are porting their existing NDS eDirectory applications to use LDAP or who are writing new NDS eDirectory applications using LDAP will find many details on how Novell's LDAP service uses the rich features of NDS eDirectory. They will also find information showing the correlation between legacy NDS Directory APIs and LDAP APIs.

Developers writing new LDAP applications will find everything they need to successfully write and deploy an LDAP application. We start with the basics of LDAP and work to advanced topics giving practical advice and code examples along the way.

Developers porting existing LDAP applications to NDS eDirectory are pro-vided with the nitty-gritty details of Novell's LDAP implementation that are invalu-able in completing a quick, successful port. From information on installing and configuring NDS eDirectory to explanations of the inner workings of NDS eDirectory, developers who already understand LDAP and need to understand NDS eDirectory will find what they're looking for.

NDS eDirectory Administrators who are responsible for deploying and administering NDS eDirectory systems using LDAP. If you've heard of LDAP but don't know what it is, we'll bring you up to speed. We'll show you how to use the Novell Import/Export Utility to load your directory with data. We'll also show you how to configure NDS eDirectory to get the best LDAP performance possible and give you lots of insider tips based on our development experience as engineers on Novell's LDAP server, client, and utilities.

Presentation

The book is organized into three parts followed by several appendixes.

Part I, LDAP Basics, introduces LDAP and Novell's LDAP server. It is an introduction to LDAP in general and Novell's LDAP implementation in particular. It presents the foundational concepts that you'll need to know as you read through the remainder of the book and shows you how to install a functioning NDS eDirectory LDAP server to use for your development efforts.

Chapter 1 provides an introductory tour of LDAP including its data model, schema, and operations. The chapter concludes with an example program that demonstrates many of the concepts discussed during the chapter. Since many of the topics discussed in this book are interrelated, Chapter 1 is also designed to provide you with a basic working vocabulary of LDAP terms, so that later chapters can assume a fundamental knowledge of LDAP as they cover their topics in depth.

Chapter 2 acquaints you with Novell's LDAP implementation. It explains how to install NDS eDirectory, including Novell's LDAP server, perform some common configuration tasks, and test that the server is properly functioning.

Part II, Coding and Development, is the heart of the book. It presents Novell's LDAP SDK and then covers all of the features of LDAP in depth, beginning with basic topics such as connecting and authenticating and moving all the way to advanced topics such as schema management and LDAP extensions. While each chapter is independent, we've included them in the order we think you'll use the information. Part II assumes you are familiar with the basic LDAP concepts presented in Chapter 1 and have access to a working version of NDS eDirectory to test your code.

In **Chapter 3**, we present the Novell LDAP SDKs and discuss the data structures and principles that overarch the remaining chapters in the section.

Chapter 4 explains how to locate, connect, and authenticate (bind) to LDAP servers. It covers several authentication options including anonymous binds, using simple passwords, and SASL mechanisms. The chapter also shows you how to establish SSL encrypted connections to an LDAP server.

Retrieving data is the most common operation performed on an LDAP server, and it is the topic of **Chapter 5**. A single operation — search — is used for all data retrieval. The chapter covers the many search options available including search filters and using LDAP URLs to describe search operations.

A directory isn't much good unless you can create new entries or modify existing entries. **Chapter 6** explains the LDAP object manipulation operations: add, modify, rename/move (moddn) and delete.

The data stored in a directory is subject to a set of rules called the schema, and your LDAP application is likely to need to extend the schema to store its information in the directory. In **Chapter 7**, we explain LDAP schema in detail and show you how to manage, read, and modify the schema.

NDS eDirectory is a distributed, partitioned, replicated directory that can store data on several cooperating servers in the same directory tree. **Chapter 8** explains how Novell's LDAP implementation implements both the chaining and referral models of name resolution to provide LDAP access to directory data stored on any server in your NDS eDirectory tree and gives advice on how to configure LDAP name resolution.

Chapter 9 explains two standard ways that LDAP can be extended: controls and extensions. It shows how to write LDAP applications that use two common controls: the Server Side Sorting (SSS) control and the Virtual List View (VLV) control. It also provides a sneak preview into the mechanics of writing your own LDAP server extension.

We cover a couple of **Advanced Topics** in **Part III**, including server administration and LDIF utilities. In the following chapters we jump into the ways that you can fine-tune and speed up your LDAP server and show how to quickly load your directory with information.

Chapter 10 covers server administration, configuration, and tuning topics including configuring SSL connections, creating indexes, and setting database cache sizes.

In **Chapter 11**, we present LDIF, a commonly used language used to represent directory data and explain the Novell Import/Export Utility which can be used to import and export LDIF data as well as perform data migration between LDAP servers.

The **Appendixes** include

- ▶ Information about the contents of the CD-ROM included with this book

- ▶ Solutions to common problems

- ▶ Resources where you can get more help

> ► A summary of the differences between NDAP and LDAP (along with a handy table showing the correlation between the two API sets)

> ► A glossary of LDAP and related terms used in the book

Conventions Used in the Book

Because LDAP is a product of the IETF, it is specified in RFCs and Internet-Drafts. We refer to these documents throughout the book. For your convenience, these documents have also been included on the CD-ROM that accompanies this book. Appendix A contains more information about the location of these documents on the CD-ROM.

There are currently several SDKs that use LDAP to talk to directories. As we designed this book, we felt that trying to demonstrate two or more of these SDKs in the book would be problematic. If we switched SDKs from example to example, we would lose continuity of thought, and showing all the examples for more than one SDK was too unwieldy to be practical. Our approach of explaining concepts first and the SDK second means that nearly all of the material in the book is equally applicable to any LDAP SDK you may choose to use. We have chosen to show our code examples in the book in Java, however code examples in the book that are identified by a listing number are also included on the CD-ROM in both Java and C versions.

LDAP is an exciting technology. We hope you'll enjoy learning about it and using it as much as we have!

Acknowledgments

There are too many people who deserve my thanks to name them all, but a few cannot go without mention. First and foremost, I'd like to thank Julie, Rachelle, Megan, Tanner, and Spencer for letting me take the time away from them to write. Second, my father and mother, Gerald and Lynda Harrison, for being "mean" enough to always make me do my best. Shirley Eldredge, Ila Hodgson, and Max Egley, for giving me a love of learning, a love of reading, and a love of writing. Steve Richins and Jim Ritchie, two of the great examples in my life. Larry Cousin and Doug Rawdon, for honing my writing skills on the rocks of the Superstition Mountains. Roger Bond, Shawn Hurley, Bill McIntyre, and Hal Kartchner for listening to my ongoing saga and never complaining, even once. And Gary Anderson, for being the first to make me read the LDAP RFCs.

— Roger

I'm very thankful to my wife Roni and my three children for the support, encouragement, and lack of complaints they gave me through my long bouts of huddling over the keyboard and for keeping vigil over my memory while I was missing. I also need to send a long overdue thanks to my parents Jerry Sermersheim and Judy Cole for patiently allowing me as a child, to systematically dismantle practically everything they owned just to see how it worked. Thanks to my friends — especially Don LaVange for grounding me with his ever-gentle smile as I would rant about one problem or another, and gurus like Ed Reed and Dale Olds who patiently explained and reexplained the directory in terms I could understand. Finally, thanks to that benevolent mystery of life for always amazing me.

— Jim

Thanks to Allison and the kids for putting up with their absentee dad. Their love and support has fueled me to finish this project. If nothing else, I've learned how to answer if anyone asks me to write a book again. Thanks to my parents, Don Trottier for giving me curiosity about the world, and Julia Stephenson for giving me faith and good sense.

Thanks to Dave Heldenbrand for being the best teacher I ever had. He presented networking concepts in a way that kept me interested, and gave me good advice when I was considering participation in this project.

— Steve

ACKNOWLEDGMENTS

Our sincere appreciation to Layne Izatt, Pat Felsted, Dave Steck, John Aurich, Dave Wilbur, Renea Campbell, Steve Merrill, Yulin Dong, Eddie Pulido, James Whitchurch, Blaine Southam, Monty Wiseman, Troy McArthur, and lots of others in NDS Engineering who supported this project, gave us advice, answered our dumb questions, and kept us technically honest. Todd Peterson, Mike Westover, Brandon Dalling, and Greg Jones for helping us work out permissions for the Novell SDKs. Darren Geddes for his input. Russ Weiser, our technical editor. Dan Marshall, Phil Richardson, and Marci Shanti at Novell Press for believing in the project and helping us work out the tough details. Ed Adams, Chandani Thapa, Cindy Lai, and all the folks at IDG Books whose professional polish made us shine!

Contents at a Glance

Contents

LDAP Basics

CHAPTER 1

An Introduction to LDAP

The *Lightweight Directory Access Protocol*, most commonly known as LDAP, is quickly emerging as the preferred Internet protocol for accessing directory information. If you're writing Internet applications today and you need to store information related to the application or the people and organizations who use it, you'll likely want to store it in a directory — a network data repository. In the past, if you wrote such an application, you would likely have had to write your own proprietary directory to store this sort of information. Today, several LDAP server implementations are commercially available and widely deployed. This, coupled with the advantage of being able to use a standard protocol to access the data stored in any of them, makes the choice to use LDAP an easy one.

In this chapter, we give you a broad overview of LDAP and most of the concepts you'll encounter in this book. First, we explore the history of LDAP and briefly discuss its future. Next, we explain how data is represented in an LDAP directory and introduce the rules governing data storage. We cover the basics of the protocol itself, including the naming conventions used for data in the directory and the way messages are sent between client and server. We then give you a brief overview of each of the LDAP operations and describe what they do. Finally, we show you how easy it is to use LDAP by presenting a sample program that reads the information from an LDAP directory.

When you finish reading this chapter, you'll have a clear idea of what LDAP is and what it can do for you. Of course, this chapter is meant to be an introduction to the protocol. In subsequent chapters, all this material is covered in depth. It's important, however, that you become familiar with the basic concepts presented here before you move on to more advanced topics, because most of them are interrelated.

What Is LDAP?

LDAP is an Internet protocol for accessing the data stored in a network directory. It is based on the OSI X.500 directory service model. Although LDAP is in its third revision and is beginning to mature, work is actively continuing in order to extend and enhance the protocol; the goal is to make LDAP fulfill its promise as a standard way for network applications to access distributed directory information from anywhere it is stored.

LDAP's Roots

LDAP is aptly named. It was originally conceived as a simpler way for personal computing applications to access information stored in directories based on the OSI X.500 directory service. Traditional X.500 clients use the *Directory Access Protocol*, DAP, which allows rich interaction between client and server but also tends to be complex. In some cases, the processing power required by X.500 clients overwhelmed the desktop computing power available. The designers of LDAP wanted something that would allow clients and client programmers to easily leverage the power of directories without all of the complexities associated with the full X.500 DAP. The resulting protocol, LDAP, provides the most useful functionality of DAP while excluding redundant, esoteric, and less-used DAP functionality. The result was a "lightweight directory access protocol."

LDAP and the IETF

The designers of LDAP chose an open forum in which to promote their protocol. The Internet Engineering Task Force (IETF) has become the home for ongoing work in the LDAP space. The IETF is the body that designs, records, and promotes the protocols used in the Internet. The IETF and its associated bodies pride themselves on an open, egalitarian approach to designing and publishing Internet protocol standards. All official and unofficial documents of the IETF, including Internet-Drafts, Proposed Internet Standards, and Internet Standards, are freely and publicly available. Anyone who is interested may participate in discussions regarding the design of Internet protocols, including LDAP. The IETF also prefers to promote standards that are free of intellectual property constraints.

The LDAP Advantage

This Internet-based, open standards approach to the development of LDAP has contributed significantly to its popularity and widespread adoption as a directory access protocol standard. Numerous vendors are shipping LDAP-compliant directory services, and many others are shipping LDAP-based directory-enabled applications. One of the primary advantages you gain by writing your directory-enabled application using LDAP is that it is then compatible with LDAP directories from many leading vendors, including Novell's LDAP implementation, which is the primary focus of this book.

Ongoing LDAP Standards Work

Although it was not a formal standard, the initial University of Michigan LDAP implementation became a de facto standard that generated interest in LDAP. In 1995, LDAPv2 was defined in Request for Comments (RFC) 1777 and RFC 1778. Since that time, work on LDAP has continued. LDAPv3 was advanced to proposed-standard status in the IETF in December 1997, in RFCs 2251–2256.

As of this writing, two working groups in the Applications Area of the IETF are actively pursuing LDAP-related work. The LDAP Extensions Working Group (LDAPEXT) is doing work to extend LDAPv3 in various ways, including the following:

▶ Defining a standard access control model

▶ Providing additional internationalization support for LDAP clients

▶ Supporting dynamic directory information

▶ Defining mechanisms for storing knowledge references within LDAP servers

▶ Specifying methods for LDAP server discovery

▶ Defining a version of LDAP that runs over connectionless protocols such as UDP

▶ Generating a standard set of LDAP application programming interfaces (APIs) for C and Java

The LDAP Duplication/Replication/Update Protocols Working Group (LDUP) is defining an architecture and associated protocols to enable replication of data across servers running different implementations of LDAP. Its charter includes

▶ Standardizing multi-master replication that allows data to be updated on any of several servers containing a copy of the data and have it replicate to all other servers that have copies of the data

▶ Standardizing master/slave replication that allows data to be stored on many servers but updated only on a single master copy; the updates then replicate to the other slave servers

▶ Defining a replication architecture

▶ Describing a replication information model

▶ Designing a replication information transport protocol

▶ Providing support for administering replicas and replication agreements

▶ Documenting the methodology and procedure for replicating updates among multiple masters

More information on IETF documents and working groups can be found at http://www.ietf.org.

Why Directories?

At this point you may be wondering what directories are and why you should want to use one in your application. Or maybe you've heard that directories and LDAP are cool technologies but no one has told you why. Please indulge us for a moment while we briefly explain the need for directories and extol their virtues.

Special-Purpose Directories

Most computer applications need to store information about their configuration, users, and so on. In the past, virtually every one of these applications kept its information within some sort of proprietary database that only that application knew how to access and interpret. Each of these databases is essentially a special-purpose directory.

One of the disadvantages of special-purpose directories is that the information is often stored in a proprietary format, so it is accessible only to the application for which it is was generated. This means that two applications needing to store similar information, such as user names, would probably duplicate at least some of the information. It is estimated that an average large corporation has more than 100 of these special-purpose directories, so the potential for data duplication and the associated hassle of maintaining the duplicate data everywhere it occurs can be tremendously costly.

Another disadvantage of many special-purpose directories is that they are not network-enabled. This prevents clients on other machines from accessing the information stored within them. Even if they are network-enabled, the network protocol they use may be proprietary, making it difficult or impossible for programmers to access the data they contain.

It is interesting to note that these problems are not confined to the corporate workspace. To alleviate these same problems, the IETF Directorate actively encourages working groups within the IETF to use LDAP directories to store configuration information.

General-Purpose Network Directories

Unlike special-purpose directories, general-purpose network directories are designed to enable data sharing among many applications. Because the directory can be accessed over a network, applications can access the data from anywhere. General-purpose directories can store a variety of information about the various entities that participate in a computer network, including organizations, users, printers, file systems, and so on. Although general-purpose directories have certain rules about what they store and how the data is structured, these rules can be extended to accommodate new uses.

In today's world, where Internet connectivity is becoming almost as common as telephone access, directory-enabled applications provide many desirable benefits. Your directory-enabled application will be easier to deploy because it can leverage existing directory information. Your directory-enabled application will be cheaper to administer because it shares common data with other directory-enabled applications rather than forcing administrators to synchronize it manually. If your application stores configuration information for each user in the directory, your users will be unchained from their desks and can access your application independent of the location where they are doing their work. This is because the directory is network centric not machine centric. And best of all, these benefits increase exponentially, rather than linearly, as more directory-enabled applications share a directory.

The LDAP Data Model

Before diving into the details of writing LDAP-enabled applications, let's take a quick look at the way data is represented in LDAP directories. Understanding the terms and concepts introduced in this chapter is key to understanding the rest of this book, but don't let us scare you. The vocabulary isn't large, and it's really not complicated. Our goal is to introduce you to all of the basic concepts underlying LDAP so that you have a base of knowledge to which you can add as you become an LDAP expert. If you're already familiar with Novell Directory Services (NDS), you'll find many familiar terms and concepts. Even if you have no previous directory experience, you'll quickly gain a solid foundation on which you can build as you continue through the other chapters in this book and beyond.

Entries, Directory Trees, and Attributes

A directory is a collection of *entries*. Generally, entries are arranged in a hierarchical fashion. For this reason, a collection of entries is called a *Directory Information Tree* (DIT), which is frequently shortened to *tree*.

Superior Entries, Subordinate Entries, and Containers

An entry that is above another entry in the tree is its *superior*, and an entry below another entry in the tree is its *subordinate*. Some entries are allowed to contain other entries. These entries are referred to as *containers*. By definition, the superior of every entry is a container.

Entry Hierarchy

Many organizations are organized as hierarchies. For instance, a corporation might be organized as shown in Figure 1.1.

The entries in a directory can be organized to precisely match the corporate hierarchy that is shown in Figure 1.1. A container entry could be used to represent Acme Corp. It, in turn, would have three other subordinate container entries, one for each of the divisions. The entries for the Consumer Products and Wholesale Products divisions would each have two additional subordinate container entries for Sales and Marketing, which would hold entries for the employees in those sales and marketing organizations. The Product Engineering division entry would also contain entries for the people employed in that division.

FIGURE 1.1

A hypothetical corporate organization

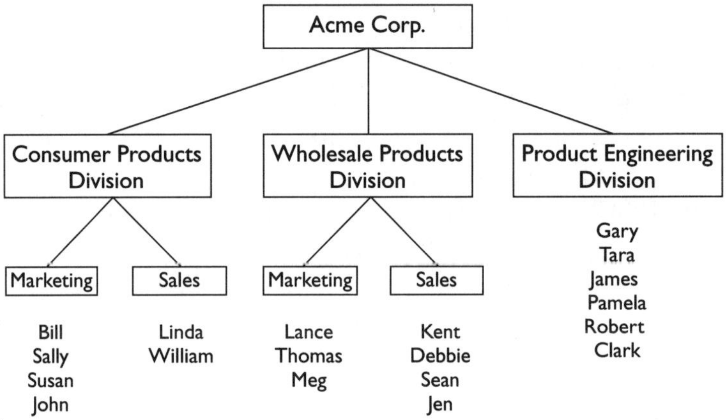

Attributes

Each entry has one or more pieces of data associated with it. These pieces of data are called *attributes*. To help you understand the idea of entries and attributes, imagine that you have an entry that is going to represent a person. The attributes of the entry would be pieces of information about that person, such as a name, an address, a telephone number, an e-mail address, a title, and so on.

Object Classes

Every entry has an attribute that specifies the *object class* of the entry, which in turn controls what other attributes can be stored in the entry. In the case of an entry for a person, you would pick an object class, such as the inetOrgPerson object class, that includes the attributes that are commonly associated with people.

Distinguished Names

Entries have several characteristics. Each entry is uniquely identified by a name called a *Distinguished Name* or DN. Every entry also has one or more attributes used to identify or name the entry. For instance, the inetOrgPerson object class uses the commonName attribute to store the naming value for entries that use it.

Attribute Values

Each attribute of an entry has one or more data *values*. Some attributes can have only one value and are thus referred to as being *single-valued*. Other attributes may have more than one value and are said to be *multi-valued*. The rules that determine whether an attribute is single-valued or multi-valued are part of the directory schema, which we'll discuss shortly. When you retrieve the attribute of an entry from the directory, you get all of the values associated with the attribute whether it is one or many.

The reason for having single- and multi-valued attributes is to help the directory model data in the real world. Some characteristics of an entity have only a single value; other characteristics may have many values. For instance, at any given time, a person has only one height. It would not make much sense to store several height values for a person. How would you even know which one to use if you did? On the other hand, a person could have several e-mail addresses, telephone numbers, or titles. If you weren't allowed to store more than one value in these attributes, you wouldn't be able to model a lot of real people very well at all.

Figure 1.2 illustrates an entry with multiple attributes, each of which has one or more values.

F I G U R E I.2

Relationship between an entry, its attributes, and their values

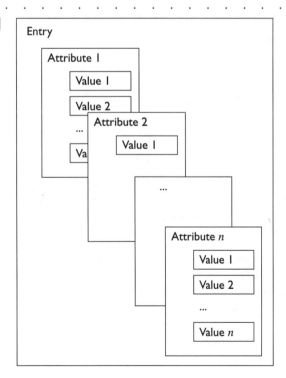

An Entry and Its Attributes

To help you better understand the relationship between an entry and its attributes, let's look at the information you might find about a person in a directory. Figure 1.1 shows a hypothetical corporate organization. The directory entry for Bill might have several attributes, some of which are single-valued and some of which are multi-valued, as in the following example:

```
Entry: Bill Smith
    Attribute: title
            Value: Division Manager
            Value: Vice President
    Attribute: employeeNumber
            Value: 123456
    Attribute: cn
            Value: Bill Smith
            Value: William Smith
    Attribute: givenName
            Value: William
    Attribute: sn (surname)
            Value: Smith
    Attribute: telephoneNumber
            Value: 415 445 4248
            Value: 415 445 4249
    Attribute: facsimileTelephoneNumber
            Value: 415 445 8290
```

In this example, Bill has seven attributes: `title`, `employeeNumber`, `cn`, `givenName`, `sn`, `telephoneNumber`, and `facsimileTelephoneNumber`.

- ► Bill's title attribute is multi-valued and has two values, Division Manager and Vice President, because Bill is a vice president of Acme Corp and also happens to manage the Consumer Products Division of the company.

- ► Bill's employee number is single valued. It doesn't make sense for an employee to have more than one employee number, so the employee number attribute can only store one value.

▶ The cn attribute stores values for an entry's "common name." Many different entry types can have a cn attribute, but in the case of entries that represent people, the cn attribute is typically the person's full name. The cn attribute is multi-valued and, in Bill's case, it has two values, Bill Smith and William Smith, because Bill's legal name is William but he generally goes by Bill.

▶ Just like the cn attribute, the givenName attribute contains two values: Bill and William, because Bill goes by more than just his given name.

▶ Although many people go by nicknames in our society, generally people have only a single surname, so the surname attribute is single-valued. The surname attribute for Bill contains the value Smith.

▶ The telephoneNumber is multi-valued, and Bill has two telephone numbers.

▶ The facsimileTelephoneNumber is a multi-valued attribute; however, Bill has only one fax number stored on his entry. This means that if Bill gets a second fax line, he'll be able to add the information to the facsimileTelephoneNumber attribute of his entry.

We'll come back to the topic of entries and their associated attributes and values in a bit, but first, we need to explain some additional concepts.

A Simple Introduction to LDAP Schema

A directory needs rules about how its data should be stored in order to ensure that data is stored in an orderly, logical fashion. Without such rules data would likely be strewn about in a chaotic mess (a lot like the papers on my desk!), and you'd have a tough time knowing how to properly add new information or find information you were looking for. Rather than leave order to chance, LDAP directories enforce a set of rules about the way the directory data is structured and stored. These rules are collectively called *schema*. Schema includes the following types of information:

- ► Syntaxes

- ► Matching rules

- ► Attribute types

- ► Object classes

- ► Naming and containment rules

We'll talk about each of these schema elements in due course.

If someone tries to store data in a way that isn't allowed by the schema, the directory rejects the attempt. This guarantees that the data your LDAP application accesses is structured according to a set of well-defined rules that your application can read from each LDAP server to which it connects.

We won't take the time to give you all of the details of LDAP schema here (we're saving that for Chapter 7), but we need to introduce you to some basic schema concepts now to help you understand the rest of the material in this chapter.

Object Identifiers

Elements of schema need to be defined in a globally unique way to prevent two different elements from inadvertently sharing the same name and thus causing confusion. To meet this need, *Abstract Syntax Notation One* (ASN.1) *Object Identifiers*, commonly referred to as OIDs, are assigned as unique identifiers for schema elements. OIDs are usually represented in *dotted-decimal* form as strings of period-separated numbers, such as 2.5.6.3 or 1.3.6.1.4.1.1466.115.121.1.27.

OIDs are allocated hierarchically, so all OIDs beginning with the same sequence of numbers are subordinate to that sequence. For instance, 2.4.6.3, 2.4.6.3, and 2.5.6.19.22.13.44 are all subordinate to 2.5.6.

Only the owner of a superior OID can define the meaning of its subordinates. For example, only the owner of 2.5.6 can define what 2.5.6.3 means. This method of assigning OIDs guarantees that all OIDs can be assigned uniquely. Each number within an OID can grow arbitrarily large, and the OID hierarchy can also be arbitrarily deep to accommodate an infinite number of unique identifiers.

Syntaxes

A *syntax* determines the type of information that can be represented by an attribute value, and it also determines the types of comparison operations that are performed on the value. LDAP has a well-defined set of syntaxes, each of which is identified by an OID. These syntaxes are defined in RFC 2252 and RFC 2256. Examples of LDAP syntaxes include INTEGER, Printable String, and Generalized Time.

For example, the INTEGER syntax would allow a value like 5782, but a string value like "abcdefg" would be invalid. INTEGER syntax would also say that the value 10 is greater than the value 2 when performing comparisons. The Printable String syntax, on the other hand, would say that a value of "10" is less than a value of "2" because it comes first in dictionary order, but wouldn't allow you to store binary, non-printing values.

Attribute Types

As we mentioned earlier, every entry has attributes associated with it. Attribute types serve as definitions for actual attributes that are stored on entries. The directory schema lists all of the *attribute types* that can be stored in the directory. Quite a few fields can be included in an attribute type, so we save a detailed discussion on all of them for Chapter 7. Right now, we show you some of the most common fields that are included in attribute types to give you a feel for what attribute types look like.

An attribute type is represented as a string value containing various fields. Only one, an OID, is required; all the other fields are optional. Some of the fields that you commonly encounter in an attribute type include the following:

- ▸ An OID that acts as a unique identifier

- ▸ A human-readable name

- ▸ Matching rules to be used for the attribute

▶ A syntax

▶ A flag that indicates the attribute is single valued

▶ A description

For example, the LDAP attribute type for a telephone number is defined as:

```
( 2.5.4.20
    NAME 'telephoneNumber'
    DESC 'Standard Attribute'
    EQUALITY telephoneNumberMatch
    SUBSTR telephoneNumberSubstringsMatch
    SYNTAX 1.3.6.1.4.1.1466.115.121.1.50{32} )
```

The OID for the telephoneNumber attribute type is 2.5.4.20, its name is telephoneNumber, and it's a standard attribute. The equality matching rule is the telephoneNumberMatch, and the substring matching rule is the telephone NumberSubstringsMatch. Attribute values must conform to the telephone number syntax identified by 1.3.6.1.4.1.1466.115.121.1.50, and implementations should allow telephone numbers with a length of at least 32 characters. Because there's no SINGLE-VALUE flag, the telephoneNumber attribute type is multi-valued. Each attribute defined by this attribute type must conform to these rules.

Here's the definition for preferredDeliveryMethod, an attribute type that is single-valued:

```
( 2.5.4.28
    NAME 'preferredDeliveryMethod'
    SYNTAX 1.3.6.1.4.1.1466.115.121.1.14
    SINGLE-VALUE )
```

Remember that the only required field is the OID field, so it's acceptable that some of the fields we discussed earlier are missing from this attribute type. This attribute type is identified by the OID 2.5.4.28. Its name is preferredDeliveryMethod, and its values must adhere to the 1.3.6.1.4.1.1466.115.121.1.14 (delivery method) syntax. Attributes of this type may store only one value.

Object Classes

When an entry is created, the object class to which it belongs must be specified; thus, every entry belongs to an object class. An entry's object class determines the kinds of attributes that can be stored in it. The directory schema lists the object classes supported by the directory.

Object Class Hierarchies

We just stated that every entry belongs to an object class, but technically, every entry actually belongs to an *object class hierarchy*. Object class hierarchies are analogous to class hierarchies in object-oriented programming languages. A Java class derived from another Java class inherits methods and data. Similarly, an object class derived from another object class inherits its attributes. An object class derived from another object class is called its *subclass*, and the object class from which it was derived is called its *superclass*.

Figure 1.3 shows the object class hierarchy for the organization and inetOrgPerson organization object classes.

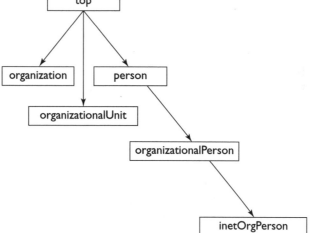

F I G U R E   1.3

Object class hierarchies for organization, organizationalUnit, and inetOrgPerson

You can see the object class to which an entry belongs by reading its objectClass attribute. The objectClass attribute is multi-valued, and when you read it, you get a value for each object class in the entry's object class hierarchy all the way back to "top."

TIP

Since it can be tricky to determine which of the objectClass values for an entry is its base object class, NDS provides an operational attribute called structuralObjectClass, which contains the base structural object class of the entry.

Object Class Definitions

Like attribute types that define attributes, object classes are defined by *object class definitions*. Object class definitions are represented by strings composed of fields. Here are some of the fields that are usually included in an object class definition:

▶ An OID that acts as a unique identifier

▶ A human-readable name

▶ A list of superior object classes from which the object class is derived

▶ An identifier telling whether the object class is abstract, structural, or auxiliary (we explain this in a moment)

▶ A list of *required attributes* that entries of the object class must have

▶ A list of *optional attributes* that entries of the object class may have

For instance, here's the object class definition for the person object class.

```
( 2.5.6.6
   NAME 'person'
   SUP top
   STRUCTURAL
   MUST ( sn $ cn )
   MAY ( userPassword $ telephoneNumber $ seeAlso $
        description ) )
```

The class is identified by the OID 2.5.6.6 and its name is "person." The top object class is a superclass of person. The person object class is structural, and it must have attribute values for the sn (surname) and cn (common name) attributes. It may also have attribute values for the userPassword, telephoneNumber, seeAlso, and description attributes.

Abstract, Structural, and Auxiliary Object Classes

There are three categories of object classes: abstract, structural, and auxiliary. You can't create entries with *abstract object classes*. While any object class can be used as a superclass, this is the sole use for abstract object classes. For instance, the "top" object class is an abstract object class, so you can't create (and thus you never see) an entry whose base object class is "top". This implies that the `objectClass` attribute for every entry always has at least two values, one of which is "top".

Structural object classes are used to create entries. This means that every entry's base object class is a structural object class.

In general, you cannot overwrite an entry's object class once it is created. For instance, an entry that is created with the object class person will always be a person. That said, *auxiliary object classes* (often shortened to just auxiliary classes or aux classes) could be used to define a set of attributes that can be added to specific entries that already exist within the tree. Auxiliary classes and their associated properties are tacked on to whatever entry they are added. Auxiliary classes on entries can also be removed.

For example, most persons in an organization are not managers. You could create a new structural subclass under person called managerPerson, which would inherit all of the attributes of the person object class and add manager-specific attributes, such as a list of direct reports. This could cause problems, though, when someone is promoted to manager. You wouldn't simply be able to change their entry's object class from person to managerPerson because that's not allowed. Instead, you'd have to create a new entry for the person, copy over the attributes it contained, then add the new manager-specific attribute values. The reverse process would have to be used for someone leaving management. That's pretty complicated.

Another approach would be to simply put the manager-specific attributes into the person object class definition as optional attributes. This has two potential problems:

- ▸ First, you'd be unnecessarily cluttering the person object class with attributes used by a small fraction of entries.

- ▸ Second, there'd be no way to guarantee that entries for managers would have values that are required for managers.

50018046

Auxiliary classes can be used to easily solve all of these problems. A manager auxiliary class could be created to contain manager-specific attributes. When a person becomes a manager, you would simply add the manager auxiliary class to that person's entry so that it would be able to contain these additional attributes. Likewise, when a person leaves a management position, you would remove the manager auxiliary class from that person's entry, thus making the entry incapable of having the attributes in the manager auxiliary class. Any attributes required for managers would be listed as required in the manager auxiliary object class definition, thus ensuring the integrity of manager entries.

Auxiliary classes are a good way for you to extend entries to include attributes needed specifically for your application.

TIP

Naming and Containment Rules

Every entry in a directory has one or more attributes that identify it in the tree hierarchy. These attributes are called *naming attributes*. The *naming rules* in the directory schema control which attribute or attributes are used as naming attributes for each object class.

Containment rules are used to impose order on the entries in a directory by limiting the object classes that are valid superiors (containers) for entries of each object class. For instance, the schema on one of my test servers states that an entry of the inetOrgPerson object class can only be contained by entries from the o (organization), ou (organizationalUnit), or domain object classes. Similarly, an entry of the ou object class can only be contained by entries from the l (locality), o, and ou object classes. Attempts to create entries where they are not allowed by containment rules will fail.

Retrieving and Updating Schema

Your application can learn what schema rules are in effect for a given server by reading a special entry called the *subschema subentry*. If the application has the rights to do so, it can also change the schema by modifying that same entry.

We discuss reading and modifying the subschema subentry in Chapter 7 and also show a utility-based method for doing these tasks in Chapter 11.

X-REF

LDAP Naming Conventions

To locate an entry in the directory, it must have a name by which it is known. As we mentioned earlier, every entry in a directory has one or more identifying attributes called naming attributes. An identifying value of a naming attribute is called a *distinguished value*.

Relative Distinguished Names

A naming attribute and its associated distinguished value are combined to form a *Relative Distinguished Name* (RDN) for an entry. An entry's RDN must be unique with respect to all of its siblings (that is, no two children of the same parent may have the same RDN). This restriction does not prevent two entries with *different* parents from having the same RDN, hence the adjective *relative* is applied to the term.

For instance, the cn (common name) attribute is a naming attribute of the inetOrgPerson class. The RDN of a user entry with the distinguished value of Janet in its cn attribute would be written as "cn=Janet". The equal sign serves as a separator between the attribute name and its value when the two are joined to form an RDN.

Distinguished Names

Even though two non-sibling entries may have the same RDN, every directory entry is uniquely identified by its *Distinguished Name* (DN). An entry's DN is composed of its RDN combined with the RDN of its parent, its parent's parent, and so on to the root of the tree.

NOTE **Before moving on, we should point out that the tree root is not an actual entry. Rather, it is an imaginary placeholder that is superior to all other entries in the tree. Because of this, a DN doesn't include an RDN for the root.**

Just as the equal sign separates components of an RDN, the comma separates RDNs within a DN. The string cn=Janet,ou=Sales,o=Acme Corp is an example of a DN.

Figure 1.4 shows a typical tree layout with an organization (o=Acme Corp) containing two organizational units (ou=Sales and ou=Marketing) and various users in each organizational unit. In this example, the RDN for each entry is formed from a naming attribute of its object class (o for organization, ou for organizationalUnit, and cn for inetOrgPerson). The DN for each entry is formed from its RDN and the RDNs of each of its superiors in the tree. Note, also, how the `objectClass` attribute is multi-valued and contains values for the entire object class hierarchy of each entry.

Uniqueness of Names

To guarantee a unique DN value for each entry in the entire directory tree, no two sibling entries may have the same RDN. If you attempted to create an entry with an RDN of cn=Tom in the ou=Sales,o=Acme Corp container in Figure 1.4, the operation would fail because there's already an entry with that RDN in that container.

This, however, does not prevent two entries in different containers from having the same RDN. For instance, in Figure 1.4, two entries have the same RDN of cn=Janet. The DNs for each of these entries are unique because one, cn=Janet,ou=Marketing,o=Acme Corp, is in the ou=Marketing container, and the other, cn=Janet,ou=Sales,o=Acme Corp, is in the ou=Sales container.

TIP

The LDAP naming convention is very similar to the naming convention used for most file systems, which like LDAP, are hierarchical in nature. One major difference, however, is that file systems names generally list elements from most significant to least significant, whereas LDAP names list elements in the reverse order, from least significant to most significant.

The Role of DNs in LDAP

Most LDAP operations have a DN parameter that specifies a directory entry that is to be used for the operation. For instance, to add an entry to an LDAP directory, you would pass the DN of the entry you want to create along with a list of attributes and attribute values you want the new entry to have. Similarly, if you wanted to delete an entry, you would pass the DN of the entry you want to delete. We talk about LDAP operations in more detail in the following sections.

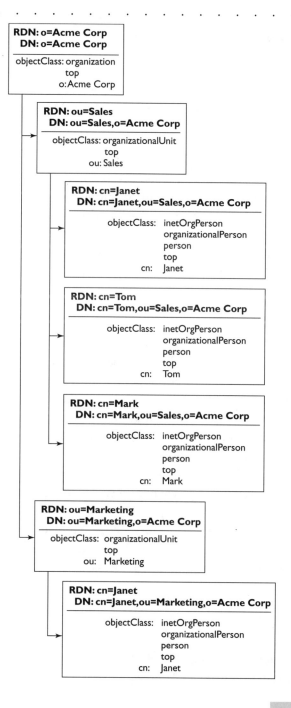

FIGURE I.4

Entries and their associated RDNs, DNs, and objectClasses

RDN: o=Acme Corp
DN: o=Acme Corp

objectClass: organization
top
o: Acme Corp

RDN: ou=Sales
DN: ou=Sales,o=Acme Corp

objectClass: organizationalUnit
top
ou: Sales

RDN: cn=Janet
DN: cn=Janet,ou=Sales,o=Acme Corp

objectClass: inetOrgPerson
organizationalPerson
person
top
cn: Janet

RDN: cn=Tom
DN: cn=Tom,ou=Sales,o=Acme Corp

objectClass: inetOrgPerson
organizationalPerson
person
top
cn: Tom

RDN: cn=Mark
DN: cn=Mark,ou=Sales,o=Acme Corp

objectClass: inetOrgPerson
organizationalPerson
person
top
cn: Mark

RDN: ou=Marketing
DN: ou=Marketing,o=Acme Corp

objectClass: organizationalUnit
top
ou: Marketing

RDN: cn=Janet
DN: cn=Janet,ou=Marketing,o=Acme Corp

objectClass: inetOrgPerson
organizationalPerson
person
top
cn: Janet

LDAP Messages

LDAPv3 is currently designed to work over any connection-oriented protocol. In practice, however, LDAP is an Internet Protocol (IP) and all implementations of which we're aware use TCP as the transport for LDAP Messages.

LDAP Requests and Responses

LDAP operations work on a request/response model. The client sends an operation request to the server. For most operation requests, the server processes the request and sends a single response back to the client indicating whether or not it succeeded. Exceptions to this model are the search operation, which can send multiple partial responses to a single request, and the unbind and abandon operations, for which no response is sent.

LDAP Message Format

Each LDAP message — request or response — is encapsulated within a message envelope, which contains the elements that are common to all protocol messages. One element in the message envelope is the message ID that uniquely identifies each outstanding request on a connection. Another element in the message envelope specifies which type LDAP request or response is contained within the message and includes all other information that must be specified for that particular request or response.

The format of LDAP messages is described using ASN.1. LDAP messages are encoded for transfer between client and server using a subset of the ASN.1 Basic Encoding Rules (BER).

RFC 2251, "Lightweight Directory Access Protocol (v3)," specifies the ASN.1 notation for all LDAPv3 messages. To help you get a feel for what this looks like, here's the ASN.1 notation for an LDAP message, as defined in RFC 2251:

```
LDAPMessage ::= SEQUENCE {
    messageID       MessageID,
    protocolOp      CHOICE {
        bindRequest     BindRequest,
        bindResponse    BindResponse,
```

```
          unbindRequest     UnbindRequest,
          searchRequest     SearchRequest,
          searchResEntry    SearchResultEntry,
          searchResDone     SearchResultDone,
          searchResRef      SearchResultReference,
          modifyRequest     ModifyRequest,
          modifyResponse    ModifyResponse,
          addRequest        AddRequest,
          addResponse       AddResponse,
          delRequest        DelRequest,
          delResponse       DelResponse,
          modDNRequest      ModifyDNRequest,
          modDNResponse     ModifyDNResponse,
          compareRequest    CompareRequest,
          compareResponse   CompareResponse,
          abandonRequest    AbandonRequest,
          extendedReq       ExtendedRequest,
          extendedResp      ExtendedResponse },
      controls         [0] Controls OPTIONAL }

MessageID ::= INTEGER (0 .. maxInt)

maxInt INTEGER ::= 2147483647 -- (2^^31 - 1) --
```

This definition essentially says, "An LDAP message is composed of a messageID followed by a protocol operation, followed by an optional set of controls for the operation." A protocol operation is a bind request, a bind response, an unbind request, or a search request . . . (and so on, through extended response). A messageID is defined as a MessageID (note the capitalized "M"), and MessageID is defined to be an integer with a range of possible values from 0 to 2^{31}-1.

Each of the protocol operations is further defined using ASN.1 notation. For instance, the delete request (which simply identifies the DN of the entry to be deleted) is defined in the following way:

```
DelRequest ::= [APPLICATION 10] LDAPDN
```

The entire ASN.1 definition of LDAP is listed in Appendix A of RFC 2251 available at `http://www.ietf.org/rfc/rfc2251.txt.`

Unless you are writing an LDAP client software development kit (SDK), an LDAP server, or a protocol decoder, you usually do not need to concern yourself with this level of detail in the protocol. The Java or C SDK you use to generate LDAP client requests provide APIs that simply accept the appropriate parameters for each LDAP operation. Behind the scenes, the SDK generates a message ID, does the BER encoding, and then sends the protocol message to the server. When a response is received from the server, the SDK also decodes the message for you.

TIP

Although you shouldn't have to think about it often, understanding the mechanisms underlying your application can help you in debugging and development. This is especially true if you have to look at wire traces containing LDAP packets, or if you create LDAP extended operations of your own, because you'll probably want to encode them using the same BER encoding that is used for standard LDAP operations.

LDAP Operations

We've now laid a sufficient conceptual foundation to introduce the operations you'll use in your LDAP application. We cover these operations in far more detail in later chapters, but reading this section is a quick way for you to get acquainted with the basics of all of the LDAP operations and to start to envision the ways you can use a directory. Because SDK implementations tend to obscure some interesting details regarding the protocol, we'll look at the operations from the perspective of client/server interaction. The program example in the last section of this chapter gives you a taste of the SDK and how it relates to LDAP operations.

LDAPv3 defines nine standard operations: bind, unbind, modify, add, delete, modify DN, compare, search, and abandon. In addition, LDAPv3 defines two mechanisms that can be used to extend the protocol.

Session Management Operations

The bind and unbind operations initiate and terminate your LDAP session. The bind operation allows you to identify yourself to an LDAP server. The unbind operation tells the server you plan to disconnect from it.

Binding to an LDAP Server

The bind operation authenticates a client to an LDAP directory. For example, in password-based authentication, the client passes the DN identifying the name of the directory object that it wants to bind, along with credentials in the form of a password. The LDAP server verifies that the proper credentials have been passed for the stated DN, and then returns a reply with a status code indicating the success or failure of the operation.

LDAP provides a standard way for clients to bind to a server using an anonymous identity. This feature is particularly handy for deploying publicly-accessible, read-only white page applications. When a client wants to bind anonymously, it simply sends an empty string as the identifying DN in its bind request.

LDAP servers typically provide two different ports that listen for incoming LDAP connections and bind requests. The first port, 389 by default, accepts connections that are unencrypted. Thus, the data that flows between the client and server on connections made to this port is in clear text form and is subject to interception while it is on the wire. The second port, 636 by default, accepts connections that are encrypted using Secure Sockets Layer (SSL). Because the data that flows between client and server on connections made to this port is encrypted, it cannot be intercepted and easily decoded.

Unbinding from an LDAP Server

The unbind operation terminates a protocol session between a client and server. Unlike most LDAP operations, no reply is sent by a server for the unbind operation. Rather, when a client sends an unbind request to a server, it may assume that the protocol session is terminated and it closes its connection to the server. The server likewise assumes that any outstanding requests for that client session are to be abandoned, and that its connection to the client may be closed.

Chapter 4 discusses the bind and unbind operations in detail.

X-REF

Entry Manipulation Operations

Entry manipulation operations allow you to add entries to the directory and delete entries from the directory, modify the attribute values of existing entries, and rename or move entries.

Adding an Entry

The add operation adds an entry to an LDAP directory. An add request takes the DN of the entry to be added, along with a list of attributes and their associated values, which the entry should have when it is created. The protocol server attempts to create the entry and replies with a status code indicating the success or failure of the operation. At a minimum, you must include values for all required attributes to successfully add an entry.

Deleting an Entry

The delete operation deletes an entry from an LDAP directory. A delete request takes the DN of the entry to be deleted. The protocol server attempts to delete the entry and replies with a status code indicating the success or failure of the operation.

Modifying an Entry's Attributes

The modify operation adds, deletes, or modifies attribute values of an existing entry. A modify request takes the DN of the entry to be modified, along with a list of attribute modifications to be made to the entry.

A single modify request can include a combination of attribute additions, deletions, and modifications. The order in which the desired modifications are specified is important, and the semantics of the modify operation require the LDAP server to perform the modifications in the order that they are specified in the LDAP request. These semantics also require the LDAP server to apply all of the modifications as a single atomic operation. If the modify operation fails for any reason, the entry must be left in the state it was in before the request was received, and the client must assume that no changes were made to the entry.

Even though a single modify request may contain many modifications—hundreds or even thousands, a single response is sent to the client indicating the success or failure of the operation.

Renaming or Moving an Entry

The modify operation, which we discussed in the last section, cannot be used to modify any of an entry's distinguished values (values that form the entry's RDN).

The modify DN operation is used for this purpose, which is, in essence, renaming. The modify DN operation can also be used to move an entry to a new location in the DIT. If the entry is a container with children, the operation moves the entire subtree below the target entry or returns an error, if the server does not support the ability to move subtrees. The rename and move functions of the modify DN operation can even be combined in a single operation request to move and rename an entry in a single step.

TIP

Some widely used LDAP servers, including the Novell LDAP server, do not currently support moving subtrees via the modify DN operation. Moving entire subtrees is not a trivial operation and may consume large amounts of servers processing resources. We recommend that you be judicious in using the ability to move subtrees even when an implementation does support this feature.

The modify DN operation takes the DN of the entry to be renamed and/or moved, its new RDN, a flag indicating whether the current distinguished value should be deleted as part of the rename, and, optionally, the DN of the new parent for the entry. The protocol server attempts to rename and/or move the entry as requested, and then replies with a status code indicating the success or failure of the operation.

X-REF

We discuss the LDAP entry manipulation functions in detail in Chapter 6.

Entry Comparison and Search and Retrieval Operations

There's not much point in storing data in a directory if you can't get it back somehow. LDAP gives you two operations to help you access the data stored within the directory. The *compare* operation enables you to see if an entry contains an attribute value, and the *search* operation allows you to find and retrieve the contents of one or more directory entries.

Checking an Entry for an Attribute Value

The compare operation sees if an entry contains a given attribute value. The compare operation takes the DN of the entry to be compared and an *attribute value assertion* (an attribute name and value). It then checks the entry to determine whether the named entry contains an attribute with the asserted value. If the attribute value assertion is true for the entry, the server returns a result of compareTrue to the client; likewise, a result of compareFalse is returned if the assertion is false.

For example, you could use a compare operation to see if the entry cn=Bob, o=Acme Corp has a `telephoneNumber` attribute with a value of 281-6653. If one of Bob's telephone numbers were 281-6653, the server would return a compareTrue result. If none of Bob's telephone numbers were 281-6653, the server would return a compareFalse result.

Searching for and Retrieving Entries

The search operation finds and reads the value of one or more entries. A search can return just the entry specified by the target DN, the target entry's immediate subordinates, or the target entry and all of its subordinates (its entire subtree).

The attributes returned for each entry are controlled by a list specifying the desired attributes to be returned. You can either explicitly request the set of attributes you want by name, or ask for all attributes from each entry. You can also limit the entries returned for a search operation by specifying a search filter that gives criteria used to compare each entry in the scope of the search. Entries that match the criteria are returned; entries that do not are filtered from the result set.

The search operation is unique in that it does not send its result as a single response. Rather, it sends zero or more intermediate responses called search entries—one for each entry that matches the search filter—and then ends by sending a search result to indicate that all entries matching the search criteria have been sent.

Other parameters can be sent as part of a search request, which provide additional control over the operation. These are beyond the scope of this chapter.

X-REF

Searching is such a rich and important LDAP feature that we've devoted all of Chapter 5 to the subject. We cover all of the details related to searching there.

TIP

As with all LDAP operations, the capability to successfully perform a search is dependent on the rights given to the identity you used when binding to the LDAP server. If you do not have read and compare rights for an entry or its attributes, you will not find the entries or attributes you request. In NDS, browse rights are given to all identities by default, but attribute read and compare rights are not given by default and must be given explicitly.

Abandoning Outstanding Operation Requests

A client may abandon any outstanding operation request with the abandon operation. The client passes the message ID of the request it wishes to have abandoned, and the server attempts to abandon the operation. No response is sent for an abandon request, and no response is sent for the abandoned operation. The client should simply expect that the requested operation has been abandoned. Even so, client implementations should be prepared to accept a response for an operation that has been abandoned, because it is possible that the response for the operation was already in transit from the server when the abandon request was issued by the client.

If a client sends an abandon request to a search operation that is in progress, the server must, upon receipt of the abandon request, immediately cease sending search entries to the client. As with other abandoned operations, no final response is sent for the search.

Extending LDAPv3

LDAPv3 was designed to be extensible in order to provide a standard expansion path for future needs of the protocol. There are two ways you can extend LDAPv3: extended operations and controls.

Extended Operations

LDAPv3 defines the extended request and extended response messages as the standard mechanism to extend the protocol with additional operations. The extended request and response messages are not really an operation, but serve as a framework upon which new protocol operations can be built.

Controls

In addition to the capability to add new operations to the protocol, LDAPv3 also allows the behavior of any LDAP operation — standard or extended — to be modified by controls. Several controls can even be stacked together on a single LDAP operation so that their individual effects are combined.

In Chapter 9, we discuss two widely used controls and give you information on writing your own LDAPv3 extensions for Novell's LDAP server.

X-REF

Synchronous and Asynchronous Requests

There are times (such as when you're updating the same entry more than once) when you need to guarantee the order in which operations are processed; at other times you may not care about the processing order of one or more operations because they are mutually independent. An LDAP client can send requests synchronously or asynchronously to meet both of these needs.

When sending synchronous operations, the client sends an operation request on a connection and waits for the corresponding response from the server before sending the next operation request. In this model, a client never has more than one outstanding operation request per connection. Because of this, the client knows that the first operation has completed before it sends the request for the second operation, and so on. This guarantees the processing order of operations. The tradeoff is that the client must wait for one response before sending the next which means that the server is sitting idle from the time it sends a reply for one response until it gets the request for the next.

To overcome this network latency, a client can send requests asynchronously. When sending asynchronous operation requests, the client does not wait for the response to one operation request before sending additional operation requests. This allows a client to have multiple outstanding requests on a single connection, and can reduce the overhead of network latency that is caused when requests are sent synchronously. It also allows a multi-processor server to make better use of its resources because it can assign one request to each processor it has available. The tradeoff is that there's no guarantee of the order in which the server processes the requests. The scheduling algorithm of the server's operating system, the relative time it takes to complete each asynchronous operation, and other factors make it relatively likely that asynchronous requests will be processed in an order different from the one in which a client sends them.

Even though it may receive responses in a different order from the corresponding requests, the client can match responses to requests because the LDAP server takes the message ID from each request and places this same message ID in the corresponding response.

Your First LDAP Program

Programming to the LDAP Java SDK is not difficult, especially because there is a straightforward correspondence between most LDAP operations and the calls to invoke them from the SDK. In the Chapter 2, we get into the details of setting up a working NDS server that you can use to run code examples against. Right now, we just want to give you a feel for the type of code you'll be writing as you develop your LDAP-enabled application.

The example in Listing 1.1 searches an LDAP directory for all entries immediately subordinate to an entry specified on the command line, and prints each entry along with its associated attributes and values. The call to connect at line 46 establishes a TCP/IP connection to the LDAP server and also performs a simple bind request using the name and password provided on the command line. The call to search at line 51 causes a search request to be sent to the LDAP server. As you recall from our earlier discussion, the server sends an intermediate search entry response for each entry matching a search request. The three nested while loops from lines 62 to 102 get the values for each attribute for each entry matching the search criteria and print them to the screen. Notice how the SDK handles all of the messy details of processing the search entry responses from the server and lets you easily access all of the information in each entry. Finally, the call to disconnect at line 109 causes an unbind request to be sent to the LDAP server and then closes the connection to the server.

LISTING 1.1

A sample LDAP search

```
1 import java.util.*;
2 import netscape.ldap.*;
3
4 public class Search {
5   public static void main( String[] args) {
6     int ldapVersion = 3;
7     String host;
8     int port = 389;
9     String loginDN;
```

Continued

```
10    String password;
11
12    LDAPConnection conn = new LDAPConnection();
13
14    String searchBase;
15    int searchScope = 2; //subtree
16    String searchFilter;
17
18    /* empty list means return all attributes */
19    String attributeList[] = null;
20
21    /* return attributes and values */
22    boolean attributesOnly = false;
23
24    if (args.length != 5) {
25      System.out.println(
26        "Usage: Search <host> <login DN> <password> "
27        + "<search base> <search filter>");
28
29      System.out.println(
30        "Example: Search acme.com "
31        + "\"cn=admin,o=Acme Corp\" "
32        + "password \"ou=Sales,o=Acme Corp\" "
33        + "objectClass=*");
34
35      System.exit(0);
36    }
37
38    host = args[0];
39    loginDN = args[1];
40    password = args[2];
41    searchBase = args[3];
42    searchFilter = args[4];
```

```
43
44    try {
45      /* Connect and bind to the ldap server. */
46      conn.connect(ldapVersion, host, port, loginDN,
47                password);
48
49      /* Perform the search */
50      LDAPSearchResults searchResults =
51        conn.search(searchBase, searchScope,
52                searchFilter, attributeList,
53                attributesOnly);
54
55      /*
56       * Get all values for all attributes for each
57       * entry.  This is done using three nested loops.
58       * The outer loop gets each entry, the middle loop
59       * get each attribute of the entry, and the inner
60       * loop gets the values for each attribute.
61       */
62      while (searchResults.hasMoreElements() == true) {
63        LDAPEntry entry = null;
64        try {
65          entry = searchResults.next();
66        }
67        catch(LDAPException e) {
68          System.out.println("Error: " + e.toString());
69          /* go to next entry after handling exception */
70          continue;
71        }
72
73        System.out.println("\n" + "Entry: "
74                          + entry.getDN());
75
76        LDAPAttributeSet attributeSet =
77            entry.getAttributeSet();
```

Continued

LISTING 1.1

A sample LDAP search
(continued)

```
78        Enumeration attributes =
79              attributeSet.getAttributes();
80
81        while (attributes.hasMoreElements() == true) {
82          LDAPAttribute attribute =
83          (LDAPAttribute) attributes.nextElement();
84          String attributeName = attribute.getName();
85
86          System.out.println("\t" + "Attribute: " +
87                          attributeName);
88          Enumeration values =
89           attribute.getStringValues();
90
91          if (values != null) {
92            while (values.hasMoreElements() == true) {
93              String value =
94                      (String) values.nextElement();
95
96              System.out.println("\t\t" + "Value: "
97                                  + value);
98            }
99          }
100        }
101      }
102    }
103    catch (LDAPException e) {
104      System.out.println("Error: " + e.toString());
105    }
106
107    if (conn.isConnected() == true) {
108      try {
109        conn.disconnect();
110      }
```

```
111        catch (LDAPException e) {
112           System.out.println("Error: " + e.toString());
113        }
114     }
115     System.exit(0);
116   }
117 }
```

You can compile this program using a command line similar to

```
javac -classpath c:\\netscape\\ldapjava\\packages\\ldapjdk.jar Search.java
```

If you ran this program with the command line

```
java -classpath c:\\netscape\\ldapjava\\packages\\ldapjdk.jar\;.
    Search 180.33.122.1 "cn=Janet,ou=Sales,o=Acme Corp" password
    c=us objectclass=\*
```

against the data contained in Figure 1.4, assuming that you replaced the LDAP server IP address, the bind DN, and the password with appropriate values, and that the bind DN is a user with sufficient rights, you'd get output like this:

```
Entry: o=Acme Corp
       Attribute: o
              Value: Acme Corp
       Attribute: objectClass
              Value: organization
              Value: ndsLoginProperties
              Value: ndsContainerLoginProperties
              Value: top

Entry: ou=Sales,o=Acme Corp
       Attribute: ou
              Value: Sales
       Attribute: objectClass
              Value: organizationalUnit
              Value: ndsLoginProperties
```

```
                         Value: ndsContainerLoginProperties
                         Value: top


     Entry: cn=Janet,ou=Sales,o=Acme Corp
             Attribute: sn
                     Value:
             Attribute: objectClass
                     Value: inetOrgPerson
                     Value: organizationalPerson
                     Value: person
                     Value: ndsLoginProperties
                     Value: top
             Attribute: cn
                     Value: Janet


     Entry: cn=Tom,ou=Sales,o=Acme Corp
             Attribute: sn
                     Value:
             Attribute: objectClass
                     Value: inetOrgPerson
                     Value: organizationalPerson
                     Value: person
                     Value: ndsLoginProperties
                     Value: top
             Attribute: cn
                     Value: Tom


     Entry: cn=Mark,ou=Sales,o=Acme Corp
             Attribute: sn
                     Value:
             Attribute: objectClass
                     Value: inetOrgPerson
                     Value: organizationalPerson
                     Value: person
                     Value: ndsLoginProperties
                     Value: top
```

```
        Attribute: cn
                Value: Mark

Entry: ou=Marketing,o=Acme Corp
        Attribute: ou
                Value: Marketing
        Attribute: objectClass
                Value: organizationalUnit
                Value: ndsLoginProperties
                Value: ndsContainerLoginProperties
                Value: top

Entry: cn=Janet,ou=Marketing,o=Acme Corp
        Attribute: sn
                Value:
        Attribute: objectClass
                Value: inetOrgPerson
                Value: organizationalPerson
                Value: person
                Value: ndsLoginProperties
                Value: top
        Attribute: cn
                Value: Janet
```

Note that if you actually run this example you'll also get ACL attribute values for each entry, but we've removed them from the output here to make it easier to read. The output we have just shown matches the information contained in Figure 1.4.

NOTE

The NDS schema requires a surname attribute on the inetOrgPerson object class, so to meet this requirement, each inetOrgPerson entry contains a surname with a value of " " in addition to the information in Figure 1.4. Also, NDS entries that contain passwords include the ndsLoginProperties object class in their object class hierarchy. They also include the ndsContainerLoginProperties object class if they are containers. These object class values are also shown in the program output as well as in the object class values shown in Figure 1.4.

Summary

This chapter covered many of the foundational concepts you need in order to quickly get up to speed in developing LDAP-enabled applications. It discussed the important role directories — especially LDAP directories — play in enabling applications in the world of Internet computing. It introduced the LDAP data model, LDAP schema concepts, the LDAP message format, the LDAP request/response model, and LDAP operations. Finally, it showed how easy it is to put all of this together into a working client program.

Chapter 2 introduces you to Novell's LDAP server and shows you how to install and configure it for your development or testing needs.

Novell's LDAP Server

Chapter 1 covered LDAP concepts and models and discussed its capabilities. At this point, you're probably anxious to get your feet wet. This chapter introduces the Novell LDAP server, helps you get one installed, and sets some basic configuration options. It then shows you how to verify that the server is running.

A Brief History of Novell's LDAP Server

In 1993, Novell shipped a product called Novell Directory Services (NDS). This directory was used by its NetWare operating system to keep track of network entities like network servers, printers, and users. NDS was built based on the X.500 recommendations that were discussed in Chapter 1. A proprietary protocol, termed *Novell Directory Access Protocol* (NDAP), was created and used to access NDS. This protocol was chosen over the *Directory Access Protocol* (DAP) described in the X.500 series due to reasons similar to those that were responsible for the creation of LDAP.

Once LDAP was defined by the IETF, Novell added it as a second access mechanism to NDS. This new access mechanism began as a separate module, which served as a gateway to NDS. With time, the LDAP mechanism has and continues to evolve as the mainstream access mechanism for NDS, while NDAP is preserved for backward compatibility.

A Difference between LDAP and NDAP Names

While managing your NDS server, you'll likely use legacy utilities that use NDAP rather than LDAP. Because of this, you may encounter some of the differences between these two protocols. These may include differences in functionality as well as naming. To avoid confusion, you should be aware of the DN form that most applications and SDKs use to name directory entries. Whereas an LDAP DN might look like cn=admin,o=administration, its NDAP counterpart would look like cn=admin.o=administration, or simply admin.administration. Note that LDAP uses a comma to separate RDNs, whereas NDAP uses a period. Also, the attribute types (cn and o) may be absent in NDAP. This is only a slight difference, but it is mentioned here because you'll be using some of these utilities soon.

Other differences between NDAP and LDAP are covered in Appendix D.

X-REF

NDS and LDAP Installation

Before going much further, you need to get an NDS server installed and configured with LDAP. Currently, NDS runs on three operating systems: Novell NetWare, Sun Solaris, and Microsoft Windows NT. This book was written with NDS version 8.50 in mind, so it's best if you're using that or a later version.

If you don't already have NDS installed, a limited-use version is included on the CD-ROM accompanying this book.

TIP

Determining the Version of NDS

If you already have NDS installed, but aren't sure what version it is, follow these steps:

If you're running NDS on NetWare, type `modules ds` from the netware command screen. You'll see the version of DS.NLM along with some other information. If you're running NDS on Windows NT, you can look at the version of DS.DLM by following these steps:

1. Locate DS.DLL in Windows Explorer (typically in \Novell\NDS).

2. Right-click the file, choose Properties, and then click the Version tab.

3. You should see a file version of 8.50 or later. (On Solaris and Linux, this functionality is currently unavailable.)

Installing from the CD-ROM

Before starting the installation process, read the quick start manual provided for your platform. For Windows NT and NetWare, this file is called QSCTAO.PDF and it's in the NDS\documentation\english\ndsedir\pdfdoc directory. For Solaris and Linux, it's called QUICK_START.HTM and is located in the NDS/Solaris and

NDS/Linux directories respectively. This document identifies the minimum system requirements for your platform and includes detailed installation instructions.

The CD-ROM contains version 8.50 of NDS for NetWare and NT, Solaris, and Linux.

NOTE

Because of the ever-changing nature of software, every detail of the installation process is not covered in this book. Instead, refer to the quick start manual that is included with your distribution of NDS. Use the following sections as you install the product to better understand the meanings of various settings along the way.

Some of the examples in this book assume you've configured your server with the same settings used in the following installation sections. If you alter these settings while installing your server, make a note of it so you can make the proper adjustments to later examples.

TIP

Installing NDS for NetWare

If you have a version of NetWare that meets the minimum system requirements, then you already have NDS installed. You can upgrade to version 8.50 on the CD-ROM or a later version by following the installation instructions in the quick start manual. Rather than downloading NDS from `www.novell.com/download/` as instructed in the quick start manual, you can specify the path to NDS 8.50 for NetWare in the NDS\nw directory on the CD-ROM.

Follow the remaining instructions in the quick start manual and restart your server when finished.

When NDS 8.00 or higher is installed on NetWare, it automatically adds the command START NLDAP to your AUTOEXEC.NCF file. If you chose not to install NDS 8.00 and have an earlier version of NDS, you need to either execute this command manually or place it in your AUTOEXEC.NCF file.

Installing NDS for NT

You can install both NDS and the ConsoleOne management utility from a single install program.

1. Run the setup program in the NDS\nt directory.

2. Mark the "Install Novell Directory Services" as well as the "Install ConsoleOne" checkboxes. The dialog box should look like Figure 2.1.

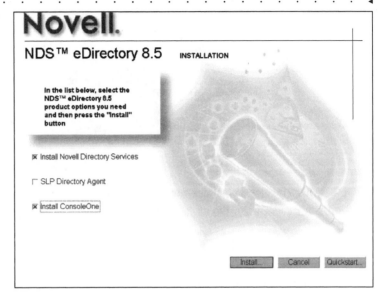

F I G U R E   2.1

NDS for NT Install program

3. The installation program installs the management utilities first. The management utilities installation is self-explanatory. Because these utilities rely on recent features of the Novell client, their installation may be preceded by an installation of the Novell client.

4. Follow the instructions until you come to the NDS for NT installation. If you need additional help, read the quick start manual provided with the installation program. Either click on Quickstart at this dialog box, or find QSCTAO.PDF in the NDS\documentation\english\ndsedir\pdfdoc directory.

5. Follow the NDS for NT installation wizard until you come to a dialog box that requests a license file. There is a license on the CD-ROM in the \NDS directory called 01234567.nfk. Change the path in the license dialog box to reflect the location of this file. The result should look like Figure 2.2.

▶ · ◀

F I G U R E   2.2

*NDS for NT Install
License dialog box*

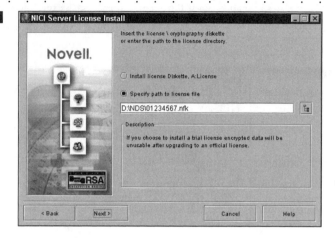

After the licensing files have been installed, you'll be instructed to reboot your computer. Do so, and the installation will continue.

6. When the installation process restarts after the reboot, you see an installation-type dialog box. Choose the "Create a new NDS Tree" radio button, unless you are installing this into an existing tree. The remaining installation instructions assume you are creating a new tree.

7. The next dialog box asks for NDS information.

a. Choose any name you wish for the Tree Name.

b. In the Server Name field, specify a server name followed by a period followed by a container name. This specifies the name and placement of the NDS server object. The NDS server object holds administrative information about this specific NDS server.

c. Choose a name for the directory administrator, and enter the password. The completed dialog box should look like Figure 2.3.

The example figure uses the name "Administration" for the server object's container as well as the administrator's container to consolidate all the administrative entries for the server.

NOTE

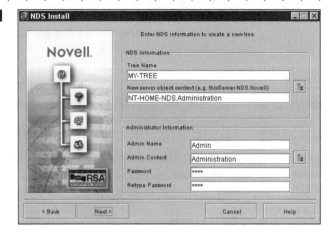

FIGURE 2.3

*NDS for NT Install, NDS
Information dialog box*

8. Next, you'll be asked whether or not the server should accept clear text passwords. To quickly and easily use the directory, select this option. You can later turn the option off, which causes the server to only accept SSL connections. SSL is covered in Chapters 4 and 10.

9. Following is a dialog box that allows you to set up a server certificate. Figure 2.4 shows this dialog box with the appropriate settings.

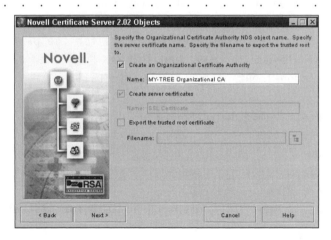

FIGURE 2.4

*NDS for NT Install, Novell
Certificate Server dialog box*

NOTE

Figure 2.4 represents the state of the installation program at the time of this writing. In the future, all checkboxes will be enabled. The tasks represented by these checkboxes can be performed at a later time and are covered in Chapter 10.

10. Follow the prompts to finish the installation. When finished, reboot the computer so the registry settings will be properly read.

Installing NDS for Solaris

Follow the directions in NDS/Solaris/quick_start.htm. The nds-install program is located in NDS/Solaris/Solaris.

1. If you are prompted to enter the path for the NICI foundation key, enter the /NDS directory on the CD.

2. Next, fill in the NDSCFG.INP file. This configuration file holds information such as the administrator's name, the NDS tree name, and so on. The following is a complete version of the configuration file. Settings that have been modified are shown in **bold** text. The settings in this file assume you are not installing NDS into an existing NDS tree.

```
#NDSCFG: Install Parameters
#Please enter the values for the following parameters and
save & quit the editor
The current or preferred values for the parameters are
displayed. You may change them.
Common Input parameters for Install

#ParamName: Admin Name and Context
#Description: The NDS name with context of the user with
admin rights to the root of the tree
#Example: Admin Name and Context=CN=admin.OU=is.O=mycompany
#Required: Required
Admin Name and Context=CN=admin.O=Administration
```

```
#ParamName: Tree Name
#Description: The name of the NDS tree the product should
be installed into
#Example: Tree Name=CORPORATE_TREE
#Required: Required
Tree Name=MY_TREE


#Parameters specific to NDS module


#ParamName: Create NDS Tree
#Description: Install a fresh NDS tree
#Example:Create NDS tree=NO
#Required: Optional
Create NDS Tree=YES


#ParamName: Server Context
#Description: The context in which the NDS server object
should reside. If the context does not exist, it is
created.
#Example:Server Context=OU=Novell.O=n
#Required: Required
Server Context=O=Administration


#ParamName: DB Files Dir
#Description: The file directory in which the NDS database
files are stored
#Example:DB Files Dir=/var/nds/dib
#Required: Optional
DB Files Dir=/var/nds/dib


#ParamName: Install LDAP
#Description: Install LDAP Services for NDS
#Example:Install LDAP=YES
#Required: Optional
Install LDAP=YES
```

```
#ParamName: LDAP Group Object
#Description: The distinguished name of the LDAP Group
object to which the LDAP Server should belong
#Example:LDAP Group
Object=cn=myLDAPgroup.ou=myContainer.o=myCompany
#Required: Optional
LDAP group Object=CN=LDAP Group.O=Administration

#ParamName: Create LDAP group Object
#Description: Create the LDAP group Object if it does not
exist. If the specified LDAP Group Object is invalid, the
default group object is created.
#Example:Create LDAP Group Object=NO
#Required: Optional
Create LDAP Group Object=YES
```

3. After editing the file, save it and close the editor, then return to the NDS installation program.

4. Enter a password for the administrator, and you're finished.

Installing NDS for Linux

The installation for Linux is the same as the one for Solaris except that the NDSCFG.INP file has an additional setting for the server's IP address.

Running NDS and LDAP

Unless you've changed the way NDS is configured on your server, it will automatically start when your server starts. There may be times, specifically while troubleshooting problems, that you'd like to stop and restart NDS or the LDAP module.

Stopping and Starting LDAP on NetWare

If you have NDS installed on NetWare, it's probably already running because NetWare uses NDS to authenticate connections from users and other servers.

If you need to stop or start NDS, enter either one of the following commands at the system console:

▸ **unload ds** stops NDS.

▸ **load ds** starts NDS.

LDAP should be running as well. If not, it may be because you have a version of NDS older than 8.00. Older versions of NDS don't automatically start the LDAP module when they load. You can manually unload and load the LDAP module by typing either one of the following at the system console:

▸ **unload nldap** stops the LDAP server.

▸ **load nldap** starts the LDAP server.

Stopping and Starting on Windows NT

On Windows NT, NDS is installed as a service and is set to automatically run when NT is started. You can stop and start NDS from the Services dialog box as follows:

1. From the Start Menu, choose Control Panel, then Services.

2. Locate the entry called NDS Server (followed by the name of your server).

3. Select the NDS Server entry and choose either Stop or Start.

4. You can also start NDS by running DHOST.EXE in the directory where NDS is installed.

WARNING

When manually starting DHost, you must use the /datafiles <dir> **command line option to point to the directory in which the Directory Information Base (DIB) files are located. The DIB files are typically located in a directory called DIBFiles directly under the directory where NDS is installed (\Novell\NDS\DIBfiles by default). Alternately, you can make the DIB file directory the working directory prior to starting DHost.**

While NDS is running, a program titled NDS Services can be used to stop and start all the NDS modules and utilities.

1. The NDS Services program may be opened at any time by running the program named NDSCons.exe. This program is located in the directory that NDS was installed in.

2. Make sure LDAP is running by selecting nldap.dlm in the NDS Services dialog box and choosing Start.

Stopping and Starting on Solaris

The installation of NDS on Solaris creates a daemon called ndsd that is automatically run when the server is started. You may use this daemon to stop and start NDS by entering either of the following commands:

- ▸ `/etc/init.d/ndsd stop` stops NDS.

- ▸ `/etc/init.d/ndsd start` starts NDS.

If you installed LDAP as part of the NDS installation, the LDAP module will automatically run when the ndsd daemon is run. You can manually unload and load the LDAP module by entering either of the following commands:

- ▸ `/etc/init.d/nldap -u` loads the LDAP module.

- ▸ `/etc/init.d/nldap -1` unloads the LDAP module.

Stopping and Starting on Linux

To stop and start NDS and LDAP on Linux, follow the same steps as shown for Solaris, but replace the directory `/etc/init.d` with `/etc/rc.d/init.d`.

Basic LDAP Configuration

While installing the LDAP module, two objects are created in the directory to hold the configuration information for the LDAP server. These are called the LDAP

Server and the LDAP Group objects. The LDAP Server object holds configuration information specific to this particular LDAP server, while the LDAP Group object contains configuration information that is shared among multiple LDAP servers. Chapter 10 details the configuration settings held by these two objects. For now, you need to make some minor adjustments to make connecting and testing the server easier.

Installing and Running the ConsoleOne Management Utility

Novell provides an NDS management utility called ConsoleOne that may be used to examine and edit the LDAP Server and LDAP Group objects. Currently, ConsoleOne will only run on a Windows platform. If you followed the Windows NT installation instructions above, it's already on your NT server, probably in the Novell\consoleone\1.2\bin directory. If you installed NDS on NetWare, it was installed in the sys:\public\mgnt\consoleone\1.2\bin directory. The Solaris and Linux NDS install programs don't copy ConsoleOne to the server, so you must install it separately on a computer running Windows 95, 98, 2000, or NT.

To install ConsoleOne on Windows, run SETUP.EXE in the NDS\nt directory on the CD-ROM and mark the "Install ConsoleOne" checkbox. The installation program may install a new Novell Client before actually installing ConsoleOne.

Using ConsoleOne

ConsoleOne displays all NDS trees and servers that you're currently logged into under the "NDS" tree view item. If you don't see your tree name listed, you need to log into your NDS tree.

1. Click NDS to enable the ability to authenticate.

2. Choose Authenticate from the File menu. You're presented with a login dialog box similar to the one in Figure 2.5.

3. Enter the tree, context, administrator user name, and password that you specified when installing NDS. The context in this case is the container that holds the administrator object.

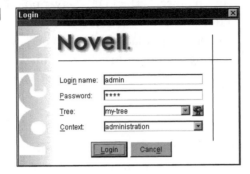

FIGURE 2.5

*ConsoleOne Login
dialog box*

4. Once logged in, find the server/container item in the ConsoleOne tree view and click it to expose its contents on the right. It should look like Figure 2.6.

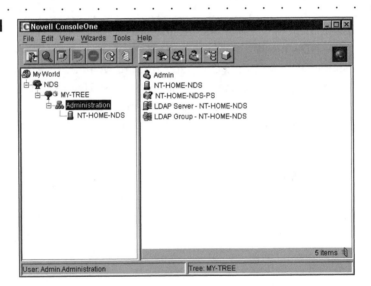

FIGURE 2.6

*A view of the server in
ConsoleOne*

5. Edit the LDAP Server object by right-clicking it and then choosing Properties.

6. Click the "Screen Options" tab on the LDAP Server object properties page and mark the checkboxes shown in Figure 2.7. These settings control which LDAP messages are output to the debug screen while the server is processing requests.

FIGURE 2.7

The Screen Options tab on the LDAP Server object properties page

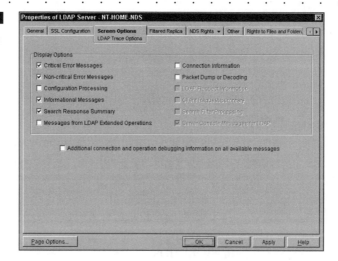

X-REF

For a full explanation of what types of messages to expect from which options, see the "LDAP Server Specific Settings" section in Chapter 10.

7. Dismiss the LDAP Server properties dialog box by clicking OK.

8. Edit the LDAP Group object by right-clicking it and then choosing Properties.

9. Mark the "Allow Clear Text Passwords" checkbox. If this is not set, the server will not allow you to bind to it unless you've established an SSL connection. Setting up SSL connections is covered in Chapter 10. Click OK to dismiss the LDAP Group properties dialog box.

WARNING

Marking the "Allow Clear Text Passwords" checkbox in a production environment is discouraged. Doing so introduces a possible security risk because anyone who has the ability to perform packet traces can examine users' passwords.

Testing the Server

Now the server is running and configured for use. You can send it some requests to make sure it's working and to get a feel for how it operates.

Running DSTrace

It's not uncommon to experience problems after initially installing a new server. Maybe it's not configured quite right, or maybe there are problems with the way the client is sending requests. To make the client aware of problems, the LDAP server sends error codes back to the client when it experiences problems. But because there are only a few dozen LDAP error codes, and they are not always descriptive enough to help you figure out a problem, an additional debug utility called DSTrace is provided with NDS.

The DSTrace utility is run on the NDS server and is used to view informational and error messages encountered by various NDS modules. It's a good idea to run this program while you're getting your feet wet, not only to quickly resolve any problems, but also to get a feel for what's going on.

NOTE

DSTrace's virtues of helping you find problems and reporting actions performed by the NDS server come with a significant performance loss. Although it's a good idea to run this utility when developing applications and trying out new features, it should be turned off when the server is being run in a production environment or when running benchmarks on your applications.

DSTrace on NetWare

If your LDAP server is running on NetWare, perform the following steps to turn on DSTrace:

1. Type `dstrace on` at the NetWare system console to load the dstrace nlm.

2. Type `dstrace` at the NetWare system console again to display a list of options.

3. Type `dstrace +ldap`. This allows LDAP messages to be sent to the trace screen.

4. You can turn off other options by typing `dstrace -<tag>`. For example, `dstrace -MISC` turns off the MISC option. On NetWare 5.1 and later, all dstrace options can be cleared by typing `dstrace clear all`.

5. To output the trace messages to a file, type `dstrace file on`; `dstrace file off` turns off file output. File output is put in the file SYS:/SYSTEM/ DSTRACE.LOG.

DSTrace on Windows NT

If your LDAP server is running on Windows NT, use the NDS Services program to start the DSTrace program. The "Stopping and Starting on Windows NT" section earlier in this chapter talks about the NDS Services program.

I. Select DSTrace in the NDS Services dialog box, then select Start.

2. Switch to the DSTrace screen and turn off the non-LDAP messages.

    a. Choose Options from the Edit menu item and then press Clear All.

    b. Mark the LDAP checkbox, and press OK to dismiss the dialog box.

DSTrace on Solaris and Linux

To turn on DSTrace when your LDAP server is running on Solaris, perform the following:

I. Enter the command `ndstrace on`. This starts DSTrace in a new window.

2. Switch to the DSTrace window and type `dstrace +ldap`. This allows LDAP messages to be sent to the trace screen.

3. You can turn off other options by typing `dstrace -<tag>`. For example, `dstrace -MISC` turns off the MISC option.

The combination of turning on DSTrace and setting the LDAP Server screen options now allows you to see diagnostics in the DSTrace screen.

Sending a Search Request

Now the trace screen is up, but because you're not asking the server to do much, there's probably not much activity. You can test whether the server is actually working by using the LDAPSEARCH utility located in the Utilities\Win32 directory on the CD-ROM (this is an .EXE file that must be run from a Windows or DOS command prompt).

From a command line, type `ldapsearch -h <server address> -b "" -s one objectclass=*`, replacing `<server address>` with the server's IP or DNS address. The result should look similar to this:

```
dn: o=Administration
o: Administration
objectClass: organization
objectClass: ndsLoginProperties
objectClass: top
```

If the utility printed an error, check Appendix B for a list of common problems and resolutions.

TIP

Congratulations! You just viewed the top-level entries in your directory. What do all those command line options for ldapsearch mean?

- The -b specifies the base of your search. In this case, the base is " ", which is used to specify no value or empty. In effect, this set the search base to the root of the directory tree.

- The -s specifies the scope of the search, which you set to one (meaning one level). This causes the search to only return entries that are one level below the base in the directory hierarchy.

- The last argument is the search filter, which you specified as objectclass=*. This causes all entries in the scope to be returned because every entry in an LDAP directory must have an objectclass attribute.

X-REF

These concepts are covered in detail in Chapter 5.

If you look at your DSTrace screen, you should see some positive-looking messages. Here's a sample:

```
DoBind on connection 0x948810
Treating simple bind request with empty DN as anonymous.
bind: dn = "anonymous"
send_ldap_result 0:: to connection 0x948810
DoSearch on connection 0x948810
begin get_filter
PRESENT
SRCH base "" scope 1 deref 0
   sizelimit 0 timelimit 0 attrsonly 0
   filter: (objectclass=*)
   attrs:
=> send_search_entry (o=Administration)
send_ldap_result 0:: to connection 0x948810
DoUnbind on connection 0x948810
```

Anonymous Bind

Notice the dn = "anonymous" in the bind message? This tells you that the server is performing an anonymous bind. In LDAP lingo, the term *bind* means to authenticate. What happened here is that you sent a search request to the server without binding first. LDAPv3 specifies that it's legal to send operations to the server without first performing a bind operation. In this case, the NDS LDAP server behaves as though you performed an anonymous bind. This is referred to as an implied anonymous bind. To force an anonymous bind, you either specify a name and no password, or an empty name and an empty or missing password while performing a bind operation.

If you'd like to test whether the server will allow you to bind as a user, modify your LDAPSEARCH command line to include a username and password using the -D and -w options respectively. Here's a sample of what the command should look like:

```
ldapsearch -D cn=admin,o=administration -w ldap -h localhost -b
"" -s one objectclass=*
```

Now you see the following bind message on the trace screen:

```
bind: dn = "cn=admin,o=administration"
```

NOTE

If you followed this example, you may have also noticed that the LDAPSEARCH command returned more attributes than before. This is because you identified yourself as the directory administrator who has more rights than an anonymous user.

Summary

At this point, you should have an NDS LDAP server up and running. You should know how to use ConsoleOne to edit the LDAP configuration objects, and know how to view debug messages in the DSTrace screen. Finally, you should know how to use the LDAPSEARCH utility to verify that your LDAP server is working.

Now that your server is functioning, you can begin to write your first programs with the LDAP SDK. The next chapter introduces that subject.

PART II

Coding and Development

CHAPTER 3

Introducing the LDAP SDK

The key to writing an LDAP directory-enabled application is the LDAP software development kit (SDK). There are LDAP SDKs available from Novell's DeveloperNet, as well as from several other companies. In this chapter, we introduce you to Novell's LDAP client SDK offerings and point you to resources on the Internet where you can read more about them and the SDKs available from other companies. We also talk about some helpful programming strategies you can use when developing your client, including multiple concurrent connections and the asynchronous LDAP operations model.

How the SDKs Work

Though the implementation details are different, each of the LDAP client SDKs that we mention in this chapter have some similarities. The job of any LDAP SDK is threefold:

▸ Expose a functional application programming interface (API) to the programmer or user in a way that makes sense for the programming language or platform that is being used.

▸ Package LDAP requests from the programmer or user strictly according to the LDAP protocol, and send those packaged requests to the LDAP server.

▸ Receive LDAP responses from the server and present them to the programmer or user according to the specified API.

Because they all utilize the LDAP standard, each of the SDKs (whether they use ActiveX, C, Java, or Perl) sends the requests to the LDAP server in the same wire format. In fact, the LDAP server has no idea whether the client is a Perl script running on Solaris or a C++ application using ActiveX controls running on Windows 2000. It doesn't matter, because the information coming to it on the wire is in the same, standard LDAP format.

You might be asking yourself if you really need to use an LDAP client SDK at all? Because LDAP is a standard, can't you just format the requests yourself in the format that the LDAP server is expecting them and send them directly on the wire to the LDAP server? The answer is, yes, of course you can. But it might be harder than it sounds. Besides having to adhere to a very strict format, all LDAP messages (both those sent to the server and those received back) are encoded according to the ASN.1 Basic Encoding Rules (BER). You *could* add the code to your client to format these messages properly, encode them, and decode them, and you'd probably learn a lot in the process, but you would be, in essence, reinventing the wheel. The work of doing those things has been done and made publicly available by several organizations already. You may as well take advantage of their effort.

How to Choose an LDAP Client SDK

Later in this chapter, we introduce the LDAP client SDKs that Novell provides, as well as several LDAP SDKs available from other organizations. In the course of your own research, you may discover other SDKs that didn't make it onto our list. Depending on the platform your application needs to run on, there are probably two, three, or even more SDKs that you can choose from. Some of them may not suit your purposes as well as others, and we'd like to help raise your awareness about the suitability of the SDK you will potentially use to develop that next "killer app."

Before You Decide

As long as they correctly conform to the LDAP protocol, *any* LDAP client SDK can be used to write a client that should work with *any* LDAP server. The two don't necessarily need to be from the same vendor. So, for example, you should be able to use the LDAP client SDKs that Novell offers to write an application that works equally well with NDS or some third-party LDAP server. Likewise, an application that uses the Netscape Directory SDK should be able to access NDS as easily as the Netscape Directory Server. One of the biggest advantages of using LDAP is that your product should be able to work with a wide range of LDAP servers.

Of course, we recommend that you do some compatibility testing with the SDK you choose, and the LDAP server you plan on accessing, to make sure that they work well together for the purpose you have planned.

A Checklist

Before you choose an LDAP client SDK, ask yourself these questions:

What Protocol Am I Going to Use?

Because you are reading this book, we assume you have already made this choice. LDAP is a good choice because it is a standard and is supported by a variety of directory servers. We only list this as a question because some directory servers also allow access through proprietary APIs. If, for example, you knew that your application would only be used to access NDS servers, you could choose to use one of the NDS-specific SDKs that Novell makes available to developers, such as the NDS Libraries for C SDK.

 See Appendix D for a comparison of LDAP and NDAP.

X-REF

One reason you might consider using an NDS-specific API would be if you needed access to NDS functionality that wasn't yet available through the core LDAP protocol or through any defined extensions. However, Novell is actively participating in defining new extensions for LDAP, and any such gaps in functionality should be quickly closed.

Which Platforms Does My Application Need to Run On?

Some LDAP client SDKs only run on one operating system, such as Windows. Others include support for three or four different platforms. The SDKs that are Java-based usually work on any platform that has a Java runtime environment available for it. Carefully consider which operating systems your application needs to support, and choose an LDAP client SDK accordingly.

What Programming Language Am I Going to Use?

There are LDAP SDKs for C, C++, and Java. There are extensions to scripted languages, such as Perl and Tcl, which enable you to perform LDAP operations. Some LDAP SDKs are implemented as ActiveX controls and can be used with Visual Basic or Delphi, or can even be embedded in a Word document.

Am I Willing to Use Early Access Software Libraries?

Many of the currently available LDAP client SDKs are very young in their product release cycle. When choosing an SDK, you need to consider whether you'd be willing to use an early access release (alpha or beta) or whether you need a more stable shipping version for use in a production environment. You should also investigate what level of support is provided for each SDK. Some SDKs are fully supported by the companies that released them, and others are not supported at all.

Am I Willing to Pay for the Use of an LDAP Client SDK?

Most LDAP client SDKs are available to download and evaluate free of charge. Some are free, no matter how you want to use them. Others require some type of licensing if you want to use them in a shipping product. If you are considering the use of a particular client SDK, refer to its Web site for licensing details.

Do I Need to Use SSL or SASL?

All of the LDAP client SDKs that we know of allow simple authentication (DN and password). However, not all of them have support for socket layer encryption, such as SSL, or for other methods of authentication, such as SASL. If you need these types of features, make sure they are in the SDK you are evaluating.

Refer to Chapter 4 for details about SSL and SASL.

X-REF

Novell's LDAP SDK Offerings

Novell provides (or will shortly) four different SDKs that can be used when writing an LDAP client:

- ▸ LDAP Libraries for C

- ▸ LDAP Libraries for Java

- ▸ LDAP Service Provider for JNDI

- ▸ LDAP ActiveX Controls

Each of these can be downloaded from Novell's DeveloperNet Web site at `http://developer.novell.com.`

We encourage you to become familiar with the layout of the DeveloperNet Web site and the services offered there. You will find many resources there to help you create directory-enabled applications, including SDKs, sample code, developer support, information on certifying your product, FAQs, white papers, and so on.

The part of the Web site that has downloadable SDKs is called the Novell Developer Kit (NDK). The NDK is divided into several sections. There is a primary download section where you can find SDKs and other tools that are recommended and supported by Novell. There is another section called Leading Edge where very new SDKs and technologies are located. The downloadable files in the Leading Edge section are usually alpha or beta product versions. There's a notice on the Leading Edge page stating that Novell doesn't recommend the use of Leading Edge technologies in a production environment, that they cannot be used in derivative software, and that Novell makes no promise to make the products available to the public in the future. You should seriously consider the goals and objectives you have for your application before using products from the Leading Edge section of the NDK.

As of this writing, the LDAP Libraries for Java and the LDAP ActiveX Controls are not yet available. However, by the time this book is printed (summer 2000), it is expected that they will be available in the Leading Edge section of the NDK.

If you are interested in either one of these, go to `http://developer.` `novell.com/ndk/leadedge.htm` **and look for them. If they are not there when you read this, they may have already moved to the supported area of the NDK at** `http://developer.novell.com/ndk/` `downloadaz.htm.`

The LDAP Libraries for C and the LDAP Service Provider for JNDI are both located in the main, supported area of the NDK. There is documentation for each of the SDKs that you can either download or read online.

You can download them from `http://developer.novell.com/ndk/` `downloadaz.htm.`

LDAP Libraries for C

The LDAP Libraries for C SDK is a good choice if you are writing an LDAP client application in C or C++. It includes libraries for use on NetWare, Microsoft Windows NT 4.0, Windows 95, and Windows 98. There are also libraries for use on Solaris and Linux, but as of this writing they are available only from the Leading Edge section of the NDK.

 The LDAP Libraries for C home page is at http://developer.novell.com/ndk/cldap.htm.

This SDK conforms to "The C LDAP Application Program Interface," which is defined in RFC 1823 (for LDAPv2) and an Internet-Draft by the same name (for LDAPv3).

Novell's LDAP Libraries for C SDK is one of Novell's first products to be released as open source and is based on the OpenLDAP project. (See the following "Other LDAP SDKs" section for additional information on OpenLDAP.) By *open source,* Novell means that they will make the source code available. People will be able to take that source code and modify it, either to add additional functionality or to fix defects. Under the terms of the open source license, those changes should then be submitted back to Novell to enable others to benefit from an improved product. The details of the open source agreement should be available soon on the DeveloperNet site.

LDAP Libraries for Java

As of this writing, Novell is working on a Java-based SDK that will probably be called LDAP Libraries for Java. Currently, Novell is planning to make it an open source product, similar to the LDAP Libraries for C SDK. By the time you read this, it should be available. Check for it in the Leading Edge section of the NDK.

The LDAP Extension Working Group of the IETF has been working on an API for Java LDAP client SDKs. It is currently in Internet-Draft form, but should become an RFC soon. Novell's LDAP Libraries for Java conforms to the API defined in this document.

If it is still an Internet-Draft when you read this, you can find it by going to http://www.ietf.org/ids.by.wg/ldapext.html **and searching for "The Java LDAP Application Program Interface." It can also be found on the CD-ROM included with this book.**

LDAP Service Provider for JNDI

Novell provides an LDAP service provider for use with the Java Naming and Directory Interface (JNDI). As its name suggests, JNDI provides a standard way for Java applications to use directory and naming services. JNDI supports several access protocols — LDAP being just one of them.

You can read about the LDAP service provider and download it at http://developer.novell.com/ndk/ldapjndi.htm. **You can read more about JNDI at** http://java.sun.com/products/jndi/.

LDAP ActiveX Controls

The LDAP ActiveX controls that Novell provides give developers a good way to add LDAP client features to an application that may already be using COM and ActiveX. As of this writing, these ActiveX controls are not yet available from DeveloperNet, but they should be there by the time you read this.

Check the Leading Edge section of the NDK at http://developer. novell.com/ndk/leadedge.htm. **You can find out more about ActiveX directly from Microsoft's Web site at** http://www.microsoft.com/com/ tech/activex.asp.

Other LDAP SDKs

We would like readers of this book to have as much information as possible about currently available LDAP SDKs. In an attempt to provide that information, we have compiled this list of other LDAP client SDKs we are aware of. If we have left any currently available SDKs off the list (which is almost a certainty), it is only because we are not aware of them.

We have not attempted in any way to give these SDKs any type of rating or review. That would be a huge undertaking and would be best performed by an independent lab. In most cases, we only tell you of the existence of an SDK and point you to the Web page where you can get more information and download the SDK.

University of Michigan

Much of the early work on LDAP was done at the University of Michigan. The tools and source code available there haven't been updated for a few years now and don't include LDAPv3 support. But most other LDAP implementations have been influenced by the University of Michigan's work.

 You can still download LDAP tools and source code from its site at `http://www.umich.edu/~dirsvcs/ldap/ldap.html`.

Netscape (Sun-Netscape Alliance, iPlanet, and mozilla.org)

One of the LDAP client SDKs that has been around the longest and has gone through the most revisions is the Netscape Directory SDK. There are both C and Java versions of this SDK (both currently at version 4.1), as well as a Perl library called PerLDAP that can give you access to LDAP operations from your Perl scripts.

The Netscape Directory SDK used to be available as a download directly from `developer.netscape.com`, and you can still find some documentation and examples there. When America Online bought Netscape, they announced a strategic partnership with Sun Microsystems to deliver e-commerce solutions and products. This partnership is referred to as the Sun-Netscape Alliance. Near the end of 1999 and the beginning of 2000, that partnership began to take shape with the introduction of a brand called iPlanet.

 The Netscape Directory SDK and PerLDAP are now available as downloads from the iPlanet Web site at `http://www.iplanet.com/downloads/developer/`. **Visit the Web site for information about use and licensing of the SDK.**

The source code for parts of the Netscape Directory SDK and PerLDAP has been made available through the open source model from mozilla.org. The Netscape Public License governs its use.

You can read the license and download the source code from http://mozilla.org/directory/.

IBM SecureWay Directory Client SDK

IBM has two LDAP client SDKs. One of them is for C programmers, and the other is for Java. The Java version uses JNDI.

 For details, check http://www.ibm.com/software/network/directory/ downloads/.

Protek Boldon James LDAP-X Toolkit

UK-based Protek Boldon James makes another ActiveX-based toolkit for creating LDAP clients and servers.

 More information is available from the company's Web site at http:// www.bj.co.uk/ldapx.htm.

OpenLDAP

The OpenLDAP Project provides an open source implementation called OpenLDAP, which includes a stand-alone LDAP server, a stand-alone LDAP replication server, libraries implementing the LDAP protocol, and utilities, tools, and sample clients.

 It is located on the Web at http://www.openldap.org/.

Python-LDAP

There is an LDAP API for the Python programming language. It currently only supports LDAPv2, but it does provide SSL capabilities.

Find out more about LDAP for Python at `http://python-ldap.`
`sourceforge.net/`.

Some Simple Examples

We've talked about quite a few of the LDAP client SDKs that are available, and
how they work on a general level. Let's look at some coding specifics now. In this
section, we present the simple example of a client connecting to the server, performing a search, parsing and printing the results, and disconnecting. We present
this example twice in Java (using both the Java LDAP SDK and the JNDI LDAP
Service Provider) and once in C.

**The following three examples, although they are in different
programming languages and use different APIs, are functionally
equivalent. The LDAP server would notice very little difference
between them.**

NOTE

Java LDAP SDK Example

This Java example uses the Netscape Directory SDK 4.0 that is referred to previously in the chapter. Using the `javac` command-line tool that comes with Sun's
JDK, this source code compiles into a Java class that can be run using the `java`
tool. You need to either set up the CLASSPATH environment variable to include
the ldapjdk.jar file that is included with the Netscape Directory SDK, or include
that file on the command-line using the `-classpath` option.

LISTING 3.1

*A search example
in Java*

```
/* MySearch.java */
/* Connect, search, print results, and disconnect example */

import netscape.ldap.*;
```

Continued

LISTING 3.1

*A search example
in Java (continued)*

```java
import java.util.Enumeration;

class MySearch {
    public static void main(String[] args) {

        /* Create the connection class that will be used
           for each call to the LDAP server */
        LDAPConnection conn = new LDAPConnection();

        try {
            /* Make an LDAPv3 connection (bind) on the standard
               LDAP port (389) as admin */
            conn.setOption(LDAPv3.PROTOCOL_VERSION,
                new Integer(3));
            conn.connect("myserver.acme.com", 389,
                "cn=admin,o=acme", "adminPass");

            /* List all the people in the sales container
               along with their user attributes and values */
            String[] wantedAttrs = {LDAPv3.ALL_USER_ATTRS};
            LDAPSearchResults results = conn.search(
                "ou=sales,o=acme", LDAPv2.SCOPE_ONE,
                "objectClass=inetOrgPerson", wantedAttrs, false);
            while (results.hasMoreElements()) {
                LDAPEntry person = results.next();
                System.out.println("\ndn: " + person.getDN());
                Enumeration attrs =
                    person.getAttributeSet().getAttributes();
                while (attrs.hasMoreElements()) {
                    LDAPAttribute attr =
                        (LDAPAttribute)attrs.nextElement();
                    Enumeration values = attr.getStringValues();
                    while (values.hasMoreElements()) {
```

```
                System.out.println(attr.getName() + ": " +
                    (String)values.nextElement());
            }
        }
    }

    /* Disconnect from the server */
    conn.disconnect();

/* Catch and print any LDAPException */
} catch(LDAPException e) {
    System.out.println(e.toString());
}
    }
}
```

JNDI LDAP Service Provider Example

Here is the same search using the LDAP Service Provider for JNDI. It differs from the previous Java example in several ways, but notice especially the Hashtable that contains the environment, and the notion of a naming context.

L I S T I N G   3 . 2

*A search example using the
LDAP provider for JNDI*

```
import java.util.Enumeration;
import java.util.Hashtable;
import javax.naming.*;
import javax.naming.directory.*;

class MyJNDISearch {
    public static void main(String[] args) {
        Hashtable env = new Hashtable();
        env.put(Context.INITIAL_CONTEXT_FACTORY,
            "com.sun.jndi.ldap.LdapCtxFactory");
```

Continued

LISTING 3.2

*A search example using the LDAP
provider for JNDI (continued)*

```
env.put(Context.PROVIDER_URL,
        "ldap:// myserver.acme.com:389");
env.put(Context.SECURITY_AUTHENTICATION, "simple");
env.put(Context.SECURITY_PRINCIPAL, "cn=admin,o=acme");
env.put(Context.SECURITY_CREDENTIALS, "adminPass");


try {
    /* Create an InitialDirContext. This will set up the
       relationship between the client and server (the
       actual bind may happen later during the search
          operation */
    DirContext context = new InitialDirContext(env);


    /* Search for the people in the sales container */
    NamingEnumeration searchResults = context.search(
                    "ou=sales,o=acme",
                    "objectClass=inetOrgPerson",
                    new SearchControls());


    /* Print search results by iterating through
        1. All entries in search results
        2. All attributes in each entry
        3. All values in an attribute */
    while (searchResults.hasMore()) {
        SearchResult nextEntry =
                    (SearchResult)searchResults.next();
        System.out.println("\ndn: " +
            nextEntry.getName());

        Attributes attributeSet =
            nextEntry.getAttributes();
        NamingEnumeration allAttrs =
            attributeSet.getAll();
```

```
        while (allAttrs.hasMoreElements()) {
            Attribute attribute =
                (Attribute)allAttrs.next();
            String attributeId = attribute.getID();

            Enumeration values = attribute.getAll();
            while(values.hasMoreElements()) {
                System.out.println(attributeId + ": "
                    + values.nextElement());
            }
        }
        }
        }
    /* Catch and print exceptions */
    } catch (Exception e) {
        System.out.println(e.toString());
    }
    }
}
```

LDAP C SDK Example

This is an example that uses the LDAP Libraries for C SDK that is available from the DeveloperNet Web site. We compiled this using Microsoft Visual C++ 6.0. Be sure to edit the project options to add the "include" directory and the correct library from the LDAP Libraries for C SDK.

LISTING 3.3

*A search example using the
LDAP SDK for C*

```
#include <stdio.h>
#include <ldap.h>

int main() {
    int        rcode, i;
```

Continued

A search example using the LDAP
SDK for C (continued)

```c
char        *dn, *attribute, **values;
BerElement  *ber;
LDAP        *ld;
LDAPMessage *results, *entry;

/* Set LDAP version to 3 */
int version = LDAP_VERSION3;
ldap_set_option(NULL, LDAP_OPT_PROTOCOL_VERSION,
   &version);

/* Initialize the LDAP session */
if ((ld=ldap_init("myserver.acme.com", 389)) == NULL) {
   printf("LDAP session initialization failed\n");
   return(1);
}

/* Bind (connect) to the server */
rcode = ldap_simple_bind_s(ld, "cn=admin,o=acme",
   "adminPass");
if (rcode != LDAP_SUCCESS) {
   printf("ldap_simple_bind_s: %s\n",
      ldap_err2string(rcode));
   ldap_unbind_s(ld);
   return(1);
}

/* Search for the people in the sales container */
rcode = ldap_search_ext_s(ld, "ou=sales,o=acme",
   LDAP_SCOPE_ONELEVEL, "objectClass=inetOrgPerson",
   NULL, 0, NULL, NULL, NULL, LDAP_NO_LIMIT, &results);
if (rcode != LDAP_SUCCESS) {
   printf("ldap_search_ext_s: %s\n",
      ldap_err2string(rcode));
```

```
    ldap_unbind_s(ld);
    return(1);
  }


  /* Print each returned entry with attributes and values */
  for (entry = ldap_first_entry(ld, results); entry != NULL;
    entry=ldap_next_entry(ld, entry)) {
    if ((dn=ldap_get_dn(ld, entry)) != NULL) {
      printf("\ndn: %s\n", dn);
      ldap_memfree(dn);
    }
    for (attribute = ldap_first_attribute(ld, entry, &ber);
      attribute != NULL;
      attribute = ldap_next_attribute(ld, entry, ber)) {
      if ((values = ldap_get_values(ld, entry, attribute))
        != NULL) {
        for (i = 0; values[i] != NULL; i++)
          printf("%s: %s\n", attribute, values[i]);
        ldap_value_free(values);
      }
      ldap_memfree(attribute);
    }
  }
  ldap_msgfree(results);

  /* Disconnect and free the LDAP structure */
  ldap_unbind_s(ld);

  return(0);
}
```

Sample Code in This Book

With the exception of another C example in Chapter 4, the previous examples
in C and JNDI are the only ones you find in this book. All of the other coding
examples use the Java LDAP SDK. We made the decision to go with Java sample

code for several reasons. First, the Java coding syntax is similar to C, and we feel C programmers will have little trouble following along. Second, the error-handling code is more efficient because of the elegant throw-catch exception model used in Java. And third, we didn't have the space to develop side-by-side examples in multiple languages.

The LDAP Libraries for C and the LDAP Service Provider for JNDI areas of the NDK have excellent examples with source code that parallel nearly all of the examples we use in this book. If you are planning to write your directory application in C, or to use the LDAP Service Provider for JNDI, we encourage you to look at that sample code, which is available on the Web at `http://developer.novell.com/ndk/cldap.htm` and at `http://developer.novell.com/ndk/ldapjndi.htm`.

TIP

The sample code and NDK downloads are also available on the CD-ROM that accompanies this book.

Programming Strategies

Most LDAP client applications communicate with an LDAP server by making a single connection to the server and then sending a series of synchronous LDAP requests to it. In this case, the term synchronous refers to the way each individual request is handled: A message containing a request is sent to the server, and then the client waits for the server to respond before sending the next request.

While the synchronous method is adequate for most client applications, there may be times when you need the flexibility of having more than one connection to the server or the performance and flexibility that an asynchronous model can provide. In this section, we discuss strategies for dealing with these needs.

Handling Multiple Synchronous Connections with Threads

You don't have to use an asynchronous model to avoid being idle while waiting for server responses. One popular method used to avoid waiting on the server is to establish more than one simultaneous connection to the LDAP server. If the ordering of operations isn't important to you, then you can perform one operation on one connection, and while you wait for it to finish, you can send another operation on another connection. Using this method, you can increase the performance of your client application without adding some of the complexity that can come with an asynchronous model.

WARNING **Whenever the LDAP server receives a request, it checks the pool of worker threads it has already allocated and either assigns the request to one of those threads or starts a new thread to handle the request. Since these threads operate independently from one another, there is no guarantee that operations will be completed in the order the server receives them. Therefore, unless your client uses a single, synchronous connection that waits for a response from the server before sending the next request, it may receive responses out of order.**

If you are planning on using multiple simultaneous connections, you should evaluate the server's capacity to handle them. Most LDAP servers are able to handle multiple simultaneous connections — some better than others. NDS currently handles more than 1,500 simultaneous connections on NetWare, 300 on NT, and 700 on Solaris.

IMPORTANT **In NDS, the administrator can limit the maximum number of concurrent connections that a user can have. If you plan on using the same user to authenticate to NDS with multiple connections, make sure that this setting is high enough to handle all of the connections you need. It can be set in ConsoleOne by going to the user's Login Restrictions tab. It can also be set, or read, through LDAP with the** `loginMaximumSimultaneous` **attribute.**

Example of Multiple Synchronous Connections with Threads

The following Java example creates ten threads. Each thread makes a connection to the server, performs a search operation, prints the DNs from the search results, and disconnects. If you run this example, you will probably notice that the results don't seem to print in any particular order. This is, in fact, one of the advantages of multi-threading. One thread doesn't have to wait for another to finish; they each go about their business and finish as system resources allow.

The Java core API specification provides some classes and methods that make dealing with multiple threads easier. We don't show them in this example, but you should take some time to explore the thread-related classes in the Java core API documentation, specifically the ThreadGroup class and the methods of the Thread class that allow for the synchronization, starting, suspending, and prioritization of threads.

Handling multiple concurrent connections

```
/* MultipleSearch.java */

import netscape.ldap.*;

class MultipleSearch {
    public static void main(String[] args) {
        /* Start 10 threads to do searches */
        for (int i = 0; i < 10; i++)
            new SearchThread("Thread" + i);
    }
}

class SearchThread extends Thread {
    public SearchThread(String name) {
        super(name);
        start();
    }

    public void run() {
        /* Create the connection class that will be used
           for each call to the LDAP server */
        LDAPConnection conn = new LDAPConnection();

        try {
            /* Make an LDAPv3 connection (bind) on the standard
               LDAP port (389) as admin */
            conn.setOption(LDAPv3.PROTOCOL_VERSION,
                new Integer(3));
```

```
conn.connect("myserver.acme.com", 389,
    "cn=admin,o=acme", "adminPass");

/* List all the people in the sales container
    along with their user attributes and values */
String[] wantedAttrs = {LDAPv3.ALL_USER_ATTRS};
LDAPSearchResults results = conn.search(
    "ou=sales,o=acme", LDAPv2.SCOPE_ONE,
    "objectClass=inetOrgPerson", wantedAttrs, false);

/* Print thread name and DNs of found entries */
String entries = "";
while (results.hasMoreElements())
    entries += results.next().getDN() + '\n';
System.out.println(getName() + " found the " +
    "following entries: \n" + entries);

/* Disconnect from the server */
conn.disconnect();

/* Catch and print any LDAPException */
} catch(LDAPException e) {
    System.out.println(e.toString());
}
    }
}
```

Performing Asynchronous LDAP Operations

Most LDAP clients communicate with the LDAP server synchronously; that is, they make a request and wait for the response. This model works quite well for most situations. However, there are times when an LDAP client may need to eke out a little more performance, and in those cases, an asynchronous model may be used.

To function properly, an asynchronous client must not care about the ordering of operations on the server. It sends the requests one after another without waiting for a response. The server processes these requests and responds, but not necessarily in the order they were received. The client gathers the responses as they are received from the server, and the programmer or user processes the (unordered) responses whenever it makes sense to do so.

To make this work, each LDAP request that is sent to the server is identified with a message ID. Typically, when a client application establishes a connection to the LDAP server, it assigns the first LDAP request message the ID of 1, and subsequent requests get the next highest number. When the server responds to each LDAP request, it puts the message ID from the request into the message ID field for the response. So, when the client receives a response, it can match the message ID and knows which request the response is for.

For the most part, the LDAP server doesn't know or care whether your client is accessing it synchronously or asynchronously. Server implementations should be written in such a way as to be able to handle more than one request at a time, but other than that, the way that a server answers a request sent to it asynchronously is the same as the way it handles a synchronous one. It performs the operation and returns the result (with a matched message ID). The actual LDAP messages containing the requests and the replies are no different. Only the timing changes.

The real change in the asynchronous model then is on the client side. Because the client neither waits for nor processes responses immediately after making a request, an LDAP client SDK that provides a way of performing asynchronous LDAP operations must have some way of storing the responses received from the server until the user or programmer either asks for and processes them, or discards them.

WARNING

Because the server does not guarantee to process requests in the order they are received, there are some LDAP operations that shouldn't be attempted asynchronously. For example, if you perform an asynchronous bind (also referred to as connect or authenticate) followed by a search, you may not actually be authenticated before the search is performed. The obvious implication of this is that without the rights you expect as an authenticated user, you might not be able to see the entries or attributes you are searching for. Even worse, the LDAP specification says that when a bind request is received, all outstanding operations on that connection must be abandoned. So, if the search request has been received but hasn't completed when the bind request is received, it will be thrown away.

The Asynchronous Interface

Most LDAP client SDKs provide a way to communicate asynchronously with the server. Check the documentation that came with your client SDK for details.

The Java LDAP API provides the following classes, methods, and interface that allow for asynchronous operation:

- **LDAPAsynchronousConnection interface:** The LDAPConnection class (which you can see in the examples in this chapter and which we cover more thoroughly in the next chapter) implements the LDAPAsynchronous Connection interface. The interface defines asynchronous versions of most of the methods in the LDAPConnection class that communicate directly with the server. It is because LDAPConnection implements LDAPAsynchronous Connection that add, bind, compare, delete, modify, rename, and search can be performed asynchronously.

- **LDAPMessage class:** LDAPMessage is the base class for request and response messages. It has fields to identify the message type, as well as the message ID and any controls. (We cover the use of controls in Chapter 9.)

- **LDAPResponse class:** LDAPResponse extends LDAPMessage and is the basis for a server's reply to a request. It adds the ability to return a result code, an error message, and a referral. (Referrals are covered in Chapter 8.)

- **LDAPExtendedResponse class:** The response to an extended LDAP operation is an LDAPExtendedResponse. (We cover the use of extended LDAP operations in detail in Chapter 9.)

- **LDAPResponseListener class:** The asynchronous versions of add, bind, compare, delete, modify, and rename take an LDAPResponseListener object as a parameter. An LDAPResponseListener gathers responses from the server until the client is ready to process them. Its getResponse method returns the LDAPResponse objects one at a time.

- **LDAPSearchResult class:** The LDAPSearchResult extends LDAPMessage and is one of the possible results that can be received from a search request. It encapsulates a single LDAPEntry object, which represents an entry in the directory.

► **LDAPSearchResultReference:** If the results of a search are not all located locally on an LDAP server, it can return a type of referral called a continuation reference as part of its reply. The LDAPSearchResultReference contains one of these continuation references. (Chapter 8 discusses continuation references and referrals in more detail.)

► **LDAPSearchListener class:** The LDAPSearchListener plays a role that is similar to the LDAPResponseListener class, but for the search method. It is capable of gathering LDAPMessage objects, including referrals, which can be checked later using the getResponse method.

Example of Asynchronous Searching

The following asynchronous example searches the containers for sales, marketing, and education one right after another without waiting for a response. The LDAPSearchListener quietly gathers the responses from the server as they are returned. After performing the three searches, we process the returned responses, printing the inetOrgPerson entries found in the three containers.

```
L I S T I N G   3.5
```
Searching asynchronously

```java
import netscape.ldap.*;
import java.util.Enumeration;

class AsyncSearch {
    public static void main(String[] args) {

        /* Create the connection class that will be used
           for each call to the LDAP server */
        LDAPConnection conn = new LDAPConnection();

        try {
            /* Make an LDAPv3 connection (bind) on the standard
               LDAP port (389) as admin */
            conn.setOption(LDAPv3.PROTOCOL_VERSION,
                new Integer(3));
```

```
conn.connect("myserver.acme.com", 389,
    "cn=admin,o=acme", "adminPass");

/* Asynchronously search the sales, marketing, and
    education containers. */
String[] bases = {"ou=sales,o=acme",
    "ou=marketing,o=acme", "ou=education,o=acme"};
String[] wantedAttrs = {LDAPv3.ALL_USER_ATTRS};
/* Do the first search and get the listener */
LDAPSearchListener listener = conn.search(
    bases[0], LDAPv2.SCOPE_ONE,
    "objectClass=inetOrgPerson", wantedAttrs, false,
    (LDAPSearchListener)null);
/* Use the same listener on subsequent searches */
for (int i = 1; i < bases.length; i++)
    conn.search(bases[i], LDAPv2.SCOPE_ONE,
        "objectClass=inetOrgPerson", wantedAttrs,
        false, listener);

/* Loop on results */
LDAPMessage msg;
while ((msg = listener.getResponse()) != null) {
    if (msg instanceof LDAPSearchResultReference) {
        String[] urls =
            ((LDAPSearchResultReference)msg).getUrls();
        // Do something with the referrals...
    }
    if (msg instanceof LDAPSearchResult) {
        LDAPEntry entry =
            ((LDAPSearchResult)msg).getEntry();
        System.out.println("\ndn: " + entry.getDN());
        Enumeration attrs =
            entry.getAttributeSet().getAttributes();
        while (attrs.hasMoreElements()) {
```

Continued

LISTING 3.5

Searching asynchronously
(continued)

```
          LDAPAttribute attr =
              (LDAPAttribute)attrs.nextElement();
          Enumeration values =
              attr.getStringValues();
          while (values.hasMoreElements()) {
              System.out.println(attr.getName() + ": "
                  + (String)values.nextElement());
          }
        }
      }
    if (msg instanceof LDAPResponse) {
        LDAPResponse res = (LDAPResponse)msg;
        int status = res.getResultCode();
        if (status == LDAPException.SUCCESS) {
            // Search was successful. Nothing to do.
        } else {
            String err =
                LDAPException.errorCodeToString(status);
            throw new LDAPException(err, status,
                res.getErrorMessage(),
                res.getMatchedDN());
        }
    }
    /* There should not be any other msg types */
}

/* Disconnect from the server */
conn.disconnect();
```

```
    /* Catch and print any LDAPException */
    } catch(LDAPException e) {
        System.out.println(e.toString());
    }
  }
}
```

Summary

Much of the work of developing an LDAP client has already been done for you and made available in the form of an LDAP client SDK. This chapter gave some ideas and pointers that should help you pick an SDK to use in writing your application. It gave examples of a simple client application in both Java and C. It also described ways of handling multiple simultaneous connections to the LDAP server and mentioned specific instances when you might consider performing LDAP operations asynchronously.

The next three chapters explore some of the most common LDAP operations that you can perform with a client SDK, such as connecting, authenticating, searching, and updating.

CHAPTER 4

Connection and Authentication

Before your client application can do anything with the information in the directory, it must connect and authenticate to the server. Authentication is a way of proving to the server that you are who you say you are, and that you are entitled to the privileges given to you by the administrator. Your client does this by establishing a connection to the LDAP server and sending a bind request.

NOTE

In LDAP-speak, the terms *authenticate* and *bind* are often used interchangeably. This is because the LDAP protocol definition gives the name *bind* to the LDAP operation that authenticates your client as a particular user, identified by its DN, in the directory. You can think of it as creating a *binding* between an authenticated identity and a connection.

In this chapter we present different ways of connecting and authenticating to an LDAP server, focusing primarily on what is referred to as a *simple bind* by providing a DN and password. We also discuss how to encrypt the connection between your client and the server by using a Secure Sockets Layer (SSL).

The TCP Network Connection

Request for Comments (RFC) 2251 states that the LDAP protocol is designed to be run over connection-oriented, reliable transports, with all 8 bits in an octet being significant in the data stream. While the RFC specifically mentions the Transmission Control Protocol (TCP), it leaves open the possibility that LDAP could be implemented on some other transport protocol.

In practice, we know of no existing LDAP implementation that uses any transport other than TCP — the same transport protocol used by connection-oriented Internet services such as Hypertext Transfer Protocol (HTTP), File Transfer Protocol (FTP), and Telnet. A detailed description of TCP is beyond the scope of this book, but the advantages of using TCP include guaranteed delivery of packets, guaranteed ordering of packets at the destination, and a guarantee that the contents of each packet received are the same as when they were sent. The individual network packets that are sent between the source and destination are combined into a stream, and this stream has the ability to regulate its own flow. If there are too many errors occurring at a faster stream rate, it has the ability to slow (or narrow) the flow until the errors are less frequent. When an error does occur in one of the packets that make up the stream, the error is detected at the TCP level, the packet is resent, and the error never makes it into the actual stream that is seen by the application.

A service using TCP listens for connection requests on a specified port. For example, the Web server at www.novell.com is on port 80, listening right now for incoming connection requests by Web browsers. By putting each service on a unique port, a single server can provide multiple services without any ambiguity. The LDAP specification recommends that an LDAP server listen for connections on port 389, but allows for the use of other ports. In order to be compliant with the LDAP specification, an LDAP client cannot assume that LDAP service will always be on port 389. It must have some way of letting the user specify the port number that should be used. For example, command-line LDAP tools typically allow the user to specify the LDAP port by providing the -p option on the command-line.

NOTE

Most LDAP servers, in addition to listening for connections on port 389, also listen on port 636. A connection on port 636 signifies that the client wants the TCP connection to use the Secure Sockets Layer (SSL) protocol to encrypt the data stream. We discuss SSL later in this chapter.

Once the TCP connection is established between a client and the server, the client may begin sending LDAP requests to the server. The first LDAP request is typically the bind operation, unless it wants the server to perform an implied anonymous bind on its behalf.

A client may establish more than one connection to the LDAP server.

X-REF

The "Programming Strategies" section of Chapter 3 has details about handling multiple connections.

The Bind Operation

While most LDAP client SDKs provide several ways to connect and authenticate to an LDAP server, they all map to a single operation in the LDAP protocol itself. The Abstract Syntax Notation One (ASN.1) definition for a bind request is discussed in RFC 2251 in the following example:

 For a closer look at RFC 2251, go to http://www.ietf.org/rfc/ rfc2251.txt **or \IETF DOCUMENTS\RFCS\RFC2251.TXT on the CD-ROM that accompanies this book.**

```
BindRequest ::= [APPLICATION 0] SEQUENCE {
        version                 INTEGER (1 .. 127),
        name                    LDAPDN,
        authentication          AuthenticationChoice }


AuthenticationChoice ::= CHOICE {
        simple                  [0] OCTET STRING,
                                -- 1 and 2 reserved
        sasl                    [3] SaslCredentials }


SaslCredentials ::= SEQUENCE {
        mechanism               LDAPString,
        credentials             OCTET STRING OPTIONAL }
```

As this definitions shows, when you bind to the LDAP server you present the LDAP version you want to communicate with (2 or 3), and the DN of the directory entry you want to bind as (the name parameter), and some means of proving that you are who you say you are (the authentication parameter). The two types of authenticating shown in this definition are *simple* and *sasl*. The simple method of authentication is to simply provide the correct password for the DN you indicated in the name parameter. The sasl method uses the Simple Authentication and Security Layer specification (SASL) as defined in RFC 2222. SASL is addressed in more detail near the end of this section.

Anonymous Bind

There may be times when you want access to a minimum level of services from an LDAP server without having to provide a DN and password. The LDAP protocol (and the SDKs) provides a way to bind anonymously to the server. To do this, send a simple bind request to the server and provide an empty string for the name and password fields. The server accepts this form of bind request as anonymous and gives you whatever level of service the administrator has allowed for anonymous users. Usually, the administrator will only allow anonymous users to view the tree hierarchy and to see the names of the objects it contains (browse rights).

NOTE

Actually, the LDAP protocol specifies that only the password field needs to be left blank to perform an anonymous bind. If the password field is blank, anything can be in the name field and it will still be treated as an anonymous bind. In practice, however, it's a good idea to provide the empty string for the name field as well, to make it completely clear that you want to bind anonymously.

The anonymous aspect of the bind operation is convenient if your LDAP server doesn't contain information that needs to be protected, and you don't want to deal with authentication issues. In Novell Directory Services (NDS), the administrator can specify exactly what rights an anonymous user has by either setting access controls for the [public] entry, or by setting up a proxy user that is used whenever someone requests an anonymous bind.

X-REF

See the "Shared Server Settings: Editing the LDAP Group Object" section in Chapter 10 for details about configuring a proxy user.

Implied Anonymous Bind

When a client connects to the server, the first request it sends is typically the bind operation. We say *typically* because LDAPv3 has the notion of an implied anonymous bind. If the client sends some other operation as the first request on a new connection, the server treats the connection as an anonymous LDAPv3 connection and performs the requested operation. All subsequent requests on that connection are also performed anonymously, until a bind operation for another identity succeeds.

SASL Bind

As we stated previously, the two types of authentication allowed by the bind operation are simple and sasl. The Simple Authentication and Security Layer (SASL) specification is defined in RFC 2222 and allows for more flexibility and strength in the ways authentication can take place. SASL isn't directly related to LDAP — it was defined with a broader target audience in mind and can be used to authenticate to a variety of different services. However, SASL is well suited for authenticating to LDAP when some method other than supplying a DN and password is desired.

 You can find RFC 2222 at `http://www.ietf.org/rfc/rfc2222.txt.`

There are various *SASL mechanisms* that have been defined, and each one performs authentication a little differently. In fact, as of this writing there are ten SASL mechanisms registered with the Internet Assigned Numbers Authority (IANA). SASL is extensible. If you came up with a new way to authenticate, you could create a SASL mechanism, register it with the IANA, and begin to use it with LDAP servers that supported that SASL mechanism.

 You can read about the defined SASL mechanisms and find links to where they are defined at `http://www.isi.edu/in-notes/iana/ assignments/sasl-mechanisms.`

NDS eDirectory 8.5 has support for the "EXTERNAL" SASL mechanism. Other mechanisms are not yet supported. Versions of NDS prior to NDS eDirectory 8.5 didn't have any SASL support. In NDS, the "EXTERNAL" SASL mechanism is used to provide client authentication, which is sometimes called mutual authentication, to the server when using SSL. When the client performs this type of a bind, it presents an X.509 user certificate to the server. The server checks the signature on the certificate to verify that it was signed by the organizational certification authority in the server's tree. If it was, the server accepts the connection as authenticated to the user specified in the DN portion of the certificate information.

WARNING

Although Novell has added support for the "EXTERNAL" SASL mechanism to NDS eDirectory 8.5, few LDAP SDKs are able to handle the PKCS#12 formatted user certificates that NDS generates. In particular, none of the LDAP SDKs currently provided by Novell are able to perform this type of authentication. Therefore, as of press time, we unfortunately have no working SASL example for this book. As the LDAP SDKs and SASL support in NDS matures, we expect that working examples will be posted on DeveloperNet at http:// developer.novell.com.

Using the SDK to Connect and Authenticate

Up to this point, we've talked about the LDAP bind operation in general terms. The Java LDAP SDK allows the client application writer to connect and authenticate to an LDAP server through an LDAPConnection object. In this section, we show you how to establish a bound connection using the SDK.

The LDAPConnection Class

If you are using the Java LDAP SDK, the way to send the bind operation to the server is to call one of the bind or connect methods of an LDAPConnection object. The definition of the LDAPConnection class looks like this:

```
public class LDAPConnection implements LDAPv3,
    LDAPAsynchronousConnection, Cloneable
```

NOTE

The Internet-Draft that defines a standard LDAP API for Java doesn't require an SDK to implement LDAPAsynchronousConnection. In practice, however, most SDKs do. The "Programming Strategies" section of Chapter 3 has details about performing asynchronous LDAP operations.

There are only two constructors for the LDAPConnection class. The first takes no parameters at all, and the second takes an object that has implemented the LDAPSocketFactory interface. We'll talk more about the LDAPSocketFactory interface later in this section.

```
public LDAPConnection()
```

```
public LDAPConnection(LDAPSocketFactory factory)
```

Once you have created an LDAPConnection object, there are several ways to actually establish the connection. The most common way is to call either the connect method by itself or the connect method followed by the bind method.

The Connect Method

There are three versions of the connect method. The parameters that they all have in common are the host and port of the LDAP server. The version that has only a host and port parameter adds that information to the LDAPConnection object. Most LDAP SDKs then wait for you to call some other method, usually the bind method, before the network connection to the LDAP server is actually made.

```
public void connect(String host, int port)
    throws LDAPException
```

The version that takes host, port, dn, and passwd as parameters establishes the connection *and* sends a bind request (using the simple bind method) at the same time.

```
public void connect(String host, int port, String dn,
    String passwd) throws LDAPException
```

The third version is the same as the second, except it also has a version parameter where a value of 2 indicates that your client will stick to LDAPv2 operations that comply with RFC 1777; a value of 3 indicates that your client will use LDAPv3 operations that comply with RFC 2251. If the server is only capable of handling LDAPv2 requests, it throws an LDAPException with the value LDAPException. PROTOCOL_ ERROR.

```
public void connect(int version, String host, int port,
    String dn, String passwd) throws LDAPException
```

Here is a simple example of using this connect method:

```
...
LDAPConnection conn = new LDAPConnection();
conn.connect(3, "ldap.acme.com", 389, "cn=admin,o=acme",
            "adminPassword");
/* Make other LDAP requests here */
conn.disconnect();
...
```

The Bind Method

If you already have an active connection to the server and you call LDAPConnection.bind, the client simply reauthenticates using the credentials you supply. It does this over the current connection without closing it. If the LDAP Connection has been connected before but is currently disconnected, calling bind reestablishes the connection and then performs the bind. If the LDAPConnection. connect method hasn't been called yet, calling bind causes the LDAPException. PARAM_ERROR to be thrown because it doesn't yet know what the host and port should be.

The first version of the bind method performs a simple bind with a DN and password.

```
public void bind(String dn, String passwd)
    throws LDAPException
```

The second version is the same as the first, except that it adds a version parameter to indicate whether you are performing LDAPv2 or LDAPv3 requests. You can use 3 as the version and still make LDAPv2 requests, but if you specify 2 for this parameter you won't be able to do things that are new in LDAPv3, such as making extended requests, using controls, and moving entries.

```
public void bind(int version, String dn, String passwd)
    throws LDAPException
```

WARNING

In the Netscape Directory SDK, there are additional versions of the bind method that take and return an **LDAPResponseListener** object. These methods make asynchronous bind requests. However, because an **LDAP** server does not guarantee to process requests in the order they are received, a bind request should never be made asynchronously. For example, if you perform an asynchronous bind followed by a search, you may not actually be authenticated before the search is performed. The obvious implication of this is that without the rights you expect as an authenticated user, you might not be able to see the entries or attributes for which you are searching. Additionally, the **LDAP** specification says that when a bind request is received all outstanding operations on that connection must be abandoned. So, if the search request has been received but isn't completed when the server begins processing the bind request, it will be thrown away. See the "Programming Strategies" section of Chapter 3 for more information about asynchronous requests.

The Clone Method

The clone method returns a new LDAPConnection that has all of the settings the original had. The original and cloned objects, however, are separate, and any change made to one does not affect the other. The exception is that if the original LDAPConnection object had an open connection to an LDAP server at the time it was cloned, the new (cloned) LDAPConnection object shares that connection. The connection remains open until either it has been closed from both LDAPConnection objects, or the objects go out of scope. If an LDAPConnection object or its clone creates a new connection to an LDAP server, however, that connection is private to the object that created it.

If your LDAP client application needs to establish multiple connections to the LDAP server, one strategy is to create an initial unconnected LDAPConnection object that has your preferred options set, and then clone that object each time your client application needs a new connection to the LDAP server.

```
. . .
LDAPConnection conn1, conn2;
conn1 = new LDAPConnection();
conn1.connect(3, "ldap.acme.com", 389, "cn=admin,o=acme",
            "adminPassword");
```

```
conn2 = conn1.clone();

/* At this point, conn1 and conn2 are separate objects, but
   are both sharing the same network connection to
   ldap.acme.com.
*/

conn1.disconnect();

/* The connection to ldap.acme.com is still active because
   conn2 hasn't disconnected yet, but it's no longer shared
   between conn1 and conn2.
*/

conn1.connect(3, "ldap.acme.com", 389, "cn=steve,o=acme",
                  "stevePassword");

/* conn1 is connected as steve, conn2 is connected as admin.
   Neither of these network connections is shared.
*/

conn1.disconnect();
conn2.disconnect();
...
```

Constraints

The LDAPConnection class uses the term *constraints* to refer to preferences that can be set on the connection. Constraints can be set on the LDAPConnection object so that any operation performed on that connection uses the same constraints. Additionally, some LDAP SDKs, such as the Netscape Directory SDK for Java, allow constraints to be specified uniquely for each operation performed. Many of the constraints that can be set apply only to searching. For that reason, we postpone a detailed discussion of constraints until the next chapter.

Two of the constraints can affect the bind operation. One is the version of the LDAP protocol that the connection will use. Most of the examples in this book call the setOption method to globally set the LDAP version to 3 before calling the connect method. The other constraint that can affect the bind operation is the timeout value. You can specify an amount of time, in milliseconds, that the LDAP client will wait for a response from the server. If the response isn't received in this time, the client abandons the operation by sending an abandon message to the server and throwing an LDAPException with the value LDAPException.LDAP_TIMEOUT.

Use the setOption or the setConstraints method to set preferences to be used by the connection. If you are using the Netscape Directory SDK for Java, you can override the connection-wide constraints for a single operation by calling a method that takes an LDAPConstraints object as a parameter. For example, to specify a timeout value of two seconds for the connection request only, you could do this:

```
...
LDAPConnection conn = new LDAPConnection();
LDAPConstraints connectConstraints = conn.getConstraints();
connectConstraints.setTimeLimit(2000);
conn.connect(3, "ldap.acme.com", 389, "cn=admin,o=acme",
             "adminPassword", connectConstraints);
...
```

The LDAPSocketFactory Interface

If a client SDK wants to add security or other features to the underlying data stream, it can do so by creating a class that implements the LDAPSocketFactory interface. Most SDKs use this interface to allow SSL connections to the LDAP server. See the following section for details about SSL.

The interface definition is very straightforward:

```
public interface LDAPSocketFactory
```

The only method specified by this interface is makeSocket. A class that implements this interface must take the host name and port number of the server and return a java.io.Socket object that has whatever feature the SDK is trying to provide, which usually means it will be an SSL socket.

```
public Socket makeSocket(String host, int port)
    throws IOException, UnknownHostException
```

The com.novell.service.ndssdk.jldap.ssl.LDAPSecureSocketFactory class provided by Novell implements this interface and returns a connected SSL socket from the makeSocket method. We introduce it and show how it is used later in the chapter.

Secure Sockets Layer

Much of what we currently do on the Internet is not secure. Because packets usually pass through several routers on the way to their destination, anyone who has access to any of those networks along the way can "snoop" into the packets that travel across them. The *Secure Sockets Layer* (SSL) protocol encrypts all of the data passing between the endpoints of a TCP socket so that someone inspecting an individual packet in midstream will not be able to decipher it.

The SSL protocol obviously has good implications for LDAP, which is a service traveling over TCP. For one thing, if the client uses the simple authentication method to pass a DN and a password to the server, that password is protected while in transit. Additionally, any information that subsequently passes between the client and the server, in the course of making requests and responding to them, is also encrypted and immune from eavesdropping.

SSL also provides a way for the server to prove its identity to the client through a certificate. When a connection is first established between a client and a server over a port used for SSL communications, a handshaking process establishes the encryption that will be used on the connection. As part of the SSL handshake process, the server sends its certificate to the client that can verify it with a trusted certification authority. Being able to verify the identity of the server prevents spoofing and man-in-the-middle attacks.

NOTE

Less common is client authentication, sometimes called mutual authentication, where the client authenticates to the server by presenting a client certificate. Some LDAP servers provide the capability to do this type of authentication through SASL. Novell has added support for client authentication through the "EXTERNAL" SASL mechanism, but as we previously mentioned, there is not yet support for this type of SASL authentication in the LDAP SDKs provided by Novell.

Connecting to Novell's LDAP Server with SSL

In order for Novell's LDAP server to communicate with a client using SSL, it must have a server certificate that it can pass to the client. There are a few ways to generate and sign a certificate that the server can use, but the most common way is to create a *certification authority* and *key material object*, also called a server certificate, on the server that is running NLDAP. Once you have done this, export the *trusted root* of the key material object and use that in your LDAP client application to verify the server certificate that gets sent to you during the SSL handshake.

It sounds a little complicated, but it's really not.

X-REF

The steps to configure your server to use SSL are described in detail in the section on Secure Sockets Layer configuration in Chapter 10.

Another way to obtain a server certificate is to apply for one from an independent certification authority, such as VeriSign or Digital Signature Trust. An independent certification authority can give your server certificate additional credibility because it is not self-generated.

Using SSL with Novell's LDAP Libraries for C SDK

Making SSL connections from your LDAP client is pretty straightforward if you are using Novell's LDAP Libraries for C SDK. There are three prerequisites:

1. Configure the server according to the instructions listed in the "Secure Sockets Layer Configuration" section of Chapter 10.

2. Export the server's trusted root certificate as described in Chapter 10. Once you have the certificate (in the form of a .DER file), you need to put it somewhere on the file system that is accessible from your client application. In Listing 4.1, we just put the TRUSTEDROOTCERT.DER file directly in the directory where our sample client application was located.

3. Install Novell Cryptography Support Modules, sometimes called Novell International Cryptographic Infrastructure (NICI), on the computer that will be running your client application.

You can find NICI installation packages for NetWare, Solaris, Linux, and Windows at http://www.novell.com/products/cryptography/.

Once you have done these three things, you can compile code similar to the one in Listing 4.1 by using the Novell LDAP Libraries for C SDK.

L I S T I N G   4 . 1

SSL connection using LDAP SDK for C

```c
#include <stdio.h>
#include <ldap.h>
#include <ldap_ssl.h>

int main()
{
    int     rcode;
    LDAP    *ld;
    char    *certPath = "TrustedRootCert.der";
    char    *host = "myserver.acme.com";
    int     port = 636;
    int     useSSL = 1;
    char    *loginDN = "cn=admin,o=acme";
    char    *loginPass = "adminpass";

    /* Set LDAP version to 3 */
    int version = LDAP_VERSION3;
    ldap_set_option(NULL, LDAP_OPT_PROTOCOL_VERSION,
        &version);

    /* Initialize the SSL LDAP session */
    if (ldapssl_client_init(certPath, NULL) < 0) {
        printf("Failed to initialize SSL client\n");
        return(1);
    }
```

Continued

```
/* Make the SSL connection */
if ((ld=ldapssl_init(host, port, useSSL)) == NULL) {
   printf("LDAP session initialization failed\n");
   ldapssl_client_deinit();
   return(1);
}


/* Bind to the server */
rcode = ldap_simple_bind_s(ld, loginDN, loginPass);
if (rcode != LDAP_SUCCESS) {
   printf("ldap_simple_bind_s: %s\n",
       ldap_err2string(rcode));
   ldap_unbind_s(ld);
   ldapssl_client_deinit();
   return(1);
}


/* Make other LDAP requests here */

/* Disconnect and free the LDAP structure */
ldap_unbind_s(ld);
ldapssl_client_deinit();

return(0);
}
```

Using SSL with the Netscape Directory SDK for C

You can use the Netscape Directory SDK for C to establish an SSL connection to Novell's LDAP server. The steps are nearly identical to the preceding for Novell's LDAP Libraries for C SDK. The primary difference is that instead of pointing directly to the TRUSTEDROOTCERT.DER file, you must first import the TRUSTEDROOTCERT.DER file into Netscape's certificate store (named cert7.db on your hard drive), and then point to that certificate store instead of the actual .DER file when you call ldapssl_client_init.

Chapter 10 describes how to import the TRUSTEDROOTCERT.DER file into Netscape's certificate store. The steps are near the end of the "Secure Sockets Layer Configuration" section.

X-REF

Using SSL with a Java LDAP SDK

Both the Netscape Directory SDK for Java and Novell's LDAP Libraries for Java, when it becomes available, will allow the client programmer/user to establish SSL connections to the server. Both require an additional, third-party Java class that implements the javax.net.ssl.SSLSocket interface. You can obtain such a class from www.phaos.com (look for their SSLava product), but Novell has licensed this package for developers to use with Novell products and makes it available from DeveloperNet.

You can find documentation, some sample code (which currently includes no LDAP-specific examples, unfortunately), and download the SDK from http://developer.novell.com/ndk/jssl.htm.

Certificates created in NDS use Rivest-Shamir-Adleman (RSA) encryption technology. The only SSL for Java package we know of that has the correct algorithms for reading these RSA-generated certificates is Novell's SSL for Java package. Therefore, the example given here requires it.

WARNING

The example we give you later in this section uses the Netscape Directory SDK for Java 4.0, along with the Novell SSL for Java package for the actual SSLSocket implementation. When Novell's LDAP Libraries for Java SDK is released, the setup to use SSL should be very similar to this example. The example also uses the Java Development Kit (JDK) version 1.2. JDK 1.1 should work as well, with some minor changes.

JDK version 1.2 is available from http://java.sun.com.

Configure the Server

If you install NetWare 5.1 or later, the installation program configures the server for you by creating a certification authority and a server certificate (key material object). It even exports the trusted root and copies it to SYS:PUBLIC\RootCert.der.

If your NDS server is running on NT, Linux, or Solaris, you need to follow the steps in the "Secure Sockets Layer Configuration" section of Chapter 10 to create a certification authority and a server certificate, and also to export the trusted root.

Put the Necessary .JAR Files in Your CLASSPATH

Besides the LDAPJDK.JAR file that comes with the Netscape Directory SDK, there are two other Java archive (JAR) files that you need in your CLASSPATH environment variable: either the NSSL1.2_EXP.JAR or NSSL1.2_DOM.JAR, and the NOVBP.JAR files. The difference between the NSSL1.2_EXP.JAR and NSSL1.2_DOM.JAR files is that the level of encryption that NSSL1.2_EXP.JAR supports allows it to be exported outside the United States. The NSSL1.2_DOM.JAR file is only available domestically. Because of recent changes to the laws governing encryption technologies, the stronger encryption should soon be widely available, and the name of the files may change to leave off the _EXP or _DOM parts.

IMPORTANT

If you are using the exportable NSSL1.2_EXP.JAR file, you should take care that the certification authority and server certificate that you create use the smaller key size (512 bits) instead of the larger size (2048 bits). When you create them in ConsoleOne, you can choose the custom create method to select the smaller key sizes. Larger key sizes won't work with NSSL1.2_EXP.JAR, and will cause an error when you try to create the SSL connection.

The other file we mentioned that needs to be in your CLASSPATH environment variable is NOVBP.JAR. This file contains several class files that create interfaces between SSL and LDAP. Some of the classes are meant to be used only with JNDI (see Chapter 3 for a description of JNDI), but the one we need for our example is com.novell.service.ndssdk.jldap.ssl.LDAPSecureSocketFactory, which creates the necessary interface between Novell's SSL for Java package, and either the Netscape Directory SDK for Java or Novell's LDAP Libraries for Java. When Novell's LDAP Libraries for Java becomes available, the NOVBP.JAR file should be included with it.

**For now, however, you can find it as a component of the LDAP
Service Provider for JNDI download at** `http://developer.`
`novell.com/ndk/ldapjndi.htm.`

Import the Trusted Root Certificate to the Client's Certificate Store

Once you have the trusted root certificate exported from your server, you need
to import it into the certificate store on the client. To import the certificate to the
local certificate store, also called a keystore, you can use the KeyTool class that
comes with JDK 1.2 or later. Alternatively, there is a keytool executable that comes
with the Java Runtime Environment (JRE) that may be used.

If you had the trusted root certificate from the server saved on a diskette as
A:ROOTCERT.DER, to import it into a new keystore file named .KEYSTORE in the
current directory you would type the following on the command line:

```
java sun.security.tools.KeyTool -import -noprompt
    -alias TrustedRoot -file a:rootcert.der
    -keystore .keystore -storepass keystorepass
```

If you leave off the –keystore parameter, the certificate is imported into your
default system certificate store. Search your drive for the .KEYSTORE file to find it.
On Windows 2000 Professional, logged in as Administrator, we found it at
C:\DOCUMENTS and SETTINGS\ADMINISTRATOR\.KEYSTORE.

Optionally Configure the SSL.PROPERTIES File

If the trusted root certificate is in a .KEYSTORE file in the current directory, or
if it is in the default system certificate store, it can be found and used automatically. If the trusted root certificate is in a certificate store that is not in one of these
two places, you can specify its location by setting up a file in the current directory
called SSL.PROPERTIES. The file is a plain text file that contains properties used
by the SSL provider. One of the properties you can set is the location of the keystore. For example, you could add a line (it could be the only line) like this:

```
ssl.keystore=C:/mydata/.keystore
```

Sample Java Source Code

Compared to the setup and configuration required, the source code is quite
simple. The following Java class, when compiled with JDK 1.2, establishes an SSL

connection to the LDAP server, assuming all of the previously described setup is complete.

L I S T I N G   4.2

*SSL connection using LDAP
SDK for Java*

```
import netscape.ldap.*;
import
com.novell.service.ndssdk.jldap.ssl.LDAPSecureSocketFactory;

public class SSLExample{
    public static void main(String[] args) {
        try {
            LDAPConnection conn = new LDAPConnection(
                new LDAPSecureSocketFactory());
            conn.connect("ldap.acme.com", 636,
                "cn=admin,o=acme", "adminpass");

            /* Make other LDAP requests here */

            conn.disconnect();
        } catch(LDAPException e) {
            System.out.println(e.toString());
        }
    }
}
```

Notice that the main difference when using SSL is that when you create an LDAPConnection object, you use the constructor that takes an LDAPSecure SocketFactory object. The only other difference between this example and one that doesn't use SSL is the port number, which needs to be 636 for an SSL connection.

Summary

Connecting and authenticating to the LDAP server through the LDAP bind operation is the first step in getting services from it. All of the rights you have to perform other LDAP operations are based on the identity with which you authenticate to the LDAP server. This chapter covered simple authentication, SASL, and SSL connections. The next chapter covers the meatiest of the LDAP operations: search.

CHAPTER 5

Searching

One of the primary benefits of a directory is the capability to search for information in it. The name Lightweight Directory Access Protocol implies the capability to retrieve information from a directory. LDAP has evolved to encompass more than a simple access protocol, but that is where its roots lie. The way you access information in an LDAP directory is to perform a search operation. Because of its flexibility, search can be one of the more complex of the LDAP operations. By the time you finish this chapter, however, you should have a good grasp of the different ways you can perform a search, when you would want to do each kind, and how to effectively implement them in your applications using the LDAP SDK.

Search Concepts

An LDAP search request originates from the client and is sent on the network to the LDAP server. If the server is able to successfully perform the search, it sends the search results, along with a result code that indicates success, back to the client. The search results consist of the distinguished names (DNs) of each entry that matched your search criteria, along with their attributes and values if requested. If the search was not successful, a result code indicating the type of error encountered is returned to the client.

The LDAP client SDK handles this exchange through its LDAPConnection.search method by either returning an instance of LDAPSearchResults or throwing an LDAPException. Before going into detail about coding specifics, we need to talk more generally about searching the directory.

The Elements of a Search Request

When you are forming your search request you'll need to decide the following few things:

- ▶ What types of entries are you looking for?

- ▶ Where in the tree structure do you want to look?

▸ Do you want to see only entries that match a certain condition or criterion?

▸ Do you want to limit the number of returned entries in case your search criteria is too broad?

▸ How long are you willing to wait for the server to finish processing the request?

▸ Do you want to see all of the attributes of the entries that get returned or only certain ones?

▸ Do you want to see the attribute values?

It sounds like a lot to keep track of, but there are really only four primary inputs that define a search request. You could rely on defaults for the others and get by. The four primary inputs are

▸ The search base

▸ The search scope

▸ The search filter

▸ The attribute list

The Search Base: Where Do You Want the Search to Start?

The search base is the distinguished name, or DN, of the entry in the tree where you would like the search to begin. For example, if you want to do a subtree search beginning at ou=sales,o=acme, then provide that as the base DN. If you want the search to begin at the root of the tree, then you provide the empty string as the search base.

The Search Scope: How Deep Do You Want the Search to Go?

The scope defines how deep the search extends from the base DN. You can choose to search just the entry specified by the base DN, all of the entries immediately subordinate to the base DN, or the entire subtree beginning with the base DN. Figures 5.1 through 5.3 show how these three different scope values would affect a search. In each example, the dark border represents the entry that is the search base, and the gray area represents the search scope.

In Figure 5.1 the base of the search is l=San Francisco. Because we are using SCOPE_BASE, the only entry within the scope is the one we specified as the base DN. This is useful if you are interested in a single entry, you already know that entry's DN, and you want to read its attributes. The LDAP SDK actually provides two methods of doing this — read and search — both of which are discussed later in this chapter.

In Figure 5.2 the base is still l=San Francisco. Using SCOPE_ONE as the scope means that the server searches one level beneath the base, not including the base itself. Therefore, the two entries representing the butchers and bakers containers are the only ones within the search scope in this example. This is useful for an application that browses a tree, only needing to see the immediate subordinates of a container at one time.

Figure 5.3 shows an example of a subtree search. The search base and all entries beneath it in the tree are searched. This is useful when you want to search a larger portion of your tree, looking for entries that match a certain criteria.

► · ◄

FIGURE 5.1

Example of SCOPE_BASE

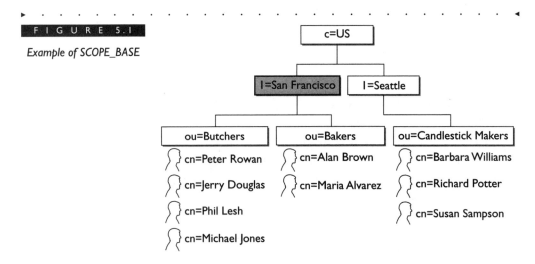

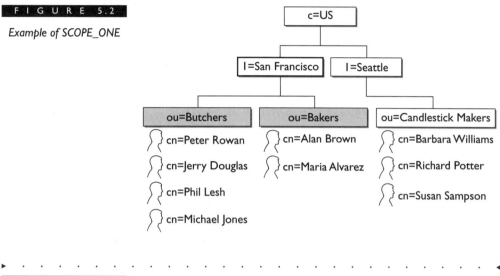

FIGURE 5.2

Example of SCOPE_ONE

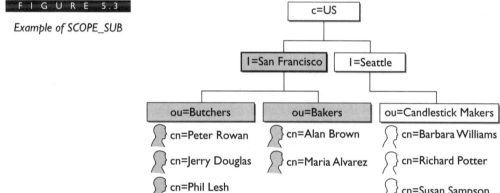

FIGURE 5.3

Example of SCOPE_SUB

The Search Filter: Which Entries Do You Want Returned?

The filter defines which entries within the scope you want the server to return to you. If you are doing a subtree search, looking for all of the people who have a first name that begins with Deb, your filter would be givenName=Deb*. The filter syntax is quite flexible but can also be complex. Filters are discussed in detail later in the chapter.

The Attribute List: Which Attributes of Those Entries Do You Want to See?

The attribute list specifies which attributes you want returned with each of the entries. You can specify that you want all attributes (the default), that you want no attributes (just the DNs), or that you want a specific list of attributes (if they exist) on the entries. For example, if you are only interested in telephone numbers and e-mail addresses you would supply telephoneNumber and mail in the attribute list. Attribute list specifics are discussed later in the chapter.

Basic Searching with the LDAP SDK

We're ready at this point to begin looking at some of the details of searching with the LDAP SDK. Some of the classes used to search an LDAP server have already been introduced in previous chapters. We'll mention these again, but we'll focus primarily on the specific methods used to search and to handle search results.

LDAPConnection Class

In Chapter 4, we discussed the details of setting up an instance of the LDAPConnection class and authenticating (binding) to the server. You may want to go back and review that chapter, especially if you are interested in secure, encrypted communications with the LDAP server or if you are unsure how to authenticate to the server.

IMPORTANT

Most LDAP servers implement some type of access control. As discussed in Chapter 4, when you connect to an LDAP server you can specify to connect anonymously or as an authenticated user. Depending on how the LDAP server is configured, there may be information in the directory that is unavailable to you based on your authentication identity and access controls. When gathering search results, the server only includes entries and attributes that you are allowed to see based on your authentication.

In this section, we focus on the methods of the LDAPConnection class that perform the search operation called search and read.

LDAPConnection.search Method

There are four versions of the search method in the LDAPConnection class. The one used most commonly looks like this:

```
public LDAPSearchResults search(
    String base,
    int scope,
    String filter,
    String attrs[],
    boolean typesOnly)
        throws LDAPException
```

Its parameters include the four primary inputs that we have already mentioned: the search base, the search scope, the search filter, and the attribute list. The fifth parameter is a boolean that indicates whether you want to see only the attribute names or their values as well. This method returns an instance of the LDAPSearchResults class, which we cover later, and it throws an LDAPException if it encounters an error.

The other three versions of the search method enable you to provide the search inputs in the form of an LDAPUrl instance and to provide additional search options through an LDAPSearchConstraints object. We cover the use of LDAPUrl and LDAPSearchConstraints later in this chapter.

LDAPConnection.read Method

The read method performs a specific kind of search. It returns the single entry specified in the DN parameter.

```
public LDAPEntry read(String DN, String attrs[])
    throws LDAPException
```

You would use this method if you already knew the DN of an entry in the tree, and you wanted to read its attribute types and values. Or, you could use this method to test for the existence of a specific entry, because it throws an exception if the DN doesn't exist.

It's interesting to note that even though the read method looks at first glance to be quite a bit different than the search method, they both invoke the same search operation on the LDAP server. The difference is that when you call the read method, the search scope is implied to be SCOPE_BASE, and the filter is set to objectclass=*. In fact, you could get the same results by calling the search method with those parameters. We talk more about scope and filter parameters later in this chapter.

Another difference to notice between search and read is that the read method returns a single LDAPEntry rather than LDAPSearchResults, which is an enumeration of (possibly many) LDAPEntry objects.

As with search, there are other versions of the read method that enable you to specify additional options in an LDAPSearchConstraint object and to specify an LDAPUrl. We discuss those later in the chapter as well.

Choosing the Search Base and Search Scope

The search concepts section of this chapter mentioned search base and search scope choices. In the search method, you need to provide these as the base and scope parameters. The allowable choices for the search scope are specified in Table 5.1.

TABLE 5.1	SCOPE VALUE	DESCRIPTION
Values of the Scope Parameter	LDAPv2.SCOPE_BASE	Only looks at the single entry specified as the base DN.
	LDAPv2.SCOPE_ONE	Looks at the immediate children of the base DN, but not at any of their children, and not the base DN itself.
	LDAPv2.SCOPE_SUB	Looks at the base DN and the entire subtree beneath it.

The DN you supply for the base parameter therefore is the single entry you want to search if the scope is LDAPv2.SCOPE_BASE, or the container you want to search if the scope is LDAPv2.SCOPE_ONE or LDAPv2.SCOPE_SUB.

Defining a Search Filter

The next parameter required by the search method is the filter parameter. There are enough different ways to define a search filter that we have devoted a section of this chapter to it later on. For now, keep in mind that a filter is something that every entry in the search scope is compared against. Those entries within the search scope that match the filter are the entries that are returned in the search results. An example of a simple filter is givenName=john, which would match all entries within the scope that had a value of john in the givenName attribute.

Specifying the Attributes to be Returned

As we mentioned earlier, the attribute list specifies the names of the attributes that you want returned along with the DNs of the entries that match the search criteria. In both the search and the read methods, the attribute list is an array of String objects that name each attribute.

To understand more about how the server decides which attributes to return, it is important to make a distinction between *user* and *operational* attributes. User attributes are all of those attributes which hold the common information that we normally associate with an entry in the tree such as cn, sn, givenName, telephoneNumber, mail, and so on. In addition to these common user attributes, there are attributes that are used and updated by the directory server; these attributes contain information such as when the entry was created or modified, who last created or modified the entry, and where the schema definition is for the entry. These are called *operational* attributes. Operational attributes hold information that the server wants to keep track of and make available to LDAP clients. Operational attributes are created by the LDAP server and usually cannot be modified directly by an LDAP client, although they can often be modified indirectly. For instance, an entry's modifyTimeStamp value cannot be changed directly by an LDAP client (an attempt to do so would fail), but its value is updated to the current time if that same client modifies the entry in some way. Section 5.1 of RFC 2252 defines the standard set of operational attributes, and Chapter 7 in this book describes their use in NDS and additional NDS-specific operational attributes.

Table 5.2 shows the different ways you can define your attribute list, allowing for both operational and user attributes, all attributes, or no attributes.

T A B L E   5.2

*Ways of Defining
Attribute Lists*

TO GET THIS...	SUPPLY THIS FOR THE ATTRS PARAMETER...
All user attributes	`null`. If `null` is provided, instead of the attrs array, user attributes on each DN that match the search criteria are returned.
A certain set of user attributes	Name each attribute as a separate element of the array. For example, to get `cn`, `sn`, and `telephoneNumber`, specify `new String[]{"cn", "sn", "telephoneNumber"}`
Operational attributes	The name of each operational attribute that you want returned must be listed as a separate element of the array. They may be listed along with specific user attributes as well.
All user attributes along with specific operational attributes	`*` or `LDAPv3.ALL_USER_ATTRS`. The asterisk indicates that you want all user attributes. You can provide this value along with a list of user attributes to be returned.
No attributes	`1.1` or `LDAPv3.NO_ATTRS`. The object identifier (OID) 1.1 by itself specifies that you only want the list of DNs returned, without any of their attributes.

Handling Search Results

When the LDAPConnection.read method is successful, it returns an instance of the LDAPEntry class representing a single entry in the directory. The LDAP-Connection.search method returns an LDAPSearchResults object which is an Enumeration of LDAPEntry objects. (Check the Java SDK documentation or the example at the end of this section if you're unfamiliar with Enumerations in Java.) Whether your application is a simple search tool, or something more complex, you need to know how to parse the information contained in LDAPSearchResults and LDAPEntry.

LDAPSearchResults Class

The search methods of LDAPConnection each return an LDAPSearchResults object which contains the search results gathered by the server. An LDAP-SearchResults object is an Enumeration of LDAPEntry objects.

```
public class LDAPSearchResults
    implements java.util.Enumeration
```

Use the nextElement and hasMoreElements methods to iterate the elements of the LDAPSearchResults as you would do with any other Enumeration in Java.

Besides the Enumeration methods, there are two methods that are unique to the LDAPSearchResults class: getResponseControls and sort.

```
public LDAPControl[] getResponseControls()
```

The getResponseControls method returns an array of controls that the server returned with the search results. See Chapter 9 to learn about controls and how to use them in your searches.

Sorting the Results

Normally, when the LDAP server returns search results, the entries are in whatever order they were found by the server process that compared them against the search filter. If it matters to you what order your search results are in, there are a couple different ways of sorting them.

You can ask the server to sort the results before they are returned to you by sending your search request with a *sort control* attached to it. If the LDAP server you are using supports the sort control and has the features you need, then using a sort control is a good way of offloading work from your client to the server.

The other way to get sorted results is to wait for the results to come back from the server and then call the sort method of the LDAPSearchResults:

```
public void sort(LDAPEntryComparator comp)
```

You can define your own class to compare entries, or you can use the predefined LDAPCompareAttrNames class. A simple example of sorting search results by common name would be

```
results.sort(new LDAPCompareAttrNames("cn"));
```

To place the results in descending order (rather than ascending) you would do this:

```
results.sort(new LDAPCompareAttrNames("cn", false));
```

To sort on both surname and given name you could do this:

```
String[] attrNames = { "sn", "givenName" );
res.sort(new LDAPCompareAttrNames(attrNames));
```

WARNING

Asking the server to sort the results for you has some limitations. To improve performance, NDS only sorts on attributes that it has internally indexed, only sorts on one attribute at a time, and only sorts in ascending order. If you want to be able to sort on non-indexed attributes, on more than one attribute, or in descending order, you should sort the results after they are retrieved by calling the sort method of LDAPSearchResults. In Chapter 10, we list the attributes that NDS indexes by default and tell you how to index additional attributes.

LDAPEntry Class

We've seen that when you perform a search, you get an LDAPSearchResults object which is an enumeration of LDAPEntry objects. Each of these LDAPEntry objects represents an actual entry in the directory and is comprised of a distinguished name and an attribute set.

You can retrieve the distinguished name of an LDAPEntry with the following method:

```
public String getDN()
```

The attribute set is returned by calling the following method:

```
public LDAPAttributeSet getAttributeSet()
```

If you want just the attributes for a given attribute name, you can retrieve them with this method:

```
public LDAPAttribute[] getAttribute(String attrName)
```

LDAPAttributeSet Class

LDAPEntry.getAttributeSet returns an instance of the LDAPAttributeSet class as defined by

```
public class LDAPAttributeSet implements Cloneable
```

This class is also used to add and modify entries and is discussed in Chapter 6. Here, however, we limit our discussion to the methods you use when handling search results.

If you want to examine only a specific attribute, you can retrieve it from the AttributeSet with this method:

```
public LDAPAttribute getAttribute(String attrName)
```

However, the more commonly used method is

```
public Enumeration getAttributes()
```

It returns an enumeration of LDAPAttribute objects. After calling this method, your application can read the set of attributes one at a time, performing some operation on each one, such as printing them out. You can see an example that does just that at the end of this section.

LDAPAttribute Class

An Attribute object contains both the attribute name and each of its values. There are accessor methods for the attribute name and for each value—either as an enumeration of strings, an array of strings, an enumeration of byte arrays, or an array of byte arrays:

```
public String getName()
public Enumeration getStringValues()
public String[] getStringValueArray()
public Enumeration getByteValues()
public byte[][] getByteValueArray()
```

The methods that return strings can be used for most attributes. The ones that return byte arrays are used for attributes that have binary values.

Factors Limiting Your Search Results

The attributes and values that you get from your search results for a given entry may not represent the entire set of attributes and values that exist on that entry in the directory. There are three things that might limit the attribute names or values that get returned to you.

1. One of the parameters of the search method is a list of attributes that you want returned. Unless you used the default for this (to request all attributes), the attributes returned are limited to the ones in your attribute list.

2. You passed true as the typesOnly parameter of the search method. In this case, the LDAPAttribute objects returned only have attribute names — no values.

3. Remember that when the server processes your search request, it only looks at entries and attributes that you have a right to see, based on your authentication and the access controls on the server. If the access controls restrict your right to see a particular attribute, that attribute and its values may not be included in the search results returned to you.

Simple Search Example

It's time for some action! This is an example to get you started. The following Java application sends a subtree search to the server. When it has the results it iterates them, printing the distinguished names, attribute names, and values of each entry that was returned. As you read farther into the chapter, see if you can expand on this example.

LISTING 5.1

A basic search example

```
/* SearchExample.java */

import netscape.ldap.*;
import java.util.*;

public class SearchExample {
```

```java
public static void main(String[] args) {
    String HOST = "ldap.novell.com";
    int PORT = 389;
    String FILTER = "sn=Hunter";
    String BASE_DN = "o=widget,c=us";
    int SCOPE = LDAPv2.SCOPE_SUB;
    String[] ATTR_LIST = null;

    LDAPConnection conn = null;
    try {
        conn = new LDAPConnection();
        conn.connect(HOST, PORT, "cn=admin,o=acme",
                     "adminPass");
        LDAPSearchResults res = conn.search(BASE_DN,
                                            SCOPE,
                                            FILTER,
                                            ATTR_LIST,
                                            false);

        /* Loop on results until finished */
        while (res.hasMoreElements()) {

            /* Get the next directory entry */
            LDAPEntry findEntry = null;
            try {
                findEntry = res.next();
            } catch (LDAPException e) {
                System.out.println("Error: " +
                                   e.toString());
                continue;
            }

            /* Print the DN of the entry */
            System.out.println();
```

Continued

A basic search example
(continued)

```
System.out.println(findEntry.getDN());

/* Get the attributes of the entry */
LDAPAttributeSet findAttrs =
    findEntry.getAttributeSet();
Enumeration attrs =
    findAttrs.getAttributes();

/* Loop on attributes */
while (attrs.hasMoreElements()) {
    LDAPAttribute anAttr =
    (LDAPAttribute)attrs.nextElement();
    String attrName = anAttr.getName();

    /* Loop on values for this attribute */
    Enumeration vals =
        anAttr.getStringValues();
    if (vals != null) {
        while (vals.hasMoreElements()) {
            String aVal =
                (String)vals.nextElement();
            System.out.println(attrName +
                "=" + aVal);
        }
    }
}

/*/ Disconnect */
if ((conn != null) && conn.isConnected()) {
    conn.disconnect();
}
```

```
    } catch(LDAPException e) {
        System.out.println("Error: "+e.toString());
    }
  }
}
```

Constraints

There are additional settings, sometimes called constraints, which can affect both client and server behavior when searching. Some of these constraints affect any operation performed on the current connection, and others affect only the search operation. The options that affect any connection operation are encapsulated by the SDK in the LDAPConstraints class, and those that are specific to searching are represented by the LDAPSearchConstraints class.

Changing Constraints for the Current Connection

If you want to change the defaults for the current LDAP session (as represented by an LDAPConnection) you can call any one of three mutator methods:

- **setOption:** Call this to change just a single option, leaving the rest unchanged.

- **setConstraints:** Call this to change your whole set of connection options.

- **setSearchConstraints:** Call this to change the set of search options for all searches on this connection.

The three mutator methods are defined within the LDAPConnection class as follows:

```
public void setOption(int option, Object value)
    throws LDAPException
```

```
public void setConstraints(LDAPConstraints cons)

public void setSearchConstraints(LDAPSearchConstraints cons)
```

There are also three accessor methods which are used to get either a single option, an instance of LDAPConstraints used on the connection, or an instance of LDAPSearchConstraints used on the connection.

▶ **getOption:** Call this to retrieve the value of any connection option.

▶ **getConstraints:** Call this to get the current set of constraints in use on the connection.

▶ **getSearchConstraints:** Call this to get the current set of search constraints in use on the connection.

The three accessor methods are defined within the LDAPConnection class as follows:

```
public Object getOption(int option) throws LDAPException

public LDAPConstraints getConstraints()

public LDAPSearchConstraints getSearchConstraints()
```

Overriding Constraints for a Single Search

There are versions of the search and read methods that take, as an additional parameter, an instance of LDAPSearchConstraints. You can use these methods to ignore the current search-related settings and use the settings you supply in the LDAPSearchConstraints object instead:

```
public LDAPSearchResults search(String base,
                                int scope,
                                String filter,
                                String attrs[],
                                boolean typesOnly,
```

```
                    LDAPSearchConstraints cons)
                    throws LDAPException

    public LDAPEntry read(String dn,
                    LDAPSearchConstraints cons)
                    throws LDAPException
```

In order to call these methods, you need to first create the LDAPSearch-Constraints object that you will pass in as the cons argument. You can do that by creating a new LDAPSearchConstraints instance and calling the constructor, but it might be easier for you to make a *copy* of the LDAPSearchConstraints object that is being used for the current connection, and then modify that copy to suit your purposes. You can do the following to accomplish that:

```
    LDAPSearchConstraints copiedConstraints =
        conn.getSearchConstraints().clone();
```

Options That Affect LDAP Searching

Table 5.3 lists the options that are part of the LDAPConstraints class along with a short description and the default value for each. Table 5.4 lists the LDAPSearchConstraints options.

TABLE 5.3

LDAPConstraints
Parameters

PARAMETER	DESCRIPTION	DEFAULT
TimeLimit	Maximum time in milliseconds (thousandths of a second) to wait for results. This time limit is not sent to the LDAP server along with the request. Rather, the LDAPConnection method using this constraint starts a timer, and if the limit is reached before it has a response it sends an abandon message to the server. (Contrast this with the serverTimeLimit parameter in Table 5.4.) Zero indicates no time limit.	0

Continued

TABLE 5.3

LDAPConstraints
Parameters (continued)

PARAMETER	DESCRIPTION	DEFAULT
doReferrals	If you set this to true, the LDAP SDK automatically follows any referrals sent from the server, performing the operation again on the referred-to server. See Chapter 8 for more information about referrals. If you want the server to be able to pass you referrals, be sure to set the LDAP version number to 3 when you connect or authenticate. If you are calling getOption or setOption, the option parameter is LDAPv2.REFERRALS.	false
rebindProc	Specifies an object of the class that implements the LDAPRebind interface. The object is used when the client follows referrals automatically. The object provides a method for getting the distinguished name and password used to authenticate to another LDAP server during a referral. Specifying null indicates the default LDAPRebind will be used if one has been assigned with LDAPConnection.setConstraints, or anonymous authentication otherwise. See Chapter 8 for more details. If you are calling getOption or setOption, the option parameter is LDAPv2. REFERRALS_REBIND_PROC.	defaults to anonymous authentication
hopLimit	When doReferrals is set to true, it is possible for one LDAP server to refer you to another LDAP server, which refers you to another, and so on. This parameter limits the number of nested referrals you are willing to follow on a single operation. See "Name Resolution Models" in Chapter 8 for more details. If you are calling getOption or setOption, the option parameter is LDAPv3.REFERRALS_HOP_LIMIT.	10

TABLE 5.4

LDAPSearchConstraints
Parameters

PARAMETER	DESCRIPTION	DEFAULT
serverTimeLimit	Maximum time in seconds that the server should spend processing the search request. If the server hits this limit it returns the search results it has collected up to the serverTimeLimit, along with the TIME_LIMIT_EXCEEDED result code. (Contrast this with the timeLimit parameter in Table 5.3, which can also be used in a search.) Zero indicates no time limit. If you are calling getOption or setOption, the option parameter is LDAPv2.TIMELIMIT.	0
dereference	Specifies when aliases should be dereferenced. Must be either LDAP_DEREF_NEVER, LDAP_DEREF_SEARCHING, LDAP_DEREF_FINDING, or LDAP_DEREF_ALWAYS from LDAPv2. If you are calling getOption or setOption, the option parameter is LDAPv2.DEREF.	LDAP_DEREF_NEVER
maxResults	Maximum number of search results to return. If the server hits this limit it returns the search results it has collected up to the maxResults limit, along with the SIZE_LIMIT_EXCEEDED result code. If you are calling getOption or setOption, the option parameter is LDAPv2.SIZELIMIT.	1000
batchSize	Sets the suggested number of results to block on during enumeration of search results. Zero means to wait until all the results are in before returning the LDAPSearchResults object. If you want to process search results as they come in, set this to 1. Other positive values will set that batch size to that number. For example, if you set it to 5, your application waits until it has five entries, processes those, and then waits for five more, following this pattern until all search result entries have been received. If you are calling getOption or setOption, the option parameter is LDAPv2.BATCHSIZE.	1

Time Limiting Options

You can use the timeLimit or serverTimeLimit options to limit the amount of time that you wait for search results. The timeLimit option waits the given number of milliseconds (thousandths of a second) before giving up and sending an abandon message to the server. The serverTimeLimit is a value sent to the server along with your search request. If the server can't collect all of the search results in the time you specify, it quits searching and returns the TIME_LIMIT_EXCEEDED result code. In both cases, the LDAP SDK throws an LDAPException.

In NDS, the administrator can also set a global time limit that is used for all LDAP searches on a particular server. To do so, run ConsoleOne with admin privileges and edit the LDAP Server object for the server you want to configure. Put the number of seconds that you want to limit searching to in the Search Time Limit field. This field can also be set through LDAP by setting the searchTimeLimit attribute on the LDAP server object. A value of zero, which is the default, means that the time spent searching is not limited by the server. You can think of the administrator-set time limit as the upper time limit for any LDAP search. If, in your application, you set the serverTimeLimit to something less than what the administrator set the limit to, then your value is used. If you set the serverTimeLimit to something greater than the administrator-set value, then the value the administrator set is used.

Limiting the Size of Search Results

With the maxResults option you can limit the number of entries that get returned when you perform a search. For example, if you set this option to 100, and 150 entries would normally match your search criteria, only the first 100 that the server finds are returned, along with the SIZE_LIMIT_EXCEEDED result code. That result code causes an LDAPException to be thrown.

As with the time limit, the NDS administrator can also set a global size limit that is used for all LDAP searches on a particular server. Use ConsoleOne to edit the LDAP Server object and add a value to the Search Entry Limit field. By default, this value is set to zero, which means that the search result size is not limited by the server.

As with the administrator-set time limit, the size limit set by the administrator is an absolute upper limit. However, if you set the maxResults option to be smaller than the administrator-set value, then your smaller value is used instead.

Alias Handling

In NDS, as well as most other LDAP servers, you have the ability to create an entry whose function is to reference or point to another entry. These types of pointer entries are called aliases. In LDAP, an alias is defined by the alias object class. It contains an attribute called `aliasedObjectName,` which holds the DN of the entry it references. When you do an LDAP search and encounter one of these aliases, the search can proceed in one of two ways. Either it can return the alias as an alias, or it can dereference the alias and return the entry that the alias points to.

The determination of how aliases are handled during LDAP searching is made by the dereference option. Table 5.5 has some additional detail about the valid values for the dereference option.

T A B L E   5.5

Alias Dereferencing Choices

VALUE OF DEREFERENCE OPTION	SEARCH BEHAVIOR
LDAP_DEREF_NEVER	Aliases are never dereferenced.
LDAP_DEREF_SEARCHING	If an alias is encountered after the base DN of the search has been located and the server is searching, that alias is dereferenced and the search resumes from the dereferenced alias. If the search scope is subtree, and the dereferenced alias has children, the search continues down that subtree. If the search scope is one level, only the dereferenced alias is examined.
LDAP_DEREF_FINDING	If an alias is encountered when resolving the base DN of the search, that alias is dereferenced and the name resolution continues from that point. Any aliases encountered below the base DN of the search are not dereferenced and are returned as aliases.
LDAP_DEREF_ALWAYS	This causes both preceding dereference behaviors to take place

Referral Handling

It is possible to configure an LDAP server to refer clients to other servers if the information they are looking for is not present locally. We talk briefly about the client options for referral handling here. In Chapter 8 we discuss both client and server referral processing options in more depth, as well as specifics about how referrals are implemented and used in NDS.

IMPORTANT

A search request is not the only operation that can return a referral. If the base DN given for any LDAP operation is not present locally, a referral could be generated. However, Novell's LDAPv3 server implementation currently supports referrals only for search operations.

There are three options that control how your application behaves when a request returns a referral to another server: doReferrals, hopLimit, and rebindProc. If doReferrals is set to true, your application attempts to automatically follow the referral to the other server. If it is set to false (which is the default), the referral is not automatically followed, but instead generates an LDAPReferralException.

IMPORTANT

Referrals can only be returned by an LDAPv3 server to an LDAPv3 client application. NDS is an LDAPv3 server, but most LDAP SDKs today default to using LDAPv2. Unless you specifically set the version of your client application to 3, the server is not allowed to send it referrals. To set the version to 3, use the connect or authenticate method that allows you to specify a version argument.

The hopLimit option controls how many consecutive referrals your application can automatically follow for a single operation. For example, if you set the hopLimit to 2, and your application receives three nested referrals in the process of resolving a single operation, an LDAPReferralException would be thrown when the third referral was received.

The rebindProc option defines how your application attempts to authenticate to other servers it gets referrals to. By default, it attempts to do an anonymous bind (with no DN or password) to the referred-to server. If you want your application to be able to authenticate with credentials, you need to provide a way for it to get those credentials (such as the user's DN and password), probably from user input, and then bind to the server to which your application was referred. This is done by defining a class that implements the LDAPRebind interface and has a method called getRebindAuthentication. When your application is automatically following a referral, it passes the hostname and port of the referred-to server to the getRebindAuthentication method, which should return an instance of LDAPRebindAuth containing the credentials that can be used to authenticate.

Details of this process can be found in the documentation for the Java LDAP SDK and also in Chapter 8.

X-REF

Search Filters

When the server executes your search request, it uses the filter to decide which entries within the scope to send back to you. When compared to the filter criteria, each entry evaluates to true, false, or undefined based on the criteria in the filter. The entries that evaluate to true are the ones that get returned in the search results. We cover this three-valued logic model in detail a little later.

The search filter syntax is defined in RFC 2254. If you still have questions about search filters after reading this section it would be a good idea to refer to that RFC. The URL is `http://search.ietf. org/rfc/rfc2254.txt`.

Different Ways a Filter Can Match

As an example, in the first section of this chapter we mentioned the filter givenName=Deb* that might be used to find all of the entries that have a given name that begins with "Deb." The type of matching used in this filter is called substring matching and is indicated by the use of a partial string together with an asterisk. Other types of matching are presence, equality, greater than or equal, less than or equal, and approximate.

Presence Matching

At times it may be useful to search for entries that have a specified attribute, regardless of what the attribute value is. If you want to test for the presence of an attribute, use the following filter syntax, replacing attrname with the name of the attribute you are checking for, as follows:

```
attrname=*
```

NOTE

Don't confuse this syntax with the assignment operator used in programming languages such as C and Java. In an LDAP filter, the equals sign immediately followed by an asterisk is used to check for the presence of the named attribute.

You might also wonder if you can search for entries that *do not* contain a certain attribute. The answer is yes, but don't try to use a not-equal-to operator. There isn't one in LDAP filters. Instead, use the standard presence-matching syntax and apply the NOT operator to it.

```
!(attrname=*)
```

We talk about other uses of the NOT operator in the following discussion of compound search filters.

Equality Matching

Equality matching is similar to presence matching, except you are looking for an *exact* value for a given attribute.

```
attrname=value
```

In order for an entry to match this filter, it must contain the named attribute, and one of that attribute's values must be the same as the value in the filter.

Substring Matching

Substring matching uses the same syntax as equality matching, but has at least one asterisk character in the value field. A value matches if it is in the same pattern specified in the filter, where zero, one, or multiple characters would replace the position of the asterisk. For example, the filter cn=*mary* would match cn=mary, cn=maryjane, cn=rosemary, and cn=summary judgment.

Greater Than or Equal, Less Than or Equal

If an attribute uses a schema type that has defined a way to compare whether one value is greater than another, then you can use greater than or equals, and less than or equals in your filter.

```
attrname>=value
attrname<=value
```

If I were looking for all entries with an account balance less than or equal to five, I would use the filter:

```
accountbalance<=5
```

There is no less than operator or greater than operator. You must use less than or equals or greater than or equals. If you were looking for all employee numbers greater than 50, just add one and use greater than or equals.

```
employeenumber>=51
```

Approximate Matching

Some LDAP servers support approximate matching. The idea is that values that are similar to the given value will match.

```
attrname~=value
```

For example, the filter sn~=smythe might match sn=smith. Some LDAP servers implement this using a soundex algorithm, such as the one described by Donald Knuth in Volume 3 of *The Art of Computer Programming*. The soundex algorithm is commonly used in genealogical research to find matches of similar surnames with different spellings. The problem with approximate matching in LDAP filters is that most of the LDAP servers that implement it use a different algorithm. The same filter applied to the same data on LDAP servers from different vendors will likely return different results.

As of this writing, NDS supports approximate matching by changing it to equality matching before evaluating. So, the filter cn~=steven would match an entry with cn=steven but not with cn=stephen. This is, in a sense, the strictest form of approximate matching.

Extensible Matching

RFC 2254 describes a way to request additional types of matching in a search filter. This is called extensible matching because it is a way of asking the server to apply matching rules that it knows about to your search. For example, suppose an LDAP server had access to a database containing variations of common first names. A matching rule could be defined to make use of this name variation database in your LDAP searches. So, if you wanted to search for all entries that had a name such as Steve, the server would return to you all entries with the names Steve, Steven, Stephen, Stevie, and so on. The syntax for a search filter that does this looks like this:

```
(cn:1.2.3.4.5:=Steve)
```

The cn indicates that the filter should be compared against the cn attribute of each entry within the search scope. The object identifier (OID) 1.2.3.4.5 is the OID for the matching rule you want to use. In this case, the matching rule would be one that was defined to look for name variations.

NOTE

As of this writing, NDS doesn't have support for extensible matching.

Compound Filters

The filter syntax enables the use of AND and OR operators for joining filter elements together. These are prefix operators and can be followed by one or more filter elements. Each of the inner elements and the whole filter must be enclosed in parentheses.

AND Operator

The AND operator is indicated by the & character and is usually used to further restrict search results. If I wanted to list only inetOrgPerson entries that had telephone numbers I could use this filter:

```
(&(objectClass=inetOrgPerson)(telephoneNumber=*))
```

All inetOrgPerson objects which also have a `telephoneNumber` attribute will be listed. Notice that in this example (as with all compound LDAP search filters) the operator comes before the filter elements rather than between them. This is referred to as a preordered expression or a prefixed expression.

OR Operator

The OR operator is indicated by the | character and is normally used to make a filter less restrictive. If you wanted to find the entry for Jim but couldn't remember if the common name began with Jim or James, you could use the filter:

```
(|(cn=jim*)(cn=james*))
```

Both the AND and the OR operators can have multiple filter elements following them. Additional examples of possible filters are

```
(&(objectClass=inetOrgPerson)(mail=*acme.com)(cn=mary*))
(|(cn=larry)(cn=moe)(cn=curley))
```

You will probably find reasons to mix the AND and OR operators in the same filter. Use parenthesis nesting to accomplish this. If you wanted to find inetOrgPerson objects which had a telephoneNumber beginning with either 555 or 556 you could use the filter:

```
(&(objectClass=inetOrgPerson)(|(telephoneNumber=555*)
(telephoneNumber=556*)))
```

NOT Operator

The NOT operator, as introduced earlier, is represented by the ! character. It can precede just a single filter element. The following filter is *not valid* because NOT is a unary operator:

```
(!(cn=larry)(telephoneNumber=*))   /*invalid filter*/
```

However, the NOT operator can be safely used in compound searches if you only apply it to a single inner element, or if you use the AND or OR operator to join inner elements before you use the NOT operator.

Here's an example of the NOT operator used in an inner filter element. If you wanted to find all of the Marys except Mary Jones you would try:

```
(&(cn=mary*)(!(sn=jones)))
```

This filter would find everyone whose name is *not* Mary Jones:

```
(!(&(cn=mary)(sn=jones)))
```

This filter would return all of the organizational units except for sales and marketing:

```
(&(objectClass=organizationalUnit)(!(|(ou=sales)
(ou=marketing))))
```

Three-Valued Logic

While processing your search request, the server applies the filter to each entry in the search scope. Based on the filter, each entry evaluates to TRUE, FALSE, or UNDEFINED. Those that are TRUE are returned in the search results, and those that are FALSE or UNDEFINED are ignored for the purposes of the search. This three-valued logic comes from LDAP's roots in X.500 and is described briefly in RFC 2251 and in more detail in X.511(93) section 7.8.1.

As a programmer you are familiar with the idea of TRUE and FALSE in assertions, but UNDEFINED might be new. A filter element evaluates to UNDEFINED when the server is not able to determine whether the assertion value matches an entry. There are several reasons this might happen: the attribute name is not recognized by the server (not defined in its schema), the assertion value cannot be parsed, or the type of filtering requested is not implemented.

The exception to the "attribute name not recognized" rule is in a presence filter. If the attribute name given in a presence-matching filter is not defined, then the filter evaluates to FALSE rather than UNDEFINED.

For example, if the server did not recognize iq as an attribute type, then the filter iq=120 would evaluate to UNDEFINED, as would iq<=99 and iq>=100. However, iq=* would evaluate to FALSE.

An UNDEFINED element in a compound search filter behaves as you might expect. Table 5.6 shows the behavior of UNDEFINED elements in a compound search filter.

TABLE 5.6	IF YOU DO THIS...	IT BECOMES...
Behavior of Undefined in Compound Filters	(&(UNDEFINED)(TRUE))	UNDEFINED
	(&(UNDEFINED)(FALSE))	FALSE
	(|(UNDEFINED)(TRUE))	TRUE
	(|(UNDEFINED)(FALSE))	UNDEFINED
	(!(UNDEFINED))	UNDEFINED

Does Case Matter?

Throughout this chapter we have typically used lowercase letters for both the attribute names and values in our search filters. You may have wondered if this is primarily a matter of style or if changing the case affects the search.

Changing the case of an attribute name or an object class name doesn't matter. We could use `telephonenumber` and `telephoneNumber` interchangeably, for example.

The case in an attribute value *usually* doesn't matter either. Most attributes have a string syntax that ignores case for the purpose of comparisons. For instance, all of the attributes in a fresh install of NDS ignore case. However, some third party applications that require you to extend the schema, or extend the schema themselves, sometimes use case-sensitive string syntaxes. Examples of attributes where case might matter could include ID strings, passwords, and UNIX file paths.

Using Object Identifiers

Internally, LDAP servers keep track of each object class and attribute type in their schema with both a name and an OID, which is a string containing a set of numbers in dotted decimal form that acts as a unique identifier. In this case, OIDs are used as unique identifiers for attribute types and object classes. OIDs were introduced in Chapter 1 and are discussed in more detail in Chapter 7.

All of our filter examples have used attribute names, but in each of those examples the attribute names could be replaced with OIDs and still work.

As an example, the OID for the `cn` attribute is 2.5.4.3. So, the following filters are identical:

```
cn=Larry
2.5.4.3=Larry
```

As a general rule, you cannot use OIDs in the value part of a filter. For example, there is no OID for the value Larry. An exception to this is when you are specifying an objectClass in your filter because object classes are optionally named by OIDs. For example, the following two filters would be treated as identical by the server:

```
objectClass=inetOrgPerson
objectClass=2.16.840.1.113730.3.2.2
```

RFC 2252 defines some common LDAP schema along with the OIDs for those schema elements. Refer to chapter 7 for a further discussion of OIDs and how to read the schema that is in use on your LDAP server.

 WARNING **The use of OIDs in your search filters greatly reduces the readability of your code and should be avoided wherever possible. RFC 2252 suggests that OIDs only be used in the case of schema elements that do not have a name assigned to them.**

LDAP URLs

Both the search and read methods of the LDAPConnection class have versions that take an instance of the LDAPUrl class. The purpose of the LDAPUrl class is to encapsulate the primary inputs for an LDAP search and to represent those parameters as a Uniform Resource Locator (URL) such as those commonly used on the Internet. The general URL format is defined in RFC 1738. An LDAP URL is defined in RFC 2255 and looks like this:

```
"ldap://" [hostName [":" portNumber]] ["/" [dn ["?" [attributes]
["?" [scope] ["?" [filter] ["?" extensions]]]]]]
```

The text in quotes indicates literal text that needs to be entered exactly. Everything else is a symbol for some element of the URL. Those elements that are within brackets are optional, but notice the nesting of the brackets. Some of the elements require that preceding ones be included as well. The portNumber defaults to 389 if omitted, which is the default port used by most LDAP servers. If the filter is omitted it defaults to objectClass=*, which means to return *all* entries in the scope. The possible values for the scope are base, one, and sub. The scope defaults to base if it is omitted. An omitted DN defaults to the root of the tree.

Let's look at an example for a typical subtree search. Suppose you are looking for the telephone numbers of all accounting department employees in the Acme company. The URL for your search might be:

```
ldap://ldap.acme.com/ou=accounting,o=acme,c=us?
telephoneNumber?sub?objectclass=inetorgperson
```

Notice that this example left off the portNumber and the extension portion of the URL. That's okay because they're both optional. An LDAP client reading an LDAP URL should default to use port 389 if the portNumber isn't present. That's the default port used by LDAP servers. Another thing that you commonly notice in LDAP URLs is that the attribute list portion is left blank. A blank attribute list indicates that you want to see *all* of the attributes for the matched entries. But because the attribute list is required if you include a scope, you have to remember to put the literal ?? between the dn and scope as a placeholder for the attribute list. The filter objectClass=inetOrgPerson means that we want to see all objects within our scope that are of class inetOrgPerson.

The nice thing about using the LDAPUrl class is that you don't have to know how to format a URL yourself. That's right. You can forget the previous few paragraphs if you want to. There are two constructors for the class that enable you to pass in all of the elements of the URL as parameters. The constructor knows how to format them into a URL.

```
public LDAPUrl(String host,
               int port,
               String dn)
```

This simplest constructor is the one you want to use if you are going to call LDAPConnection.read, or if you want to do a SCOPE_BASE search with the filter objectclass=*. It specifies the host, port and base DN, but uses the defaults for the search scope, search filter, and attribute list. The default scope is base, the default filter is objectClass=*, and the default attribute list is a zero-length string which causes *all* attributes to be returned. It doesn't actually put these defaults in the URL string. It leaves them off, which has the same effect as using the defaults.

If you want to specify parameters for a full search, use the following constructor for the URL:

```
public LDAPUrl(String host,
               int port,
               String dn,
               String attrNames[],
               int scope,
               String filter)
```

This version creates a full LDAP URL that can be used with the LDAP-Connection.search method to do a search that includes an attribute list, a scope other than the default base, and a filter.

If you already have a formatted URL string and want to turn it into an LDAPUrl object there's a constructor for that, too.

```
public LDAPUrl(String url)
   throws MalformedURLException
```

This constructor is useful if you are accepting user input from a URL location (as in the Location window of a web browser. Be aware that if the URL is not correctly formatted, the constructor throws an LDAPException.MalformedURLException.

Once the LDAPUrl is created, it can't be edited. There are no *set* methods. There are methods to *get* each of the components of the URL, however, as shown in Table 5.7.

TABLE 5.7

*Methods to Retrieve the
Components of the LDAPUrl*

METHOD	RETURN TYPE	DESCRIPTION
getAttributeArray()	String	Returns an array containing the attributes named in your attribute list.
getAttributes()	Enumeration	Returns an Enumeration containing the attributes named in your attribute list.

METHOD	RETURN TYPE	DESCRIPTION
getDN()	String	Returns the base DN for the search.
getFilter()	String	Returns the search filter.
getHost()	String	Returns the IP address or DNS name of the LDAP server.
getPort()	int	Returns the port number. This should usually be 389.
getScope()	int	Returns one of SCOPE_BASE, SCOPE_ONE, or SCOPE_SUB, which are members of the LDAPv2 interface.
getUrl()	String	Returns the string representation of this LDAPUrl.

The Compare Operation

Everything up to this point in the chapter has been related to the search operation, but this last section of the chapter focuses on another, lesser known LDAP operation — compare. Compare is used when you want to verify information you think you already know about an entry. In essence, you ask if something about a particular entry is true, and the LDAP server replies either that it is or it isn't.

The compare operation takes two inputs: the DN of an entry, and an attribute-value pair. If that attribute and value exist on the entry, the server returns a result code indicating true for the comparison. If the supplied attribute isn't on the entry, or if the supplied value doesn't match any of the values for that entry, then a result code indicating a false comparison is returned.

The LDAPConnection.compare Method

To perform the compare operation with the LDAP SDK, you call one of the compare methods of the LDAPConnection class. The simplest takes a DN parameter and an LDAPAttribute object that contains the attribute-value pair to be compared. It returns a boolean indicating whether or not the attribute and value exist on the entry.

```
public boolean compare(java.lang.String DN,
                       LDAPAttribute attr)
       throws LDAPException
```

The other version of the compare method also takes an LDAPConstraints object.

```
public boolean compare(java.lang.String DN,
                       LDAPAttribute attr,
                       LDAPConstraints cons)
       throws LDAPException
```

WARNING

The compare operation only supports comparing for a single attribute value at a time. If the LDAPAttribute object you supply to the compare method contains more than one value, the comparison could yield unpredictable results.

If you have loaded the LDIF file that is on the CD-ROM that accompanies this book, then the following bit of Java code should print: Compare returned true.

```
...
String DN = "cn=Phyllis Winters,ou=Promotion,l=New York,c=US";
String attrName = "telephoneNumber";
String attrVal = "+1 914 555 0002";

LDAPConnection conn = new LDAPConnection();

try {
   conn.connect("ldap.acme.com", 389,
                   "cn=admin,o=acme", "adminPass");

   if (conn.compare(DN, new LDAPAttribute(attrName, attrVal)))
      System.out.println("Compare returned true.");
   else
      System.out.println("Compare returned false.");
```

```
    conn.disconnect();
} catch(LDAPException e) {
    System.out.println(e.toString());
}
    ...
```

Summary

The search operation is powerful and flexible. After reading this chapter, you should understand the concepts of searching in the directory, and how to perform searches and compares using the LDAP SDK.

We covered the use of the LDAPAttribute, LDAPAttributeSet, LDAPEntry, LDAP-SearchResults, LDAPConstraints, LDAPSearchConstraints, and LDAPUrl classes. We also covered the search, read, and compare methods of LDAPConnection. There are quite a few methods and members of these classes that were not mentioned. You should review the documentation that comes with the LDAP SDK to be sure you understand these classes.

Most of the methods we described in this chapter also have versions that use LDAPResponseListener objects and can be used asynchronously. Chapter 3 contains more information about performing LDAP operations asynchronously.

If you want to understand more details about LDAP searching than what were discussed here, you may want to look at RFC 2251. You can download RFC 2251 from the IETF Web site at `http://search.ietf.org/rfc/rfc2251.txt`. Section 4.5 of that RFC covers the search operation.

The next chapter explores the details of updating directory information through the add, modify, modifyDN, and delete LDAP operations.

CHAPTER 6

Updating the Directory

For a directory to do much good, someone needs to populate it with useful entries, update those entries as necessary, and delete entries that are no longer needed. In this chapter, we examine in detail the four LDAP operations that can be used to do just that: add, modify, rename, and delete.

► · ◄

Jumping Right In

One of the best ways to learn about the use of the update methods is to simply dive in and use them. Let's begin by taking a quick look at the classes and methods that are covered in this chapter.

To use any of the update methods, you begin by establishing a connection to an LDAP server. The LDAPConnection class implements the LDAPv3 interface, which defines methods for add, modify, rename, and delete. So, once you have an LDAPConnection object, you can perform these operations by calling the appropriate methods on that object.

First Glance at the Update Methods

To introduce the methods that are used in updating the directory, let's look at a simple example of adding a new entry, performing some operations to it, and then deleting it. Don't worry if you see things we haven't covered yet. This is just a first glance. We talk about each step in detail later in the chapter.

```
...
LDAPConnection conn = new LDAPConnection();

try {
    conn.connect("myldapserver.novell.com", 389,
        "cn=admin,o=novell", "adminPassword");

    /* Create a new, empty attribute set */
    LDAPAttributeSet attrSet = new LDAPAttributeSet();

    /* Create an array of values for the "objectClass"
```

```
    multi-valued attribute */
String[] attrValues = {"top", "person",
    "organizationalPerson", "inetOrgPerson"};

/* Add the new attribute "objectClass" and values to the
    attribute set */
attrSet.add(new LDAPAttribute("objectClass", attrValues));

/* Add other attributes to the set */
attrSet.add(new LDAPAttribute("cn", "smcdonald"));
attrSet.add(new LDAPAttribute("givenName", "Susan"));
attrSet.add(new LDAPAttribute("sn", "McDonald"));
attrSet.add(new LDAPAttribute("fullName",
    "Susan McDonald"));

/* Create the entry in the directory */
conn.add(
    new LDAPEntry("cn=smcdonald,o=novell", attrSet));

/* Create a new attribute that we will add to the entry.
    Note: This attribute could have been included when we
        first created the entry, but this is an example
        of modifying an entry that already exists. */
LDAPAttribute attr = new LDAPAttribute("title", "C.F.O.");

/* Create a modification object that specifies that we
    want to add the title */
LDAPModification mod = new LDAPModification(
    LDAPModification.ADD, attr);

/* Perform the modification (adding the title) */
conn.modify("cn=smcdonald,o=novell", mod);

/* Suppose Susan married, and followed the traditional
    custom of taking her husband's last name of Thompson */
ModificationSet modSet = new ModificationSet();
```

```
modSet.add(LDAPModification.REPLACE,
    new LDAPAttribute("sn", "Thompson"));
modSet.add(LDAPModification.REPLACE,
    new LDAPAttribute("fullName", "Susan M. Thompson"));
conn.modify("cn=smcdonald,o=novell", modSet);

/* Don't forget about the naming attribute (cn) for this
    user. We want to change that (and thereby the DN
    as well). */
conn.rename("cn=smcdonald,o=novell",
    "cn=sthompson,o=novell", true);

/* To delete an entry from the directory, do this... */
conn.delete("cn=sthompson,o=novell");

conn.disconnect();
} catch(LDAPException e) {
    System.out.println(e.toString());
}
...
```

DN and LDAPConstraints

Before we get into the unique details of each of the methods used to update the directory, let's mention the two things they all have in common. First, they all take a DN parameter. The DN is either the distinguished name of the entry that the operation is to be performed on or, in the case of the add method, the distinguished name of the entry to be added.

The second common parameter that many of these methods take is an instance of LDAPConstraints. You'll remember from Chapter 5 that LDAPConstraints encapsulates options that define additional behaviors when performing an LDAP operation. For example, you can set the amount of time you are willing to wait for a response from the server, or you can set options that define the behavior of your client if it receives a referral.

Take another look at the "Constraints" section in Chapter 5 to remind yourself of the options that are available.

X-REF

Keep in mind that the options available through LDAPConstraints can also be set on the LDAPConnection object so that all LDAP operations performed on that connection have the same options. Providing an LDAPConstraints object when calling individual update methods is typically used as a way of temporarily overriding the options set on the connection.

Schema Requirements

Whenever you add or modify entries, the schema imposes certain requirements. As an example, most object classes have one or more required attributes as well as a list of optional ones. If you are adding a new entry, you need to include all of the required attributes, and if you are modifying an entry, you have to make sure you don't delete a required attribute.

In Chapter 7 we cover schema issues in detail. But we need to bring up a few things now to avoid some of the schema-related pitfalls of updating the directory.

Object Classes

When you create an entry in the directory, you define the type of object you are creating by specifying one or more values for the `objectClass` attribute. Each of the object classes, as well as all of the attribute types that can be used when creating an entry, is defined as the directory schema. In NDS, the schema definitions for each object class and attribute type can be read by performing an LDAP search on the special entry cn=schema.

For details about reading the schema in NDS as well as other LDAP servers, skip ahead to Chapter 7.

X-REF

Abstract, Structural, and Auxiliary Object Classes

Each object class is defined to be abstract, structural, or auxiliary. Only structural object classes can be used to actually create an entry in the directory. Abstract object classes are meant only for structural ones to inherit from. Auxiliary object classes are a way of extending the capabilities of an existing object. So, auxiliary object classes can be added to an existing entry or included in the list of values for the objectClasses attribute at the time the entry is created. We cover this distinction in detail in the next chapter.

IMPORTANT

An entry cannot be based on more than a single structural object class. When the entry is created, and you list the values of ObjectClass, that list should have only one structural object class and any auxiliary object classes that you want to extend it with. The exception to this is that all of the object classes that a structural object class inherits from may also be included. For example, if I create an entry with the object class inetOrgPerson, I can also list organizationalPerson, person, and top as values of the objectClass attribute because inetOrgPerson is inherited from those.

Mandatory and Optional Attributes

Most directory services (NDS included) have a concept of mandatory attributes and optional attributes. When you create an entry of a certain object class, you have to initially give it at least all of the mandatory attributes for that object class. If you attempt to create an entry without including all of the mandatory attributes, an error is returned. Specifically, the add method throws LDAPException.OBJECT_CLASS_VIOLATION.

For example, in LDAP a required attribute of the object class "person" is sn. If sn isn't one of the attributes in the LDAPAttributeSet that creates the LDAPEntry, then the LDAPConnection.add method throws LDAPException.OBJECT_CLASS_VIOLATION. Similarly, if you attempt to add an attribute that is not allowed because it's not listed in the set of mandatory or optional attributes for the object class you're working with, you get the same error.

You can see which attributes are mandatory and which are optional by checking the schema definition for any given object class. The definitions of many common object classes can be found in RFC 2256, and, as we mentioned at the beginning of this section, you can read the specific object class definitions for any object class used in NDS by reading the cn=schema entry. When you read an object class definition, you'll notice a section labeled "MAY." This section lists the optional attributes that are allowed on the particular object class. If there are mandatory attributes for the object class, they are listed in the section labeled "MUST."

NOTE

If the object class is inherited from another object class, any mandatory and optional attributes of that object class are also carried on to this one. Look at the SUP section of the object class definition to see which object classes this one inherits from.

As an example, the definition for "person" (which inetOrgPerson inherits from) looks like this:

```
( 2.5.6.6 NAME 'person' SUP top STRUCTURAL MUST ( sn $ cn )
   MAY ( userPassword $ telephoneNumber $ seeAlso $
   description ) )
```

It has two mandatory attributes, sn and cn, and four optional attributes, userPassword, telephoneNumber, seeAlso, and description. It is structural and inherits from top.

RDNs and Naming Attributes

Chapter 1 briefly mentioned the concept of naming attributes, and it becomes important to understand when you are adding an entry to the directory or renaming an existing one. In NDS, the object class definition defines which attributes are candidates to be used as the naming attribute — that is, as the relative distinguished name (RDN). For example, if I create an inetOrgPerson object for Larry Jones, the common practice is to use cn as the naming attribute. So, I would begin the new DN with an element that began with cn.

```
cn=ljones,ou=sales,o=acme
```

It could be noted that in the previous DN, each of the comma-separated elements specifies an RDN for an entry, and the attribute listed in front of the equals sign is the naming attribute for the particular entry. Therefore, cn=ljones is the RDN for the user, and cn is the naming attribute. Likewise, ou=sales is the RDN of the sales container, and ou is the naming attribute for that entry.

Typically, you would include the naming attribute among the LDAPAttributeSet when you define an entry. (We talk more about the LDAPAttributeSet later in the chapter.) However, NDS is quite forgiving in this regard. If you attempt to create an entry, and you specify the DN of the new entry as cn=ljones,ou=sales,o=acme but forget to include the attribute-value pair cn=ljones in the LDAPAttributeSet, NDS derives this attribute and value from the given DN and creates it for you. Therefore, although cn is a mandatory attribute, it can be left out of the LDAPAttributeSet as long as you specify it as the naming attribute in the DN.

Multi-Valued RDN

An interesting LDAP concept, and one not often used, is that of a multi-valued RDN. Typically, only one value attribute-value pair is specified as the naming value to be used in the RDN. However, LDAP provides for a way to specify more than one attribute-value in the RDN. It is done by separating the attribute-value pairs in the RDN portion of the DN with the plus character (+). The following DN is an example of one that has two different attribute-value pairs in its RDN:

```
cn=steve+uid=ssmith,ou=sales,o=acme
```

This entry is not known as cn=steve,ou=sales,o=acme, nor is it known as uid=ssmith,ou=sales,o=acme. The full DN, including both parts of the RDN, must be specified when referring to this entry. This technique is sometimes used to more uniquely identify entries.

Structure Rules

The schema also defines which object classes can be containers and what types of entries can exist within each type of container. For example, an organization container can only exist at the root of the tree, or within a country or locality. Again, Chapter 7 describes structure rules in more detail, but we mention it here because it becomes important to know as you add and move entries in your directory.

In NDS, the object class definitions for object classes that are not containers have the keyword X-NDS_NOT_CONTAINER. In addition, each structural object class definition (for both containers and non-containers) has a section labeled X-NDS_CONTAINMENT that lists each type of container that an object of that type can exist in.

NOTE

Even though it follows X.500 directory standards, NDS is somewhat unique in defining strict structure rules. Many LDAP servers freely allow any object to be the parent of any other object.

Adding Entries

The add method populates the directory with new objects. There are two versions of the add method. The first simply takes an LDAPEntry object.

```
public void add(LDAPEntry entry) throws LDAPException
```

The second takes the LDAPEntry object and an LDAPConstraints object.

```
public void add(LDAPEntry entry, LDAPConstraints cons)
    throws LDAPException
```

An LDAPEntry object (see Figure 6.1) represents an object in the directory and thus consists of the DN for the entry and an LDAPAttributeSet object. The LDAP-AttributeSet is a collection of LDAPAttribute objects. Each LDAPAttribute object consists of an attribute name and one or more values.

▶ . . . . ◀

The anatomy of an
LDAPEntry object

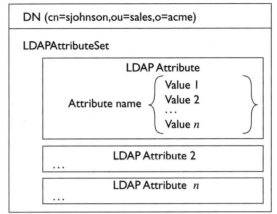

LDAP Entry

DN (cn=sjohnson,ou=sales,o=acme)

LDAPAttributeSet

LDAP Attribute

Attribute name { Value 1, Value 2, ..., Value *n* }

LDAP Attribute 2
...

LDAP Attribute *n*
...

Let's look again at the code used near the beginning of this chapter, and specifically the code to add a new entry to the directory:

```
...
/* Create a new, empty attribute set */
LDAPAttributeSet attrSet = new LDAPAttributeSet();

/* Create an array of values for the "objectClass"
   multi-valued attribute */
String[] attrValues = {"top", "person",
   "organizationalPerson", "inetOrgPerson"};

/* Add the new attribute "objectClass" and values to the
   attribute set */
attrSet.add(new LDAPAttribute("objectClass", attrValues));

/* Add other attributes to the set */
attrSet.add(new LDAPAttribute("cn", "smcdonald"));
attrSet.add(new LDAPAttribute("givenName", "Susan"));
attrSet.add(new LDAPAttribute("sn", "McDonald"));
attrSet.add(new LDAPAttribute("fullName",
```

```
   "Susan McDonald"));

/* Create the entry in the directory */
conn.add(
   new LDAPEntry("cn=smcdonald,o=novell ", attrSet));
...
```

Notice when we define the values for the objectClass attribute that we name four different object classes. This is because inetOrgPerson inherits from organizationalPerson, which inherits from person, which inherits from top. Following the LDAP protocol specification, NDS doesn't require that you list all four values. You could just list inetOrgPerson and successfully create the entry. But if you look at the entry in the directory after it is created, you'll see that organizationalPerson, person, and top were all added as well. We use a simpler LDAPAttribute constructor for the remaining attributes because they are only being populated with a single value.

The DN of the LDAPEntry object that is used to add the entry to the directory represents the name of the new directory object. This name must be unique, and the parent of the entry must already exist. In this example, the object o=novell must already exist in the directory, and there must not already be a cn=smcdonald under the o=novell container; otherwise, the add operation throws LDAP-Exception.ENTRY_ALREADY_EXISTS.

Modifying Entries

Existing entries can be modified in several ways. You can choose to add a new optional attribute to the entry, add a value to an existing attribute (if the attribute allows multiple values), delete one or more values from an attribute, replace a set of attribute values with new ones, and so on. The modify method (or, more accurately, the modify operation of the LDAP protocol) is flexible enough to allow each of these types of changes. It also allows you to make a single change or to perform multiple changes all at once.

The most simple version of the modify method takes the DN of the entry and a single LDAPModification object.

```
public void modify(String dn, LDAPModification mod)
    throws LDAPException
```

```
public void modify(String dn, LDAPModification mod,
    LDAPConstraints cons) throws LDAPException
```

When multiple modifications are to be performed, the modifications are grouped together by creating an LDAPModificationSet object.

```
public void modify(String dn, LDAPModificationSet mods)
    throws LDAPException
```

```
public void modify(String dn, LDAPModificationSet mods,
    LDAPConstraints cons) throws LDAPException
```

LDAPModification Class

At the heart of the modify operation is the LDAPModification class. It is made up of two elements: the operation type and an LDAPAttribute. The operation type specifies whether the modification should add given attribute values, delete them, or replace all the values of the specified attribute with the values given.

LDAPModification.ADD

When LDAPModification.ADD is used for the operation type, the modify method adds the given attribute and values to the entry. The LDAPAttribute you provide must include at least one value. If the attribute already exists on the entry, and it allows more than one value, the new value or values are added. If the attribute does not yet exist on the entry, and if the attribute is an allowed optional attribute, then the attribute is created and the specified values are added.

The values in the given LDAPAttribute object must be unique, and they cannot already exist on the entry. If you try to add an attribute value that already exists on the entry, the LDAPException.ATTRIBUTE_OR_VALUE_EXISTS is thrown.

LDAPModification.DELETE

The LDAPModification.DELETE operation type deletes attribute values, or an entire attribute, from an entry. If the LDAPAttribute parameter specifies an attribute type, but no values, the entire attribute is deleted from the entry (along with whatever values it had). If the LDAPAttribute parameter does include specific values, then only those values are removed from the attribute.

An attribute cannot exist on an entry without at least one value. As soon as the final value is deleted, the entire attribute is removed from the entry.

IMPORTANT

Mandatory attributes cannot be removed from an entry. If this is attempted, an LDAPException.OBJECT_CLASS_VIOLATION is thrown. Likewise, distinguished attribute values (the attribute value or values that form the RDN of directory entries) cannot be removed using the modify operation. See the following "Renaming and Moving Entries" section if you'd like to rename an entry.

LDAPModification.REPLACE

The LDAPModification.REPLACE operation type indicates that you want to replace all attribute values that currently exist for the given attribute with the new values you specify. If the attribute type is not already on the entry, then the attribute is created and the values added. If an attribute type but no values are specified, it means you want to delete the specified attribute if it exists on the entry.

LDAPModificationSet Class

As the method definitions indicate, multiple modifications can be performed in the same operation by adding multiple LDAPModification objects to an LDAPModificationSet object. The LDAPModificationSet class includes methods to add LDAPModification objects, to remove them given an attribute name, to remove the element at a specific index, to count the LDAPModification objects, and to return the LDAPModification object at a specified index.

Multiple modifications that are contained in an LDAPModificationSet are guaranteed to be processed atomically. That is, either all of the modifications are applied, or, if any of them cause an exception, the exception is thrown and none of the changes are applied.

NOTE

When you use LDAPModificationSet to encapsulate more than one modification in a single request, the entire set gets sent to the server at the same time. The LDAP server processes the modifications in the order that they were added to the

LDAPModificationSet object. Therefore, an LDAPModificationSet containing modifications to add and then delete an attribute value is different than a set containing modifications to delete and then add an attribute value.

For example, because of the order, these two LDAPModificationSet objects behave very differently, although they contain the same modifications:

```
LDAPModificationSet modSet1 = new LDAPModificationSet();
modSet1.add( LDAPModification.ADD,
    new LDAPAttribute("title", "Software Engineer"));
modSet1.add( LDAPModification.DELETE,
    new LDAPAttribute("title", "Software Engineer"));

LDAPModificationSet modSet2 = new LDAPModificationSet();
modSet1.add( LDAPModification.DELETE,
    new LDAPAttribute("title", "Software Engineer"));
modSet1.add( LDAPModification.ADD,
    new LDAPAttribute("title", "Software Engineer"));
```

In the preceding example, modSet1 first adds the title Software Engineer and then immediately deletes it. The other LDAPModificationSet, modSet2, attempts to delete the title Software Engineer, and then adds it back.

TIP

We have mentioned that modifications cannot violate schema rules. For example, a mandatory attribute cannot be deleted from an entry. The exception to this rule is that when multiple modifications are grouped in an LDAPModificationSet and sent to the server as a single modify operation, individual modifications can temporarily violate schema rules as long as the entire set leaves a valid entry when finished.

Renaming and Moving Entries

The rename method has two primary uses. It can be used to rename an entry. It can also be used to move an entry. You can do one, or the other, or both at once.

To rename an entry, you give it a new RDN. To move it, you specify a new parent container. Let's look at the different versions of the rename method:

```
public void rename(String dn, String newRDN,
    boolean deleteOldRDN) throws LDAPException

public void rename(String dn, String newRDN,
    boolean deleteOldRDN, LDAPConstraints cons)
    throws LDAPException

public void rename(String dn, String newRDN,
    String newParentDN, boolean deleteOldRDN)
    throws LDAPException

public void rename(String dn, String newRDN,
    String newParentDN, boolean deleteOldRDN,
    LDAPConstraints cons) throws LDAPException
```

A Closer Look at the Rename Method

Each of these methods has three parameters in common: dn, newRDN, and deleteOldRDN. The dn parameter is the DN of the entry you want to rename or move. The newRDN is the new relative distinguished name (RDN) that you want the entry to have. For example, if you have an entry cn=steve,o=novell, the RDN is the first element of the DN, or cn=steve. If I wanted this entry to be cn=stephen,o=novell, then I would make the newRDN parameter cn=stephen. The deleteOldRDN parameter is a boolean value that indicates whether you want to delete the old RDN value when you add the new one. In our previous example, if I were to set deleteOldRDN to false, then after doing the rename, I would have an entry with the DN cn=stephen,o=novell, but it would have two values for the cn attribute: stephen and steve.

Continuing our example, the value of cn that is used within the DN is stephen. That is the attribute and value that has been designated as the *naming attribute* for this entry. Because cn is a multi-valued attribute, it can have other values (steve in this case), but only the one specified in the DN is used as the naming value.

If, when calling rename, you set deleteOldRDN to true, then the old naming value is removed entirely from the entry and replaced with the newRDN.

NOTE

You cannot give an entry a name that some other entry within the same container already has. In other words, the RDNs of all sibling entries must be unique.

Using the Rename Method to Move an Entry

Two of the versions of the rename method have the additional parameter newParent. This parameter specifies a new parent container for the entry, effectively moving its location within the directory structure. You can choose to rename and move an entry at the same time, just rename it, or just move it.

TIP

If you only want to rename an entry (without moving it), call one of the methods without the newParent parameter. If you only want to move an entry (without renaming it), then call a method with the newParent parameter and supply the current RDN as the newRDN parameter.

WARNING

We have pointed out that the rename method can be used to both rename an entry, and to move it. The renaming part of that operation has been in LDAP since the beginning, but the move part of the operation is new to LDAPv3. Therefore, if you are planning to use the rename method to move an entry, you must set your client version to LDAPv3 before you connect to the server. If you connect as LDAPv2, the server ignores the newParent parameter and only does the rename portion of the operation. Refer to Chapter 4 for information on how to set your client version to LDAPv3.

Leaf versus Non-Leaf Entries

The behavior of the rename method differs somewhat between leaf and non-leaf entries. A "non-leaf" entry is a container that is not empty.

If you attempt to rename a non-leaf entry (but not to move it), the container *will be* renamed. A side effect of this operation is that the DN of all of the entries contained within the renamed container will be changed to reflect the new name of the parent. For example, if I had an entry named cn=larry,ou=sales,o=acme, and

I changed the name of the sales container to "marketing," then Larry's DN would change as well to cn=larry,ou=marketing,o=acme.

When you ask for an entry to be moved by giving it a new parent, most directory services (including NDS) check if you are asking to move a non-leaf entry. Because of the internal complexities involved in moving a non-leaf entry (especially when partitioning is involved), NDS won't allow it. If attempted, the rename method throws LDAPException.UNWILLING_TO_PERFORM.

Deleting Entries

The LDAPConnection.delete method is very straightforward. The simpler of the two versions has only one parameter — the DN of the entry you want to delete. As long as you are properly authenticated as someone who has rights to delete the entry, and as long as that entry is a leaf entry, the entry is deleted.

```
public void delete(String dn) throws LDAPException
```

With an LDAPSearchContraints Object

The other version of delete allows an LDAPSearchConstraints object to be used when the LDAP server is locating the entry to be deleted.

```
public void delete(String dn, LDAPConstraints cons)
    throws LDAPException
```

IMPORTANT

LDAP doesn't allow you to delete a container unless it is empty. If you attempt to delete a container that isn't empty, the delete method throws LDAPException.NOT_ALLOWED_ON_NONLEAF.

Using Recursion to Delete a Subtree

We have mentioned that if you try to delete a non-leaf entry, the delete method throws LDAPException.NOT_ALLOWED_ON_NONLEAF. One simple way to get around this is to write a method that uses the programming technique of *recursion* to delete the subtree.

The following code listing defines a class that extends the LDAPConnection class to add a method called deleteSubtree. We call it LDAPEnhancedConnection. To use this class, you would create an instance of LDAPEnhancedConnection and use it as you would normally use LDAPConnection, except that you can now call the deleteSubtree method as well. We wrote a simple application that uses this class, and have made it available on the CD-ROM that accompanies this book. You'll find it in the Examples\Listings\Chapter 6\Listing 6.1 directory. You'll also find the same example written in C in that directory.

 Keep in mind that recursion can be dangerous because it can quickly cause your application to run out of memory. The following technique only works on very small or flat subtrees.

WARNING

LISTING 6.1

*Using recursion to delete
a subtree*

```
/* LDAPEnhancedConnection.java */

import novell.ldap.*;

class LDAPEnhancedConnection extends LDAPConnection {
    public void deleteSubtree(String DN)
    throws LDAPException {

        /* Get a list of all subordinate entries and call
           deleteSubtree on each one*/
        String[] attrs = {LDAPv3.NO_ATTRS};
        LDAPSearchResults results = search(DN,
            LDAPv2.SCOPE_ONE, "objectclass=*", attrs, true);
        while (results.hasMoreElements())
            deleteSubtree(results.next().getDN());

        /* No more subordinates, delete this leaf node */
        delete(DN);
    }
}
```

Summary

The LDAPConnection class contains the methods you need to make updates to the directory: add, modify, rename, and delete. This chapter covered the use of each of these, and gave some coding examples to help you get started with them in your own application. Chapter 11 presents an alternative way of updating your directory — LDIF. The next chapter explores the use of schema in an LDAP directory server, and specifically in NDS.

CHAPTER 7

Schema Management

In previous chapters, you learned how to find, create, delete, and modify entries in the directory. The way these entries look — their form and their arrangement in the directory — is controlled by something called schema. In this chapter, you learn about what the LDAP schema is and does, and how to read and change it.

The first section gives a complete view of what the LDAP schema is. After you've become somewhat familiar with LDAP schema, the second section — "Differences between Standard LDAP and NDS LDAP Schema" — helps you understand how the NDS LDAP schema is different from standard LDAP. If you've had experience with the NDS schema using Novell's older proprietary APIs, the third section — "Differences between NDS LDAP and NDS NDAP Schema" — will prove helpful. The last three sections are about managing the schema. They show how to use an existing management tool, how to use LDAP schema APIs, and finally, they provide a schema browser utility written in LDAP.

▶ . . . . ◀

Defining the Way Things Are: LDAP Schema

In Chapter 1, the LDAP schema was introduced. We talked about the elements of the schema, what each element is used for, and how they are ultimately used to create directory entries. Here, we recap and hopefully answer any questions you may have.

X-REF

If you haven't yet, it's a good idea to read "A Simple Introduction to LDAP Schema" in Chapter 1.

In broad strokes, the LDAP Schema is a set of rules that governs the following aspects of a directory:

▶ The data types — or syntaxes — known to the directory (integer, string, DN, and so on)

▶ Which syntax is used for which attribute

> ► Which attributes must and may be present in a specific entry

> ► Where instances of specific entries may exist in the directory tree, and how they're named

Elements of the Schema

In this chapter, we cover four elements of the LDAP schema: object classes, attribute types, syntaxes, and matching rules. The first three elements specify rules for the way an entry is put together — what it can and can't hold. Syntaxes describe the format of attribute values, attribute types control the characteristics of attributes, and object classes describe the attributes and other factors that make up specific entries. The last one — matching rules — determines the ways attribute values are compared during search and compare operations.

Figure 7.1 helps you visualize the relationship between schema elements and the way those schema elements affect entries in the directory.

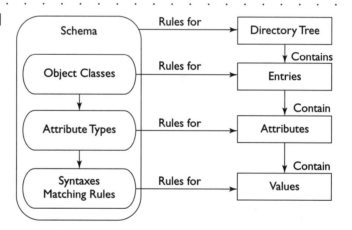

FIGURE 7.1

Relationships between schema elements and directory elements

The schema elements appear on the left, and lines are drawn to show which parts of the directory they control.

The Subschema Subentry

We know what you're thinking: The term schema is abstract enough, and now you want to talk about a subschema? Well, you can relax; the term subschema comes about in order to support multiple schemas in the directory tree. The way LDAP was defined allows for different logical sections of the tree to be governed by its own schema. While each separate schema specification is known as a sub-schema, the union of all these subschema specifications makes up the schema in its entirety. As of this writing, we know of no LDAP server, including NDS, which supports multiple subschemas. So for the sake of your sanity, just think of sub-schema and schema as synonymous. The other new term — subentry — does imply something we haven't talked about yet, and it *is* supported by LDAP servers.

A subentry is the entry analog of an operational attribute, in the respect that it is not normally returned from a search operation. A subentry is a directory entry that you must specifically ask for in order to see, usually by performing a base scope search on that entry with a special filter. Each subschema — or the entire directory schema in the case of NDS — is held in a subentry. That's right, every object class, attribute, and syntax, and each matching rule, name form, and struc-ture rule are all in one little entry.

X-REF

For more information on operational attributes, see the "Specifying the Attributes to be Returned" section in Chapter 5.

The first time you open this genie's bottle of a schema entry, you'll likely be taken aback by its complexity and the sheer amount of information it contains — you won't be alone. Don't worry, though; we break things down into understand-able components so you can effectively manage them.

Finding and Reading the Schema

As was mentioned earlier, the schema is found in a special entry called a sub-schema subentry. In order to read the schema, you must first discover the DN of the subschema subentry, then perform a base scope search on the entry and use the filter (objectclass=subschema). LDAP describes two ways in which you can find the DN of subschema subentries; one is to specifically ask for the subschemaSubentry operational attribute of a normal directory entry. This will return the DN of the subschema subentry in effect for that entry. The other is to examine the subschemaSubentry attribute of the root DSE.

Reading the subschemaSubentry Attribute in the Root DSE

To advertise certain functionality and settings, LDAP servers use the root DSE — a server-specific entry at the root of the directory. One of the attributes in the root DSE is called subschemaSubentry. It holds the DNs of all the subschema subentries that the server knows about. You can read this value by using the ldapsearch utility found in the Utilities directory on the CD-ROM.

For more information on the root DSE, see the "Read Only Information: The Root DSE" section in Chapter 10.

X-REF

Type `ldapsearch -h <server address> -b "" -s base objectclass=* subschemaSubentry`, replacing `<server address>` with the server's IP or DNS address. The result should look like this:

```
dn:
subschemaSubentry: cn=schema
```

The current version of NDS only uses one global schema for the entire directory, which is why you only see one value here. Future versions may allow you to create different schema entries that control different parts of the tree.

Reading the subschemaSubentry in Effect for an Entry

As an alternative to reading the root DSE, you can read the subschemaSubentry in effect for any directory entry simply by asking for that attribute to be returned from a search operation. For example, typing `ldapsearch -h <server address> -b "o=administration" -s base objectclass=* subschemaSubentry`, replacing `<server address>` with the server's IP or DNS address, should return something like this:

```
dn: o=administration
subschemaSubentry: cn=schema
```

Reading the Schema

Now that you've discovered the name of the subschema subentry, you can read the schema entry by typing `ldapsearch -h <server address> -b "cn=schema" -s base objectclass=subschema`, replacing `<server address>` with the server's IP or DNS address.

You should receive a mass of cryptic-looking information — the following is a printout of a portion for reference. Our discussion in the next few sections helps you decipher it.

```
objectClasses: ( 2.16.840.1.113719.1.27.6.3 NAME
'ndsPredicateStats' DESC 'Standard ObjectClass' SUP top
STRUCTURAL MUST (cn $ ndsPredicateState $ ndsPredicateFlush )
MAY (ndsPredicate $ ndsPredicateTimeout ) X-NDS_NAMING 'cn' X-
NDS_CONTAINMENT ('country' 'locality' 'organization'
'organizationalUnit' 'domain' ) X-NDS_NOT_CONTAINER '1' X-
NDS_NONREMOVABLE '1' )
attributeTypes: ( 2.5.4.35 NAME 'userPassword' DESC 'Standard
Attribute' SYNTAX 1.3.6.1.4.1.1466.115.121.1.40{128} )
```

The Format of Schema Elements

The schema entry may hold up to eight attributes. Each attribute is multi-valued and contains the definitions of particular schema elements. These definitions are human-readable strings (we show what they look like in a moment). The set of attributes that may be held in the schema entry are

- ► `objectClasses`

- ► `attributeTypes`

- ► `ldapSyntaxes`

- ► `matchingRules`

- ► `matchingRuleUse`

- ▶ `ditContentRules`

- ▶ `ditStructureRules`

- ▶ `nameForms`

As of this writing, NDS only provides values for the `objectClasses`, `attributeTypes`, and `ldapSyntaxes` attributes. We talk about these three first, followed by the others.

The following sections detail the way that each schema element is put together, and we hope that it will take a bit of the mystery away from that blob of arcane data you watched fly by in the previous example. These descriptions are taken from RFC 2252, and are in *Backus-Naur Form* (BNF). If you don't know how to read BNF, don't worry; we explain it along the way. Just be aware that any time a word or symbol is quoted in BNF, such as "`NAME`", it means that the word or symbol appears exactly like that. Other words, such as `qdescrs`, are to be replaced by something else.

The first thing you'll notice as you read about the format of the following schema elements is that each schema value starts and ends with matched parentheses. You'll also notice that an Object Identifier (OID) identifies each value. We introduced OIDs in Chapter 1; let's review them before proceeding: An OID is simply a unique set of numbers used to identify something. In the directory world, they uniquely identify object classes, attribute types, and other schema elements. If you own an OID — let's say you own 1.2.3.4 — you can assign any number beyond that to anything you like. You can also assign a *subarc* to someone else. For example, you could assign 1.2.3.4.100 to your neighbor. Now he has an OID and is free to do what he likes with it. If you need to extend the schema on your directory server and add some of your own object classes or attribute types, you'll need your own OID.

You can find more information about OIDs, along with a repository of many known OIDs, at `http://www.alvestrand.no/objectid/`. **You can get your own from the Internet Assigned Numbers Authority (IANA) at** `http://www.isi.edu/cgi-bin/iana/enterprise.pl`. **You can also get one from Novell by logging on to** `http://developer.novell.com/engsup/schreg2c.htm`.

The objectClasses Attribute

The first schema attribute we talk about is the `objectClasses` attribute. Values of this attribute define specific object classes. The syntax used to store and transmit these values is the Object Class Description syntax. An example of one such object class is (2.5.6.2 NAME 'country' SUP top STRUCTURAL MUST c MAY (searchGuide $ description)). The formal definition, in BNF, of what an object class looks like is found in section 4.4 of RFC 2252 and summarized here.

NOTE

The following definition contains line breaks. This has only been done to make it more readable. The actual values don't contain any line breaks, which makes them horribly unreadable.

```
ObjectClassDescription =
    "(" whsp
    numericoid whsp         ; ObjectClass identifier
    [ "NAME" qdescrs ]
    [ "DESC" qdstring ]
    [ "OBSOLETE" whsp ]
    [ "SUP" oids ]          ; Superior ObjectClasses
    [ ( "ABSTRACT" / "STRUCTURAL" / "AUXILIARY" ) whsp ]
                            ; default structural
    [ "MUST" oids ]         ; AttributeTypes
    [ "MAY" oids ]          ; AttributeTypes
    whsp ")"
```

It may not be apparent how the object class example (2.5.6.2 NAME 'country' SUP top STRUCTURAL MUST c MAY (searchGuide $ description)) was built from that definition. Let's go over each field of the definition while referring to our object class example of country.

▶ This and all other values in the schema are enclosed in parentheses. There's white space, typically a space character, separating the parentheses from the rest of the object class (whsp stands for white space).

The only required field is the object identifier (numericoid) assigned to this object class. All other fields are optional (which is what the brackets [] mean). The OID in the example is 2.5.6.2.

▸ The word NAME is followed by one or more quoted textual names for the object class (this is what qdescrs means). In the example, only one name — 'country' — is specified. If more than one name appeared, it would look like NAME ('name1' 'name2'). That is, both names are single-quoted with a space between them, and the whole thing is enclosed in parentheses. When an object class has more than one name, the first name in the list is typically considered its name, while the remaining names are aliases. You may use any of the names when referring to an object class, but expect to see the first name returned from any operation that would return the name of an object class. This same principal holds true for the other schema elements.

▸ A quoted description may follow the word DESC. If the example had this field, it might look like DESC 'represents a country'.

▸ The word OBSOLETE will appear in any object class that isn't used anymore. These have typically been replaced by a newer version of that object class.

▸ All the superclasses in this object class' class hierarchy are listed after the word SUP. The example has only one superclass: top. If it had more, they'd be listed as SUP (class1 $ class2). Each superclass name is separated by a $, and the entire list is surrounded by parentheses. Also note that each element is surrounded by white space. There may be one or more space characters present. In the ObjectClassDescription definition, the value for this field is called oids; RFC 2252 states that each value may either be the numeric OID that identifies the superclass or the textual name that names the superclass. The example uses the textual name but could have used the OID 2.5.6.0. The LDAP RFCs state that it is preferable to use textual names here.

See the "Object Class Hierarchies" discussion in Chapter 1 for a better understanding of superclasses.

X-REF

▸ Next, the object class' type is specified as ABSTRACT, STRUCTURAL, or AUXILIARY. Structural classes are the only ones that you can use to create entries with. An abstract object class is just a building block object class with which — by subclassing — you can build other object classes. Auxiliary classes are a convenient way to update an existing entry to include more attributes. If a class type is not specified, the default class STRUCTURAL is assumed.

X-REF

> **Refer to the "Abstract, Structural, and Auxiliary Object Classes" section in Chapter 1 for more information about these types.**

▸ A list of mandatory attributes appears after the word MUST. If there are multiple values here, they are grouped inside parentheses and separated by the $ character, as in MUST (attr1 $ attr2). These values are the names of attributes that must exist in an entry of this object class. So, if you want to create a country, the example above states that it must contain a c attribute; otherwise, the directory won't allow you to create it. Also note that if you are modifying an entry, you cannot delete all the values of any MUST attribute. To satisfy the schema, at least one value must always be present.

▸ Finally, the word MAY is followed by a list of all the allowed optional attributes. The format is the same as the list of MUST attributes. This list represents the attributes that can be held by entries of this object class but don't have to be. In other words, if you created a country entry, you're allowed to specify a description and a searchGuide attribute. You're not allowed to specify an attribute not listed in the MUST or MAY lists unless the attribute is included in the MUST or MAY list of a superclass.

NDS objectClasses

NDS predates LDAP, and as such, there are a few differences between the schema models. These differences are documented in the Internet-Draft draft-sermersheim-nds-ldap-schema-00.txt.

NDS has defined its own NDSObjectClassDescription, which augments the ObjectClassDescription described previously. It does this by using special X- fields.

The architects of LDAP foresaw the need for certain LDAP implementations to extend the amount of data an object class holds. To meet this need, LDAP specifies that new, private fields may be added, as long as the name starts with X- and the following value is a qdstrings (either a single quoted string or a list of quoted strings in parentheses). If any LDAP server or client encounters these special values and doesn't understand it, it must ignore the X- name and the following value(s). This same concept is also applied to other schema elements such as attribute types and syntaxes.

WARNING

Some early LDAP client SDKs and LDAP applications fail to ignore the special X- data while reading the schema. You can force NDS to not emit this data by marking the Enable Non-Standard Client Schema Compatible Mode option in the LDAP Server object. See the section on "LDAP Server Specific Settings" in Chapter 10 for instructions.

Here's the definition of the NDSObjectClassDescription:

```
NDSObjectClassDescription = "(" whsp
   numericoid whsp        ; ObjectClass identifier
   [ "NAME" qdescrs ]
   [ "DESC" qdstring ]
   [ "OBSOLETE" whsp ]
   [ "SUP" oids ]     ; Superior ObjectClasses
   [ ( "ABSTRACT" / "STRUCTURAL" / "AUXILIARY" ) whsp ]
                      ; default structural
   [ "MUST" oids ]    ; AttributeTypes
   [ "MAY" oids ]     ; AttributeTypes
   [ "X-NDS_NOT_CONTAINER" qdstrings ]
                      ; default container ('0')
   [ "X-NDS_NONREMOVABLE" qdstrings ]
                      ; default removable ('0')
   [ "X-NDS_CONTAINMENT" qdstrings ]
   [ "X-NDS_NAMING" qdstrings ]
   [ "X-NDS_NAME" qdstrings ] ; legacy NDS name
   whsp ")"
```

As you can see, it's the same as the ObjectClassDescription defined by LDAP except for the addition of five X- fields, which we enumerate here:

▶ The word X-NDS_NOT_CONTAINER is followed by either a ('0') or a ('1') — parentheses and quote marks included. This value controls whether or not entries of this object class can have child entries in the tree hierarchy. If this field is absent (neither X-NDS_NOT_CONTAINER nor the value following it are present), or if the value is set to ('0'), entries of this object class are considered container entries and may have child entries in the hierarchy. If the value following X-NDS_NOT_CONTAINER is ('1'), entries of this object class are leaf entries and can never have subordinate entries.

▶ X-NDS_NONREMOVABLE is followed by a value that determines whether entries of this object class may be deleted or not. If the value following X-NDS_NONREMOVABLE is a ('0'), or if this entire production is missing, entries of this object class may be deleted (as long as access controls and the tree structure permits it). If the value is ('1'), entries of this object class cannot be deleted. Clients cannot set or modify this value.

▶ The word X-NDS_CONTAINMENT is followed by a list of other object classes. Only an entry that is of one of the object classes listed here may be a parent entry to entries of this object class. For example, if the list of object classes here are ('o' 'ou'), then entries of this object class could be contained under organization and organizational units in the tree hierarchy. If you don't specify the set of X-NDS_CONTAINMENT object classes when defining an object class, the set will automatically be populated with ('c' 'o' 'ou' 'l' 'domain').

▶ Following X-NDS_NAMING is a list of all attribute type names that may be used to name entries of this object class. Naming attributes are used to form the RDN of an entry. If this field is not supplied when defining an object class, it will automatically be filled with a list of all MUST and MAY attributes, which use any of the following syntaxes: Country String, Directory String, IA5 String, and Printable String. An example value is ('cn' 'l' 'st').

▸ X-NDS_NAME is followed by a value that contains the legacy NDS name for this object class. An example is ('LDAP Server'). Because NDS was created before LDAP was defined, it sometimes doesn't adhere to the exact same rules as LDAP. One such LDAP rule is that the names of schema elements cannot contain anything other than ASCII letters, the hyphen character, and a semicolon. NDS allows spaces, colons, and others. For this reason, some schema elements will have LDAP names that are different from the NDS names that they were first known as. We talk more about these differences and how to map between LDAP and NDS names later in the chapter.

The attributeTypes Attribute

This holds all the attribute types that are defined for the directory. The syntax used to store and transmit attribute types is called the Attribute Type Description. An example attribute type value is (2.5.4.9 NAME 'street' EQUALITY case IgnoreMatch SUBSTR caseIgnoreSubstringsMatch SYNTAX 1.3.6.1.4.1.1466.115. 121.1.15{128}). The formal definition is found in section 4.2 of RFC 2252 and summarized here. Note that the following definition contains line breaks. This has only been done to make it more readable. The actual values don't contain any line breaks.

```
AttributeTypeDescription = "(" whsp
   numericoid whsp                      ; AttributeType identifier
   [ "NAME" qdescrs ]                   ; name used in AttributeType
   [ "DESC" qdstring ]                  ; description
   [ "OBSOLETE" whsp ]
   [ "SUP" woid ]                       ; derived from this other
                                        ; AttributeType
   [ "EQUALITY" woid                    ; Matching Rule name
   [ "ORDERING" woid                    ; Matching Rule name
   [ "SUBSTR" woid ]                    ; Matching Rule name
   [ "SYNTAX" whsp noidlen whsp ] ; Syntax OID
   [ "SINGLE-VALUE" whsp ]              ; default multi-valued
   [ "COLLECTIVE" whsp ]                ; default not collective
   [ "NO-USER-MODIFICATION" whsp ]; default user modifiable
   [ "USAGE" whsp AttributeUsage ]; default userApplications
   whsp ")"
```

```
AttributeUsage =
  "userApplications"      /
  "directoryOperation"    /
  "distributedOperation"  /      ; DSA-shared
  "dSAOperation"                 ; DSA-specific
```

As with the Object Class Description, the only required fields are the surrounding parentheses and the numeric OID. Each field of the Attribute Type Description is discussed:

▶ The first field contains the OID assigned to this attribute type. In the example of the street attribute type above, the OID is 2.5.4.9.

▶ The word NAME is followed by one or more quoted textual names for the attribute type. In the example, only one name, 'street', is specified. If more than one name appeared, it would look like NAME ('name1' 'name2'). That is, both names are single-quoted with a space between them, and the whole thing is enclosed in parentheses.

▶ A quoted description may follow the word DESC. If the example had this field, it might look like DESC 'A street address'.

▶ The word OBSOLETE will appear in any attribute type that isn't used anymore. These have typically been replaced by a newer version of that attribute type.

▶ If this attribute type is derived from another attribute type, the name of the supertype follows the word SUP. Attribute types may be inherited from other attribute types in the same way object classes can inherit from other object classes. When an attribute type inherits from another, it is said to be an attribute *subtype*. The attribute it inherits from is its *supertype*. An example of this subtyping can be seen in attributes that represent names (cn, givenName, title, and so on). They all have a common supertype called name. Those attribute types have the value SUP name in their schema values. Unlike object class hierarchies, an attribute may only inherit from one other attribute; thus, only one SUP value is permitted here. NDS does not currently support attribute supertypes.

▶ Next, one or more matching rules are specified. The matching rules are EQUALITY, ORDERING and SUBSTR. Each one, if specified, will be followed by a matching rule name. These matching rules tell the directory how to perform comparisons when processing search and compare requests. You'll notice that most attribute types have at least an EQUALITY matching rule.

- The EQUALITY rule defines how two values of this attribute type are to be compared for an exact match. The street attribute type example above uses caseIgnoreMatch as its EQUALITY matching rule. This means that uppercase and lowercase differences are ignored when any street attribute in an entry is evaluated for equality.

- An ORDERING rule will allow you to perform search operations with the <= and >= operators in the search filter. That is, it's used when determining whether a value is greater or less than another value.

- The SUBSTR matching rule defines the way in which substring matches work. The example attribute type of a street has a caseIgnoreSubstrings Match matching rule. This enables you to perform substring matches when searching. For example, the LDAP search expression (street=122 E*) will match any street address that starts with 122 E or 122 e.

▶ The syntax of an attribute is specified by its OID following the word SYNTAX. The street example above specifies 1.3.6.1.4.1.1466.115.121. 1.15{128}. You'll notice that this OID looks a bit different than others you've seen so far (the definition calls it a noidlen rather than an oid). This has a value enclosed in braces at the end that represents an upper bound for the attribute. In this case, the syntax is a string, so the upper bound here means that no street address is allowed to have more than 128 characters. If this were a numerical syntax (such as INTEGER), it would mean that no value greater than 128 is allowed. Rather than using a name, like other elements (SUP, MUST, MAY, and so forth) have, the syntax must be specified by a numeric OID. You can look up the names of most of these syntaxes in section 4.3.2 of RFC 2252.

NOTE

The way an attribute is stored and, more importantly, transferred over the wire, is defined by its syntax. An attribute's syntax describes the form of the attribute. For example, there is an attribute type called modifyTimestamp. **The** modifyTimestamp **attribute stores the last time an entry was modified. The syntax for this attribute type is Generalized Time. The Generalized Time syntax defines a very specific format for time. It looks like YYYYMMDDHHMMSSZ. If you were to represent April first, at 10:32 a.m. in the year 2000, the value would be 20000401 1032Z (the Z means that it's in Greenwich Mean Time). The reason LDAP uses such tightly controlled and highly specified syntaxes is a good one because you need to be sure that the attribute values you send over LDAP to the directory are exactly what the directory expects. You also need to be sure that when you ask for a value, LDAP will deliver it exactly as you expect it. Finally, you want to create applications that will work without modification regardless of the implementation of the LDAP server they talk to. Tight control on attribute value format (syntax) ensures that all of these needs are met.**

▶ If the word SINGLE-VALUE is included in the attribute type, this attribute is only allowed to contain one value. Otherwise, the default is that attributes can contain multiple values.

▶ The word COLLECTIVE states that this attribute is collective. Collective attributes are defined by X.500 and not implemented by most LDAP servers (including NDS). Collective attributes are attributes that are shared among multiple entries. They are defined and updated in a subentry, and may affect all the entries in the subtree specification for that subentry. They are included or excluded from entries by using DIT content rules. To fully understand collective attributes, you would need a much deeper foundation of knowledge and that is beyond the scope of this book.

▶ A read-only attribute has the word NO-USER-MODIFICATION in its attribute type. This field is typically reserved for attributes used by the server.

▶ Finally, userApplications, directoryOperation, distributedOperation, or dSAOperation follows the word USAGE. These tell you what the attribute is used for.

NOTE

Most attributes are used for applications; thus, userApplication typically follows the USAGE field. userApplication is the default, so if you don't see the USAGE statement at all when reading an attribute type, you'll know that it's an ordinary user attribute. The other three values specify that this is an operational attribute and is typically used by the server. Operational attributes aren't normally seen by end-users and must be specifically asked for by name if a client wishes to receive them (see the "Specifying the Attributes to be Returned" discussion in Chapter 5). The value directoryOperation means that the attribute is used for directory operations or holds directory specific values (access control information is a good example). The distributedOperation **attributes hold DSA (or server) information and are shared among all servers holding replicas of the entry. (We talk about replicas in Chapter 8.) The** dSAOperation **attributes also hold DSA information, but are local to a server. They are not replicated to other servers.**

NDS Attribute Types

For the same reasons discussed in the preceding NDS objectClasses section, NDS has created its own version of the attribute type description and called it NDSAttributeTypeDescription. Here it is with its additions:

```
NDSAttributeTypeDescription = "(" whsp
    numericoid whsp                 ; AttributeType identifier
    [ "NAME" qdescrs ]              ; name used in AttributeType
    [ "DESC" qdstring ]             ; description
    [ "OBSOLETE" whsp ]
    [ "SUP" woid ]                  ; derived from this other
                                    ; AttributeType

    [ "EQUALITY" woid              ; Matching Rule name
    [ "ORDERING" woid              ; Matching Rule name
    [ "SUBSTR" woid ]              ; Matching Rule name
```

```
        [ "SYNTAX" whsp noidlen whsp ] ; Syntax OID
        [ "SINGLE-VALUE" whsp ]         ; default multi-valued
        [ "COLLECTIVE" whsp ]           ; default not collective
        [ "NO-USER-MODIFICATION" whsp ]; default user modifiable
        [ "USAGE" whsp AttributeUsage ]; default userApplications
        [ "X-NDS_PUBLIC_READ" qdstrings ]
                              ; default not public read (0')
        [ "X-NDS_SERVER_READ" qdstrings ]
                              ; default not server read ('0')
        [ "X-NDS_NEVER_SYNC" qdstrings ]
                              ; default not never sync ('0')
        [ "X-NDS_NOT_SCHED_SYNC_IMMEDIATE" qdstrings ]
                              ; default sched sync immediate ('0')
        [ "X-NDS_SCHED_SYNC_NEVER" qdstrings ]
                              ; default schedule sync ('0')
        [ "X-NDS_LOWER_BOUND" qdstrings ]
                              ; default no lower bound('0')
                              ;(upper is specified in SYNTAX)
        [ "X-NDS_NAME_VALUE_ACCESS" qdstrings ]
                              ; default not name value access ('0')
        [ "X-NDS_NAME" qdstrings ]     ; legacy NDS name
        whsp ")"


    AttributeUsage =
      "userApplications"     /
      "directoryOperation"   /
      "distributedOperation" /      ; DSA-shared
      "dSAOperation"                ; DSA-specific
```

Again, this definition is the same as the one specified by LDAP other than the addition of some X- fields. There are eight additional elements in the NDS attribute type. In each case, a default behavior is given. That default is used when an attribute type doesn't contain the field.

▸ X-NDS_PUBLIC_READ is followed by ('0'), which signifies false, or a ('1'), which signifies true. Setting this value to true indicates that anyone can read the attribute without read privileges being assigned. Using ACLs to restrict the access to this attribute will be ineffective.

▸ Following X-NDS_SERVER_READ is either ('0'), meaning false, or ('1'), meaning true. When this is true, other servers can read the attribute even if access control has not been set up to allow that server to read the attribute. Clients cannot set or modify this value.

▸ A ('0') signifying false or a ('1') signifying true follows X-NDS_NEVER_ SYNC. Here, true indicates that this attribute is never sent to (synchronized on) other replicas. Clients may not set or modify this value.

▸ X-NDS_NOT_SCHED_SYNC_IMMEDIATE is followed by either ('0') (false) or ('1') (true). By default, any update to an attribute value will cause a replica synchronization session to occur within 10 seconds. If this flag is set to true, updates to this attribute won't immediately initiate a synchronization session; instead, a synchronization session will be initiated within 30 minutes. At that time, the updates will be replicated to other servers.

▸ Valid values that follow X-NDS_SCHED_SYNC_NEVER are ('0') (false), and ('1') (true). If this flag is set to true, updates to this attribute will not cause a synchronization session to be scheduled. Note that this flag does not prevent the attribute from being synchronized like the X-NDS_NEVER_ SYNC does. Once a synchronization session is initiated by another process, the updates to this attribute will be replicated. Clients cannot set or modify this value.

▸ X-NDS_LOWER_BOUND is followed by a quoted uint32string in parentheses, such as ('12'). While the upper bound of a value is specified by the upper bound value in braces following the SYNTAX OID, this value represents the lower bound of a value. LDAP only allows for an upper bound (see the definition of noidlen in RFC 2252). The lower bound of LDAP attributes is either assumed to be 0, or a special syntax is created that spec-ifies a minimum number or number of characters.

For example, it was necessary in LDAP to create a special syntax for country that states that the value is exactly two characters. In NDS, this can be done by setting both the lower and upper bounds to 2.

▸ Following X-NDS_NAME_VALUE_ACCESS is either ('0') (false) or ('1') (true). This is specified only when the attribute uses a Distinguished Name syntax. When true, it specifies that the subject, or user, must have management rights (write permissions on the acl attribute) to the entry that is being added or removed from this attribute, which the DN names. In other words, if this is set to true on a DN attribute called 'friends' in my user entry, I can't add your DN to my list of friends unless I have write permissions to your acl attribute. For those familiar with legacy NDS access APIs, this is the "Write Managed" flag.

▸ X-NDS_NAME is followed by a value that contains the legacy NDS name for this attribute type. One example is telephoneNumber. This attribute is called Telephone Number in the NDS schema. Refer back to the discussion of the X-NDS_NAME field that NDS added to the object class description to understand why this is needed.

The ldapSyntaxes Attribute

This attribute holds all the possible syntaxes that this server is capable of supporting. Unlike attribute types and object classes, the set of syntaxes can't be changed. In other words, you can't add or delete syntaxes. The format of a syntax is called Syntax Description. An example syntax is (1.3.6.1.4.1.1466.115.121. 1.15 DESC 'Directory String'). The formal definition is found in section 4.3.3 of RFC 2252 and summarized here. Note that the following definition contains line breaks. This has only been done to make it more readable. The actual values don't contain any line breaks.

```
SyntaxDescription = "(" whsp
    numericoid whsp
    [ "DESC" qdstring ]
    whsp ")"
```

This is considerably less complicated than the definition of object classes and attribute types, and if you suffered through the explanation of either of those, you'll have no problem understanding the elements of this one.

- As with all other schema elements, a syntax description requires a numeric OID to identify it. The example uses 1.3.6.1.4.1.1466.115.121.1.15. If you look at section 4.3.2 of RFC 2252, it is in the table of well-known syntaxes.

- The only other bit of information is the description following the word DESC. Note that the description of a syntax is usually just a human-readable name. In the example above, the description reads 'Directory String'.

There is only one difference between the LDAP syntax description and the NDS syntax description, and that is the addition of an X-NDS_SYNTAX field. This is followed by a number such as ('9'). NDS identifies and documents all syntaxes with a single number (rather than an OID). This number represents the legacy NDS syntax.

```
NDSSyntaxDescription = "(" whsp
    numericoid whsp              ; Syntax identifier
    [ "DESC" qdstring ]          ; description
    [ "X-NDS_SYNTAX" qdstrings ]; legacy NDS syntax identifier
    whsp ")"
```

Differences between Standard LDAP and NDS LDAP Schema

This section describes some minor differences between the schema as it is defined by LDAP and the way NDS has chosen to represent its schema through LDAP.

Additional Syntaxes

NDS supports all the standard syntaxes defined in RFC 2252 and defines a few more specialized ones. Most of these are complex syntaxes—meaning they're made up of more than one part. For example, NDS defines a syntax called Tagged

Name and String. Values of this syntax are made up of a number, a DN, and a string. A complete listing and description of these syntaxes may be found in section 5 of the Internet-Draft draft-sermersheim-nds-ldap-schema-00.txt. Table 7.1 lists the additional syntaxes introduced.

Syntaxes Coupled with Matching Rules

When the original X.500 recommendations defined schema concepts, it tied matching rules to syntaxes. So when you define a syntax, you also define a matching rule to be used for values of that syntax and associate the two. This was the model adopted by NDS and has stuck ever since. Later versions of X.500, and LDAPv3 that is based on these later versions, have slightly adjusted the way this association is made. In LDAP, you specify a syntax and matching rules as part of an attribute type. This way, you can have one attribute type that uses Directory String syntax and a caseIgnoreMatch equality matching rule, and have another attribute type that uses the same syntax but a caseExactMatch equality matching rule.

NDS has a static set of syntaxes (as do most other LDAP directories). When you create a new attribute type, NDS looks at the syntax and the matching rules you specified and makes a best-fit mapping to one of its internal syntaxes. For example, one NDS syntax is called Case Ignore String; if you create an attribute type and specify a Directory String syntax and a caseIgnoreMatch equality rule, NDS will use the Case Ignore String syntax for this attribute. This model has worked fine historically, but there is the possibility that you might pick a syntax and matching rule combination that doesn't map to any NDS syntax. In this case, the syntax will be used to find the best fit, and the matching rule you specified will not be used. If you add an attribute type to the schema and want to know if this kind of thing has happened, read the attribute type after adding it to see what was actually stored.

Additional Flags and Identifiers

In the previous sections, you read about various additional NDS fields that have been added to schema elements, and you already know a bit more about the reason for the X-NDS_NAME.

Naming Rules

One mechanism described by X.500 that is implemented a bit differently in NDS is the way the naming attributes are specified for an object class. Naming rules control the attributes that make up DNs. In X.500, this is done by using *Name Forms*. In LDAP, name forms are another element of the schema called nameForms. Each name form rule holds a list of naming attributes and a specific object class. To find out which attributes may be used to name an entry, you must find the name forms rule that is in effect for that object and examine its list of attributes.

Rather than make you do this, NDS has included the naming rules in the object class itself. This is done using the X-NDS_NAMING field. This field is followed by the list of valid naming attributes. Most object classes only specify a single attribute as the naming attribute. For example, the naming attribute for a locality is `l`, for organizationalUnit it's `ou`, and for country it's `c`. Users are typically named by their `cn` attribute.

Structure Rules versus Containment

Another X.500 concept is called structure rules. These rules mandate the way the hierarchy of a tree is laid out. This helps you make sure your tree models the real world. An example is using structure rules to make it impossible to allow a country object to exist under a printer object. The way this is achieved in X.500 directories is through using *DIT Structure Rules*. These rules are held in the schema as another set of values in an attribute called `ditStructureRules`. Each structure rule points to a specific name form rule, which in turn points to a specific object class. The structure rule also points to one or more superior structure rules. The superior structure rules point indirectly to the object classes that are allowed to be parents to objects of this object class in the tree hierarchy.

This is all a bit complicated, so to simplify things, NDS chose to tie structure rules to object classes rather than make you go through all that indirection. The X-NDS_CONTAINMENT field in an object class lists all the other possible object classes to which this object can be directly subordinate in the tree hierarchy. For example, the organizationalUnit object class lists locality, organization, domain, and organizationalUnit in its set of containment classes. This means that an organizationalUnit entry can only appear directly underneath an entry that is a locality, organization, domain, or another organizationalUnit.

Another field—X-NDS_NOT_CONTAINER—specifies whether entries of an object class can be used as containers. By default, all object classes are container classes. (Their entries can have subordinate entries in the tree hierarchy.) If this field is set, the entries created with the object class will remain leaf node objects.

▶ . . . . ◀

Differences between NDS LDAP and NDS NDAP Schema

Unlike the previous section, this section highlights the differences between the way the NDS schema is represented through LDAP and through NDAP. This section is particularly useful for anyone who is already familiar with the way NDS's schema is represented through legacy APIs. It is also useful for people who use management utilities that use NDAP as their access protocol.

Names

Although it doesn't present a horrible problem, one of the most obvious differences between the way the schema is represented through NDAP versus LDAP is the allowed character set used to build names for object classes and attribute types. LDAP has tighter restrictions on what characters can appear in these names—only ASCII letters and hyphens. A large number of the schema names in NDS deployments contain spaces, underscores, and colons. This problem has been dealt with by allowing LDAP-friendly names to be assigned or "mapped" to existing NDS names. We discuss this further in the "Managing the Schema" section in this chapter.

Identifiers

NDS identifies attribute types and object classes by OIDs, just like LDAP does. The only difference is that legacy NDS APIs and applications call this identifier an ASN.1 ID rather than an OID.

Syntaxes

There are approximately 60 LDAP syntaxes defined in IETF RFCs, and there are 28 syntaxes in use by NDS. Some of the NDS syntaxes are functionally equivalent to one or more LDAP syntaxes; other NDS syntaxes are not like any LDAP syntax, and some LDAP syntaxes are not like any NDS syntax. The sets of these two syntaxes look like Figure 7.2.

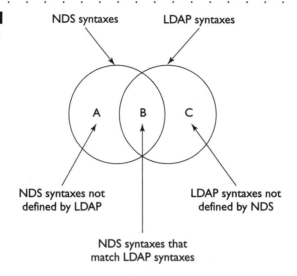

FIGURE 7.2

The sets of NDS and LDAP syntaxes

NDS syntaxes   LDAP syntaxes

A   B   C

NDS syntaxes not
defined by LDAP

LDAP syntaxes not
defined by NDS

NDS syntaxes that
match LDAP syntaxes

The circle on the left represents the complete set of NDS syntaxes. The circle on the right represents the complete set of standard LDAP syntaxes. Set A represents all NDS syntaxes that are functionally different from any standard LDAP syntax. Set B represents all NDS and standard LDAP syntaxes that are functionally the same, though they're typically named differently. Set C represents all the standard LDAP syntaxes that are functionally different from any NDS syntax. Let's talk about what NDS has done to blend this into one big happy circle.

NDS Syntaxes New to LDAP

Set A represents all the NDS syntaxes that are completely different from anything ever defined in LDAP. We talked about this set of syntaxes briefly in the previous section. Novell has redefined these syntaxes in terms of LDAP and published the definitions in the Internet-Draft draft-sermersheim-nds-ldap-schema-00.txt. The draft assigns OIDs to the syntaxes, gives many of them new names, and provides the instructions needed to encode values of each syntax for transfer over the wire. Table 7.1 contains the set of these syntaxes and illustrates some differences between the way they were named and identified with legacy NDS APIs and the way they are now named and identified with LDAP APIs. Refer to the previously mentioned draft if you need to understand how a value of one of these syntaxes is supposed to be formatted.

TABLE 7.1	NDS NAME	NDS ID	LDAP NAME	LDAP OID
Novell Specific LDAP Syntaxes	Case Ignore List	6	Case Ignore List	2.16.840.1.113719. 1.1.5.1.6
	Net Address	12	Tagged Data	2.16.840.1.113719. 1.1.5.1.12
	Octet List	13	Octet List	2.16.840.1.113719. 1.1.5.1.13
	Email Address	14	Tagged String	2.16.840.1.113719. 1.1.5.1.14
	Path	15	Tagged Name And String	2.16.840.1.113719. 1.1.5.1.15
	Replica Pointer	16	NDS Replica Pointer	2.16.840.1.113719. 1.1.5.1.16
	Object ACL	17	NDS ACL	2.16.840.1.113719. 1.1.5.1.17
	Timestamp	19	NDS Timestamp	2.16.840.1.113719. 1.1.5.1.19
	Counter	22	Counter	2.16.840.1.113719. 1.1.5.1.22
	Back Link	23	Tagged Name	2.16.840.1.113719. 1.1.5.1.23
	Typed Name	25	Typed Name	2.16.840.1.113719. 1.1.5.1.25

NDS Syntaxes that Match LDAP Syntaxes

Set B represents the functional intersection of the NDS and standard LDAP sets of attributes. Table 7.2 shows the relationship between these syntaxes.

TABLE 7.2	NDS NAME	NDS ID	LDAP NAME	LDAP OID
Mappings Between NDS and Standard LDAP Syntaxes	Distinguished Name	1	DN	1.3.6.1.4.1.1466.115. 121.1.12
	Case Exact String	2	IA5 String	1.3.6.1.4.1.1466.115. 121.1.26
	Case Ignore String	3	Directory String	1.3.6.1.4.1.1466.115. 121.1.15

	NDS NAME	NDS ID	LDAP NAME	LDAP OID
T A B L E 7.2 *Mappings Between NDS and Standard LDAP Syntaxes (continued)*	Printable String	4	Printable String	1.3.6.1.4.1.1466.115.121.1.44
	Numeric String	5	Numeric String	1.3.6.1.4.1.1466.115.121.1.36
	Boolean	7	Boolean	1.3.6.1.4.1.1466.115.121.1.7
	Integer	8	Integer	1.3.6.1.4.1.1466.115.121.1.27
	Octet String	9	Octet String	1.3.6.1.4.1.1466.115.121.1.40
	Telephone Number	10	Telephone Number	1.3.6.1.4.1.1466.115.121.1.50
	Facsimile Telephone Number	11	Facsimile Telephone Number	1.3.6.1.4.1.1466.115.121.1.23
	Postal Address	18	Postal Address	1.3.6.1.4.1.1466.115.121.1.41
	Class Name*	20	Directory String	1.3.6.1.4.1.1466.115.121.1.15
	Stream*	21	Binary	1.3.6.1.4.1.1466.115.121.1.5
	Time*	24	Generalized Time	1.3.6.1.4.1.1466.115.121.1.24
	Hold**	26	<Deprecated>	2.16.840.1.113719.1.1.5.1.0
	Interval*	27	Integer	1.3.6.1.4.1.1466.115.121.1.27

*These NDS syntaxes don't have exact LDAP counterparts, but they aren't different enough from the LDAP syntaxes to which they're mapped to warrant a new LDAP definition.

**The NDS Hold syntax has been deprecated. If an existing entry has an attribute value of this syntax, it may be read but not updated. No attributes may be defined with this syntax.

LDAP Syntaxes Not Matching NDS Syntaxes

There are numerous standard LDAP syntaxes that don't have exact NDS counterparts. NDS supports all of these by simply mapping them to either Case Ignore String or more commonly, Octet String. This allows attribute values to be stored and read from the directory, but values of these syntaxes will not be checked for integrity. For example, if you stored your street address in an attribute that uses the JPEG syntax, NDS will allow it, but chances are, a client trying to read that attribute back will run into problems because it thinks it's reading a JPEG image. We won't take the time to list these syntaxes. If an LDAP syntax is not found in one of the tables above, it's either mapped to Octet String or Case Ignore String.

Attribute Types

If you're familiar with NDS attribute types (most NDS references call them attribute type definitions), and you've looked over the NDSAttributeType Description earlier in this chapter, you've seen most of the differences that exist between their representations in legacy APIs and applications and their LDAP representations. We go over each difference here.

Syntax and Matching Rules

Because NDS associates matching rules to syntaxes, NDS attribute types don't actually store matching rules. When you examine an NDS attribute type using LDAP, you won't see any matching rules displayed.

Also, when a syntax is specified for an attribute type with legacy NDS APIs, the NDS syntax ID is used rather than the LDAP OID. You can see how NDS has mapped between NDS syntax IDs and LDAP OIDs in Table 7.1 and 7.2.

Constraint Flags

This is where NDS and LDAP really start to differ. NDS has found the need to allow certain flags to be associated with each attribute type. Table 7.3 contains a list of those flags, named as they are in legacy NDS APIs. The list shows how each constraint flag is accessed through LDAP. They are exposed as additional fields that begin with the name X- in the NDSAttributeTypeDescription. We discussed the fields of the NDSAttributeTypeDescription earlier; here's the definition again for your reference:

```
NDSAttributeTypeDescription = "(" whsp
  numericoid whsp
  [ "NAME" qdescrs ]
  [ "DESC" qdstring ]
  [ "OBSOLETE" whsp ]
  [ "SUP" woid ]
  [ "EQUALITY" woid ]
  [ "ORDERING" woid ]
  [ "SUBSTR" woid ]
  [ "SYNTAX" whsp noidlen whsp ]
  [ "SINGLE-VALUE" whsp ]
  [ "COLLECTIVE" whsp ]
  [ "NO-USER-MODIFICATION" whsp ]
  [ "USAGE" whsp AttributeUsage ]
  [ "X-NDS_PUBLIC_READ" qdstrings ]
  [ "X-NDS_SERVER_READ" qdstrings ]
  [ "X-NDS_NEVER_SYNC" qdstrings ]
  [ "X-NDS_NOT_SCHED_SYNC_IMMEDIATE" qdstrings ]
  [ "X-NDS_SCHED_SYNC_NEVER" qdstrings ]
  [ "X-NDS_LOWER_BOUND" qdstrings ]
  [ "X-NDS_NAME_VALUE_ACCESS" qdstrings ]
  [ "X-NDS_NAME" qdstrings ]
  whsp ")"

AttributeUsage =
  "userApplications"     /
  "directoryOperation"   /
  "distributedOperation" /
  "dSAOperation"
```

TABLE 7.3	NDS ATTRIBUTE CONSTRAINT FLAG	LDAP ATTRIBUTE TYPE FIELD
NDS Attribute Constraint Flags	DS_SINGLE_VALUED_ATTR DS_SIZED_ATTR* DS_NONREMOVABLE_ATTR*	SINGLE-VALUE
	DS READ ONLY ATTR DS HIDDEN ATTR* DS_STRING_ATTR*	NO USER MODIFICATION
	DS_SYNC_IMMEDIATE	X-NDS_NOT_SCHED_SYNC_ IMMEDIATE
	DS_PUBLIC_READ	X-NDS_PUBLIC_READ
	DS_SERVER_READ	X-NDS_SERVER_READ
	DS_WRITE_MANAGED	X-NDS_NAME_VALUE_ ACCESS
	DS_PER_REPLICA	X-NDS_NEVER_SYNC
	DS_SCHEDULE_SYNC_NEVER	X-NDS_SCHED_SYNC_NEVER
	DS_OPERATIONAL	USAGE directoryOperation -or- USAGE dSAOperation

* Novell found it unnecessary to expose these NDS Attribute constraints through LDAP.

Limits

NDS allows you to specify a lower bound as well as an upper bound for attribute values. For example, the cn attribute has a lower bound of 1 and an upper bound of 64. This means that values of this attribute may be from 1 to 64 characters long. LDAP only allows you to specify an upper bound. NDS exposes this functionality in the NDSAttributeTypeDescription X-NDS_LOWER_BOUND field.

Object Classes

As with attribute types, there are a number of differences in the way certain aspects of object classes are represented in NDAP and LDAP.

Flags

Much like the way attribute types in NDS employ constraint flags, object classes use object class flags to specify extra information about the object class. Table 7.4 lists those flags along with their corresponding access methods in LDAP. In LDAP, these flags are exposed as additional fields that begin with the name X- in the NDSObject ClassDescription. We discussed the fields of the NDSObjectClass. Description earlier; here's the definition again so you don't have to flip back to reference it.

```
NDSObjectClassDescription = "(" whsp
    numericoid whsp
    [ "NAME" qdescrs ]
    [ "DESC" qdstring ]
    [ "OBSOLETE" whsp ]
    [ "SUP" oids ]
    [ ( "ABSTRACT" / "STRUCTURAL" / "AUXILIARY" ) whsp ]
    [ "MUST" oids ]
    [ "MAY" oids ]
    [ "X-NDS_NOT_CONTAINER" qdstrings ]
    [ "X-NDS_NONREMOVABLE" qdstrings ]
    [ "X-NDS_CONTAINMENT" qdstrings ]
    [ "X-NDS_NAMING" qdstrings ]
    [ "X-NDS_NAME" qdstrings ]
    whsp ")"
```

TABLE 7.4	NDS OBJECT CLASS FLAG	LDAP OBJECT CLASS FIELD
NDS Object Class Constraint Flags	DS_CONTAINER_CLASS	X-NDS_NOT_CONTAINER
	DS_EFFECTIVE_CLASS	STRUCTURAL
	DS_NONREMOVABLE_CLASS DS_AMBIGUOUS_NAMING* DS_AMBIGUOUS_CONTAINMENT*	X-NDS_NONREMOVABLE
	DS_AUXILIARY_CLASS	AUXILIARY
	DS_OPERATIONAL_CLASS**	

*This is not needed in LDAP.

**This is not yet supported in LDAP.

Containment

When you create an object class with legacy NDS APIs, you specify a list of containment object classes. This list determines where instances of this object class may reside in the directory tree. The X-NDS_CONTAINMENT field in the NDSObjectClassDescription does this in LDAP.

Naming

The X-NDS_NAMING field in the NDSObjectClassDescription holds a list of all the naming attributes for this object class. These are the attributes that are allowed to be used in the RDN of instances of this object class.

Default ACL

With legacy NDS APIs, you could specify a default access control list for an object class. These access control settings are applied by default to all new instances of an object class. This feature is not yet supported by LDAP.

Managing the Schema

If you're writing simple LDAP applications such as browsers and address books, you may never need to add to the schema. If, on the other hand, you write a custom application, chances are you'll need to define a few new object classes and attributes.

Why Change Schema Elements?

Let's say that you have a circle of friends who are all musicians and you want to write a directory-enabled application that keeps track of them. You would need to create a new object class, probably called musician, which holds attributes that are specific to musicians, such as instruments played, disciplines, and so on. This could be done by either subclassing another object class (person would be a good choice), or by creating an auxiliary class to hold the extra attributes.

The "Abstract, Structural, and Auxiliary Object Classes" section of Chapter 1 talks about auxiliary classes.

X-REF

Most applications being written today tend to modify the schema for very similar reasons as those listed in the preceding paragraph. The object classes that represent real-life objects are the ones that tend to get customized. There are two popular ways to do this: Use the iNetOrgPerson object class or use auxiliary classes. Many directories — NDS included — use the iNetOrgPerson object class to represent people. iNetOrgPerson is defined in the RFC 2798. An application that needs to add its own set of user data will either subclass iNetOrgPerson or create an auxiliary class that can be added to any desired user. The latter method (using auxiliary classes) tends to be a better design choice in most situations. This is because an auxiliary object class doesn't require that another object class already exist in the schema before it's defined (which a subclass does). Another benefit is that an auxiliary class is simply added to directory objects that already exist. If you create a new object class, existing directory objects won't be able to take advantage of its features, unless you provide some kind of migrate utility.

Adding Schema Elements

This is the most common schema modification that applications make. Typically this is done when an application is being installed for the first time, or it may be done as a separate step, prior to installing an application that uses the new schema elements. If a new address book application, which requires schema additions, is being rolled out to employees at Company X where there is a single directory, the schema only needs to be extended once. In this case, it would be impractical to cause the installation program to attempt to extend the schema; rather, the schema should be extended once before the application is installed on any workstation. On the other hand, if a single application — such as a payroll system — is being deployed, it may make sense to extend the schema at install time.

Deleting Schema Elements

The act of deleting object classes and attribute types isn't something you find yourself doing very often. Typically, an application is written that needs additional schema, not less. In fact, deleting any schema elements brings with it the risk of rendering another application useless. You might need to delete some schema elements while you're in the development stage of writing an application due to design changes and such.

WARNING

You might receive errors when deleting an object class or attribute type because other things currently depend on it. If an attribute type is currently in the **MUST** or **MAY** list of any object class, you cannot delete that attribute type — you must first either delete the object class or remove the attribute type from it in order to remove the dependency. Similarly, if an object class is in use by any directory object, you cannot delete that object class.

Modifying Schema Elements

Although NDS allows you to modify an existing object class or attribute type, doing so to a schema element defined in a standards document is strongly discouraged by Novell, the IETF, and the ITU. If you need to modify an object class or attribute type, you should always create a new one and assign it a new OID. The reason for this is to maintain interoperability. The whole reason OIDs are used to identify schema elements is so that everyone (servers and clients) knows what everyone else (other servers and clients) means when they say that this is the 2.5.6.0 object class. If you alter the meaning of an object class, by adding or removing attributes, you may compromise the integrity of your directory deployment.

TIP

If you find you need to modify an existing object class, consider using an auxiliary object class instead. Many times, using an auxiliary object class is a better alternative than modifying an existing object class.

Mapping LDAP Names to NDS Names

To work around the issue of name differences that have been mentioned earlier, Novell's LDAP implementation provides a mechanism that allows you to specify a mapping between NDS schema names and LDAP schema names. For example, the NDS attribute called `Telephone Number` can be — and is — mapped to the LDAP attribute called `telephoneNumber`. In effect, what happens is that an NDS attribute type or object class already exists, and an LDAP name is assigned to it. The schema element remains the same; only its name is augmented with an LDAP-friendly version.

In versions prior to NDS 8.38, it was required that for each NDS object class and attribute type, you provide an LDAP name mapping. This requirement has been removed in version 8.38 . Since then, as long as a schema element's NDS name follows LDAP naming rules — that is, it contains only ASCII letters and hyphens — no mapping needs to exist. For example, if an attribute type is named `BX:Relative Density`, it's not a valid LDAP name. To access this attribute through LDAP, you need to map it to something like `bxRelativeDensity`.

The entire schema that ships with NDS comes pre-mapped to LDAP-friendly names. If you upgrade NDS, the installation program also auto-generates maps between existing NDS names to LDAP names.

We discuss two ways that you can map LDAP schema names to NDS schema names later in this chapter. If you stick to LDAP names when adding attribute types and object classes, you won't have to worry about doing this.

You can also map well-known LDAP attribute types and object classes to existing and slightly dissimilar NDS schema elements. In some cases, this has already been done for you. Take, for instance, the most commonly used NDS object class — User. LDAP doesn't define a User object class. Instead, there is person, organizationalPerson, and iNetOrgPerson. NDS maps inetOrgPerson to User when it is installed. We talk about the problems this creates in just a moment.

Many-to-One Mappings

More than one LDAP name may be mapped to a single NDS schema element. An example of this can be found in the default object class mappings provided by NDS. As far as NDS is concerned, the LDAP groupOfNames and groupOf UniqueNames object classes are effectively the same and both are mapped to the NDS object class called Group. By the same token, both the LDAP attribute types called description and multiLineDescription are mapped to Description.

Effects of Name Mapping

Aside from allowing access to schema elements that are not named with LDAP-compliant names, you must be aware of other effects.

Providing a map between an LDAP object class name and an NDS object class affects the following notable things:

- The values of an entry's `objectClass` attribute contain the LDAP names rather than the NDS names. When reading this attribute or when searching for, or updating, it, expect to see and specify the LDAP versions of the object class name.

▶ When reading the schema, the LDAP name is used to name the object class. You also see the LDAP object class name if it's used in a superclass hierarchy of another object class. This implies that if you extend the schema by subclassing an existing object class, you must specify the LDAP name of the existing object class.

Mapping between an LDAP attribute type name and an NDS attribute type may affect more than you imagined. The following are scenarios that are affected by attribute type mappings:

▶ All operations requiring a DN — which includes almost every operation — may be affected. The attribute type you specify in an RDN must be specified by the LDAP name. If you created a mapping to the NDS CN attribute type, and specified cName as the LDAP name, DNs would have to look something like cName=admin,o=administration rather than cn=admin, o=administration. This causes problems when applications assume that an entry will be named by cn, which many do. Keep this in mind when mapping attributes that are likely to be used as naming attributes.

▶ The preceding principle also applies to any attribute that uses a Distinguished Name syntax. Because these attributes contain DNs, those DNs will contain RDNs that use LDAP names in the attribute part. For example, there may be an entry in the tree that represents a group of people in the directory. The attribute that holds the list of people would use a Distinguished Name syntax. Let's say a user name in that group is cn=marge,o=officers. If cName were mapped to cn, that value would change to cName=marge,o=officers.

▶ Of course, the attributes specified in a search filter are LDAP names. Also, if you specify attributes to be returned from a search, they must be the LDAP name of the attribute. If your search operation specifies that all attributes are to be returned, and an attribute has a mapping, the LDAP name will be returned.

▶ If there are multiple LDAP names mapped to a single NDS name, the first one that was mapped will be returned from a search unless another one was specifically requested in the attributes to be returned list.

▸ The update operations add and modify both allow you to specify attributes; these attributes must be specified by their LDAP names.

General Cautions

In some cases, providing a map between an LDAP name and an NDS name will cause a problem. The problem occurs when the LDAP name represents a well-known schema element and the NDS schema element isn't exactly the same as what was defined in LDAP. One example of this problem, which may manifest itself, is actually due to NDS providing a mapping between the LDAP object class inetOrgPerson and the NDS object class User. This is because the definition of inetOrgPerson doesn't exactly match that of User. For example, you may read the `objectClasses` attribute of an entry, find out it's an inetOrgPerson, try to update the employeeNumber, and receive an error from the server because inetOrgPerson is actually just mapped to User—which doesn't allow the `employeeNumber` attribute.

The same holds true for attribute types. If the definitions of both attribute types don't match exactly, think twice before mapping them. For some time, there were instructions floating around on newsgroups, telling people they needed to map the LDAP attribute type uid to CN in NDS. The reason was that a popular address book application performed searches on the `uid` attribute when trying to look up names. Typical NDS deployments didn't have a value for uid, so the search would fail, thus the suggestion to "redirect" uid to CN. This presents a horrible problem later. Once the `CN` attribute was effectively called `uid` in LDAP, LDAP applications that read or modified the `cn` attribute failed to function.

Using ConsoleOne to Modify the Schema

If you'd like to modify the schema for your directory, you can do so by using the ConsoleOne management utility that comes with NDS, or you can write your own management utility using LDAP. ConsoleOne has the advantage of already having been written and tested, but has the disadvantage of using NDAP, thus requiring you to run Novell's NetWare client. Here, we demonstrate the use of ConsoleOne to modify the schema. Later, we introduce the LDAP operations used to perform the same tasks and present a schema browser utility that uses LDAP.

If you want to follow along with the examples in this section, you need to install ConsoleOne. You may have already done this.

X-REF

The instructions for installing ConsoleOne are in Chapter 2 under the heading "LDAP Installation." You'll also find instructions in Chapter 2 on how to run this utility and locate your directory tree in the "Using the ConsoleOne Management Utility" section.

Once you've located and highlighted your tree, you can select Schema Manager from the Tools menu. The Schema Manager is shown in Figure 7.3.

NOTE

ConsoleOne uses the NDAP protocol to talk to NDS, and as such, all attribute types and object classes are named by their NDS names rather than their LDAP names.

F I G U R E 7.3

ConsoleOne's Schema Manager

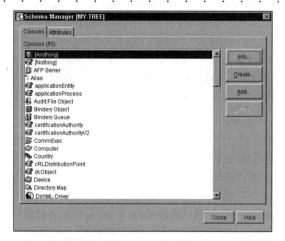

From here, you're able to manage object classes and attributes by choosing one of the tabs at the top of the dialog box. ConsoleOne refers to object classes as classes and attribute types as attributes. The Classes tab page has four buttons on the right. Info lets you read an object class, Create lets you create a new object class, Add allows you to add optional attributes to an existing object class, and Delete lets you remove an existing object class. The Attributes tab has three buttons, Info, Create, and Delete , and their functions are the same as those on the Classes tab.

Reading Schema Elements

Select the Info button to read a specific object class or attribute type. Refer to Figure 7.4 for a screen shot of an object class information dialog box. ConsoleOne calls this the Class Manager dialog box, presumably because you can optionally add attributes to the object class from the dialog box shown in Figure 7.4.

FIGURE 7.4

ConsoleOne's Class Manager

In the upper left, the class flags are listed. These flags correspond to the flags listed in Table 7.4.

The list in the upper right displays all of the object classes that are containment classes for this class. An instance of this class may be contained in the tree hierarchy by an instance of any of the classes listed here.

The "Attributes" list contains all the attributes that this object class contains — including attributes derived from all superclasses. An attribute listed here is optional (one listed in the MAY list of the object class) unless there is a check mark in the Mandatory column. Attributes that are marked Mandatory are those listed in the MUST list of the object class. The Naming column is used to mark the attribute(s) that name instances of this object. Attributes in the Naming column are those listed in the X-NDS_NAMING list of the object class.

The ASN1 ID text box at the bottom shows the OID of the object class.

On the right, there are two buttons. The Info button brings up a view of the currently selected attribute. The Add Attribute allows you to specify additional optional attributes.

Adding Schema Elements

If you'd like to add a new object class or attribute type, choose the Create button on the right of the Schema Manager dialog box. This will spawn a wizard that will step you through the process. The process is fairly painless, so we won't take the time here to cover each option the wizard presents you with. Just be aware that the terms used in this utility may not be the terms used in LDAP. Refer to the section titled "Differences between NDS LDAP and NDS NDAP Schema" if you have questions about the meaning of a term.

Deleting Schema Elements

Deleting schema elements is easy, provided you make sure they're not being used anywhere. If an object in the tree is currently using an object class, you cannot remove that object class from the schema. Likewise, if an attribute type is listed in an object class, you cannot remove that attribute type. If you try to delete a schema element that has a dependency, you'll receive an error message.

Before trying to remove an object class, it's a good idea to search the directory for any object using it. You could use the command line search utility to do this. Type `ldapsearch -h <server address> -b "" -s sub objectclass=<myObjectClass>`, replacing `<server address>` with the server's IP or DNS address and `<myObjectClass>` with the name of the object class you wish to delete. If any results are returned, you have to delete those entries before removing the object class from the schema.

Before deleting any attribute, remove it from any object class that is listing it in its set of `MUST` or `MAY` attributes. Discovering which object classes contain an attribute is a bit trickier; you must dump all the object classes into a file and then use the find feature of your editor to locate the attribute. You can get a list of the object classes by typing `ldapsearch -h <server address> -b "cn=schema" -s base objectclass=subschema objectclasses`, replacing `<server address>` with the server's IP or DNS address. Use whatever tools you have to search for the attribute type name.

Select the object class or attribute type you wish to delete and press the Delete button. Answer yes on the following dialog box to confirm the deletion before it is removed.

Mapping Novell LDAP to the Novell Schema

If, for whatever reason, you've created an object class or an attribute type with a name that is invalid for LDAP, you can use ConsoleOne to map an LDAP-friendly name to it. You can also map well-known LDAP attribute types and object classes to existing NDS schema elements. In some cases, this has already been done for you. Take for instance the most commonly used NDS object class—User. LDAP doesn't define a User object class. Instead, there is person, organizationalPerson, and iNetOrgPerson. NDS maps inetOrgPerson to User when it is installed.

The mappings are held in a couple of attributes in the LDAP Group object. Find the LDAP Group object in your tree, right-click it, and then choose Properties. There are two tabs at the top of this dialog box—Attribute Map and Class Map—which you can use to create or remove mappings.

Mapping Attribute Types

Select the Attribute Map tab to reveal the current attribute mapping table. It looks like Figure 7.5.

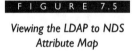

FIGURE 7.5

Viewing the LDAP to NDS Attribute Map

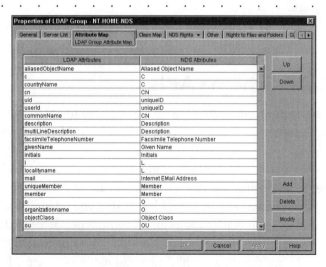

The Up and Down buttons in the upper right let you move a mapping in the table. This specifies which mapping is to be used when a many-to-one mapping exists. For instance, you can see two mappings for the NDS attribute C — one for c and one for countryName. When using search to read an object that has a C attribute, the attribute returned to the client will be c rather than countryName if countryName was not specifically requested in the attribute list. This is because c is higher in the list than countryName.

Press the Add button to produce the dialog box shown in Figure 7.6.

 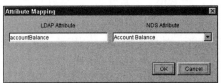

Adding an Attribute Mapping

FIGURE 7.6

Type the name of the LDAP attribute in the left edit field, then choose an NDS attribute from the list on the right. Press OK or Cancel to dismiss the dialog box. The modify button brings up a dialog box similar to the Add dialog box.

Mapping Object Classes

Mapping an object class works exactly like mapping an attribute type. Make sure the NDS object class or attribute exists before attempting to map it to an LDAP name.

LDAP Schema APIs

In this section, we cover the Java classes used to access and modify schema elements and show how to use those classes to build your own schema management tool.

As was mentioned earlier, the entire schema is actually held in one object in the directory. This being the case, you could use standard LDAP APIs to read and modify the schema. The only problem is that you'll have to write a fairly complex string parser if you want to turn an attribute type such as (2.5.6.2 NAME 'country' SUP top STRUCTURAL MUST c MAY (searchGuide $ description)) into a structured class that your application can easily deal with. Luckily, the Java SDK has already defined and implemented a complete set of schema-related classes that enable you to read all aspects of the schema without having to write a single parse routine. This point is illustrated by the example listings on the CD-ROM. There is approximately four times as much code for Listing 7.1 using the C libraries as there is using the Java libraries.

Overview of LDAP Schema APIs

There are four classes with which to read and modify the schema:

- The LDAPSchema class reads the schema object in the directory. This is done by calling its fetchSchema() method. Once you've fetched the schema, you can use this class to get the list of syntaxes or a specific syntax, get the list of attribute types or a single attribute, and so on. One problem with this approach is that if another process updates the schema, you'll have an outdated view of it. If you write applications that use this class, you should provide a way to refresh your application's local copy of the schema, in which case you'd call fetchSchema() again.

- The LDAPSchemaElement class is an abstract class that is subclassed by specific schema element classes such as LDAPAttributeSchema and LDAPObjectClassSchema. LDAPSchemaElement gives access to things that are common among schema elements, such as the OID, the name, and the description.

- The LDAPAttributeSchema methods give you access to a specific attribute type contained in an instance of the LDAPSchema class. With the LDAP-AttributeSchema class, you can get an attribute type's syntax, matching rules, upper and lower bounds, and so on. You can also use it to create or modify attribute types.

- The LDAPObjectClassSchema class enables you to read an object class' super classes, mandatory and optional attributes, and type. You also use it to create or modify object classes.

Fetching the Schema

As you read above, before you begin to read specific schema elements, you need to use the LDAPSchema class to fetch the entire schema from the directory. The following code snippet shows how to fetch the schema. It's from the DumpSchema example on the CD-ROM found in the Examples\Listings\Java\Chapter 7\ DumpSchema folder. There is a C version in the Examples\Listings\C\Chapter 7\DumpSchema folder:

```
LDAPConnection conn = new LDAPConnection();
LDAPSchema schema = new LDAPSchema();
LDAPArgs args = new LDAPArgs("DumpSchema");

try {
    args.populate(arguments);

    /* Connect to server */
    conn.connect(args.getHost(), args.getPort());

    if (args.getPassword() != null) {
        conn.bind(args.getDN(), args.getPassword());
    }

    /* Read the schema */
    schema.fetchSchema(conn);
```

That's pretty simple. Now the LDAPSchema object (schema) has been populated with the entire schema for the directory. In this case, the fetchSchema method queried the root DSE for its subschemaSubentry attribute, then it used that value to read the schema.

Alternately, you could call schema.fetchSchema(conn, o=administration). This form of the method takes a DN, which is queried for its subschemaSubentry attribute rather than the root DSE. This is useful when there are multiple schemas in effect for the directory tree. Most LDAP server implementations — including NDS — only use a single, global schema, so calling either version of the method will return the same results. To maintain your application for the long term, we recommend that you use this method when possible so that you're sure to get the correct schema for the directory entry you're concerned with.

Now that you've populated the LDAPSchema object with the entire schema, you can read specific elements.

Reading Schema Elements

Attribute types are represented by the LDAPAttributeSchema class. You can get an enumeration of LDAPAttributeSchema objects by calling the getAttributes method of the LDAPSchema object. If you're interested in reading a particular attribute type and you know its name, use the getAttribute method of the LDAPSchema class.

Once you have an LDAPAttributeSchema object, you can read its OID, description, syntax, and other fields. This code builds on the previous snippet by enumerating all the attributes in the schema and printing each one's name and syntax:

```
/* Get an enumeration of all attribute types */
Enumeration enum = schema.getAttributes();

System.out.println("Attribute Types:");

/* Read each attribute type */
while (enum.hasMoreElements()) {
    LDAPAttributeSchema attr =
                (LDAPAttributeSchema)enum.nextElement();
    System.out.println("\t" + attr.getName());
    System.out.println("\t\tSyntax: " +
                    attr.getSyntaxString());
}
```

The same kind of code can be used to print out fields of an object class. Instead of calling the getAttributes() method of LDAPSchema, call getObjectClasses(). This will result in an enumeration of LDAPObjectClassSchema objects.

You may notice that there are no accessory methods for the NDS-specific fields of the different schema elements. For example, there isn't an obvious way to get a list of all the naming attributes for an object class. The LDAPSchemaElement class has a catchall method called getQualifier that can be used to read implementation-specific fields of schema elements. This method returns the values for that field in an array of String objects. So, for instance, this code could be used with the code above to print out all the object classes along with their naming attributes:

```
/* Get an enumeration of all object classes */
enum = schema.getObjectClasses();

System.out.println("Object Classes:");

/* Read each object class */
while (enum.hasMoreElements()) {
    LDAPObjectClassSchema oc =
            (LDAPObjectClassSchema)enum.nextElement();

    /* Print the name */
    System.out.println("\t" + oc.getName());

    /* Get the list of naming attributes */
    String [] naming = oc.getQualifier("X-NDS_NAMING");

    if (naming != null) {
        System.out.println("\t\tNaming Attributes:");

        /* Print each naming attribute */
        for (int i = 0; i < naming.length; i++) {
            System.out.println("\t\t\t" + naming[i]);
        }
    }
}
```

Modifying the Schema

All modifications to the schema are done through three methods of the LDAPSchemaElement class: add, remove, and modify. The add and remove methods act on the implicit object. In other words, if the object elem represents a schema element, and you call elem.remove(conn), the schema element represented by elem will be deleted. The modify method also works on the implicit object, but takes another LDAPSchemaElement as a parameter. The element passed in the parameter list replaces the element represented by the implicit object. In other words, if elem represents a schema element, and you call elem.modify(conn, newElem), the schema element represented by elem is replaced by newElem.

NOTE

Under the covers, these schema modification methods are simply making modifications to the appropriate attribute values in the subschema subentry.

Adding and Deleting Schema Elements

To create a new attribute type or object class in the schema, you instantiate the proper schema element object and then call its add method. For example, to create a new attribute type, first create a new LDAPAttributeSchema object, supplying the fields you want, then call its add method. Here is some code that does just that. It assumes the object conn is an LDAPConnection object that is connected to the directory and bound as an identity, which has sufficient rights to update the schema.

```
LDAPAttributeSchema attr = new LDAPAttributeSchema(
    "MyNewAttribute",              /* Name */
    "1.2.3.4",                     /* OID */
    "This is my new attribute",    /* DESC */
    "1.3.6.1.4.1.1466.115.121.1.15",/* SYNTAX */
    FALSE,                         /* SINGLE_VALUE */
    null,                          /* SUP */
    null)                          /* alternate names */

/* add attribute to schema */
attr.add(conn);
```

Simple? Well, if you think that was easy, look at what you need to do to delete it.

```
attr.remove(conn);
```

When removing a schema element, the OID value is the only one that is looked at by the directory. All other values are ignored, so you can specify null (FALSE if it's a boolean type) if you like.

You may receive an error when deleting schema elements. See "Deleting Schema Elements" in the previous section for more information.

NOTE

Changing Schema Elements

Changing an existing schema element consists of reading the schema, getting the object you wish to change, creating a new object that represents the changed object, then applying the change. In this example, we want to add an additional optional attribute type to the Jedi object class. In this case, the new optional attribute type is called midoclorianCount. Notice that when we construct the new object class, we simply use the values from the existing one except in the case of the field that we want to modify (optional attributes).

LISTING 7.1

Code fragment from
ModifyJedi.java

```
LDAPConnection conn = new LDAPConnection();
LDAPSchema schema = new LDAPSchema();

try {
    /* Connect to server */
    conn.connect( "localhost", 389,
        "cn=admin,o=administration", "secret");

    /* Read the schema */
    schema.fetchSchema(conn);

    /* Get the Jedi object class */
    LDAPObjectClassSchema oc = schema.getObjectClass("jedi");

    /* Add the new optional attribute to the existing list */
```

```
Enumeration eOldMays = oc.getOptionalAttributes();
Vector vNewMays = new Vector();
while (eOldMays.hasMoreElements()) {
    vNewMays.addElement(eOldMays.nextElement());
}
vNewMays.addElement("midoclorianCount");
String [] newMays = new String [vNewMays.size()];
vNewMays.copyInto(newMays);

/* Create a new object class using the
 * new optional attribute list. Populate other
 * fields with old values
 */
Enumeration eOldMusts = oc.getRequiredAttributes();
Vector vNewMusts = new Vector();
while (eOldMusts.hasMoreElements()) {
    vNewMusts.addElement(eOldMusts.nextElement());
}
String [] newMusts = new String [vNewMusts.size()];
vNewMusts.copyInto(newMusts);
LDAPObjectClassSchema newOC = new LDAPObjectClassSchema (
    oc.getName(),
    oc.getOID(),
    oc.getSuperior(),
    oc.getDescription(),
    newMusts,
    newMays);

/* Ensure all other qualifiers are copied */
Enumeration qNames = oc.getQualifierNames();
while (qNames.hasMoreElements()) {
    String qName = (String)qNames.nextElement();
    newOC.setQualifier(qName, oc.getQualifier(qName));
}
```

Continued

LISTING 7.1

Code fragment from
ModifyJedi.java (continued)

```
/* Apply the modification to the directory */
oc.modify(conn, newOC);


} catch (LDAPException e) {
    System.out.println(e);
}
```

Mapping Novell LDAP to the Novell Schema

Now that you've seen how to read and update schema elements, you could write a replacement for the Schema Manager in ConsoleOne. One feature that you would be missing is the ability to map LDAP schema names to NDS schema elements. This is done by adding a schema element and specifying the NDS name in the X-NDS_NAME field. In this example, we map the LDAP attribute retinalScan to the NDS attribute Scan Of Retina.

LISTING 7.2

Code fragment from
NDSNameMap.java

```
/* Create an attribute type that represents
 * the NDS attribute called "Scan Of Retina"
 * (this assumes there is already an NDS
 * attribute called "Scan Of Retina")
 */
LDAPAttributeSchema at = new LDAPAttributeSchema(
    "retinalScan",                    /* LDAP name */
    "1.2.3.4",                        /* OID (ignored)*/
    "",                               /* DESC (leave blank) */
    "1.3.6.1.4.1.1466.115.121.1.40",/* SYNTAX (ignored, but
                                      *  must be valid) */
```

```
         false,                       /* SINGLE_VALUE */
         null,                        /* SUP (leave null) */
         null);                       /* aliases (leave null) */

/* Add the NDS name using the setQualifier method*/
at.setQualifier("X-NDS_NAME", new String[]{"Scan Of Retina"});

/* Add the attribute type */
at.add(conn);
```

You may also remove a name mapping by following the same example, but using the delete method instead of the add method.

A Schema Management Utility Example

Now that you've learned all about the LDAP schema, you should be able to write your own complete schema manager utility that talks LDAP, right? This utility should be able to replace the one in the ConsoleOne management utility and come with the benefit of not requiring a Novell NetWare client in order to operate.

We know what you're thinking; this book is a real page-turner! You just can't put it down and write a schema manager utility (tempting as that sounds)!

Well, okay. We got things started by including a schema browser utility on the CD-ROM. The source is in the \Examples\Applications\ Java\SchemaManager\SRC directory, and the finished classes are in the \Examples\Applications\ Java\ SchemaManager directory. You should be able to modify these classes to build a fully functional schema management utility.

The main class is called SchemaManager. To run it, type **java SchemaManager -h <server address> -D <admin DN> -w <admin password>**, replacing the appropriate command line arguments.

The utility uses the APIs discussed in this section to read and modify the schema.

Summary

If you made it this far, congratulate yourself. Getting a good understanding of the schema is one of the hardest tasks you'll likely undertake in LDAP. You now know what the schema is and which schema elements control what parts of the directory. Better still, you know how to read and manipulate the schema to your liking. This knowledge will be essential as you travel the road of creating directory-enabled applications.

CHAPTER 8

Partitions, Replicas, and Referrals

There are times when it is not convenient or possible to store all of the entries for a directory on a single physical server. For instance, most large companies have offices around the globe. When these companies deploy enterprise-wide directories, it is more convenient for users in Hong Kong to be able to access their regularly-used directory entries from a local server than to have to access them over a wide area network (WAN) link to the company's headquarters in Los Angeles. Similarly, the users in Los Angeles want their entries to be stored on a server in Los Angeles, not on a server in Hong Kong or New York. In other cases, the number of entries in a directory may exceed the capabilities of a single server, or the number of simultaneous users on the system may exceed its processing or storage capabilities. Even though NDS is a highly scalable directory service capable of running on very powerful hardware and storing many millions of entries on a single server, there are still practical limits that can be exceeded. In these situations, the directory tree is spread across multiple servers in a distributed fashion.

Most NDS deployments have several servers that collectively work together to form the DIT. The data is partitioned and replicated. Partitioning and replication provide a number of benefits: locality of reference for data, protection against catastrophic data loss, and high availability. There's a potential downside, though: The data your LDAP client wants may not be on the server to which it is connected. Worse still, the data may not be on any single server; entries may be spread across two or more servers. This chapter explains how distributed directories, particularly NDS, work and it demonstrates the LDAP features that allow your application to locate the data within the tree even when these conditions occur.

NDS Partitions and Replicas

NDS allows you to distribute directory data along two dimensions: partitions and replicas. When you deploy NDS, you can divide the directory tree into sets of entries. Each of these sets is called a *partition*. A partition can be stored on any server that is a member of the directory tree, and several partitions can be stored on a single server.

You can also create more than one copy of each partition. Each copy of a partition is called a *replica*.

Partitions

Partitions divide an NDS tree into logical pieces that can be individually managed. In its simplest form, a partition is composed of a container entry and all of its subordinate entries. When an NDS tree is first created, it has a single partition — the root partition, which includes all of the entries in the tree.

When a new partition is created, the structure of the entries in the tree remains constant, but the partition from which it is taken changes. All entries in the newly created partition are effectively removed from the original partition. Thus, in the general case, a partition is composed of a container entry and all of its subordinate entries down to the containers that serve as partition roots for subordinate partitions.

Imagine that you have a tree with the entries shown in Figure 8.1. Before any partition operations are performed, all of the entries are in a single partition called the [Root] partition.

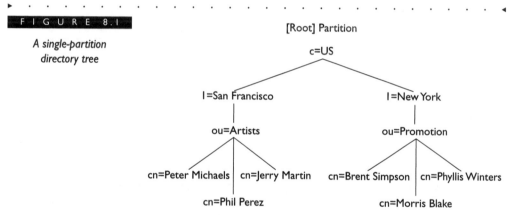

FIGURE 8.1

A single-partition directory tree

If you create a new partition at l=New York, the tree has two partitions, as shown in Figure 8.2. The [Root] partition still exists, but it contains fewer entries than before. Even so, the tree structure has not been affected; the entries in the tree are the same as before. The only change to the tree is the creation of the partition and the division of entries between the new subordinate (child) partition and the superior (parent) partition from which they were taken.

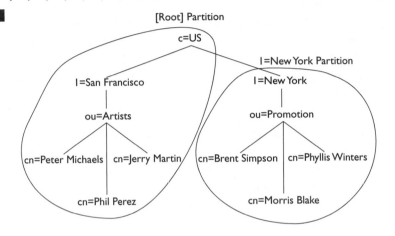

F I G U R E   8.2

A partition directory tree with two partitions

Replicas

Replicas are copies of partitions. While partitions allow you to divide the data stored in your directory into logical sets, replicas allow you to store multiple copies of partitions on various servers throughout your directory tree. Using replicas, you can store entries on servers that are close (from a network perspective) to the users who access them. This allows you to simultaneously provide the advantages of locality of reference for several geographically separated groups who might use the entries.

In general English usage, the term *replica* **refers to an exact reproduction of something. This usage implies that a replica of a thing cannot exist by itself; its existence depends on the existence of the original from which it was copied. While it is not completely proper English usage, it is more convenient for us to refer to any copy of a partition as a replica, even if it is the only copy of the partition.**

NOTE

Replicas have the added benefit of providing fault tolerance to your directory tree. If a server in your tree has a catastrophic failure, the directory entries stored on that server can be restored to the faulty server's replacement from other servers in the tree that have replicas of those entries. In the meantime, when you attempt to locate an entry that was stored on the faulty server, NDS can find another server containing a replica of the same partition in which the entry resides and give you the data from that server.

Replication

When a new replica of a partition is created, NDS sends all of the entries stored in the partition to the server where the new replica resides. When changes are made to an entry, NDS sends the information about these changes to every replica containing that entry. In this way, all replicas are kept up-to-date. The process of sending this entry information between replicas is referred to as *replication*.

Let's go back to the directory tree illustrated in Figure 8.2. Imagine that two servers, server A and server B, are in the tree and each holds a replica of the partition at l=New York,c=US. Your LDAP client binds to server A and adds a new entry, cn=Morris Blake, ou=promotion, l=NewYork,c=US. At the instant that the new entry has been added, the information in the two l=New York replicas is different. Server A has the new entry and server B does not. This condition does not last long, however, since the next time that replication occurs between server A and server B, the information about the new cn=Morris Blake entry is sent from server A to server B to keep them in sync. Figure 8.3 illustrates this process.

FIGURE 8.3

Replication in a directory tree

Step 1: cn=Morris Blake is added to Server A

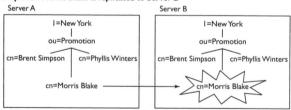

Step 2: cn=Morris Blake is replicated to Server B

Final state: cn=Morris Blake is both Server A and Server B

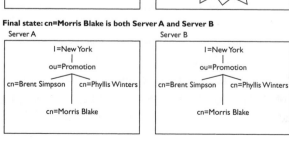

NDS Replica Types

There are four types of replica: master, read/write, read-only, and filtered. While read operations can be performed against any replica type, other operations can only be performed on certain replica types.

▶ **Master Replicas:** The first replica of any partition is the master replica. In addition to being readable and writeable, the master replica is the authoritative source of information regarding the replica. When you want to perform a partitioning operation (such as creating or deleting a partition), the master replica orchestrates the change so that it occurs properly on all machines containing replicas of the affected partition.

▶ **Read/Write Replicas:** In addition to the master replica, NDS allows other replicas to be read/write. This feature allows you to store writeable replicas of directory data wherever they are needed.

NOTE

One interesting side effect of having multiple writeable replicas of a partition is that it is possible to change an entry in a replica. Before the information regarding the change can be replicated to the other replicas, another change might be made to the same entry on another replica. NDS replication uses timestamps to resolve this potential conflict between changes and ensure that the last changes made are the ones left on all replicas in the tree.

▶ **Read-only Replicas:** As their name implies, update operations cannot be performed on read-only replicas. You can use read-only replicas to provide fast, local access to data that won't need to be updated frequently by the clients that access it from that location.

▶ **Filtered Replicas:** Filtered replicas are a new feature in NDS version 8.5 that provide a way to store a subset of a partition's entry information in a replica. Filtered replicas can be read/write or read-only. When you create a filtered replica, you can filter both the object classes of entries stored in the replica and the attribute types that are stored in each entry. These filters are independent of each other, so it's possible to get a subset of attributes for all entries, all attributes for a subset of entries, or a subset of both attributes and entries.

NOTE

Providing a local, read-only replica of a partition doesn't preclude clients from doing updates. It just means that updates have to be made on a writeable replica that is on a different server (possibly across a slower network connection) than the clients would normally use for reading the same entries. As we show later in this chapter, whenever **NDS** gets ready to perform an operation on an entry, it must first find a copy of the entry. When **NDS** is locating an entry for an update operation, it looks for a writeable copy of the entry so that the update will not fail due to the replica being read-only.

TIP

When you use a filtered replica to filter object classes or attribute types, or both, you can dramatically reduce the total size of the data that is stored on the filtered replica (compared to the total size of the unfiltered data). This makes filtered replicas an ideal tool for solving administrative needs, such as creating a single white pages directory server that holds a subset of the attributes of every **inetOrgPerson** (**NDS User**) entry in an entire tree.

Creating and Managing NDS Partitions and Replicas

You can create and manage partitions and replicas using Novell's ConsoleOne utility. By default, ConsoleOne starts in Console View mode. In order to manage partitions and replicas, you need to switch to the Partition and Replica View by clicking Partition and Replica View on the View menu.

TIP

When you're using ConsoleOne in the Console View mode, there may be **NDS** entries with names that are truncated. Although the control for doing so is invisible, you can expand the width of the display column by slowly moving your cursor to the right from the rightmost edge of the displayed names. When the cursor is over the invisible control, it changes to an arrow that points left and right. Click and hold the primary mouse button and drag the mouse to resize the column.

Figure 8.4 shows the ConsoleOne utility in Partition and Replica View mode.

FIGURE 8.4

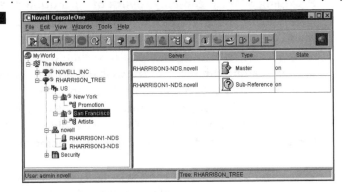

The ConsoleOne utility
in Partition and Replica
View mode

When you select a tree object on the left side of the console screen, the right side of the console screen displays a list of servers in the tree that hold a replica of the [Root] partition. When you select a server object on the left side of the console screen, you see a list of the replicas that it holds on the right side of the console screen.

NOTE

Partition and replica operations usually involve more than one server in the NDS tree. Because of this, these operations may take some time to complete. In cases where a server that is affected by a partition or replication operation is down or cannot be contacted for some other reason, the operation won't complete until contact can be established. To keep you from having to wait for partition and replica operations to complete, the ConsoleOne user interface allows you to close the dialog box it displays while they are in progress. If you decide to close the dialog box, NDS keeps track of the requested pending operation and completes it in the background.

Creating a Partition

To create a partition, you simply select the container that you want to be the root of the new partition; then click Edit, Create Partition. A Create Partition dialog box pops up, asking you to confirm the creation of the partition. After you confirm your intent by clicking OK, a Creating Partition dialog box appears until the operation is complete. If you choose not to wait for the operation to complete, simply click Close to dismiss the dialog box, and the partition creation operation completes in the background.

Merging a Partition into Its Parent

To merge a partition back into its parent partition, you select the entry that is the partition root; then click Edit, Merge Partition. A Merge Partition dialog box pops up asking you to confirm the merge operation. After you confirm your intent by clicking OK, a Merging Partition dialog box appears until the operation is complete. If you choose not to wait for the operation to complete, simply click Close to dismiss the dialog box, and the merge operation completes in the background.

Adding a Replica to a Server

To add a replica of a partition to a server, select the entry that is the partition root on the left side of the console screen, and then click Edit, Add Replica. An Add Replica dialog box pops up. You need to use the browser button to the right of the Server field to select the server where you want the replica to reside and select a radio button to specify the replica type. After you confirm your intent by clicking OK, the operation takes place in the background.

Removing a Replica from a Server

To remove a replica of a partition from a server, you must select the entry that is the partition root on the left side of the console screen. At this point, the replicas of that partition are listed on the right side of the console screen. Select the replica you want to delete; then click on Edit, Delete Replica. After you confirm your intent by clicking OK, the operation takes place in the background.

When the delete replica operation begins, the state of the replica is displayed as *dying*. When the operation is complete, the deleted replica shows as a subordinate reference. (You will have to click View, Refresh for the display to change correctly, because ConsoleOne doesn't poll NDS to get state transitions.) We discuss subordinate references in detail in just a moment.

TIP

Note that every partition must have a master replica, therefore a replica cannot be removed if it is the master for a partition. If you want to remove the master replica of a partition, first change one of the other replicas of the partition to be the master (see the next section). If there are no other replicas of the partition, you must first create another replica and make it the master replica, or you must merge the replica back into its parent.

Changing the Replica Type

To change a replica's type, for instance, from read/write to read-only, select the replica on the right hand side of the ConsoleOne screen and then click Edit, Change Replica Type. On the Change Replica Type dialog box, pick the new type for the replica and then click OK.

Replica Types and Filtered Replicas

If you choose a filtered replica type, you need to define the filter you want to be used on the Change Replica Type dialog box by clicking Create/Edit Filter. This is also how you modify an existing filter for a filtered replica type.

Name Resolution and Knowledge References

We're going to shift gears a bit here. Now that we have shown you how entries can be partitioned and replicated among various servers participating in a single directory tree, we're going to explain how NDS finds a specific entry. As we've shown in previous chapters that cover LDAP operations, almost every LDAP operation takes a DN identifying a target entry as a parameter. The first step in performing each of these operations is to find a copy of the target entry somewhere in the tree. This process is known as *name resolution*. Once a copy of the target entry has been found, the operation can be performed on the entry.

Partition Boundaries

In order to be able to find any entry on any server in the tree, NDS has to keep track of which entries are stored in each of the partitions in the tree. This book-keeping is simplified because the entries in a partition are all subordinate to the partition's root-most entry. This entry is called the *partition root*, and it is the upper boundary of a partition. The lower boundary of a partition is marked by the partition roots of subordinate partitions (if the partition has subordinate partitions) and leaf entries in the tree. By simply keeping track of the root entries for every partition in the tree, NDS can determine the partition that an entry lies within.

Subordinate References and NDS Replica Rings

In addition to knowing the boundaries for each partition, NDS must also keep track of the servers on which each of a partition's replicas are stored and the replica type of each replica. This information allows NDS to locate every copy of every entry in the tree and acts as the glue that combines the entries on multiple servers into a single directory tree.

Here's how it works: By definition, every replica of a partition has a copy of the partition root. In addition to these copies of the partition root, every server maintains a special copy of the partition roots for all partitions immediately subordinate to the replicas that it stores. These special copies of the partition root are called *subordinate references*. Figure 8.5 shows that server B has two subordinate references: one for the l=San Francisco partition and another for the l=New York partition. In NDS, each partition root has an attribute that lists the addresses of all of the servers where it is stored, including the servers that have just a subordinate reference to the replica root. This information is called a *replica ring*.

NDS External References

Whenever an NDS server references an entry that is not stored locally, a special pseudo-entry is created as a placeholder for that entry. These pseudo-entries are called *external references*, and they do not contain any attributes for the entry except for the entry's object class and name. External references are not accessible by clients; they are used by NDS for its own bookkeeping. For the purposes of our discussion in this chapter, you should be aware that one reason external references are created on a server is because placeholders are needed for entries between the tree root and the root of any replicas contained on the server. If the server contains a replica of the [Root] partition, then no external references are needed for this purpose, although it's very likely that external references will still be created on the server for other reasons that are beyond the scope of this discussion. For instance, servers A and C in Figure 8.5 would have an external reference for the entry c=US to act as a placeholder above l=SanFrancisco and l=New York, which are the partition roots on servers A and C respectively. No external reference for c=US would be stored on server B because it actually contains the c=US entry.

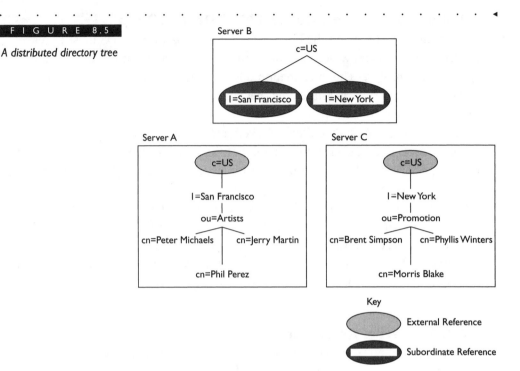

FIGURE 8.5

A distributed directory tree

Resolving a Name

To help you see how the process of name resolution works, suppose that you bind to NDS server B in Figure 8.5 and request an LDAP modify operation on the entry cn=Phyllis Winters,ou=Promotion,l=New York,c=US. The first step that NDS takes is locating a copy of the entry. To resolve the name, NDS works its way from the root of the tree down to the entry it is looking for. In this case, NDS finds the c=US entry locally, then it finds a subordinate reference for the l=New York,c=US entry. It now knows that the entry cn=Phyllis Winters,ou=Promotion,l=New York,c=US must be in the l=New York,c=US partition or one of its subordinates. The replica ring on the l=NewYork,c=US contains the addresses of both server B (because it has a subordinate reference for l=New York,c=US) and server C (because it has a replica of the l=New York,c=US partition). When server C is contacted to resolve the name cn=Phyllis Winters,ou=Promotion,l=New York,c=US, NDS once again works its way down from the root of the tree, finding first the external reference to c=US, and then the entry for l=New York, ou=Promotion, and finally the entry, cn=Phyllis Winters. Once the cn=Phyllis Winters entry is located, the LDAP operation can proceed.

There are times when name resolution requires contacting several servers to locate an entry. Suppose that you bind to server A in Figure 8.5 and request the same modify operation for the entry cn= Phyllis Winters,ou=Promotion,l=New York,c=US.

NDS works its way down from the root of the tree and finds an external reference to c=US. It then hits a dead end because no information for l=New York is contained on server A. NDS checks the replica ring on the partition root for the root-most replica on server A, which, in this case, is l=San Francisco. This replica ring contains the addresses of both server A (because it has a replica of the l=San Francisco,c=US partition) and server B (because it has a subordinate reference for l=San Francisco,c=US). The fact that server B has a subordinate reference to l=San Francisco means that server B has a replica of the partition immediately superior to l=San Francisco. When server B is contacted to resolve the name cn= Phyllis Winters,ou=Promotion,l=New York,c=US, the process shown in the previous example is repeated. In short, NDS finds the subordinate reference to l=New York on server B that points to server C, where the object is finally located and the operation can proceed.

· ◀

Name Resolution Models

In the two name resolution examples we just presented, we glossed over some important details involved in the name resolution process with a bit of hand waving, although it might have been subtle enough that you didn't notice it. In each of those examples we used language such as, "When server A is contacted to resolve the name . . . . " Now that we've pointed it out, you might be wondering *who* contacts server A to resolve the name. The answer to that question is the key differentiator between the two basic name resolution models — chaining and referrals — that we present in this section. One of these models is server-centric and the other is client-centric. Each has relative merits and shortcomings.

Chaining

Chaining is essentially a server-based name resolution protocol. In the *chaining* model of name resolution, an LDAP client issues a request to an LDAP server. The LDAP server attempts to find the target entry locally. If the entry cannot be found, the LDAP server uses the knowledge references it has stored to contact another LDAP server that knows more about the DN than it does. The second server may not have the entry and may give information for yet another server. This process continues until the first server finally contacts a server that holds a replica of the entry.

NOTE Early versions of Novell's LDAP implementation that supported a choice of name resolution options used the term *traversal* instead of *chaining* in the LDAP administration snap-ins to ConsoleOne and NWAdmin. The current implementation now uses the term chaining in both the server implementation and administration tools, and in this book we use the term chaining exclusively.

Once an entry is located in the chaining model, NDS handles all the details of completing the operation. Even if the target entry is on a remote server, NDS hides this fact from the client. In this situation, the server to which the client is connected locates the remote server containing the target entry, and then authenticates to the remote server using the same identity with which the LDAP client is bound. That done, it acts as proxy for the client and requests the remote server to complete the operation and then reports the result of the operation to the client just as if the entry had been stored locally.

Let's put this idea of chaining in everyday terms. Imagine that you've long had a lawyer for your small business. Your lawyer is very capable of handling routine day-to-day legal contracts and related issues for your business. One day you realize that your small business has grown substantially and you need to do some estate planning to ensure that all your hard work won't be lost to a whim of fate. Your lawyer's a good one, but unbeknownst to you, he's not a specialist in estate planning. He's also a little proud, and when you ask him to help you do your estate planning, he doesn't want to admit that it's out of his range of expertise. He tells you he'll draw up some papers and get back to you. Then as soon as you leave his office, he calls another lawyer from his firm and asks for the name of a lawyer specializing in estate planning. The second lawyer suggests that he call a third lawyer at a firm across town who specializes in estate planning. The first lawyer contacts the third lawyer and contracts with her to do all of the work to set up your estate plan. Once the papers are drawn up, your lawyer calls you back and gives you a fantastic estate plan, conveniently forgetting to mention the help he received from his other two associates. You now have an estate plan, and you're none the wiser; as far as you can tell, you have the smartest lawyer on the planet, and he has a satisfied client. By *chaining* his expertise with that of other lawyers he knows, your lawyer has nicely satisfied your legal needs.

Chaining between directory servers works in much the same way. Suppose that you establish an LDAP connection to server A (see Figure 8.5) and search for the entry cn= Phyllis Winters,ou=Promoters,l=New York,c=US. Server A knows it doesn't contain cn=Phyllis Winters, but it knows that another server above it might have knowledge of this entry. It contacts server B, who determines that server C might have the entry. Server B tells server A to contact server C. Once server A asks server C for the entry, server C returns the entry's data to server A, who passes it back to your LDAP application. As far as your LDAP application can tell, the entry existed on server A, because server A gave you the entry you asked for. What you don't see is the fancy footwork going on behind the scenes, but you don't care because you have the entry you asked for.

Advantages of Chaining

The biggest advantage of chaining is that it hides all name resolution details from the client. The client simply connects to a server, binds, and performs an operation.

While chaining, the server automatically takes care of reauthentication. This is a problem that is sometimes tricky to solve at the client because you don't want to the store passwords needed for authentication any longer than necessary, but you don't really want to prompt the user for a password at each referral.

Functionally, the LDAP client cannot tell whether the target entry is on the server to which it is connected or to another server in the tree, because the server to which it is connected acts as a proxy for the client, if needed. Chaining literally gives your LDAP clients one-stop shopping for all of their directory access needs.

Chaining is also useful in deploying LDAP in existing NDS installations, especially those with NDS versions that don't include LDAP services, because it works seamlessly even when some servers in the NDS tree don't support LDAP services. We talk about this in more detail later in this chapter.

Disadvantages of Chaining

Ironically, the biggest advantage of chaining is also its biggest disadvantage. The fact that chaining leaves the server in charge of what is happening while it is acting as proxy for the client can lead to problems. If chaining requires establishing connections with several different servers before the target entry is located or if any of these connections are across slow WAN links, the client can be left without feedback of any kind for an extended period of time. If the operation happens to be a search operation that returns many entries and those entries have to be sent across a WAN link, the operation can be very time consuming. This can cause timeLimitExceeded errors to occur for LDAP operation requests that are slow in completing..

Another case where chaining can be a disadvantage is when several servers are equally capable of progressing the operation. In this case, the server acting as a proxy for the LDAP client must make a decision about which server to contact next. There is no way for it to know of any preference the LDAP client might have, so it must make the decision on its own. When NDS encounters this situation, it attempts to sort the list of servers by the cost associated with contacting them. For load-balancing purposes, it then randomly chooses among the servers with the lowest cost. This means that two requests to operate on the same entry might actually be processed on different NDS servers. This is usually not a problem, but it does move the LDAP client a small step farther from being in control of what's going on.

Referrals

To leave the client in charge of its fate, a client-centric form of name resolution called *referrals* was designed. In the referral model of name resolution, an LDAP client issues a request to an LDAP server. The server attempts to find the target entry of the operation locally. If it cannot, it uses the knowledge references it has to generate a referral to another server that knows more about the entry and returns the referral information to the LDAP client. The LDAP client then establishes a connection to the server specified in the referral and retries the operation. If the second LDAP server has the target entry of the operation, it performs the operation; otherwise, it also sends a referral back to the client. This continues until the client contacts a server that has the entry and can perform the desired operation, or until an LDAP server returns an error indicating that the entry doesn't exist.

Let's go back to the lawyer analogy we used to explain chaining. Your small business is growing and you recognize the need to do some estate planning to protect your assets. You approach your lawyer for help in this regard. He knows that this is outside of his specialty, so rather than hide his lack of expertise from you, he sends you to a colleague in his firm whom he thinks knows more about estate planning. You contact the second lawyer and make an appointment to meet together, but during your initial consultation, the second lawyer also realizes that your needs are beyond his experience and ability. The second lawyer refers you to a dynamite estate-planning lawyer at a firm across town. You meet with the third lawyer and explain what you need. She draws up the required papers and delivers them directly to you when she has completed them. You have the legal advice you need (in fact, it's the same advice you got via chaining), but you had to do some extra work on your own to contact the right people.

Imagine that the servers in the scenario of Figure 8.5 were configured to return referrals instead of chaining. You establish an LDAP connection to server A and search for the entry cn= Phyllis Winters,ou=Promoters,l=New York,c=US. Server A knows it doesn't contain cn=Phyllis Winters, but it knows that another server above it might have knowledge of the entry you are searching for. It sends you a referral to server B. You would then establish a connection to server B and repeat the search request for cn= Phyllis Winters,ou=Promoters,l=New York,c=US. Server B knows server C might have the entry, and sends you a referral to server C. Finally, you establish a connection to server C and repeat the search request for cn= Phyllis Winters,ou=Promoters,l=New York,c=US. Since server C actually has the entry, it returns the entry's data to your LDAP application. At each step along the way, your LDAP application has complete control over whether it continues completing the search operation it began. At any time, if it decides to abandon the effort to search for cn= Phyllis Winters,ou=Promoters,l=New York,c=US, it can simply decide not to follow a referral.

Advantages of Referrals

In the referral model, the client is completely in control. At every stage of the name resolution process, the client knows exactly what is going on, and this enables it to make better decisions or provide feedback to the user if desired. If the client is given a referral for a server that it doesn't wish to contact, it can simply not contact that server or it can prompt a user before following the referral.

Referrals often use network resources more efficiently than chaining. When a server chains on behalf of a client, the results of the operation pass back through the server on their way to the client. If the requested operation were a search with lots of entries, this data would be transmitted across the network twice: once between the server actually holding the data and the server doing the chaining, and then again from the server doing the chaining to the client. If the client used referrals instead of chaining, it would get the results of the operation directly from the second server, and the data would only have to be transferred once.

When a server receives a request to perform an operation on an entry that is not stored locally, it may know of several other servers that are equally capable of progressing the operation. In this case, the referral returned to the client contains information for each of these other servers. To continue the operation, the client must contact one of the servers from this list. In the referrals model, the client can be smart about which server it picks from the list, or it can ask for user feedback about which server to pick from the list. Referrals leave the client in control of its behavior.

Another advantage of using referrals is that once you know where an entry is stored, you can go directly back to the server that has it. In the chaining model, this information is hidden, so you can't use it, although the first server may have access to it and be able to use it to increase its efficiency on your behalf. In our legal example, this would be like needing some more estate planning advice after getting the initial papers from the lawyer. In the chaining case, you'd contact the first lawyer since you presumed he had done the work, and he would contact the third lawyer either directly or indirectly via the second lawyer, depending on how forgetful he is. Either way, though, your request would have to pass through the first lawyer, who's acting as an intermediary. In the referral case, you'd know that you got your original advice from the third lawyer, and you could contact her directly for additional help without your first lawyer's help or knowledge.

Disadvantages of Referrals

In spite of their undisputed usefulness, referrals do have some disadvantages. First, putting the client in control means that the client has to be smart. It needs to recognize referrals in the first place and then it has to know how to follow them. Because of the way the LDAP protocol is structured, there's no operation specifically for name resolution, although a base-level search can be used to approximate it in some cases. When LDAP clients receive a referral, they generally establish a connection to the referral and then bind and reissue the operation request. If the operation request fails because the desired entry is not stored locally, the work to complete the bind was essentially wasted because it wasn't needed. The way to work around this is for the client to do an anonymous base-level search for the target entry of the operation before binding, but this adds additional complexity to the client's job. There are times when this approach will fail if the anonymous user doesn't have browse rights to the target.

In fact, even connection establishment to follow referrals can introduce additional overhead to the chaining model. Because NDS treats name resolution as a public operation without access control restrictions, NDS avoids establishing connections by reusing any established connection between two servers while it is doing name resolution. Only when NDS has located the server that actually contains the target entry does it create a connection to that server specifically for the LDAP client and authenticate that connection with the client's identity.

Another potential disadvantage of referrals is that LDAP referrals were not made an official part of the protocol until LDAPv3. LDAPv2 clients don't recognize referrals, or they use an obsolete, non-standard method for recognizing referrals. Depending on how much control you have over the clients used in your environment, you may find this to be a problem in deploying referrals.

The decision about when to use chaining and when to use referrals is probably one of the most complex administrative decisions you'll have to make when deploying the Novell LDAP service. We provide additional guidance later in this chapter to help you make this decision.

As a client developer, you'll want to make sure that your application is enabled for referrals in order to give administrators the freedom to choose whichever method works best for their needs.

TIP

LDAP Referrals

Referrals didn't become an official part of LDAP until the v3 specification. This occurred, in part, because early LDAP server implementations were actually gateways to X.500 directory services. With the LDAP gateway acting as a single point of interaction with an entire X.500 tree, there was no need for referrals. As vendors began implementing and deploying native LDAP protocol servers, the need for a mechanism to glue more than one server onto a tree arose. With no standard protocol element defined for the purpose, a common workaround used by v2 servers was to send a special error result and put the referral information into the errorMessage section of the response. The usefulness of the feature led to it being formally provided for in LDAPv3. This section explains the protocol-layer support for LDAPv3 referrals. It also briefly describes the most common v2 implementation of LDAP referrals.

LDAPv3 Referral Response

Most LDAP operations have a target entry specified by a DN parameter in the operation request. When the target entry for an LDAP operation isn't stored on the LDAP server receiving the operation request, one of the following three things happens:

▶ First, the LDAP server may be able to authoritatively determine that the target entry doesn't exist at all. In this case, the LDAP server returns a result code of noSuchObject, which is defined to have a decimal value of 32.

▶ Second, if the LDAP server is capable of chaining, it may choose to chain on behalf of the requesting client in order to complete the operation. In this case, the operation is completed and the result of the operation is returned to the client as if the LDAP server had stored the target entry locally.

▶ Finally, if the LDAP server is capable of referring, it may choose to return a referral result to the client indicating that the client should contact a different server and ask it to perform the requested operation.

Every LDAP operation that returns a response to the client can return a referral result. These operations are

▶ Bind

▶ Search

- ▶ Modify

- ▶ Add

- ▶ Delete

- ▶ ModifyDN

- ▶ Compare

- ▶ Extended

LDAPv3 Protocol Definition of Referrals

The response for every LDAP operation includes an element named LDAP-Result, which contains the fields needed to support referral responses. Listing 8.1 is an abbreviated listing of the ASN.1 definition of LDAPResult.

LISTING 8.1

```
1     LDAPResult ::= SEQUENCE {
2         resultCode        ENUMERATED {
3             success                         (0),
4             operationsError                 (1),
5             protocolError                   (2),
6             timeLimitExceeded               (3),
7             sizeLimitExceeded               (4),
8             compareFalse                    (5),
9             compareTrue                     (6),
10            authMethodNotSupported          (7),
11            strongAuthRequired              (8),
12                -- 9 reserved -
13            referral                        (10),  -- new
14            adminLimitExceeded              (11),  -- new
15            unavailableCriticalExtension    (12),  -- new
16            confidentialityRequired         (13),  -- new
```

Continued

(Continued)

```
17              saslBindInProgress           (14),  -- new
18
19                      ...
20
21              entryAlreadyExists           (68),
22              objectClassModsProhibited    (69),
23                   -- 70 reserved for CLDAP -
24              affectsMultipleDSAs          (71),  -- new
25                   -- 72-79 unused -
26              other                        (80) },
27                   -- 81-90 reserved for APIs -
28       matchedDN       LDAPDN,
29       errorMessage    LDAPString,
30       referral        [3] Referral OPTIONAL }
31
32   Referral ::= SEQUENCE OF LDAPURL
33
34   LDAPURL ::= LDAPString -- limited to characters
35                           -- permitted in UR
```

The first element of LDAPResult defined on line 2 is a resultCode. When the server performs an operation, it sets the resultCode to a value indicating the success or failure of the operation. Lines 3 to 26 contain an abbreviated listing of the ASN.1 definition of the possible result codes. The last element of LDAPResult, defined on line 30, is an optional referral. When a server wants to return a referral result rather than perform an operation, it sets the resultCode for the operation for referral (defined on line 13) to have a decimal value of 10, and puts the referral information into the referral element.

Up to this point in our discussion of referrals, all of our examples have shown referrals with a single server, but it's possible that several servers could contain copies of the target entry. For example, in the case of NDS, you can have a replica of a partition on every server in the directory tree. To support this general case, the referral element of LDAPResult on line 30 is defined to be a Referral (notice the difference in capitalization). On line 32, Referral is defined to be a sequence, or list of LDAPURLs. The definition is completed on line 34, where an LDAPURL is defined as a string that is formatted in such a way as to be a valid LDAP URL as defined in RFC 2255.

X-REF

If you're not already familiar with the syntax and semantics of LDAP URLs, you might want to read the "LDAP URLs" section in Chapter 5.

Referrals in LDAPv2

Although referrals were not officially defined as part of LDAPv2, you should be aware that a nonstandard but commonly-used protocol extension was made to LDAPv2 to support referrals. This extension used the errorMessage field of the version 2 LDAPResult, similar to the version 3 errorMessage field defined on line 29 of Listing 8.1, to pass the referral information between the LDAP server and client. This extension worked because LDAPv2 clients that supported this extension knew to look for the referral information in the errorMessage field, and LDAPv2 clients that did not support the extension simply treated the URLs in the errorMessage field as an error message string. Two LDAPv2 implementations that support this extension are the Netscape and University of Michigan implementations. Other LDAP server and client implementations based on the University of Michigan source code are also likely to support this LDAPv2 extension.

Continuation References

The search operation is unique in that it does not send its result as a single response. Rather, it sends zero or more intermediate responses, one for each entry, followed by a search result indicating the success or failure of the search operation. The intermediate responses for each entry are called *search entries*.

X-REF

For more information on this topic, see the "LDAP Operations" section of Chapter 1 and the "Handling Search Results" section of Chapter 5.

In the previous section of this chapter, we discussed how referrals are generated when the target entry of an operation is not stored on the server that receives an operation request for that entry. This mechanism works perfectly for operations that involve only a single entry. The search operation, however, can have a scope that includes more than a single entry. It's possible that the scope of a one-level or subtree search includes entries on more than one server. When this situation occurs, a special sort of referral is generated to tell the client how to find the entries that are within the scope of the search but that are not on the local machine. This special referral is called a *continuation reference*.

How It Works

As with other LDAP operations, when an LDAP server receives a search request, it locates the target entry for the search. If the target entry is not stored locally, the LDAP server simply sends a search result with a result code of referral and a list of referral URLs back to the requesting client.

If the target entry is stored locally, the LDAP server starts the search operation. For each entry that falls within the search scope, matches the search filter, and is stored locally, the LDAP server sends a search entry response containing the requested entry information for the entry to the client. If the LDAP server determines that there is an entry that is within the search scope that is not stored locally, it sends a continuation reference response to the client. When the LDAP server has responded with search entries or continuation references for all of the entries (of which it has knowledge) that lie within the search scope, it signals that it has completed processing the search operation by sending a search result response. At any time after it receives a continuation reference, the client can contact a server listed in the continuation reference to get the requested entries that the original LDAP server could not supply. Depending on the scope of the search and the way that data is divided among servers, the client may have to recursively repeat the process of following continuation references to get all of the desired entries.

An Example

Suppose you work for the Acme corporation and deployed a directory tree with two partitions as shown in Figure 8.6.

► **Referral Result:** If you bind to server1.acme.com and send a search request with a base DN of c=us, you get back a referral result with a referral of ldap://server2.acme.com because the base DN is not on the local server.

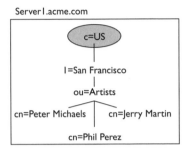

FIGURE 8.6

The Acme Corporation Directory Tree

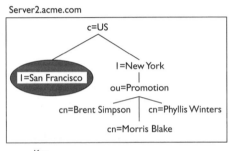

▶ **Continuation References:** If you bind to server 2.acme.com and send a search request with a baseDN of c=us and a search scope of subtree, you get back the following:

```
SearchResultEntry
    for c=US


SearchResultEntry
    for l=New York,c=US


SearchResultReference {
    ldap://server1.acme.com/l=San Francisco,c=US
}
```

```
SearchResultEntry
    for ou=Promotion,l=New York,c=US

SearchResultEntry
    for cn=Brent Simpson,ou=Promotion,l=New York,c=US

SearchResultEntry
    for cn=Phyllis Winters,ou=Promotion,l=New York,c=US

SearchResultEntry
    for cn=Morris Blake,ou=Promotion,l=New York,c=US

SearchResultDone
    with a resultCode value of success
```

Special URL Formatting Rules for One-Level Search

When an LDAP server sends a continuation reference for a one-level search, the LDAP URLs contained within the continuation reference have a slightly different form than the LDAP URLs contained within continuation references returned for a subtree search. In this case, a scope of base must be appended to the LDAP URLs to indicate that when the client follows the continuation reference it should perform a base search for the entry listed in the URL.

If you bind to server 2.acme.com and send a search request with a base DN of c=us and a search scope of one-level, you get back the following:

```
SearchResultEntry
    for c=US

SearchResultEntry
    for l=New York,c=US

SearchResultReference {
  ldap://server1.acme.com/l=San Francisco,c=US??base
  }
```

Notice the ??base appended to the URL in the SearchResultReference, which tells the client that when it resumes the search on server1.acme.com that it should do a base search to complete the search operation. In this case, a base search for l=San Francisco,c=US is precisely what is needed to complete the one-level search begun at c=US.

LDAP Name Resolution Options in NDS

Several options are available to control the name resolution process for LDAP search operations in NDS. While doing name resolution for search operations, you can choose to always chain, always refer, or use a hybrid of chaining and referrals. We explain how each of these options work, and give you pointers on when you'll want to use each of them. The specifics of how to configure these options on the LDAP Group object are discussed in Chapter 10.

IMPORTANT

The name resolution options discussed in this section apply only to LDAP search operations. All other operations in Novell's LDAP implementation currently use chaining as the only available name resolution method.

Background

To understand and compare each of the name resolution options provided by Novell's LDAP implementation, you should have a basic understanding of the knowledge reference mechanism used within NDS because LDAP referrals for NDS are based on this mechanism.

NDS Knowledge References

NDS has always been a distributed, partitioned, and replicated directory service. To do name resolution, NDS has always maintained knowledge references in the replica rings of each partition root and the subordinate references to partition roots. These knowledge references are essentially a list of network addresses that can be used to contact each server that holds a copy of the partition root or a subordinate reference to it. Each of these network addresses has an associated network transport type, such as IP or IPX, so that the server knows which network protocol to use when contacting a server associated with one of these addresses.

Using NDS Knowledge References to Chain

When Novell's LDAP server is configured to chain and it resolves the name of an entry that is stored locally, NDS automatically establishes a connection to one of the network addresses that it thinks contains the entry or has additional information about its location. If the entry is not found on the second server, the first server reads the knowledge references on the second server and uses them to contact another server that it thinks contains the entry or has additional information about its location. This continues until the first server establishes a connection with a server that actually holds a replica of the entry, or until the first server authoritatively determines that the entry does not exist in the tree. Once the entry is found, the first server asks the server storing the entry to perform the requested LDAP operation on the entry.

Using NDS Knowledge References to Generate LDAP Referrals

Novell's LDAP server leverages the fact that the NDS servers in the tree already know how to find any entry in the tree regardless of the server on which it resides. When the LDAP service starts running, it registers a network address with NDS in the form of an LDAP URL that informs NDS that entries on the server can be accessed via LDAP. This is much like adding a new network card to the server and informing NDS of the network address of the card. Registering this URL adds a new address of type URL to the list of addresses that already exist in the replica ring of each replica on the server. Like other attribute values, this new URL address is replicated throughout the tree so that it can be used during name resolution.

When the LDAP server is configured to return referrals and it resolves the name of an entry, LDAP asks NDS to give it URL transport addresses of the servers where the entry can be found. If the entry is on the local server, the LDAP server performs the requested LDAP operation on the entry. If the entry is not on the local server, the LDAP server uses the LDAP URLs returned from the resolve name operation to generate a referral list that it sends back to the client. If it wants to do so, the client then connects to one of the servers in the referral list and repeats the LDAP operation request.

NOTE

When the LDAP service shuts down, it also deregisters the LDAP URL addresses that it registered on startup so that NDS knows that it can no longer contact the server via the LDAP URL transport. This implies that when NDS performs a name resolution operation for an entry contained on a server that is not running the LDAP service, no referral can or will be generated for that server because NDS doesn't have the information needed to generate the referral.

The Always Chain Option

The Always Chain option works precisely as its name implies. When a search operation is received, the LDAP server automatically chains whenever it needs to locate an entry in the tree that is not stored locally. When the entry has been located, the LDAP server acts as a proxy for the LDAP client. It authenticates to the remote server using the same identity with which the LDAP client is bound, and then continues the search operation on the remote server. All search entries and the search result are sent back to the LDAP client via its connection to the LDAP server that received the original search request. At the risk of restating the obvious, referrals and continuation references cannot and will not be returned when the Always Chain option is selected.

The Always Chain option is a good choice in the following situations:

▶ You never want referrals to be sent to LDAP clients.

▶ You can't or don't want to run the LDAP service on some NDS servers in your tree.

▶ You want to imitate the name resolution behavior of older implementations of Novell's LDAP service that did not support referrals.

▶ You are experiencing problems that may be related to referral generation or referral processing.

TIP

If you have a problem that you suspect is related to referral generation or referral processing, you can use the Always Chain option to stop referral generation. If the problem disappears, this confirms that the issue is related to referrals. The Always Chain option can also be used as a temporary workaround while you resolve the referrals issue.

> At least one replica of every partition in your NDS tree is on a server on the same local area network (LAN).

> You want to ensure maximal backward compatibility with older versions of NLDAP and NDS that are running in the same tree.

> LDAP clients that cannot follow referrals are binding as version 3. Technically, this is improper behavior, but it can happen.

Except for cases where you know you want referral support to deal with issues such as allowing the LDAP client to give feedback as it traverses a slow WAN link, the Always Chain option is a no-hassle choice. It takes care of virtually every administrative, interoperability, and backward compatibility issue related to name resolution in a single step. For this reason, Always Chain is the default option selected when Novell's LDAP server is initially installed.

TIP

Novell's implementations of LDAP previous to NDS 8 (NLDAP versions less than 3.10) did not support referrals and chained exclusively. The chaining behavior in these older versions of NLDAP is identical to the chaining behavior selected by this option in newer versions of NLDAP. Search is also the only operation for which you can configure name resolution in Novell's current LDAP implementation. All other operations use the same chaining behavior we just described.

The Always Refer Option

As its name implies, the Always Refer option causes the LDAP server to send referrals whenever it needs to locate an entry that is not stored locally during a search operation. If the entry is the base object of the search, a referral result is returned. If the entry is subordinate to the base object of the search, a continuation reference is returned. The Always Refer option prevents chaining from occurring during the processing of LDAP search operations. To complete the search operation, the LDAP client has to follow each referral received from the LDAP server.

When you select the Always Refer option, you can also specify a default referral whose value is stored in the LDAP Group Object. When an entry is not on the local server and NDS cannot locate a referral to a server that contains the entry for which it is resolving a name, it sends the URL in the default referral field as a last resort. If nothing is specified in the default referral field, then an error of noSuchObject is sent.

The Always Refer option is a good choice when you always want to get referrals for non-local entries. This implies that you never want or need chaining to occur.

TIP

For the Always Refer option to work properly, the following conditions must be met:

▶ At least one replica of every partition in the tree is contained on an NDS server that's running a version of the Novell LDAP service that supports referrals.

You should be aware that for NDS 8.5, the versioning scheme for NLDAP has changed to bring the versions of all NDS components into alignment. With the NDS 8.5 release, the version number for NLDAP will jump from 3.x to 85.x. Also, the lowest version of NLDAP that supports referrals is 3.10. Due to bug fixes made since that release, we recommend using versions of NLDAP 3.16 or higher when a referrals support option (either Always Refer or Refer When Possible) is configured.

IMPORTANT

▶ All LDAPv3 clients being used are capable of handling referrals. Generally, a client that binds as v3 should be capable of handling referrals since it is technically improper for a v3 client to not support referrals.

Novell's LDAP server does not support the non-standard **LDAPv2** referral behavior implemented by some other vendors. When an **LDAP** client binds with a version of 2, chaining is used exclusively for that client, and referrals are never sent to it.

TIP

The Refer When Possible Option

In the LDAP Group properties page in ConsoleOne, this option is labeled, "Refer to NDS LDAP servers that support referrals, and chain to NDS servers that don't." The Refer When Possible option attempts to send referrals to the client instead of chaining whenever it is possible to do so. If NDS cannot find an LDAP server with a registered URL containing the remote entry, the LDAP server chains to complete the operation. In a sense, this option uses chaining as a fail-over mechanism for referrals.

This option is a good choice when you want to support referrals as much as possible but you also want to ensure seamless backward compatibility with older versions of NDS and LDAP.

TIP

The Refer When Possible option should be used in the following situations:

▸ You want referral support, and some partitions do not have a replica on NDS servers running versions of LDAP that support referrals.

▸ You have an NDS tree that has some servers that aren't running versions of LDAP that support referrals, and you want a "configure once and forget about it" option that supports referrals.

Strictly speaking, if you ensure that at least one replica of every partition is on an NDS server running a version of LDAP that supports referrals, the Refer When Possible is functionally equivalent to the Always Refer option, but choosing the Refer When Possible option is a good defensive measure when your NDS tree includes one or more NDS servers that are not running Novell's LDAP service. The Refer When Possible option enables chaining to automatically take care of a situation where a partition operation inadvertently creates a situation where a partition no longer has a replica on an NDS server that supports LDAP referrals.

TIP

Work In Progress

Although referrals were important enough to be included as standard protocol elements in LDAPv3, work is continuing in this area to fully define the way this information is stored in LDAP servers and the semantics associated with the information. The LDAP protocol in RFC 2251, along with the definition of the LDAP URL in RFC 2255, define the way that referrals are sent to clients. One piece missing from this specification is the way that referral information is stored and managed inside the LDAP server. One of the objectives of the LDAP Extensions Working Group of the IETF is to define the way that referral information is to be stored within LDAP servers, along with methods that LDAP clients can use to read and write this information when the need arises.

As of this writing, two Internet-Drafts offering similar approaches for referral storage and access are under consideration. These drafts are "Named Referrals in LDAP Directories" and "Referrals and Knowledge References in LDAP Directories."

You can find "Named Referrals in LDAP Directories" at http://www.
ietf.org/internet-drafts/draft-ietf-ldapext-namedref-00.txt **and**
"Referrals and Knowledge References in LDAP Directories" at
http://www.ietf.org/internet-drafts/draft-ietf-ldapext-
knowledge-00.txt.

The proposed storage mechanism that seems likely to be adopted at this time is based on the use of a special attribute named ref which can be placed on an entry. When the LDAP server is performing name resolution in preparation to fulfill an LDAP operation request, and the target entry contains the ref attribute, the LDAP server uses the URL values stored in the attribute to generate a referral to the client. Similarly, during a one-level or subtree search, any entries within the scope of the search that contain the ref attribute cause a continuation reference to be sent to the client. Along with the ref attribute, a new control, manageDSAIT, is defined. The manageDSAIT control can be placed on normal LDAP operations such as add, delete, modify, and search, to allow LDAP clients with the proper authority to read and write the actual URL values inside of ref attributes. Without this control, there would be no way to manage the referral information stored in the tree because a referral would be generated whenever you tried to perform an operation on the entry.

Some LDAP servers are already using a referral storage model similar to the ones defined in these two drafts. In the absence of a clear standard in this area, Novell has chosen to leverage the referral storage mechanisms that it already has in place to support the referral responses defined in RFC 2251. For search requests, this implementation is fully compatible with RFC 2251 and is compatible with providing a referral storage and access mechanism that is standards-based as these Internet-Drafts progress along the IETF standards track.

LDAP SDK Referral Support

The LDAP SDK provides you with several options for handling referrals received by your LDAP application. When your application receives a referral you can choose to handle it in one of the following ways:

▶ Automatically follow the referral using the anonymous identity.

▶ Automatically follow the referral after authenticating to the LDAP server you are referred to by using an application-provided method.

▶ Manually handle the referral by catching the LDAPReferralException generated when a referral is received and automatic referral handling is disabled.

Enabling and Disabling Automatic Referral Handling

Referral handling policy can be set as a constraint on a single operation or it can be set as an option for all operations on an LDAP connection.

NOTE

Although the LDAP SDK documentation says that automatic referral handling is the default, we recommend that you explicitly set the referral handling policy you want your application to use in order to ensure that you get the behavior you desire.

Constraint-based Referral Handling

You can use the LDAPConstraints object to change the referral behavior of a single operation. The setReferrals method of the LDAPConstraints object allows you to set the referral handling mode. Pass a value of false to disable automatic referral handling, and pass a value of true to enable automatic referral handling. Listing 8.2 is an example that enables referrals using a constraint:

LISTING 8.2

```
try {
   LDAPSearchConstraints constraint =
        new LDAPSearchConstraints();

   /* Connect and bind to the ldap server. */
   conn.connect(ldapVersion, host, port, loginDN,
        password);

   /* Enable automatic referral following. */
   constraint.setReferrals(true);

   /* Perform the search. */
   LDAPSearchResults searchResults =
   conn.search(searchBase, searchScope,
        searchFilter, attributeList,
        attributesOnly, constraint);

   /*
    * Get each of the entries matching the search
    * criteria and print its DN.
    */
   while (searchResults.hasMoreElements() == true) {

      /* Process each search entry... */

   }
} catch (LDAPException e) {
```

Continued

LISTING 8.2

(continued)

```
    System.out.println("Error: " + e.toString());
}
```

Alternatively, several of the LDAPConstraint and LDAPSearchConstraint constructors allow you to specify a doReferrals value during object instantiation.

Connection-based Referral Handling

To change the referral behavior for all operations on a connection, use the setOption method of the LDAPConnection object to set the LDAPv2.REFERRALS option on the connection. Just as with constraints, a value of true allows the client to automatically follow referrals, and a value of false prevents the client from automatically following referrals. Listing 8-3 is an example.

LISTING 8.3

```
try {
    /*
     * Automatically follow referrals for all
     * operations performed on this connection.
     */
    conn.setOption(LDAPv3.REFERRALS, new Boolean(true));

    /* Connect and bind to the ldap server. */
    conn.connect(ldapVersion, host, port, loginDN,
            password);

    /* Perform the search. */
    LDAPSearchResults searchResults =
    conn.search(searchBase, searchScope,
            searchFilter, attributeList,
            attributesOnly);

    /*
     * Get each of the entries matching the search
```

```
    * criteria and print its DN.
    */
    while (searchResults.hasMoreElements() == true) {
       /* Process each search entry... */
    }
} catch (LDAPException e) {
    System.out.println("Error: " + e.toString());
}
```

Automatically Following Referrals as Anonymous

By default, when the LDAP SDK automatically follows referrals, it does so using the anonymous identity. In this mode, whenever a referral is received by the LDAP client, the SDK binds anonymously (no username or password are specified) to the next server and then continues the operation. This approach works well in cases where the anonymous identity has sufficient rights to do everything your application needs it to do, such as reading publicly accessible data for a white pages application. But there are times when access controls prevent the anonymous identity from doing the desired work. In these cases, you need to authenticate as you follow referrals.

Automatically Following Referrals with Authentication

To simplify the work required to follow referrals with authentication, the LDAP SDK defines an interface called LDAPRebind that can be used to provide authentication information (name and password) to the client when it is following referrals. All you have to do is define a class that implements the LDAPRebind interface and then specify an object of this class to be used when the client needs to bind to a server to which it has been referred. In the following discussion, we refer to this object as the *rebind object*.

TIP

NDS uses the IP address to specify the host in referral URLs, for example, ldap://137.65.180.203:389/ **rather than** ldap://server1. acme.com:389. **This means that when you're comparing host names from NDS LDAP referrals, you need to either compare to the IP address or convert the IP address to a DNS name before doing the comparison.**

Listing 8.4 is an example implementation of a simple class that implements LDAPRebind.

LISTING 8.4

```java
import netscape.ldap.*;

public class SampleLDAPRebind implements LDAPRebind {
    private String dn;
    private String password;
    private LDAPRebindAuth sampleRebindInfo;

    public SampleLDAPRebind() {
        dn = "cn=admin,c=us";
        password = "password";
    }

    public LDAPRebindAuth
        getRebindAuthentication(String host, int port) {

    if (  host.equalsIgnoreCase("137.65.188.203")
        && (port == 389) ) {
        /*
        * Return rebind credentials based on a matched
        * host name.
        */
        sampleRebindInfo = new LDAPRebindAuth(dn, password);
    } else {

        /*
        * Return default rebind credentials of anonymous.
        */
        sampleRebindInfo =
            new LDAPRebindAuth( "", "" );
    }
```

```
        return sampleRebindInfo;
    }
}
```

The key to the LDAPRebind interface is the getRebindAuthentication method. When the client receives a referral, the SDK passes the host and port information from the referral to the getRebindAuthentication method in your rebind object. Your implementation of getRebindAuthentication is responsible for returning an LDAPRebindAuth object that contains valid credentials for the host and port.

We discuss how the SDK uses LDAPRebind and LDAPRebindAuth at greater length in a moment, but first we need to show you how to use a rebind object. Just like with other referral processing options, you can specify a rebind object as one of the constraints on an operation or as a connection option that applies to all operations that use the connection.

Constraint-based Rebinding

The setRebindProc method of the LDAPConstraints object allows you to specify the object of a class implementing LDAPRebind that should be used to rebind.

The example in Listing 8.5 enables referrals using a constraint. Note that our rebind object uses the sampleLDAPRebind class we defined in the last code example.

LISTING 8.5

```
SampleLDAPRebind rebind = new SampleLDAPRebind();
LDAPSearchConstraints constraints =
        new LDAPSearchConstraints();

/* Connect and bind to the ldap server. */
conn.connect(ldapVersion, host, port, loginDN,
        password);

/*
 * Enable automatic referral following using
 * the rebind object to get the DN and credentials
 * used when a referral is received whenever these
 * constraints are applied to an operation.
```

Continued

LISTING 8.5

(continued)

```
 */
constraints.setReferrals(true);
constraints.setRebindProc(rebind);

/* Perform the search. */
LDAPSearchResults searchResults =
      conn.search(searchBase, searchScope,
              searchFilter, attributeList,
              attributesOnly, constraints);
```

Connection-based Rebinding

You can use the setOption method of the LDAPConnection object to set the LDAPv2.REFERRALS_REBIND_PROC option on the connection. Just as with constraints, you pass an object of a class implementing LDAPRebind. Listing 8.6 is an example:

LISTING 8.6

```
SampleLDAPRebind rebind = new SampleLDAPRebind();
LDAPSearchConstraints constraints =
      new LDAPSearchConstraints();

/*
 * Enable automatic referral following using
 * the rebind object to get the DN and credentials
 * used when a referral is received for all operations
 * on this connection.
 */
conn.setOption(LDAPv3.REFERRALS, new Boolean(true));
conn.setOption(LDAPv3.REFERRALS_REBIND_PROC, rebind);

/* Connect and bind to the ldap server. */
conn.connect(ldapVersion, host, port, loginDN,
      password);
```

```
/* Perform the search. */
LDAPSearchResults searchResults =
        conn.search(searchBase, searchScope,
          searchFilter, attributeList,
          attributesOnly, constraints);
```

The SDK Rebind Algorithm

Once you've specified a rebind object to be used, here's what happens during an LDAP operation that generates a referral from a server:

1. The client receives a referral from an LDAP server. The referral is in the form of an LDAP URL that contains a host name and port information.

2. The client creates a new LDAPConnection object.

3. The client finds your rebind object by calling the getRebindProc method.

4. The client invokes the getRebindAuthentication method of the rebind object and passes in the host and port from the referral.

5. Your getRebindAuthentication method obtains the appropriate DN and password by some means, such as user intervention, lookup, and so on, and puts the information into an LDAPRebindAuth object and returns the LDAPRebindAuth object.

6. The client retrieves the DN and password from the LDAPRebindAuth object using the getDN and getPassword methods.

7. The client connects to the host and port specified in the referral URL.

8. The client passes the DN and password to the authenticate method of the LDAPConnection object in order to authenticate itself to the server.

Manually Handling Referrals

There may be times when you don't want referrals to be handled automatically by the SDK, even with the assistance of the LDAPRebind interface. In these cases, simply disable automatic referral handling (see the previous "Enabling and Disabling

Automatic Referral Handling" section). Once you do this, an LDAPReferralException is thrown whenever a referral is received. You can then process the referrals in your exception handler.

Listing 8.7 demonstrates how you set up your code to manually handle referrals as part of an LDAPReferralException.

LISTING 8.7

```
try {
    LDAPSearchConstraints constraints =
        new LDAPSearchConstraints();

    /* Connect and bind to the ldap server. */
    conn.connect(ldapVersion, host, port, loginDN,
        password);

    /* Disable automatic referral following. */
    constraints.setReferrals(false);

    /* Perform the search. */
    LDAPSearchResults searchResults =
        conn.search(searchBase, searchScope,
            searchFilter, attributeList,
            attributesOnly, constraints);

    /*
     * Get each of the entries matching the search
     * criteria and print its DN.
     */
    while (searchResults.hasMoreElements() == true) {
        LDAPEntry entry = null;
        try {
            entry = searchResults.next();
        } catch(LDAPException e) {
            System.out.println("Error: " + e.toString());
```

```
        /*
         * Go to the next entry after handling exception.
         */
        continue;
      }

      System.out.println("Entry: " + entry.getDN());
    }
  } catch(LDAPReferralException e) {
    /* Handle search references. */
    LDAPUrl urls[] = e.getURLs();

    for (int i = 0; i < urls.length; i++) {
      System.out.println(
            "received referral: " + urls[i]);

      /*
       * handle URL manually here
       */
    }
  } catch (LDAPException e) {
    System.out.println("Error: " + e.toString());
  }
```

Limiting Referral Hops

Another aspect of referral processing that you can control is the number of referral hops that can be taken before a name is resolved. *Referral hops* are the number of referrals received in resolving a single name. For instance, if you request an LDAP operation from LDAP server X and it refers you to LDAP server Y, it counts as one hop. If server Y in turn refers you on to LDAP server Z, this counts as two hops, and so on.

Constraint-based Hop Limits

To limit the number of allowed referral hops on a single operation, use the setHopLimit method of the LDAPConstraints object like this:

```
LDAPSearchConstraints
constraints = new LDAPConstraints();

constraints.setHopLimit(3);
constraints.setReferrals(true);

/* Perform the search. */
LDAPSearchResults searchResults = conn.search(searchBase,
        searchScope, searchFilter, attributeList,
        attributesOnly, constraints);
```

If you prefer, you can pass a hop limit into several of the constructors for LDAPConstraints and LDAPSearchConstraints objects.

Connection-based Hop Limits

To change the referral hop limit for all operations on a connection, use the setOption method of the LDAPConnection object to set the LDAPv2.REFERRALS_ HOP_LIMIT option on the connection like this:

```
Boolean useReferrals = new Boolean(true);
Integer hopLimit = new Integer(3);

conn.setOption(LDAPv2.REFERRALS_HOP_LIMIT, hopLimit);
conn.setOption(LDAPv2.REFERRALS, useReferrals);

/* Connect and bind to the ldap server. */
conn.connect(ldapVersion, host, port, loginDN, password);

/* Perform the search. */
LDAPSearchResults searchResults = conn.search(searchBase,
        searchScope, searchFilter, attributeList,
        attributesOnly);
```

When the Hop Limit Is Exceeded

If the number of allowed hops is exceeded, an LDAPReferralException is thrown.

Summary

Directory administrators are able to spread data across many servers for performance and fault tolerance by using distributed and replicated directories. Name resolution is the key to a distributed directory implementation because it enables your application to find any directory entry regardless of its physical location. In this chapter we presented two name resolution methods: chaining and referrals. We explained the relative merits and disadvantages of each of these name resolution methods and explained how Novell's LDAP server implements both of these name resolution models. We explained the three configuration options you have for name resolution in Novell's LDAP server: exclusive chaining, exclusive referrals, or a hybrid model. Finally, we showed you how you can process referrals in your application when it's running in an environment where LDAP referrals are generated.

In the next chapter, we cover another advanced topic: LDAP controls and extensions.

CHAPTER 9

Controls and Extensions

One of the weaknesses of LDAPv2 was its inability to be extended by adding new operations or by modifying the behavior of existing operations in a standard way. The only standard way to extend LDAPv2 was to create a new version of the protocol. As we showed in Chapter 8, when LDAPv2 implementers needed to provide protocol support for referrals, they had to overload the error message field of LDAP response in a non-standard way to shoehorn the feature into the protocol.

To overcome these problems and provide a path for future expansion of the protocol, LDAPv3 was designed to be extensible. To accomplish this, the architects of LDAPv3 provided two separate mechanisms for extending LDAP in two different ways:

- Controls can be used to modify the behavior of an LDAP operation.

- Extended operations can be used to define new LDAP operations. This chapter explains LDAPv3 support for controls and extended operations. We discuss the controls supported by Novell's LDAP implementation and how you can use them in your LDAP-enabled applications. We conclude with some forward-looking information to help you write your own server-side extensions for future NDS releases.

Controls

Controls are simply additional pieces of information that can be sent with an LDAP message. The information in a control tells the LDAP server to modify the default behavior of the operation contained in the message in some way.

A Fable

Once upon a time, the fast-food industry created the Fast-Food Protocol (FFP) to expedite the placing and filling of orders at fast-food restaurants everywhere. Among the operations defined in FFP was the "OrderHamburger" operation. If someone wanted a hamburger, he could go into any FFP-compliant restaurant, walk up to the counter, and issue the OrderHamburger operation request. In response, a standard hamburger was then quickly made and served. FFP was fantastic; everyone loved the ease with which they could get their fast food.

Being anxious to keep up with every innovation in his industry, the owner of a certain fast-food restaurant adopted FFP in his restaurant. One day, this restaurant owner realized that he would be able to sell a lot more hamburgers if his patrons could customize their hamburgers instead of having to order a standard hamburger with a fixed set of condiments. Unfortunately, this culinary innovation was not anticipated when FFP was originally designed; FFP would have to be extended somehow to handle this new need.

One way to add this feature to the protocol would be to revise the protocol and redefine the OrderHamburger operation to include additional parameters that would allow the requester to specify the desired condiments. The restaurateur realized that this might create some backward compatibility problems, however, because some restaurants might not adopt the new version of FFP for a while. Fast-food customers would then have to know how to speak the old and new versions of FFP to buy hamburgers at any FFP-compliant restaurant. It was even possible that some FFP restaurants wouldn't see a need to offer anything other than a standard hamburger and would never update their systems to the new version of the protocol. Customers who only knew the new version of the protocol would not be able to order food from these restaurants.

Fortunately, the designers of FFP had known that they wouldn't be able to anticipate every new idea in the fast-food industry, so they had made FFP extensible. One of the extensibility features of FFP was the ability to add information to any existing operation in a standard way, via an operation control. Ordering a customized hamburger was still essentially ordering a hamburger, so it made sense to simply add control information to the protocol request that specified the customizations that should be made to a standard hamburger.

The innovative restaurateur decided to use the FFP control feature to extend the existing OrderHamburger operation by defining the CondimentControl, which contained a list of condiments that should be added to the standard hamburger and a list of condiments that should be left off of the standard hamburger. The original OrderHamburger request hadn't changed at all, but its meaning could now be modified by making an OrderHamburger request and including a CondimentControl in that request. Customers were happy because they could get what they wanted on their burgers, and the restaurateur was happy because he'd found a way to add value to his business without having to violate the rules of the FFP standard.

Features of Controls

While the fable is a bit fanciful, it illustrates how LDAP controls work. Any LDAP operation — including extended operations — can be modified by a control. Here are the basic features of controls:

▶ **Controls allow you to extend or modify the behavior of existing operations:** In the fable, the CondimentControl added new functionality to the OrderHambuger operation. In real life, controls are defined to do things like request that the results of a search operation be sorted by the server, or modify a delete operation to delete an entire subtree.

▶ **Controls maintain backward compatibility:** In the fable, modifying the OrderHamburger operation directly by adding condiment fields to it would have changed the OrderHamburger operation so that existing FFP servers wouldn't understand it.

NOTE   Because the information for a control is appended to an operation in a standard way, LDAP servers know to look for control information. Even if an LDAP server doesn't recognize a control sent with an operation, it can still understand the original operation and make some decisions accordingly. (In the next section we show you the details of how control information is appended to LDAP operations.)

▶ **Controls can be reused:** In the fable, the CondimentControl was used to modify the OrderHamburger request, but once it was defined, the restaurant owner probably would have realized that it could also be used to modify other FFP requests, such as the OrderChickenFilletSandwich operation and the OrderSubSandwich operation.

NOTE   The same thing is true of LDAP controls. The behavior of a control can be defined to modify a single operation or it can be defined to modify many operations. In fact, you can even define how one or more existing controls will modify a new extended operation at the time you define it.

▸ **Control information can be included in LDAP responses as well as LDAP requests:** In the fable, when a customer included the Condiment Control as part of an OrderHamburger operation request, the operation response (the actual hamburger) was also modified to include new response information in the form of condiments that were added or removed from the standard hamburger.

NOTE

This capability is also available in LDAP controls. Some LDAP controls only include information in the operation request. Other LDAP controls include information in both the operation request and response. It's even legal to define a control that would only include information in an LDAP response. For instance, one (non-NDS) LDAP server implementation adds a control to the bind response when a password is about to expire in order to inform the client of the need to pick a new password.

▸ **The controls supported by an LDAP server are advertised in its root DSE:** In the context of our fable, this would be analogous to having restaurants that supported the CondimentControl post signs near their entrance advertising that they supported. This would let people know that they could use the CondimentControl when ordering.

NOTE

Every control supported by an LDAP server is listed in its root DSE. Your LDAP application can query the root DSE to determine which controls are available for your use.

▸ **Controls can be critical or non-critical:** In the context of our fable, it's possible that someone would go to a restaurant that didn't support the CondimentControl and make an OrderHamburger request with a CondimentControl. If the person didn't require that the CondimentControl be recognized, he'd just get an ordinary standard hamburger. If the person did require the CondimentControl be recognized, the restaurant staff would politely inform him that they didn't support the CondimentControl. If the person really wanted a hamburger "his way" he'd have go to another restaurant, one that supported the CondimentControl.

The same sort of thing is possible with LDAP controls. You can choose to specify that a control is critical to your request. If you specify that the control is not critical and the LDAP server cannot support the control, the LDAP server simply ignores the control and completes the LDAP request as though it had no control. If you do specify that the control is critical and the LDAP server cannot support the control for some reason, the server returns an unavailableCriticalExtension result code that causes the LDAPConnection object to throw an LDAPException.UNAVAILABLE_ CRITICAL_EXTENSION, and you'll have to take an alternative action.

Sometimes, even though a server supports a control, it may not be able to support the control in the way you request. For instance, the Server Side Sorting control, which we discuss later in this chapter, can only be used with a search operation. If you try to include a Server Side Sorting control on any other operation and you specify that the control is critical, the server won't process your request. As another example, the Server Side Sorting control also generally requires that the server have a sorted index for the attribute you request the LDAP server to sort on. Even though the server supports the Server Side Sorting control, you might ask it to sort entries using an attribute that isn't indexed. In this case, the server can't give you sorted results. If you said the control was critical, the server will refuse to perform your search request and will send an unavailableCriticalExtension result code back to your program. On the other hand, if you said the control was not critical, the server would still perform the search request but ignore the Server Side Sorting control and send back unsorted search results.

▶ **Controls can be "stacked":** In our fable, imagine that an OrderComboMeal operation was defined in FFP. This operation request would allow you to specify your choice of sandwich and drink and the response would be the sandwich, the drink, and an order of fries. Certainly, before long, someone would define the BigSize control for the OrderComboMeal operation to make the size of the drink and fries bigger. The CondimentControl would still be useful in this scenario because it would allow the requester to specify condiments on whatever sandwich was ordered for the combo meal. You could then send both a BigSize control and a CondimentControl with the OrderComboMeal operation request when you want both customizations at once.

When you specify multiple controls in a single operation, we say that the controls are *stacked*. In some cases, the proper behavior of a certain set of stacked controls is obvious or intuitive. In other cases the proper behavior may need to be defined. A server might support two controls independently but not support them when they're stacked together. It's also possible for one control to depend on being stacked with another control to work properly. Later in this chapter, we discuss the Virtual List View (VLV) control, which depends on being stacked with the Server Side Sort (SSS) control.

▶ **Controls can be standard or proprietary:** The restaurateur of our fable might choose to keep the condiment control proprietary to give his restaurant a competitive advantage. However, in the interests of furthering the Fast-Food Protocol and ensuring the widespread adoption of the control, it's likely that he would contribute the design of his condiment control to the FFP community. If the idea of a CondimentControl really caught on, it's likely that every fast-food restaurant would want to implement support for the control. A standard way of adding condiments would serve the interests of the FFP community far better than several proprietary controls that all did the same basic thing.

There are times when it may be appropriate to make a control proprietary. For instance, if a control defines specialized functionality that only certain LDAP clients should understand, you may not want to publish the details of your control. In other cases where you have a proprietary control, it is a useful courtesy to publish an informational Internet-Draft to the LDAP community to publicly document how it works. When you design a new control with general applicability to the LDAP community, you should document it in an Internet-Draft and submit it to the IETF, where it can eventually become a standard based on the IETF community's input.

The End of the Story

It wouldn't be fair to make you read so much about our fabled restaurateur without telling you the end of his story, so here it is. In almost no time, the CondimentControl made our hero's restaurant the most successful one in town.

While all of the other restaurants were busily adopting his CondimentControl as an industry standard, he franchised his restaurant, using the Fast-Food Protocol as one of the key elements of standardization for the restaurant chain.

The restaurant owner presides over an empire of FFP-compliant fast-food restaurants, but he saw that the custom fast-food market was being saturated by all of the competition moving into the market space he had defined. He sold his restaurant chain for millions at the peak of the excitement and became a semi-retired venture capitalist specializing in financing fast-food startups and consulting on deployments of the Fast-Food Protocol.

The LDAPv3 Control Syntax

Even though we've already explained the features of LDAPv3 controls, we feel it's important for you to understand the formal way that LDAPv3 controls are defined so that you can visualize what's happening when you use controls. The following LDAPMessage is essentially a wrapper for every LDAP operation request and response. One or more controls can be added to the end of any LDAP message as shown in line 24:

```
1 LDAPMessage ::= SEQUENCE {
2 messageID        MessageID,
3 protocolOp       CHOICE {
4       bindRequest      BindRequest,
5       bindResponse     BindResponse,
6       unbindRequest    UnbindRequest,
7       searchRequest    SearchRequest,
8       searchResEntry   SearchResultEntry,
9       searchResDone    SearchResultDone,
10      searchResRef     SearchResultReference,
11      modifyRequest    ModifyRequest,
12      modifyResponse   ModifyResponse,
13      addRequest       AddRequest,
14      addResponse      AddResponse,
15      delRequest       DelRequest,
16      delResponse      DelResponse,
```

```
17        modDNRequest      ModifyDNRequest,
18        modDNResponse     ModifyDNResponse,
19        compareRequest    CompareRequest,
20        compareResponse   CompareResponse,
21        abandonRequest    AbandonRequest,
22        extendedReq       ExtendedRequest,
23        extendedResp      ExtendedResponse },
24 controls        [0] Controls OPTIONAL }
25
26 Controls ::= SEQUENCE OF Control
27
28 Control ::= SEQUENCE {
29        controlType       LDAPOID,
30        criticality       BOOLEAN DEFAULT FALSE,
31        controlValue      OCTET STRING OPTIONAL  }
```

Controls are an optional element of LDAPMessage (note the use of the OPTIONAL keyword on line 24). The ASN.1 syntax definition on lines 26–31 shows that the controls element of LDAPMessage is a sequence of Control elements. Control is further defined to have three elements: controlType, criticality, and controlValue.

▸ **controlType.** This is an ASN.1 OID that uniquely identifies the control.

▸ **criticality.** This is a flag that tells whether the control is a critical part of the request or if it can be ignored by a server that doesn't support the control.

▸ **controlValue.** This is an optional element that contains additional data for the control when it is present.

The designer of the control defines the data values allowed in the controlType and controlValue fields. The application generating an LDAP message that includes the control supplies the value of the criticality field.

Detecting Supported Controls

Before you use a control, you should check to see if the server supports it. You do this by reading the `supportedControl` attribute of the root DSE for the server to see if it contains the OID value for the control you want to use. Here's an example of how you could do this on an LDAPConnection object that has been instantiated, connected, and bound to an LDAP server:

```
try {
    String searchBase = "";
    int searchScope = LDAPv3.SCOPE_BASE;
    String searchFilter = "objectclass=*";

    /* Get just the list of supported controls. */
    String attributeList[] = {"supportedControl"};

    /* return attributes and values */
    boolean attributesOnly = false;
    boolean found = false;

    /* request OID for the Server Side Sorting control */
    String controlOID = "1.2.840.113556.1.4.473";

    /* Perform the search */
    LDAPSearchResults searchResults =
            conn.search(searchBase, searchScope,
                searchFilter, attributeList,
                attributesOnly);

    /*
     * Since we're searching the root DSE,
     * there will be only one entry.
     */
    LDAPEntry entry = searchResults.next();
```

```
LDAPAttributeSet
        attributeSet = entry.getAttributeSet();
Enumeration attributes = attributeSet.getAttributes();

/*
 * Since we specified a single attribute in our
 * attribute list, there will be only one attribute.
 */
LDAPAttribute attribute =
        (LDAPAttribute) attributes.nextElement();
String attributeName = attribute.getName();

Enumeration values = attribute.getStringValues();

if (values != null) {
    while (values.hasMoreElements() == true) {
        String value = (String) values.nextElement();
        if (value.compareTo(controlOID) == 0) {
            System.out.println("Control " + controlOID +
                    " is supported.");
            found = true;
            break;
        }
    }
}
if (found == false) {
    System.out.println("Control " + controlOID +
                " isn't supported.");
}
} catch (LDAPException e) {
    System.out.println("Error: " + e.toString());
}
```

TIP

This code example could be simplified a great deal if you could simply use the LDAP compare operation to check for the `supportedControl` **attribute value you are looking for. Unfortunately NDS currently doesn't allow you to compare against values in the root DSE. You may also encounter this problem with other server implementations, so it's good defensive programming to use a search request to read the** `supportedControl` **attribute and then compare the** `supportedControl` **attribute values against the OID you're looking for as we've just shown.**

Including Controls in an LDAP Request

In the Java LDAP SDK, you can specify a control as a constraint to an operation or as an option on the connection object. When you use a constraint to specify a control, it only applies to the operations that also include the constraint. When you use a connection option to specify a control, the control is subsequently added to every operation on that connection.

IMPORTANT

The netscape.ldap package that you've imported when using standard LDAP operations provides only general support for controls via the LDAPControl class. To have access to classes that are implemented for specific LDAPv3 controls, such as the Server Side Sorting and Virtual List View controls, you need to import the netscape.ldap.controls package in addition to the netscape.ldap package.

The next few examples use the Server Side Sorting and Virtual List View controls to demonstrate some general points about using controls. We discuss both of these controls in detail later in this chapter, so don't get bogged down in the details of each specific control. Instead, we'd like you to focus on the main point of each example.

Specifying a Control Using Constraints

To specify a control using constraints, you need to create a control object and a constraint object. You then use the setServerControls() method of the constraint object to add the control to the constraint. Here's how you would specify the Server Side Sorting control using a constraint.

```
String attrname = "cn";

/* Create a sort key to specify the sort order. */
LDAPSortKey sortOrder = new LDAPSortKey(attrname);


/*
 * Create a server sorting control using that sort key,
 * and specify that it is critical.
 */
LDAPControl sortControl =
    new LDAPSortControl(sortOrder, true);

/* Create search constraints to use the control. */
LDAPSearchConstraints constraints =
    new LDAPSearchConstraints();

/* And add the control to the constraints. */
constraints.setServerControls(sortControl);

/* Perform the search. */
LDAPSearchResults searchResults = conn.search(searchBase,
    searchScope, searchFilter, attributeList,
    attributesOnly, constraints);
```

Specifying a Control Using a Connection Option

To specify a control using a connection option, you first create a control object. You then use the setOption() method of the connection object to add the control to the connection.

WARNING

When you specify a control using the connection option, the control is included on every LDAP operation request made using the connection. In some cases, this may be the behavior you want, but generally a control can only be used on certain operations, so it's usually better to use constraints to include the control with only the operations it applies to.

Here's how you would specify the Server Side Sorting control using a connection option:

```
String attrname = "cn";

/* Create a sort key to specify the sort order. */
LDAPSortKey sortOrder = new LDAPSortKey(attrname);


/*
 * Create a server sorting control using that sort key,
 * and specify that it is not critical.
 */
LDAPControl sortControl =
    new LDAPSortControl(sortOrder, false);


/*
 * Add the SSS control to the connection's options
 * so that every operation on this connection will
 * send the control.
 */
conn.setOption(conn.SERVERCONTROLS, sortControl);

/* Perform the search. */
LDAPSearchResults searchResults = conn.search(searchBase,
    searchScope, searchFilter, attributeList,
    attributesOnly);
```

Stacking Controls

When you want to combine more than one control in a single operation, you do so by passing an array of control objects to the setServerControls() method of the constraint or to the setOption() method of the connection. Here's how you would stack the Server Side Sorting control and the Virtual List View control using constraints:

```
LDAPControl controls[] = new LDAPControl[2];
String attrname = "cn";

/* Create a sort key to specify the sort order. */
LDAPSortKey sortOrder = new LDAPSortKey(attrname);

/*
 * Create a server side sorting control using that
 * sort key, and specify that it is critical.
 */
controls[0] =
    new LDAPSortControl(sortOrder, true);

/* Create a virtual list view control. */
controls[1] =
    new LDAPVirtualListControl(1, 0, 5, 0);


/* Create search constraints to use the controls. */
LDAPSearchConstraints constraints =
    new LDAPSearchConstraints();

/* And add both controls to the constraints. */
constraints.setServerControls(controls);

/* Perform the search. */
LDAPSearchResults searchResults = conn.search(searchBase,
    searchScope, searchFilter, attributeList,
    attributesOnly, constraints);
```

Controls Supported by NDS

Novell's LDAP implementation currently supports two widely used controls: the Server Side Sorting (SSS) control and the Virtual List View (VLV) control. In this section, we explain how each of these controls works and show you how to access these controls via the LDAP SDK.

IMPORTANT

The SSS and VLV controls are only defined for use with the search operation. They can't be used with any other operation.

The Server Side Sorting Control

The Server Side Sorting (SSS) control allows you to tell the LDAP server to return the entries for a search operation in sorted order. The SSS control is especially handy when the number of entries matching your search criteria is large because it removes the burden of sorting them at the client. Furthermore, if the entries are indexed in sorted order at the server, the server doesn't have to sort them either; it can simply use its index to retrieve each of the entries in the sorted order you request.

Using Sort Keys

The control is designed to allow you to specify a list of sort keys. Each sort key contains the following information:

- The attribute for the sort key.

- An optional ordering rule, which is a matching rule that is valid for the attribute type of the sort key. If the ordering rule is not specified, the server uses the default ordering matching rule defined for the attribute type of the sort key.

- An optional reverse ordering flag. When this flag has a value of true, entries are sorted in the reverse order. If the flag is omitted, it defaults to a value of false and the standard ordering is used.

IMPORTANT

First, NDS currently only allows you to specify a single sort key. It also requires that you have an index (typically a value index) defined for that sort key. More information on creating indexes is available in the section "Speeding up Searches: Creating Indexes" of Chapter 10. Second, the ordering rule and reverse order options of the Server Side Sort control are not currently supported in NDS. Finally, all of the entries in the subtree of the base DN of your search request must be stored locally on the server receiving the search request with the SSS control for SSS control support to be available. If you issue a search request with an SSS control that does not meet any of these requirements, the request will fail.

SSS Control Tips

If the SSS control cannot meet your application's needs for sorting, you can also sort the entries from a search operation at the client. While client-side sorting is less efficient than server side sorting, especially in cases where a large number of search entries are returned, it can be used to overcome several of the current limitations of NDS's SSS control. You can do client-side sorting without an index, you can sort on more than one attribute, and you can sort in reverse order.

X-REF

A discussion of client-side sorting can be found in the "Sorting the Results" section of Chapter 5.

If you experience slow performance using an SSS control (especially in very large trees), it may be due to the search filter you are using. If the search filter includes any attributes besides the primary sort key attribute for the SSS control, NDS may not be able to use its indexes as efficiently, thus slowing the performance of your search. If you're experiencing performance problems in this scenario, a good first step in diagnosing this condition is to change your search filter to include only the attribute in the sort key to see if performance improves. If it does, it's a good indicator that you're in this situation. If you can, try adjusting your search filter to improve the performance of your search request.

The LDAPSortControl Class

The Java LDAP SDK provides direct support for the SSS control via the LDAPSortControl class. The LDAPSortControl class is simple to begin with, and even then, you'll probably only use a subset of the constructors and methods it provides.

Constructors

The LDAPSortControl has three constructors:

```
LDAPSortControl(LDAPSortKey key, boolean critical)
LDAPSortControl(LDAPSortKey[] keys, boolean critical)
LDAPSortControl(String oid,
                boolean critical, byte[] value)
```

For now, you'll probably only use the first of these constructors. Because only one sort key is allowed in Novell's current implementation, there's no need to use the second method, which allows you to specify multiple sort keys. The third constructor is used to create an SSS response object, which you'll probably never need to do unless you're subclassing the LDAPSortControl class.

Methods

Some methods of the LDAPSortControl that you may want to use include:

```
String getFailedAttribute()
int getResultCode()
String toString()
```

You can use the getFailedAttribute() method to get the name of the sort key that caused the control to fail. You can use this information to give feedback to the client if an attribute specified as a sort has not been properly indexed for use with the SSS control.

The getResultCode() method gives you the result code for the SSS control itself. This may provide additional diagnostic information regarding the reason for a failure when using the SSS control. You can get details on every possible failure and its meaning from the SSS control Internet-Draft.

The toString() method returns a string representation of the control that you can use for debugging purposes.

At the time of this writing, the Server Side Sorting control draft is has been approved for RFC status but it has not yet been published as an RFC. The latest draft is available at http://www.ietf.org/internet-drafts/draft-ietf-ldapext-sorting-03.txt.

Using the SSS Control

Using the SSS control is very straightforward, because its only input parameter is one or more sort keys. We've already shown you three examples using the SSS control in the "Including Controls in an LDAP Request" section earlier in this chapter. Because the SSS control is required to use the Virtual List View (VLV) control, we also show you a more complete example, using the SSS control in the "Using the VLV Control" section later in this chapter.

The Virtual List View Control

A virtual list view is a device employed in user interface design that enables you to create the illusion that a large set of items in a list has been presented to the user in a scrolling window. Rather than actually loading the list with an extremely large number items, you only load the list with enough contiguous items to fill the view window. As the user navigates through the list, you regenerate the set of items displayed in a way that makes it appear that the entire list is actually stored in the scrolling window.

How a Virtual List View Works

To help you understand the concept of a virtual list view, imagine you have a list containing 10,000 items, and you want to display them in a scrolling window with room to display 25 lines. Figure 9.1 shows a list of names with a scrolling window superimposed over it.

FIGURE 9.1

A scrolling window superimposed over a list of names

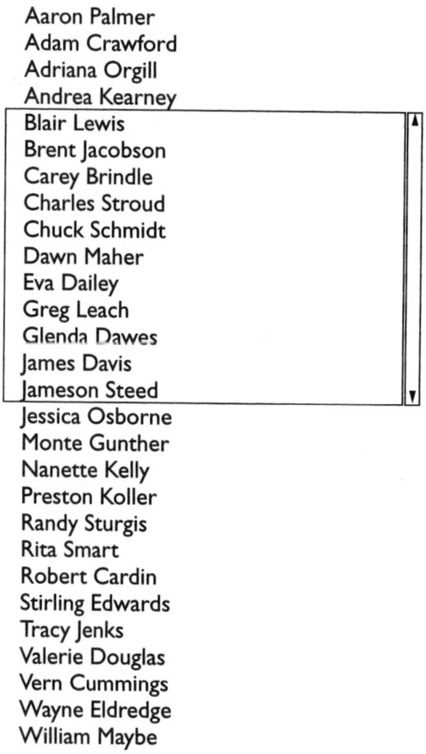

Aaron Palmer
Adam Crawford
Adriana Orgill
Andrea Kearney
Blair Lewis
Brent Jacobson
Carey Brindle
Charles Stroud
Chuck Schmidt
Dawn Maher
Eva Dailey
Greg Leach
Glenda Dawes
James Davis
Jameson Steed
Jessica Osborne
Monte Gunther
Nanette Kelly
Preston Koller
Randy Sturgis
Rita Smart
Robert Cardin
Stirling Edwards
Tracy Jenks
Valerie Douglas
Vern Cummings
Wayne Eldredge
William Maybe

One option would be to retrieve all 10,000 items and place them in the scrolling list. Alternatively, you could use a virtual list view by doing the following:

▶ When the user first opens the scrolling window, you would put items 1 through 25 from the full set of items into the scrolled window.

▶ If the user pages down once, you would replace items 1 to 25 in the scrolling window with items 26 to 50.

▶ If the user then presses the up arrow key three times, you would replace the contents of the scrolling window with items 23 to 47.

▶ If the user moves the slider on the scrolled window to the bottom, you would put the last 25 items (9,976 to 10,000) into the scrolling window.

▶ You could choose to support *typedown*, a feature that allows the user to type in one or more alphanumeric characters that match the beginning of the list item they want to see. When the user types in the characters "Jo", you'd find the first entry in the list that begins with "Jo" and display it so that it would be centered on the scrolled window with 12 entries from the list preceding it and 12 entries from the list following it.

You could be clever, and refine the process we just described to make it more efficient. For instance, you could avoid having to retrieve items 23 to 47 in the third action in the preceding example if you always had 35 list items instead of 25 and centered your 25-line window over the 35 items it contained. In this case, there would be five invisible items preceding and five invisible items following the displayed items. When the user pressed the up arrow key three times, you'd just scroll the window up three lines, which would leave two invisible lines above the window and seven invisible lines following it.

Now that you understand what a virtual list view is, let's turn our attention to the LDAPv3 VLV control. The client-server interaction using the VLV control requires communication in both directions, so we need to discuss both the VLV request and response controls.

The LDAPv3 VLV Request Control

The LDAPv3 VLV request control is used to modify the LDAP search operation so that you can retrieve search entries from an LDAP server in precisely the manner needed to support the virtual list view functionality we just described.

IMPORTANT

The VLV request control must always be used in conjunction with the SSS control because its behavior depends on the entries being provided in sorted order. Whenever we talk about sending a VLV request control, it is implied that the SSS request control is also included in the search request. You can read more about the SSS control in the "Sever Side Sorting Control" section earlier in this chapter.

The ASN.1 encoding of the VLV request control is:

```
VirtualListViewRequest ::= SEQUENCE {
    beforeCount    INTEGER (0..maxInt),
```

```
afterCount      INTEGER (0..maxInt),
CHOICE {
   byoffset [0] SEQUENCE {
      offset          INTEGER (0 .. maxInt),
      contentCount    INTEGER (0 .. maxInt)
   },
   greaterThanOrEqual [1] AssertionValue },
contextID      OCTET STRING OPTIONAL }
```

When you include the VLV control in a search request, the LDAP server returns a contiguous subset of the entries that match the specified search criteria. This subset is grouped around a target entry. You can choose the number of entries before and after the target entry that you want the LDAP server to send back.

You can specify the location of the target entry in one of two ways:

▶ **By an offset into the list:** Offsets are transmitted between the client and server as ratios of offset to total count. Using offset ratios, as opposed to using absolute offsets, deals with cases where the server may only have an approximate value for the total count, or where the actual number of entries is changing due to updates being made to the directory. Later, we explain how this works in more detail.

▶ **By a value assertion:** The target entry is the first entry in the list with a value of the primary sort key greater than or equal to the asserted value. If "Jo" were given as the value assertion and the primary sort key was cn, the first entry in the list whose common name begins with the letters "Jo" is the target entry. If no common name begins with the letters "Jo," the target entry is the first entry in the list with a value that is greater than "Jo."

NOTE

If no entry has a value that satisfies these criteria, there is no target entry. When this occurs, the server sets the value of the target position to the value of the content count plus one in the VLV response control.

The VLV Response Control

When you send a search request with a VLV request control, the search entries returned by the server represent the subset of the total set of entries that you requested based on the search criteria alone. The VLV response control is included as part of the SearchResultDone message sent from the server to the client.

The ASN.1 notation for the VLV response control is as follows:

```
VirtualListViewResponse ::= SEQUENCE {
    targetPosition    INTEGER (0 .. maxInt),
    contentCount      INTEGER (0 .. maxInt),
    virtualListViewResult ENUMERATED {
        success (0),
        operationsError (1),
        unwillingToPerform (53),
        insufficientAccessRights (50),
        busy (51),
        timeLimitExceeded (3),
        adminLimitExceeded (11),
        sortControlMissing (60),
        offsetRangeError (61),
        other (80) },
    contextID    OCTET STRING OPTIONAL }
```

The VLV response control includes the following:

- The target position containing the numerical position of the target entry in the entire set of entries matching the search criteria

- The content count, which is a total count of the entries that matched the search criteria (this total may be approximate)

- A result code that tells the success or failure of the control

- An optional server context

NOTE

If a server context is provided, the client application should send the most recently received context on the next search request for the same virtual list view in order to help the server know how to properly process the requests. The LDAPVirtualList class that we discuss in a moment takes care of this bookkeeping for you by automatically returning the last context sent by the server in the next request that uses the same instance of the class.

How the Target's Index Is Computed

Because the content count is only approximate, The VLV control computes the index of the target using a ratio of the client's index and the client's content count. The formula used by the server to compute the index of the target is as follows:

```
Si = Sc * (Ci / Cc)
```

where

▸ Si is the actual index of the target entry computed by the server. (This is the index of the target entry you get back from the server.)

▸ Sc is the server's estimate of the content count.

▸ Ci is the desired index of the target entry submitted by the client.

▸ Cc is the client's submitted content count.

If the server's content count is stable and you use the content count you received from the server's most recent VLV response in your next VLV request, then Sc = Cc and the target index, Si, will also be Ci — the index you requested.

There are three special cases for computing the target's index that you need to know:

▸ When you send a client content count of zero (Cc = 0), it means you have no idea what the content count actually is. In this case, the server uses its own content count in place of the one you supplied.

▶ When you specify a target index of one (Ci = 1), it always means that the target is the first entry in the list.

TIP

You can use the formula Si = Sc * (Ci / Cc) to jump a certain percentage of the way into the list. For instance if you wanted to jump 50 percent of the way (approximately), you could send values of 50 for the start index (Ci=50) and 100 for the contentCount (Cc=100).

▶ When you specify a target index equal to the content count (Ci = Cc) it means you want the target to be the last entry in the list. The only time that the target index can be zero (Ci = 0) is when the content count is also zero (Cc = 0). This is a good way to say that you want the last entry when you don't have a content count yet.

IMPORTANT

Because the content count is only approximate, you must write your application in a way that does not depend on the count being exact or you may get unexpected or undesirable results. That said, the LDAP server does all it can to provide consistent data from one request to the next. If your VLV application uses the offset method to move to a new target index a small (200 items or less) distance from the current target index, the Novell LDAP server calculates the new offset exactly. This means that cases where you scroll up or down a few lines or do a page up or a page down will work correctly.

The LDAPVirtualListControl Class

The Java LDAP SDK makes using the VLV control very straightforward by providing the LDAPVirtualListControl class.

SMART LINKS

At the time of this writing, the Virtual List View control draft is available at `http://www.ietf.org/internet-drafts/draft-ietf-ldapext-ldapv3-vlv-04.txt`**.**

Constructors

The LDAPVirtualListControl has four constructors.

```
LDAPVirtualListControl(int startIndex, int beforeCount,
                    int afterCount, int contentCount)
```

```
LDAPVirtualListControl(int startIndex, int beforeCount,
                       int afterCount, int contentCount,
                       String context)

LDAPVirtualListControl(String jumpTo,
                       int beforeCount, int afterCount)

LDAPVirtualListControl(String jumpTo,
                       int beforeCount, int afterCount,
                       String context)
```

The first two constructors are used when you want to specify a target entry at an exact offset into the list. The last two constructors are used when you want to specify a target entry using typedown. Table 9.1 explains each of the parameters for these constructors.

TABLE 9.1	PARAMETER	DESCRIPTION
VirtualListControl Constructor Parameters	startIndex	The index of the target entry to be returned.
	beforeCount	The number of entries before the target entry that you want returned.
	afterCount	The number of entries after the target entry that you want returned.
	contentCount	The total number of entries the client assumes the server has. When the client sets this value to 0 (zero), the server uses its own content count for computing the ratio and the startIndex is the actual index of the target entry returned.
	jumpTo	An LDAP attribute value assertion. The target entry is the first entry with a value greater than or equal to the attribute value assertion.
	context	The server-generated context that should be sent back by the client on subsequent search requests for the same virtual list view.

Methods

The LDAPVirtualListControl class also provides the following methods to enable you to access and modify the class's data:

```
'int getAfterCount()

int getBeforeCount()

String getContext()

int getIndex()

int getListSize()
```

The getIndex() method retrieves the index of the target entry, and the getListSize() method retrieves the current value of the content count. In both of these methods, the value you retrieve will be one returned by the server if you've issued a search request with this VLV control since you last set the values otherwise, they'll be the values you provided.

These methods enable you to modify the class's data:

```
void setContext(String context)

void setListSize(int listSize)

void setRange(startIndex, int beforeCount, int afterCount)

void setRange(String jumpTo,
              int beforeCount, int afterCount)
```

The setListSize() method enables you to set the content count. The other methods are self-explanatory.

Finally, the toString() method enables you to convert the class's data into string format for debugging purposes:

```
String toString()
```

Using the VLV Control

The following example shows how you could use the VLV control (along with the SSS control) to get the first 25 entries matching the search criteria, the last 25 entries matching the search criteria, and 25 entries centered around the first entry with a value greater than or equal to "Jo". Notice how each time you want another set of data, you simply adjust the parameters for the range of items you want to retrieve from the list and search again using the same connection and controls.

```
import java.util.*;
import netscape.ldap.*;
import netscape.ldap.controls.*;

public class Search
{
  public static void main( String[] args)
  {

    ...

    try
    {
      LDAPSearchResults searchResults;
      conn.connect(ldapVersion, host, port,
          loginDN, password);

      LDAPControl controls[] = new LDAPControl[2];

      /*
       * Create a virtual list view control.
       *
       * We want the first 25 entries from the virtual
       * list. To get this, our target offset is 1,
       * with a beforeCount of 0, an afterCount of 24.
       *
       * The contentCount is 0 since we this is our
```

```
 * first use of the VLV control and we don't yet
 * have a contentCount).
 */
LDAPVirtualListControl vlvControl =
    new LDAPVirtualListControl(1, 0, 24, 0);


/* Create a sort key to specify the sort order. */
LDAPSortKey sortOrder = new LDAPSortKey("cn");



/*
 * Create a server side sorting control using that
 * sort key, and specify that it is critical.
 */
controls[0] =
    new LDAPSortControl(sortOrder, true);


controls[1] = vlvControl;


/* Create search constraints to use the controls. */
LDAPSearchConstraints constraints =
    new LDAPSearchConstraints();


/* And add both controls to the constraints. */
constraints.setServerControls(controls);


/* Perform the search. */
searchResults = conn.search(searchBase,
    searchScope, searchFilter, attributeList,
    attributesOnly, constraints);


/* Print the name of each entry. */
System.out.println("\nFirst 25 entries...\n");


while (searchResults.hasMoreElements() == true) {
  LDAPEntry entry = searchResults.next();
```

```
        System.out.println("Entry: " + entry.getDN());
    }


    /* Get the last 25 entries from the list. */
    vlvControl.setRange(vlvControl.getListSize(), 24, 0);


    /* Perform the search. */
    searchResults = conn.search(searchBase,
        searchScope, searchFilter, attributeList,
        attributesOnly, constraints);


    /* Print the name of each entry. */
    System.out.println("\nLast 25 entries...");


    while (searchResults.hasMoreElements() == true) {
LDAPEntry entry = searchResults.next();
        System.out.println("Entry: " + entry.getDN());
    }



    /*
     * Get 25 entries centered around the first entry
     * beginning with "Jo".
     */
    vlvControl.setRange("Jo", 12, 12);


    /* Perform the search. */
    searchResults = conn.search(searchBase,
        searchScope, searchFilter, attributeList,
        attributesOnly, constraints);


    /* Print the name of each entry. */
    System.out.println(
        "\n25 entries centered around \"Jo*\"...");


    while (searchResults.hasMoreElements() == true) {
```

```
      LDAPEntry entry = searchResults.next();
      System.out.println("Entry: " + entry.getDN());
    }

  } catch (LDAPException e) {
    System.out.println("Error: " + e.toString());
  }



  if (conn.isConnected() == true) {
    try {
      conn.disconnect();
    } catch (LDAPException e) {
      System.out.println("Error: " + e.toString());
    }
  }
  System.exit(0);
  }
}
```

LDAPv3 Extensions

The first part of this chapter shows how adding control information can customize LDAP operations. This part of the chapter explains how new operations can be added to the LDAP protocol using LDAP extensions.

LDAP extensions are simply a framework that allows you to define new LDAP operation requests and responses in a standard way. This makes it possible to add new functionality to the protocol in a way that maintains backward compatibility with existing LDAPv3 clients and servers. When an LDAP extended operation is employed, its syntax and semantics must be predefined so that both the server and the client understand the operation. An LDAP extended operation may be applicable to only a specific LDAP server implementation, or it may be a standard operation defined in an RFC.

There are three elements of protocol that define the framework for LDAP extensions: the LDAP extended request, the LDAP extended response, and the LDAP extended partial response.

LDAP Extended Request

The LDAP extended request is used for clients to issue operation requests to LDAP servers. Here's the ASN.1 definition for extended requests:

```
ExtendedRequest ::= [APPLICATION 23] SEQUENCE {
    requestName      [0] LDAPOID,
    requestValue     [1] OCTET STRING OPTIONAL }
```

As you can see, there's not much to the extended request; it's just a framework that can be used to transmit data.

▸ The requestName is an ASN.1 object ID that uniquely names the operation.

▸ The requestValue, if it's needed at all, can contain arbitrarily complex data. The data in the requestValue is defined in ASN.1 syntax and Basic Encoding Rules (BER) encoded for transmission, just like the data for other LDAP operations.

LDAP Extended Response

The LDAP extended response is used to send responses from the server to the client. The ASN.1 definition for extended responses looks like this:

```
ExtendedResponse ::= [APPLICATION 24] SEQUENCE {
    COMPONENTS OF LDAPResult,
    responseName     [10] LDAPOID OPTIONAL,
    response         [11] OCTET STRING OPTIONAL }
```

Like the extended request, the extended response is just a framework for response data.

▸ The element COMPONENTS OF LDAPResult allows the extended response to behave like other LDAP responses by including a result code as well as matched DN, error message, and referral information, if they're needed.

▸ The responseName is an ASN.1 object identifier that uniquely identifies the response.

NOTE

The responseName is optional; this allows the server to send an error result when it receives an extended request that it doesn't recognize. In this case, the error protocolError (decimal 2) is sent in the resultCode field of the LDAPMessage to tell the client that the extended request cannot be processed.

▸ Like the requestValue in the extended request, the response, if needed, can be arbitrarily complex. Its structure is defined in ASN.1, and it is transmitted on the wire in BER encoded form.

Unsolicited Notifications

You may be interested to know the LDAPv3 specification uses the extended response for one of its own protocol elements. An LDAP server can send an extended response to a client without first receiving an extended request. When this occurs, the response is called an *unsolicited notification*. By definition, unsolicited notifications must always use a message ID of zero. Unsolicited notifications let the client know of an unusual condition in the LDAP server or in the connection between the client and the server. To make it possible for clients to distinguish unsolicited responses from other LDAP messages, LDAP clients generally use message IDs beginning at one for their LDAP requests.

Notice of Disconnection

RFC 2251 defines one unsolicited notification: the notice of disconnection. When a server is about to terminate the connection to a client due to an error condition, it may first send a notice of disconnection in order to help the client know that the connection is being deliberately closed due to an error condition, not to a network failure. When a client receives a notice of disconnection, it must not send any more data on the connection. The final state of any outstanding requests on that connection is undefined; the client must not assume that they are completed or unfinished.

The responseName for the notice of disconnection is 1.3.6.1.4.1.1466.20036. The response field is absent, and the resultCode indicates the reason for the disconnection.

The possible values for resultCode that can be sent by the LDAP server, along with their meanings, are given in Table 9.2

TABLE 9.2	RESULTCODE	DESCRIPTION
Unsolicited Notification Result Codes and Their Meanings	ProtocolError	The server has received data from the client in which the LDAPMessage structure could not be parsed.
	strongAuthRequired	The server has detected that an established, underlying security association that protects communication between the client and server has unexpectedly failed or been compromised.
	unavailable	This server has stopped accepting new connections and operations on all existing connections, and it will be unavailable for an extended period. The client may use an alternate server.

After the LDAP server sends a notice of disconnection, it must close the connection. After a client receives a notice of disconnection, it must immediately stop transmitting data on the connection. The client may also abruptly close its connection to the server if it chooses to do so.

NOTE

As of this writing, neither the Novell LDAP C SDK implementation nor the IETF drafts for the C and Java LDAP SDKs provide a way for your client application to receive unsolicited notifications. Fortunately, the client SDKs handle connection timeouts and other connection failures, which allow your client to detect a disconnection even though you can't get the notice of disconnection directly. It is likely that the need to handle unsolicited notifications will be addressed in future drafts of the IETF LDAP SDKs.

LDAP Extended Partial Response

The extended request and extended response are defined in RFC 2251. These two protocol elements are sufficient to support a request and response model that has one response for each request. There may be times, however, when an extended operation needs to be able to send multiple responses for a single request. The LDAP search operation is an example of such an operation.

To generalize the LDAPv3 extension mechanism, a third element of protocol that supports LDAP extensions has been proposed. This protocol element, called the extended partial response, provides a way to send multiple intermediate responses to an extended request. The ASN.1 definition for the extended partial response looks like this:

```
ExtendedPartialResponse ::= [APPLICATION 25] SEQUENCE {
    responseName      [0] LDAPOID OPTIONAL,
    response          [1] OCTET STRING OPTIONAL }
```

Like the extended response, the extended partial response is just a framework for response data.

- ▸ The responseName is an ASN.1 object identifier that uniquely identifies the response.

- ▸ The response, if needed, can be arbitrarily complex. Its structure is defined in ASN.1, and it is transmitted on the wire in BER-encoded form.

- ▸ Because the ExtendedPartialResponse is an intermediate response, there is no result information. This parallels the way that the SearchResultEntry and SearchResultReference intermediate responses work in relation to the SearchResultDone response.

When an extended operation is defined to use the extended partial response, the client sends an extended request operation to the server. The server processes the request and sends zero or more extended partial responses back to the client. Finally, the server sends an extended response to the client to indicate that the operation is complete.

Current Status of Extended Partial Response

As LDAP implementers have gained experience with the protocol, they have proposed a number of changes to RFC 2251; these changes would clarify certain points, fix errata, and so forth. Among these requests is the proposal for an extended partial response. The authors of RFC 2251 have indicated that a revision to RFC 2251 will be written to address these requests. We anticipate that the extended partial response will be included as a standard element of protocol in that revision of RFC 2251.

You can read all of the details on extended requests and responses in section 4.12 of RFC 2251. At the time of this writing, the LDAPv3 Extended Partial Response Internet-Draft is available at `http://www.ietf.org/internet-drafts/draft-rharrison-ldap-extPartResp-01.txt.`

▶ · ◀

Implementing Your Own Extensions

The term *extension* has several meanings. In the context of the discussion we've just completed, it refers to the specification of an extended request and its associated extended response. The term can also refer to the code that performs the server-side processing for an extended request, and then sends back the appropriate responses to the client.

While support for some extended requests are built directly into the LDAP server code, it's also possible to write server-side plug-in modules that can process extended requests. This gives you the capability to extend Novell's LDAP server in order to handle an extended request that it doesn't support natively. In this section, we use the term extension to mean one of these server-side plug-ins that implements the protocol handler for an LDAP extended operation.

Even though the processing semantics for an extended request must be the same for each implementation of an extension on various vendor's LDAP servers, an extension plug-in often needs to have a fairly intimate knowledge of the inner workings of the LDAP server it is extending. For this reason, among others, there is currently no standard set of developer APIs for writing extensions. If you choose to implement an extension plug-in, you'll probably have to do some rewriting for every LDAP platform on which you want to support your extension. That said, the LDAP world is evolving at a rapid pace, and it's possible that some standard developer APIs for this purpose will be available by the time you read this book.

IMPORTANT

NDS eDirectory 8.5 is the first release of Novell's LDAP server that supports LDAP extended requests. Because this is such a new feature, the engineers for the product wanted to gain some working experience with server-side LDAP extension support before providing an SDK to third-party developers. The LDAP extensions that are part of NDS eDirectory 8.5 are currently for use by NDS. Based on the experience that the NDS engineering team has to date, we can give you some information about how third-party LDAP extensions are likely to be supported in future releases of NDS. We hope that this information proves useful to you in the future, when this capability is made fully available.

Request and Response OIDs

Before you can write your own extension, you need request and response OIDs. You have several options for getting OIDs for your LDAP extension. Here are a couple of possibilities:

▶ The Internet Assigned Numbers Authority (IANA) at `http://www.isi.edu/cgi-bin/iana/enterprise.pl`.

▶ Novell's developer OID registry at `http://developer.novell.com/engsup`

WARNING

While you're in the process of developing a new extension, you may be able to get by temporarily without an assigned OID. It is extremely critical that you always use a properly registered unique OID for any extension that is used outside of a development-lab setting, in order to ensure that it does not conflict with other extensions. This caution applies equally to all protocol and schema elements that are identified by OIDs.

Current Best Practice

In the past, it was common for an LDAP extended request and its associated extended response to share the same OID. Recently, there appears to be a decided shift away from this practice. Currently, most LDAP extension designers are using separate OIDs for the LDAP extended request and response. Because OIDs are an unlimited resource, we advise you to follow this trend.

Server-Side Extension SDK

As of this writing, Novell plans to provide a server-side developer SDK for writing LDAP extensions in the near future. The SDK will probably provide functions for doing things like encoding and decoding BER elements, performing low-level operations on NDS, and sending replies back to the client. If you write your extension to this SDK, taking proper care to write portable code, it will be portable to all platforms that support NDS. For performance reasons, the language for the API set in the SDK will almost certainly be C rather than Java.

 When the Novell LDAP server-side developer kit becomes available, you'll be able to get it from Novell's developer Web site at http://www.developer.novell.com.

Extension Entry Points

Although we can't peer into the future and tell you precisely what APIs will be in the server-side developer SDK, we do know that your extension module will have to provide three well-known entry points in order to allow communications between the NDS server and the extension module you provide.

The three entry points are as follows:

> ▶ **An initialization function:** This function is called when the LDAP server first loads your extension module. Even if your extension module services more than one extended request, this function is called just once. The LDAP server does not continue initializing until the thread that calls this function returns from your initialization function; the LDAP server assumes that all necessary initialization for the module is completed when the initialization function returns.

▶ **A request handler function:** This function is called when the LDAP server receives an extended request for your handler. The OID of the extended request and its accompanying BER-encoded data are passed to this handler, which is responsible for decoding the request, validating the data, processing the request, and sending an appropriate response to the client. If the module services more than one extended request, this handler must take the appropriate action based on the value of the request OID.

▶ **A cleanup function:** This function is called just before the LDAP server unloads your extension module. Your module is unloaded if all extended requests that it services have been disabled (see the next section) and the LDAP server is reconfigured or shutting down. The LDAP server does not continue cleaning up until the thread that calls this function returns from your cleanup function; the LDAP server assumes that all cleanup for the module is completed when the cleanup function returns.

Registering Extensions with NDS

The NDS LDAP server needs a way to know which LDAP extensions should be loaded when it starts up or reconfigures. This information is stored in the `extensionInfo` attribute on the LDAP Server object.

X-REF

We discuss the LDAP Server object in more detail in Chapter 10.

The `extensionInfo` attribute is a case-insensitive, multi-valued string attribute. Each value of the attribute contains data in the following form:

```
status#extensionRequestOID#extensionResponseOID#moduleName
```

The status value is either E for enabled or D for disabled. The two extension OIDs are the standard representation, in dotted decimal notation, of the OID of the request and its associated response. The moduleName is a string representation of the process name for the extension handler. The values are separated by the # character. White space is not allowed.

When the LDAP server starts up or reconfigures itself, it reads the extension Info attribute to see which extension modules need to be started and stopped. Extensions that are currently loaded and available are listed in the server's root DSE.

Installing Your Extension

Currently, NDS looks for the binaries (NLMs, DLMs, or shared objects) for LDAP extension plug-ins in the same directory where the NDS module is located. On NetWare, this is the SYS:\SYSTEM directory. On Windows NT, this is the NDS directory immediately following the point where you choose to install NDS. On Solaris and Linux, this is the /usr/lib/nds-modules directory.

Using LDAP Extensions in Your Application

To take advantage of extended operations, you need to be able to issue extended operation requests from your LDAP application and properly receive and decode the corresponding responses. In this section, we discuss how you can accomplish this.

Detecting Supported Extensions

The way to tell which extensions are currently available on a given server is to read the supportedExtension attribute of the root DSE. The code example in the previous "Detecting Supported Controls" section in this chapter shows how you can search the root DSE. In that example, the only modifications needed to check for an extension instead of a control are to change the value of attributeList from supportedControl to supportedExtension and adjust the printed output from the program to print the word "extension" instead of "control."

ASN.1

Every LDAP operation request and response is represented in Abstract Syntax Notation One (ASN.1). ASN.1 is a notation for representing abstract data types. The following are some elements of ASN.1:

▸ Simple data types such as integers, strings, and booleans.

▸ Structural building blocks such as sequences, sets, and choices.

▸ The ability to define arbitrarily complex data types in terms of other data types.

For instance, here's the ASN.1 syntax for an LDAP search request, along with some of the definitions for elements referenced by the definition. In the interest of brevity, we haven't provided all of the productions for the elements of Filter because we don't need them to make our point.

```
1 SearchRequest ::= [APPLICATION 3] SEQUENCE {
2     baseObject      LDAPDN,
3     scope           ENUMERATED {
4        baseObject            (0),
5        singleLevel           (1),
6        wholeSubtree          (2) },
7     derefAliases    ENUMERATED {
8        neverDerefAliases     (0),
9        derefInSearching      (1),
10       derefFindingBaseObj   (2),
11       derefAlways           (3) },
12    sizeLimit       INTEGER (0 .. maxInt),
13    timeLimit       INTEGER (0 .. maxInt),
14    typesOnly       BOOLEAN,
15    filter          Filter,
16    attributes      AttributeDescriptionList }
17
18 LDAPDN ::= LDAPString
19
```

```
20 LDAPString ::= OCTET STRING
21
22 AttributeDescriptionList ::= SEQUENCE OF
23      AttributeDescription
24
25 AttributeDescription ::= LDAPString
26
27 Filter ::= CHOICE {
28    and             [0] SET OF Filter,
29    or              [1] SET OF Filter,
30    not             [2] Filter,
31    equalityMatch   [3] AttributeValueAssertion,
32    substrings      [4] SubstringFilter,
33    greaterOrEqual  [5] AttributeValueAssertion,
34    lessOrEqual     [6] AttributeValueAssertion,
35    present         [7] AttributeDescription,
36    approxMatch     [8] AttributeValueAssertion,
37    extensibleMatch [9] MatchingRuleAssertion }
```

Much like data types in a programming language, elements in ASN.1 are named, and each element has a data type.

Here are some things to note about this ASN.1 example:

▸ The SEQUENCE keyword (line 1) means that a SearchRequest is an ordered collection of one or more types.

▸ The INTEGER (lines 12 and 13) and BOOLEAN (line 14) are simple data types that are part of ASN.1.

▸ The baseObject is defined as an LDAPDN (line 2), which is defined to be an LDAPString (line 18); LDAPString is defined to be an OCTET STRING, or an array of bytes (line 20), which is another intrinsic ASN.1 data type.

▸ The ENUMERATED keyword used for the scope and derefAliases elements indicates that they are enumerated data types that can only have certain values. These values are named and enumerated within the definition (lines 3 – 11).

▶ SearchRequest has two elements — filter and attributes — that are themselves complex data types.

▶ The CHOICE keyword (line 27) indicates that a filter must be made from one of the 10 options listed in lines 28 to 37.

▶ The definition of Filter demonstrates how an element can be described recursively (lines 28 – 30).

▶ The SET OF keywords (lines 28 and 29) indicate an unordered collection of zero or more occurrences of a given type.

▶ When you BER encode an ASN.1 data type, the output includes three parts: a tag specifying the data type, a length, and the data value. In addition to the tag specifying the data type, there are also cases where an additional tag must be specified before the ASN.1 element in order to allow the ASN.1 element to be encoded and decoded without ambiguity. A *tag* is an element enclosed in square brackets, [ ]; the number inside the square brackets is the unique identifier.

▶ For example, the Filter element defined on lines 27 – 37 allows you to choose one of 10 elements. Both the "and" and "or" choices are defined to be SET of Filter. To make it clear which choice is being encoded, and also to aid in decoding, the ASN.1 definition includes a tag in the form of a number enclosed in square brackets — that is, [1], [2], [3], and so on, before each choice. When you encode the Filter element, you'll first create a tag specifying which of the choices you're encoding, followed by the normal BER encoding for that choice. In some cases a context is required with a tag, which is the reason for the APPLICATION keyword in the tag on line 1.

▶ The SEQUENCE OF keywords (line 22) indicate that an Attribute DescriptionList is composed of an ordered collection of zero or more occurrences of an AttributeDescription.

As this example has shown, ASN.1 provides a rich range of expression for specifying abstract data types. If you're interested, you can see the entire ASN.1 definition for LDAPv3 in Appendix A of RFC 2251.

Basic Encoding Rules

The Basic Encoding Rules (BER) are a way of representing or encoding a set of values for an ASN.1 data type as an array of bytes. BER encoding is machine-neutral, so it is a nice way to represent data for networking protocols where machines with different byte ordering schemes will need to communicate with each other.

Distinguished Encoding Rules and BER

Some ASN.1 types are allowed to be BER encoded in more than one way, thus there are several valid encodings that might be produced depending on the way you actually choose to perform their encoding. To simplify encoding and decoding LDAP messages, LDAP uses a subset of BER called the Distinguished Encoding Rules (DER), which adds some restrictions to BER that guarantee a unique encoding for each set of values represented by an ASN.1 data type.

NOTE

Even though DER is used to encode LDAP messages, the term BER is used almost universally when referring to the rules used for encoding ASN.1 data types for LDAP messages, presumably because DER is a subset of BER. We follow the same convention throughout this book.

Essentially, the Distinguished Encoding Rules guarantee a single unique encoding by specifying which encoding choice you must take when the Basic Encoding Rules would give you an option of more than one choice.

You can find a quick introduction to ASN.1 syntax at http://www.isi.edu/gost/brian/security/asn1.html.**You can also get additional information on ASN.1 notation and BER encoding in "A Layman's Guide to a Subset of ASN.1, BER, and DER," available in PostScript format at** ftp://ftp.rsa.com/pub/pkcs/ps/layman.ps **or in text format at** ftp://ftp.rsa.com/pub/pkcs/ascii/layman.asc.

SDK Support for BER Encoding and Decoding

To send and receive any LDAP message, your LDAP application has to encode and decode BER values. For all of the standard LDAP operations, the LDAP SDK handles the BER encoding of your operation requests and the BER decoding of the server's responses behind the scenes and allows you to set and get the information using standard Java data types. Similarly, the Java SDK provides convenience classes for the commonly-used LDAPv3 controls that do all of the required BER encoding and decoding for you. However, if you're writing client-side support for your own extension or for an extension that isn't yet supported by your LDAP SDK, you have to do your own BER encoding and decoding.

IMPORTANT

As of this writing, there is no standard Java SDK for encoding and decoding BER elements, and no Internet-Drafts covering this topic have been submitted to the IETF. Netscape's Java SDK does include the netscape.ldap.ber.stream package for encoding and decoding BER elements, but the package has some deficiencies, including minimal documentation, and its need to be used by a subclass of netscape.ldap.LDAPControl to generate a BER-encoded array of data from some of the classes in the ldap.ber.stream package. When Novell releases its Java SDK, we anticipate that it will include a package similar in many respects to the netscape.ldap.ber.stream class, but there may be some significant differences. With this in mind, we'll show some examples using the netscape.ldap.ber.stream package to give you a feel for what is involved in encoding and decoding BER elements.

The ldap.ber.stream Package

The ldap.ber.stream package includes classes that correspond to every element of ASN.1 notation. We just introduced you to several ASN.1 elements, including sequences, sets, choices, enumerated types, integers, booleans, and tags. The ldap.ber.stream package has classes for each of these types and others. For instance, you use the BERSequence class to encode and decode an ASN.1 SEQUENCE element, and you use the BERInteger class to encode and decode an ASN.1 INTEGER element.

Table 9.3 lists ASN.1 simple data types and the BER classes used for encoding them.

TABLE 9.3	ASN.1 DATA TYPE	BER CLASS
Simple ASN.1 Data Types and Their Associated BER Classes	BitString	BERBitString
	Boolean	BERBoolean
	Enumerated	BEREnumerated
	Integer	BERInteger
	NULL	BERNull
	NumericString	BERNumericString
	ObjectID	BERObjectId
	OctetString	BEROctetString
	PrintableString	BERPrintableString
	Real	BERReal
	VisibleString	BERVisibleString

Table 9.4 lists ASN.1 data types used for grouping and tagging other ASN.1 elements and the BER classes used for encoding them.

TABLE 9.4	ASN.1 DATA TYPE	BER CLASS
ASN.1 Data Types Used for Grouping and Tagging Other ASN.1 Elements and Their Associated BER Classes	Choice	BERChoice
	Sequence	BERSequence
	Set	BERSet
	Tagged element	BERTag

BER Encoding Example

Let's put all of this together and show you an example of how to encode the data for an ASN.1 element. Here's part of the ASN.1 definition for the LBURP protocol, as defined in `http://www.ietf.org/internet-drafts/draft-rharrison-lburp-02.txt`.

```
LBURPOperationRequestValue ::= SEQUENCE {
     sequenceNumber INTEGER (1 .. maxInt),
     updateOperationList UpdateOperationList
}


UpdateOperationList ::= SEQUENCE of CHOICE {
     addRequest        AddRequest,
     modifyRequest     ModifyRequest,
     delRequest        DelRequest,
     modDNRequest      ModifyDNRequest,
}


DelRequest ::= [APPLICATION 10] LDAPDN


LDAPDN ::= LDAPString


LDAPString ::= OCTET STRING
```

In this example, we're only going to use delete requests in the UpdateOperation List, so we aren't including the ASN.1 definitions for AddRequest, Modify Request, and ModifyDNRequest here. You can see them in RFC 2251, if you're interested in the details.

The following Java class demonstrates how you would encode an LBURP OperationRequestValue containing an UpdateOperationList with two delete requests:

NOTE

If you don't have a lot of experience with ASN.1 and BER encoding, it's possible that some of this example, especially the part dealing with the BERTag class constructor, may be confusing. Even so, simply reading this example should help you get a feel for how BER encoding is done. If and when you need to actually do BER encoding in your own application, we recommend that you do some additional study on ASN.1 and BER encoding (see a previous Smart Links icon for sources). This will help you to understand what each of these classes is doing and how they are encoding the data.

```java
import netscape.ldap.*;
import netscape.ldap.ber.stream.*;

public class EncodeLBURP extends LDAPControl {
        /* The tag value for the Delete operation. */
        final int TAG_DELETE_REQ = 10;

        /*
         * We need to have an instance of the
         * LBURPEncode class in order to call
         * the flattenBER() method.
         */
        LBURPEncode lburp = new LBURPEncode();

        BERSequence updateOperationListBer =
         new BERSequence();

        BERTag deleteOp = new BERTag(
            BERTag.APPLICATION | BERTag.PRIMITIVE
                | TAG_DELETE_REQ,
            new BEROctetString(
              "cn=Bob,ou=Artists,l=San Francisco,c=US"),
            true);
        updateOperationListBer.addElement(deleteOp);

        deleteOp = new BERTag(
            BERTag.APPLICATION | BERTag.PRIMITIVE
                | TAG_DELETE_REQ,
            new BEROctetString("cn=Fred,ou=Promotions,c=US"),
            true);
        updateOperationListBer.addElement(deleteOp);

        /*
         * Normally, the sequenceNumber is incremented for
```

```
 * each LBURP operation request.  We just use a
 * value of one here to demonstrate how you encode
 * an integer.
 */
int sequenceNumber = 1;
BERSequence LBURPOperationRequestBer =
        new BERSequence();

LBURPOperationRequestBer.addElement(
        new BERInteger(sequenceNumber));

LBURPOperationRequestBer.addElement(
        updateOperationListBer);

byte[] LBURPOperationRequestValue =
        lburp.flattenBER(LBURPOperationRequestBer);

/* Now you could use the LBURPOperationRequestValue
 * as the valus in the constructor for the
 * LDAPExtendedOperationClass.
 */
...

} catch (Exception e) {
   System.out.println("Error: " + e.toString());
}
System.exit(0);
   }
}
```

Here are some points that we'd like you to note about this example:

▸ We imported the netscape.ldap.ber.stream package to have access to all of the BER classes used in this example.

▸ There's no public method for generating a BER-encoded array of bytes in the netscape.ldap.ber.stream package for constructed ASN.1 data types, so you need to use the flattenBER method of the LDAPControl class on the LBURPOperationRequestBer. Because LDAPControl.flattenBer() is a protected method, you must subclass the LDAPControl class in order to use it. This is why the LBURPEncode class in this example extends LDAPControl.

▸ When we create the BERTag for each of the delete operations, we perform a bitwise-OR of three values — BERTag.APPLICATION, BERTag.PRIMITIVE, and TAG_DELETE_REQ — to create the actual tag value.

  • BERTag.APPLICATION indicates that the tag is application-specific.

  • BERTag.PRIMITIVE indicates that the tag is for a primitive data type, as opposed to a constructed data type.

  • TAG_DELETE_REQ is the value of the tag given in the ASN.1 definition for DelRequest.

NOTE   The BERTag class inherits the **APPLICATION** and **PRIMITIVE** fields from BERElement. It also inherits the **CONTEXT** and **CONSTRUCTED** fields, which are used in forming various tag values, from BERElement. The document "A Layman's Guide to a Subset of ASN.1, BER, and DER," referenced in a Smart Links icon displayed previously in this chapter, explains the meanings of these terms and the way they are used in constructing BER tags.

BER Decoding Example

Just as you must BER encode data before you can send it on the wire, when you receive an extended request, you need to BER decode the data so you'll be able to use it in your application. Here's the ASN.1 definition for the LBURPOperation-ResponseValue that corresponds to the LBURPOperationRequestValue used in our previous example:

```
LBURPOperationResponseValue ::= SEQUENCE of OperationResult

OperationResult ::= SEQUENCE {
```

```
        operationNumber          INTEGER,
        ldapResult LDAPResult
}


LDAPResult ::= SEQUENCE {
    resultCode      ENUMERATED {
        success                      (0),
        operationsError              (1),
        protocolError                (2),


            ...


        entryAlreadyExists           (68),
        objectClassModsProhibited    (69),
            -- 70 reserved for CLDAP --
        affectsMultipleDSAs          (71), -- new
            -- 72-79 unused --
        other                        (80) },
            -- 81-90 reserved for APIs --
    matchedDN       LDAPDN,
    errorMessage    LDAPString,
    referral        [3] Referral OPTIONAL }

Referral ::= SEQUENCE OF LDAPURL

LDAPURL ::= LDAPString -- limited to characters
                       -- permitted in URLs


LDAPString ::= OCTET STRING
```

The following example shows how you would decode an LBURPOperation-ResponseValue. If you read the example and compare it to the ASN.1 definition we just presented, you'll see that there's a one-to-one correspondence between each element of the ASN.1 definition and the Java statements that decode each element.

NOTE

To simplify this example, we assume that there is only one Operation Result in the LBURPOperationResponseValue. This example could easily be generalized to handle multiple OperationResult elements by adding a loop around the code that gets and processes the OperationResult. This is similar to the way we use a loop to handle the sequence of LDAPURLs.

```java
import java.io.*;
import netscape.ldap.*;
import netscape.ldap.client.*;
import netscape.ldap.controls.*;
import netscape.ldap.ber.stream.*;


public class DecodeLBURPSnippet {
    public static void main(String[] args) {
        try {
            /*
             * berValue contains the BER encoded data
             * received from the extended response.
             *
             ***********************************************
             * You MUST put a value in berValue before  *
             * attempting to do the decode.              *
             ***********************************************
             */
            byte [] berValue = ...

            /*
             * Get the ber encoded array into an input stream
             * so that we can convert it into BER classes.
             */
            ByteArrayInputStream inStream =
                    new ByteArrayInputStream (berValue);

            /* Create the LDAP tag decoder. */
            JDAPBERTagDecoder decoder = new JDAPBERTagDecoder();
```

```
int[] nRead = new int[1];
nRead[0] = 0;

/*
 * Read the input stream into a BERSequence
 *
 * This corresponds to the top-level
 * LBURPOperationResponseValue sequence for
 * the ASN.1 definition.
 */
BERSequence lburpOpRespValSeq =
      (BERSequence) BERElement.getElement(decoder,
            inStream, nRead);

/*
 * Print out some debugging information
 * about this sequence.
 */
System.out.println("read " + nRead[0] +
      " bytes for sequence string");

System.out.println("sequence contains " +
      lburpOpRespValSeq.size() + " elements");
System.out.println(lburpOpRespValSeq.toString());

/*
 * Get the OperationResult sequence out of the
 * LBURPOperationResponseValue.
 */
BERSequence opResultSeq =
      (BERSequence) lburpOpRespValSeq.elementAt(0);

/*
 * Get the operationNumber out of the OperationResult.
 */
```

```java
int operationNumber =
      ((BERInteger)
            (opResultSeq.elementAt(0))).getValue();

System.out.println("operationNumber = " +
      operationNumber);

/* Get the LDAPResult out of the OperationResult. */
BERSequence ldapResultSeq =
      (BERSequence)(opResultSeq.elementAt(1));

/* Get the resultCode out of the LDAPResult. */
int resultCode =
      ((BEREnumerated)
            (ldapResultSeq.elementAt(0))).getValue();

System.out.println("resultCode = " + resultCode);

/* Get the matchedDN out of the LDAPResult. */
BEROctetString matchedDNOctet =
      (BEROctetString)(ldapResultSeq.elementAt(1));
if (matchedDNOctet.getValue() != null) {

   String matchedDN =
         new String(matchedDNOctet.getValue(),
               "UTF8" );

   System.out.println("matchedDN = " +  matchedDN);
} else {
   System.out.println("matchedDN = null");
}

/* Get the errorMessage out of the LDAPResult. */
BEROctetString errorMessageOctet =
```

```
        (BEROctetString)(ldapResultSeq.elementAt(2));
if (errorMessageOctet.getValue() != null) {

    String errorMessage =
            new String(errorMessageOctet.getValue(),
                "UTF8" );

    System.out.println("errorMessage = " +
            errorMessage);
} else {
    System.out.println("errorMessage = null");
}

/*
 * Check for optional referral element in LDAPResult.
 */
if (ldapResultSeq.size() == 4) {
    /* We have a referral element, so process it. */
    BERTag tag = (BERTag)(ldapResultSeq.elementAt(3));
    BERSequence referralSeq =
            (BERSequence)(tag.getValue());

    String referral;

    System.out.println("decoding " +
            referralSeq.size() + " referrals");

    /* Get each of the LDAPURLs out of Referral. */
    for (int i = 0; i < referralSeq.size(); i++) {

        BEROctetString referralOctet =
                (BEROctetString)(referralSeq.elementAt(i));
        if (referralOctet.getValue() != null) {
            referral =
```

```
                        new String(referralOctet.getValue(),
                            "UTF8" );
                System.out.println("referral = " + referral);
            } else {
                System.out.println("referral = null");
            }
        }
      }
    } catch (Exception e) {
        System.out.println("Error: " + e.toString());
    }
    System.exit(0);
  }
```

Here are some points that we'd like you to note about this example:

▶ We imported the netscape.ldap.ber.stream package so that we'd have access to all of the BER classes used in this example.

▶ There is no direct support for converting a byte array into BER elements, so we created an input stream from the byte array and read the input stream into a BERSequence.

▶ We imported netscape.ldap.client package to have access to the JDAPBER-TagDecoder class. This class provides hints on how to interpret the application-specific ASN.1 tags for LDAP.

TIP

The toString( ) method provided in each of the BER classes is a very useful development and debugging tool. When you call the toString() method for a BERElement or one of its subclasses, the method decodes the entire BER and presents the information in English form. We used toString() as a way of seeing what's inside a BERElement as a guide in decoding it properly, and also as way to ensure that we actually decoded it properly at each step of the decoding. The converse of this is also true; toString() can also be used to verify that you've encoded a BER the way you expected to at each step of its construction.

The LDAPExtendedOperation Class

The Java SDK uses the LDAPExtendedOperation class to represent the information for both the extended operation request and the response. As you might guess from the ASN.1 notation for extended requests and responses that we showed earlier, the class is very simple: it contains an OID and a value.

The class includes a single constructor:

```
LDAPExtendedOperation(String oid, byte[] vals)
```

and two accessor methods:

```
public String getID()
public byte[] getValue()
```

The byte array you pass into the LDAPExtendedOperation constructor is a BER encoded representation of the ASN.1 definition for the LDAP extended request defined for this extension. Similarly, the byte array returned by the getValue() accessor method is a BER encoded representation of ASN.1 definition for the LDAP extended response defined for this extension.

Making an Extended Request from the Client

To issue an extended operation request, you need to create an LDAP-ExtendedOperation object, and then pass it as a parameter to the extended Operation() method of the LDAPConnection class. The extendedOperation() method returns an LDAPExtendedOperation object that contains the extended operation response.

An Example

One LDAP extension available in the NDS eDirectory 8.5 is the refresh server extension. If you modify elements of the LDAP server's configuration (see Chapter 10), you need to tell the LDAP server to reconfigure itself. Here's a way to do it from an LDAP client:

```
/* Connect and bind to the ldap server. */
conn.connect(ldapVersion, host, port, loginDN, password);
```

```
/*
 * 2.16.840.1.113719.1.27.100.9 is the OID for the extension
 * that tells the Novell LDAP server to reconfigure itself.
 */LDAPExtendedOperation extendedReq =
        new LDAPExtendedOperation(
                "2.16.840.1.113719.1.27.100.9", null);


LDAPExtendedOperation extendedResp =
        conn.extendedOperation(extendedReq);
```

Getting Extended Response Values

The extended request in our example didn't require any extended request or response data. You could use the following code snippet to include a request value and get back the corresponding response value:

```
/*
 * Generally, reqValue will contain a BER encoded value.
 * See the BER encoding example above for information on
 * creating BER encoded values.
 */
byte reqValue[] = ...

LDAPExtendedOperation extendedReq =
        new LDAPExtendedOperation("OID", reqValue);

LDAPExtendedOperation extendedResp =
        conn.extendedOperation(extendedReq);

System.out.println("Extended Response OID: " +
        extendedResp.getID());

byte respValue[] = extendedResp.getValue();


/*
 * Generally, respValue will contain a BER encoded value.
```

```
* At this point you'll need to decode it.  See the BER
* decoding example above for information on decoding BER
* values.
*/
```

Summary

The designers of LDAPv3 designed the protocol for longevity by providing two standard ways to extend it. Controls allow you to modify the behavior of existing operations, and extensions allow you to add new operations to the protocol. We showed you how controls and extensions fit into the protocol, explained and demonstrated the controls supported by NDS 8.5, and gave you information you need to write LDAP extensions of your own in future releases of NDS. This chapter concludes Section II of this book. If you've read this entire section, you now know how every LDAP operation works and how the Java LDAP SDK supports the use of those operations in your programs.

The final chapters of the book concentrate on advanced topics relating to system administration and tuning.

PART III

Advanced Topics

CHAPTER 10

LDAP Configuration and Administration

Most computer applications allow you to configure certain properties or options to your liking. Novell's LDAP server is no exception. While many applications keep track of these settings in configuration or information files, the LDAP server uses the directory. In fact, the LDAP server is a perfect example of a directory-enabled application.

In this chapter, we mainly concern ourselves with the options and settings you can change that affect the way the server behaves. We also go over additional things that can be done to increase the performance and scalability of your server.

If you followed the installation sections in Chapter 2, you already know that most of these settings are found in two objects — the LDAP Server and the LDAP Group. To review, the LDAP Server object holds configuration options that apply to a specific server (things such as port settings and debug options). The LDAP Group object holds configuration information that is shared among multiple LDAP servers in the tree; these include referral options and schema mappings.

Server Specific Settings: Editing the LDAP Server Object

As you read earlier, the LDAP Server object holds all the configuration information that applies to a specific LDAP server. If you have more than one LDAP server that participates in your tree, you'll have multiple LDAP Server objects in the directory — each one corresponding to a specific LDAP Server. When NDS is installed, it creates an NDS Server object. You chose the name and location for this object (the installation program provides a default that is typically the name of your server machine). When the LDAP server portion of NDS is installed, it creates the LDAP Server object in the same place that it created the NDS Server object and names it `LDAP Server - <NDS server name>`, where `<NDS server name>` is the name of your NDS Server.

The easiest way to view and update the options stored in the LDAP Server object is through ConsoleOne. From ConsoleOne, locate the LDAP Server object you wish to view, right-click it, and choose Properties.

If you haven't used ConsoleOne to manage your directory yet, you may want to browse the "LDAP Configuration" section in Chapter 2.

X-REF

You'll notice that the properties page consists of a tab pane. The first four tabs — General, SSL Configuration, Screen Options, and Filtered Replica — hold the configuration settings for the LDAP server. The other tab panels hold information that is standard for every entry in the directory.

The first tab (General) is represented in Figure 10.1 and allows the settings described in the following sections.

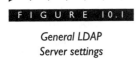

F I G U R E   10.1

*General LDAP
Server settings*

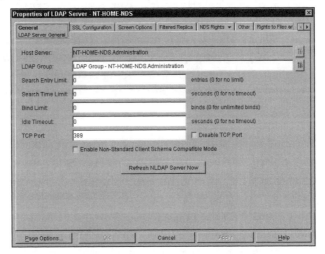

General Settings

Most of the settings on this panel set default constraints for LDAP operations. We enumerate each setting and give a brief description of its use.

For a full discussion on constraints, see Chapter 5.

X-REF

▶ **Host Server:** This field simply shows the name of the NDS Server object with which this LDAP server is associated. This field should not be changed unless the value is empty.

▶ **LDAP Group:** This associates this LDAP Server object with a particular LDAP Group object.

▶ **Search Entry Limit:** Restricts the number of search responses the server returns from any single search request. A value of 0 here means that the server allows an unlimited number of search responses to be returned. This setting and the next one — Search Time Limit — prevent users from hogging resources on the server.

TIP

If yours is a publicly available server, you may want to seriously consider setting a restriction here to prevent someone launching a denial of service attack. If a user is able to cause the server to process hundreds or thousands of complex searches that return thousands or millions of entries, it may effectively block other processes from efficiently happening. Another reason you might want to restrict the number of entries from being returned is that you don't feel comfortable letting someone easily "download" the entire contents of your directory.

▶ **Search Time Limit:** Tells the server how long (in seconds) it should continue to search and return search entries for any single search request. A value of 0 means that the server should never timeout a search request.

▶ **Bind Limit:** Sets the maximum number of LDAP connections the server allows to be open at one time. The value 0 means there is no limit. Setting this value may help in a situation where the number of active connections overwhelms the server. Once the bind limit has been reached, new bind requests will fail.

NOTE

If the bind limit is 0 (unlimited) or is a very high number, you may not witness that number ever being reached. There may be server-imposed restrictions on the number of open connections, which may take effect before the LDAP bind limit is reached. See the following section on NDS and OS Tuning for more details.

▸ **Idle Timeout:** Some LDAP clients may open a connection to the server, send a few requests, and never unbind. This setting allows the server to close connections after there hasn't been any LDAP traffic on a connection for the specified amount of time. If a connection is idle for the amount of time (measured in seconds) specified here, the server sends an unsolicited notification with a notice of disconnect to the client and then shuts down the connection. Here again, a 0 means there is no timeout.

▸ **TCP Port:** The name TCP port is a bit of a misnomer. All connections to Novell's LDAP server are made over TCP/IP. This setting controls the port that is used for cleartext or non-encrypted LDAP communications. Non-encrypted LDAP connections are typically made on port 389. If you have a conflict, such as two LDAP servers running at the same IP address, you can configure the Novell LDAP server to use a different port here.

WARNING

If you change the TCP port, you need to ensure that all the LDAP applications that talk to this server also use the new TCP port. Otherwise, the LDAP client applications fail to communicate with the server.

▸ **Disable TCP Port:** For security reasons, you may want to prohibit users from communicating to your LDAP server over the cleartext port. Marking this checkbox does just that. It causes the server to stop listening for LDAP connections on the TCP port set above.

▸ **Enable Non-Standard Client Schema Compatible Mode:** Some older SDKs have problems parsing the schema from LDAP directories. To work around these shortcomings, Novell has identified the problems and allows you to cause the server to return schema elements in a format that can be parsed by these non-standard client SDKs. If an application you have encounters a problem while reading the schema from Novell's LDAP server, check this box.

Finally, there's a "Refresh NLDAP Server Now" button on this screen. When the LDAP server is started, it reads this configuration information and stores it internally. If you make changes to any of the configuration information, the LDAP server needs to reread this information — which is what the Refresh NLDAP Server button is used for. If you don't click this button after making changes, ConsoleOne issues a refresh command to the LDAP server when you click OK or Apply.

SSL Configuration

If you switch to the SSL Configuration tab, you see the panel in Figure 10.2. This panel configures the LDAP server to use Secure Sockets Layer (SSL) connections to encrypt the data that flows between the client and the server.

FIGURE 10.2

SSL Configuration settings for the LDAP Server

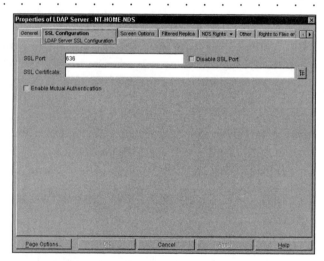

The SSL Port may be changed to avoid conflicts with other LDAP servers that may be running on the same machine. The default SSL Port is 636.

WARNING

If you change the SSL Port, you need to ensure that all the LDAP applications that talk to this server also use the new SSL Port. Otherwise, the LDAP client applications fail to communicate with the server.

If for some reason you'd like to force the server to not communicate over SSL, you may disable it by checking the Disable SSL Port checkbox.

The SSL Certificate edit box names the server's SSL Certificate used during an SSL handshake. We're going to talk about how to create one of these certificates — and how to configure your server and client to use SSL in just a moment.

Marking the Enable Mutual Authentication checkbox causes the server to ask the client for its certificate during the SSL handshake and, if needed, authenticates the client using the client's certificate.

Screen Options

The Screen Options panel is illustrated in Figure 10.3 and provides a way for you to control the types of messages that are output to the debug trace screen while the server is processing requests.

We talked about the debug trace screen (DSTrace) in Chapter 2 and showed you how to use it.

X-REF

You can turn on all the options if you like, or to cut down on traffic, just the ones you need to troubleshoot a particular problem. The following is a list of the options and what types of messages they control.

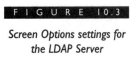

F I G U R E 10.3

Screen Options settings for the LDAP Server

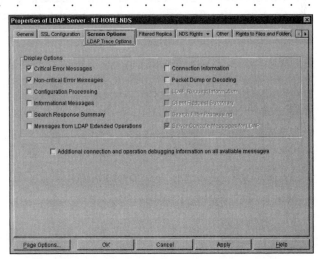

▸ **Critical Error Messages:** Corresponds to messages that are reported when a severe error is encountered. These errors typically signal a condition that causes the server to stop responding.

▸ **Non-critical Error Messages:** These are the set of all errors that are either caused by erroneous user data and requests, or non-critical errors that the server encounters that cause an operation to fail.

▸ **Configuration Processing:** This allows messages relating to the server updating its configuration data. You see these messages when starting or refreshing the LDAP server.

▸ **Informational Messages:** This allows messages that don't signal an error condition but that otherwise provide useful information. Examples include search time and size limit exceeded, operations starting and stopping, and so on.

▸ **Search Response Summary:** This allows messages that are related to search results to be sent to the trace screen. This is here as a separate option because the search operation is very complex and can generate a great deal of traffic (and subsequently a lot of trace messages).

TIP

If you're experiencing a problem with search, you might find it helpful to turn just this flag on to cut down on the amount of messages you need to wade through.

▸ **Messages from LDAP Extended Operations:** This allows informational messages from LDAP extended operations to be displayed.

▸ **Connection Information:** This allows messages associated with LDAP connections to be displayed. The amount of information you get when this option is on can be rather large. This information is typically only useful if you're having connection-related problems.

▶ **Packet Dump or Decoding:** Enabling this causes all BER-encoded packets that are received by the server to be displayed. This generates a tremendous amount of data. This is useful if you suspect the client is sending erroneous data.

WARNING

Turning on "Packet Dump or Decoding" may put sensitive information such as passwords on the trace screen or in the trace file, so use caution when using this option.

▶ **Additional connection and operation debugging information on all available messages:** This causes some low-level connection and operation information to be prepended to each operation. This is useful when you have many operations flowing into the server and need to track a specific operation. The format of the data displayed is: (`<connection identifier>:< message identifier>:<operation tag>`), where:

- `<connection identifier>` is a hexadecimal number that represents the connection that this operation is taking place on. This number is helpful when you have many clients sending requests and you need to track the behavior of a particular client.

- `< message identifier>` is a hexadecimal number that corresponds to the messageID sent in the LDAP request by the client. This information is helpful when tracing asynchronous operations sent by a client.

- `<operation tag>` is a hexadecimal number that represents the operation being serviced. This number corresponds to the actual operation value of the LDAP request.

WARNING

Turning on any of the trace messages causes a performance decrease. Trace messages are to be used as an aid in resolving problems and should normally be left off.

You may see other options on this screen that are disabled, as shown in Figure 10.3. These are options that were available in earlier versions of the server and only exist for backward compatibility with old servers.

Filtered Replica

This panel only contains the following set of radio buttons:

- ▸ Do Not Include Filtered Replica In Search

- ▸ Search Using Filtered Replica

Filtered replicas are new to NDS 8.5. A filtered replica is a replica that holds only a portion of the entries that belong in that part of the tree. If you do not allow search operations to include filtered replicas, they won't return any entries in that replica. Otherwise, they search any filtered replicas and return matched entries.

X-REF

There's a good discussion about filtered replicas in Chapter 8 if you'd like more information.

Shared Server Settings: Editing the LDAP Group Object

The LDAP Group object provides a convenient way to configure a set of options and have them apply to multiple LDAP Servers. In a single-server environment, this doesn't do much for you, but when you have many servers that participate in your tree, it reduces the busy work of reconfiguring a set of objects every time you want to make a change.

To edit the LDAP Group object from ConsoleOne, locate the LDAP Group object, right-click it, and choose Properties. You see a dialog box like the one in Figure 10.4. The first four tab panels — General, Server List, Attribute Map, and Class Map — are the ones that hold the settings for the LDAP Group object.

General Settings

On the General tab panel, you see some referral-related options, an option to allow clear text passwords, and a way to specify a proxy username — we talk about each setting next.

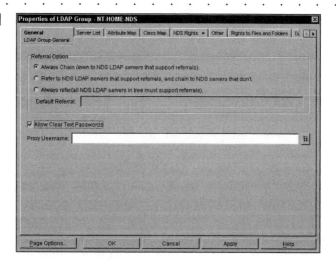

FIGURE 10.4

General settings for the
LDAP Group

Referral Options

To understand referrals, you first need to know about partitions and replicas. We summarize that information here.

The best way to learn about these concepts is by reading Chapter 8, where we discuss referrals and referral options at length.

X-REF

In short, a partition is a portion of the directory hierarchy that is sectioned off from all the rest and is *mastered* by one or more replicas. In other words, the directory tree may be logically segmented into different parts — like a jigsaw puzzle. Each piece of the puzzle resides on one or more LDAP servers. A server knows about the servers that hold the pieces of the puzzle that join to its piece; this information is held in reference objects.

If you need information about an object that resides on a different server, your server can either examine the reference object and retrieve the information from the other server, or it can simply return the reference to you in the form of a referral to tell you where to get the information for yourself.

You see three options in the Referral Option box:

- ▶ **Always Chain:** This tells the server to always do the work of chasing referrals on the client's behalf — this only works when the other servers in the tree are NDS servers. If your directory tree is made up of all NDS servers, this option is nice because it takes care of authenticating to the other servers using your public and private key-pairs. This frees your client from having to rebind to a new server every time it gets a referral.

TIP

Another reason you may want to choose this option in an NDS-only tree is if you have older versions of NDS servers in your tree that don't talk LDAP. When a server is traversing on your behalf, it uses NDAP to talk to the other NDS servers in the tree.

- ▶ **Refer to NDS LDAP servers that support referrals, and chain to NDS servers that don't:** This option attempts to return LDAP referrals to you if it can, but fail-over to chaining if it runs into a portion of the tree that isn't serviced by an LDAP server. If you know your tree is made up of some NDS servers that do not talk LDAP, but you want referrals to be returned whenever possible, choose this option.

- ▶ **Always Refer:** Choosing this option forces the server to always return referrals and never traverse to another server on your behalf. This works best in an environment where you know all your servers speak LDAP and are running versions of LDAP capable of returning referrals.

TIP

You may want to choose this option if you'd like to give your clients more control over when and when not to follow a referral. For instance, you may have a network that spans the globe. If you allow the server to chase referrals on your behalf, you may end up waiting quite a while for a subtree search to complete because it has to contact other servers that are on the other side of the world. If you have an environment where all your servers don't speak LDAP and this option is set, you won't see any portions of your tree that are only held on non-LDAP servers. To avoid this, configure at least one of your LDAP servers that supports referrals to hold a replica of the information that is held on the non-LDAP servers.

The Default Referral text field allows you to specify a default referral to be used when you've chosen the Always Refer option. This could be used when you have an LDAP server in your directory tree that doesn't use standard references. To specify a default referral, type the URL of the server to refer to in this field. (LDAP URLs are covered near the end of Chapter 5.) Only the host, port, and DN parts of the LDAP URL are used here. If I wanted to set a default referral to my server at home, I would enter `ldap://myserver.myhome.net:389`.

When NDS cannot locate a referral to a server that contains an entry, it sends the URL in the default referral field as a referral. If nothing is specified in the default referral field, then a noSuchObject error is sent.

NOTE

Allow Clear Text Passwords

The simple form of an LDAP bind is achieved by sending your DN and unencrypted password to the server. As you can imagine, sending your password over the Internet can be very risky. Because this presents such a security problem, the Novell LDAP server won't allow you to bind this way by default; you must first check the Allow Clear Text Passwords option.

If Allow Clear Text Passwords is unchecked, your simple bind request fails unless it's made over an SSL connection (see the discussion of SSL earlier in this chapter). You may want to allow clear text passwords over the normal unsecured TCP connection if you're working in a test environment or if you are not worried about security. We did just that when we installed the server in Chapter 2.

If the TCP port is disabled (see the preceding LDAP Server Settings), you won't be able to bind with a clear text password—regardless of what you set this option to.

NOTE

Proxy Username

By default, when a user performs an anonymous bind (doesn't specify a password), a special pseudo-object in the directory calculates access control for that user. This object is termed [Public]. You may see the word [Public] when you're setting access control rights. By default, this pseudo-object can browse the entire tree hierarchy and read a limited number of attributes on entries. The attributes that [Public] can read are those that have the X-NDS_PUBLIC_READ option set to true.

For more information on this topic, see Chapter 7.

X-REF

If you'd like to have an anonymous bind use a different object in the tree, you can specify that object in the Proxy Username field. By doing this, you can restrict the types of objects and attributes that anonymous users can access by setting the appropriate access controls on the proxy user object.

The proxy username must be a DN. To easily select an object, click the directory browser button to the right of the text field. A dialog box appears that allows you to choose an object in the tree.

The Proxy Username DN appears in NDAP form — that is, it is dot-separated instead of comma-separated, and the RDNs don't require types (such as cn=). The Proxy User object must be one that does not have a password.

NOTE

Server List

The next tab panel lists all the LDAP Server objects with which this LDAP Group object is associated. When you install a Novell LDAP server, a single LDAP Group object and a single LDAP Server object are created, and the two are associated. If you've installed multiple Novell LDAP servers in your tree and want to use a single LDAP Group object to store the shared settings for all the LDAP servers, use the Add button on this panel to add the remaining LDAP Server objects.

When an LDAP Server object is added to this list, the LDAP Group setting in that LDAP Server object is reset to the name of this LDAP Group. An alternate way to make this association is to set the desired LDAP Group name in the LDAP Server object.

Attribute and Class Maps

We covered Attribute and Class name mapping in Chapter 7 and showed how to use ConsoleOne to make the mappings. To recap: LDAP schema element names, specifically the names of object classes and attribute types, are more restrictive than NDS names. The Attribute and Class Map tab panels provide a way to map legal LDAP schema names to existing NDS schema names.

Refer to Chapter 7 if you need more specific information about schema name mapping.

X-REF

Read Only Information: The Root DSE

Version 3 of the LDAP protocol defined a standard way for an LDAP server to advertise certain information about itself, such as where the schema is located, what extensions and controls it supports, and so on. This is done through a special unnamed entry at the root of the tree called the *root DSE*. The root DSE holds information that is specific for the particular server you are connected to. This entry is not returned to the client as part of any normal search operation because it's not really an entry in the tree.

To read this entry, you perform a special search on an LDAPv3 server, specifying no name (an empty string) for the base DN, a scope of base, and use the filter "(objectclass=*)". This causes the server to return the root DSE as an entry consisting of a set of operational attributes. You may use the ldapsearch utility located in the Utilities directory on the CD-ROM to read this entry by typing `ldapsearch -h <server address> -b "" -s base objectclass=* subschemaSubentry`, replacing `<server address>` with the server's IP or DNS address.

The Standard Root DSE Operational Attributes

RFC 2251 and RFC 2252 specify a set of standard attributes that LDAP servers should return from the root DSE. These are:

▸ `namingContexts`: This attribute holds the names (DNs) of the roots of all the partitions that this server holds replicas of. If the server holds replicas of the entire tree, it contains an empty value.

Partitions are covered in Chapter 8.

X-REF

► `altServer`: This attribute holds the names of other servers that may be contacted in the event that this server is unavailable. These server names are in the form of a URL.

See the "LDAP URLs" section of Chapter 5 for more information on the way LDAP URLs look.

X-REF

► `supportedExtension`: This attribute holds the OIDs of all the LDAPv3 extended requests and responses that this server supports. IETF Internet-Drafts and RFCs that define LDAPv3 extended operations always assign a numeric OID to them as identifiers. This attribute may be examined to see which ones the server knows about and supports.

► `supportedControl`: Like the `supportedExtension` attribute, this attribute holds the OIDs of the LDAPv3 operation controls that it supports.

Chapter 9 covers LDAPv3 controls and extended operations.

X-REF

► `supportedSASLMechanisms`: If the server supports SASL authentication mechanisms, they are listed as values of this attribute.

► `supportedLDAPVersion`: This holds values of the version of the LDAP protocol supported by this server. LDAPv3 servers will often list 2 as well as 3 in this attribute, signifying that you may send LDAPv2 requests as well as LDAPv3 requests to it.

► `subschemaSubentry`: This holds the name (DN) of the entry or entries that are subschema entries for this server. The subschema entries hold the schema for the directory or for a part of the directory.

Chapter 7 discusses schema and subschema subentries.

X-REF

Novell-Specific Root DSE Attributes

Although the Novell LDAP server advertises information through the standard root DSE attributes where applicable, there is much more information that needs to be conveyed to an LDAP client. Novell has defined a few more attributes that it uses to advertise LDAP server-specific data in the root DSE. These are:

- `vendorName`: This holds a string that signifies the maker of the LDAP server. In Novell's case, this is "Novell, Inc."

- `vendorVersion`: This holds the version number of the server. Oftentimes, an LDAP server contains certain anomalies that must be worked around. These anomalies are fixed in subsequent versions of the server and may cause the work-around for the previous problem to malfunction. LDAP client application writers may use this attribute to better understand when their programs need to work around a particular bug.

- `directoryTreeName`: This holds the name of the NDS tree that this server is part of.

Secure Sockets Layer Configuration

When a connection is made between the LDAP client and server, it can be either an unencrypted or an encrypted connection. The protocol used to encrypt an LDAP connection is called Secure Sockets Layer (SSL).

An Overview of the SSL Protocol

The SSL protocol was originally defined by Netscape and has been accepted by the IETF as a way to securely transmit data over TCP/IP. The SSL protocol runs between the TCP/IP and LDAP protocols, as shown in Figure 10.5.

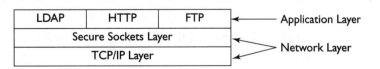

FIGURE 10.5

The SSL Protocol runs below LDAP and above TCP/IP.

The SSL protocol uses public/private key technology and X.509 certificates to perform the following tasks:

▸ Authenticate the server to the client

▸ Authenticate the client to the server (optionally)

▸ Encrypt the data that flows between the client and the server

The first two tasks take place during the *SSL handshake*. This is a sequence of events that takes place between the client and server that initializes and starts the SSL session.

Server Authentication

When performing an SSL handshake, the client is able to use the certificate sent by the server to ensure that the server you're talking to is really the server you intended to talk to. This step always happens during an SSL handshake because it is seen as a necessary security measure.

Client Authentication

In the same manner as server authentication, the server may request that the client send its certificate, which the server then uses to verify that the client is a valid entity in the LDAP directory. Client authentication is optional in the SSL protocol and is configurable on the server by marking the Enable Mutual Authentication checkbox on the SSL Configuration tab of the LDAP Server property page in ConsoleOne. When mutual authentication is used, the LDAP server uses the client certificate to authenticate the connection. This method of authentication is oftentimes preferred because the user's password doesn't have to be sent with the bind operation.

SSL Data Encryption

Once the authentication has happened, the TCP/IP connection is secured from prying eyes. This is done by using secrets and keys passed back and forth during the SSL handshake. Nearly a dozen different cipher mechanisms may be used to encrypt the data. The mechanism used for any one SSL session is agreed upon during the SSL handshake. We won't take the time to cover the cipher mechanisms here, save to say that the RSA mechanism is the one typically used by most SSL-enabled clients and servers, including Novell's. Another benefit of SSL data transfer is that the protocol ensures that the data integrity has not been compromised. In other words, it prevents someone from tampering with the data as it is sent between the client and server.

The SSL Handshake

A number of messages must be sent between the client and server before SSL data encryption begins. This exchange is called the SSL handshake. We won't go into all the details of what is sent back and forth; instead, refer to Figure 10.6 while we highlight the important pieces in the sequence, as follows:

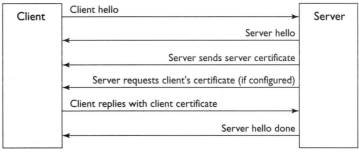

FIGURE 10.6

The SSL handshake

1. The client initiates the SSL handshake by sending an SSL hello message to the server. The message contains some preliminary data that is used by the server.

2. The server replies with its own SSL hello message with similar data. The server also sends its certificate so that the client can authenticate it.

3. The client performs a number of tests on the server's certificate to authenticate the server. These tests include:

   a. Ensuring that the certificate is valid

   b. Ensuring that the client trusts the Certificate Authority that issued the server's certificate

c. Comparing parts of the certificate to a copy of the certificate that the client previously obtained from the server

If the client cannot authenticate the server, the handshake is aborted.

NOTE

4. If the server is configured to do so, it sends a request for the client's certificate.

5. If requested, the client sends its certificate along with its digital signature to the server and the server attempts to authenticate the client. Among the steps used to authenticate the client, the server:

a. Validates the digital signature passed to it by using the public key in the certificate

b. Ensures that the certificate has not expired

c. Ensures that the server trusts the Certificate Authority that issued the client's certificate

d. Uses the subject name in the certificate to authenticate the user to the LDAP directory

6. After all authentication has completed, the server sends an SSL hello done message to the client.

Getting the Server Certificate

As you can see from the preceding steps, the client needs to have a copy of the server certificate if it is going to authenticate the server. To get a copy of the server's certificate, you must:

▸ Create a *Certificate Authority* (CA) in the directory.

▸ Use the CA to create a Key Material object.

▸ Export the server certificate using the key material.

Some or all of these things may have happened when you installed the server. In case these things didn't happen, the following directions will guide you through the process.

Creating a CA

A Certificate Authority is an entity that creates and digitally signs X.509 certificates. You may be familiar with some of the better-known certificate authorities such as Verisign. NDS allows you to create your own Certificate Authority so that you may have a centralized source of certificates within your directory.

Before creating the CA, you must make sure that Public Key Infrastructure (PKI) services are running. On NetWare, type `load PKI`. On NT, select pki.dlm from the NDS Server Console and click Start. On Solaris, type `npki start` from the /etc/init.d directory to run the PKI daemon. On Linux, type `npki start` from the /etc/rc.d/init.d directory to run the PKI daemon. If PKI services aren't running on the server with which the CA is associated, the CA will not be created.

Use ConsoleOne to create a CA. From ConsoleOne, click the tree icon that represents your tree. This should expose one or more containers in the list on the right, including one called Security. Select the Security container and from the menu, choose File, New, Object.

A dialog box appears that contains a list of all the objects that you're able to create at this point in the directory. Select the one named NDSPKI:Certificate Authority and click OK.

The next dialog box that appears is shown in Figure 10.7. From this dialog box, you must specify a server with which to associate the CA, as well as a name for the CA.

Click the directory browser button to the right of the Host server text field to facilitate choosing a host server. The host server is the NDS server that does all the work when a new certificate is to be created or signed. In Figure 10.7, we chose the same NDS server that was created during our installation by double-clicking the Administration container in the selection dialog box to move into that container.

Give the CA a name and click Next and then Finish. After ConsoleOne has finished creating the CA object, you are able to view it in the Security container.

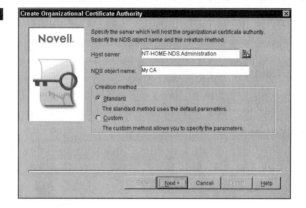

FIGURE   10.7

*Creating a
Certificate Authority*

Creating the Key Material Object

Now that you have a CA, you may create what is known as the *Key Material* object. The key material object exports the server certificate so that your client can authenticate it when performing an SSL handshake.

In ConsoleOne, select the container that contains the server associated with your CA. In our example, it's the Administration object. Next, choose New, Object from the File menu. This produces a New Object dialog box. From the Class list in the New Object dialog box, select NDSPKI:Key Material and then click OK. A dialog box called Create Server Certificate (Key Material) appears, as shown in Figure 10.8.

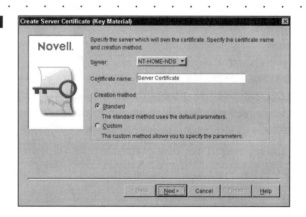

FIGURE   10.8

*Creating the
Server Certificate*

Select the name of the server associated with the CA you just created; then enter a name for the certificate. Choose Next and then Finish to complete the creation of the certificate.

IMPORTANT

The Create Server Certificate wizard allows you to optionally check a Custom creation method option. Do this if your browser software or SDK version uses a smaller key size (is of a lesser encryption strength) than your NDS software. Doing this allows you to specify the key size used to create the certificate. If your server's certificate uses a larger key size than your browser software, your browser or SDK will not be able to consume the certificate.

Associating the Key Material with the LDAP Server

Now that you have a key material object, it needs to be associated with the LDAP server. This way, when you attempt to make an SSL connection with the server, it knows which certificate to send to you to be authenticated.

Right-click the LDAP Server object; then choose the SSL tab. Click the directory browser button to the right of the SSL Certificate text window and choose the key material object you just created. Click OK to dismiss this dialog box.

Exporting the Server Certificate

For your client to authenticate the server, it must have a copy of the server certificate handy. You must export the certificate to your disk so that you can later import it to the appropriate client certificate database.

Select the new key material object and then choose Properties from the File menu. Select the Certificates tab; then click Export. You see a dialog box like the one in Figure 10.9. Make sure the format of the certificate is in DER format.

F I G U R E 10.9

Exporting the Server Certificate

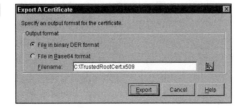

Before clicking the Export button on this dialog box, you may need to change the extension of the filename. If you are using the certificate with the SDK or with any Netscape tools, such as Netscape Navigator, change the extension to .x509, as shown in Figure 10.9. If you are using it with Microsoft products, such as Microsoft Internet Explorer, leave it as a .der extension. Note the name and location of the file to be exported, and then click the Export button to copy the file to your disk.

Importing the Server Certificate

Now that you have a copy of the server certificate on disk, you may need to import it into a certificate database before applications or SDKs can use it. Chapter 4 talks about what you need to do with the certificate on the client side before consuming it with SDK calls. Here we go over the method used to import it for use by one popular browser's address book.

Importing for Use by Netscape Navigator

If you'd like to use Netscape's Navigator and Communicator with Novell's LDAP server, you can use Netscape Navigator itself to import the server certificate. From a browser window, choose Open Page from the File menu. Either type the name of the .x509 file or click Choose File to select the certificate that was exported to your disk; change the file type to All Files (*.*) so that you can see the file.

IMPORTANT

If you are running Netscape Navigator in a Windows environment, you need to extend your registry before importing the server certificate. To do this, open the file called X509.REG in the directory that NDS was installed in.

Upon opening the certificate, a New Certificate Authority wizard is launched. Click the Next button until you come to the dialog box shown in Figure 10.10.

Check the "Accept this Certificate Authority for Certifying network sites" option (you may check the others as well if you wish); then click Next and follow the instructions until the wizard is done. After finishing this, you'll be able to make secure connections to your LDAP server with Netscape's Address book.

FIGURE 10.10

Importing the Server Certificate into Netscape Navigator

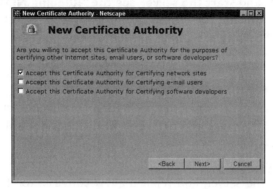

LDAP Server Command Line Options

There are no startup options for LDAP at this time; only a few command line directives are available on NetWare. To see the command line directives, type `ldap help` at the console screen on NetWare. You'll notice that only three commands are available at this time: LDAP Refresh, LDAP Refresh Immediate, and LDAP Help.

LDAP Refresh Immediate

The LDAP server reads all its configuration settings from the directory when it starts up and stores those settings in memory for quick retrieval. This works great until you happen to change a few settings. If you change any LDAP configuration settings through the ConsoleOne management utility, ConsoleOne sends a message to the LDAP server instructing it to refresh itself, meaning that the LDAP server rereads the settings from the directory. On the other hand, if you update some LDAP configurations with some other tool or API, you need to force the server to refresh itself. You may do this by typing `LDAP Refresh Immediate` at the console screen on NetWare. This command is unavailable on Solaris and NT. To refresh an LDAP server running on Solaris or NT, either stop and start the server, or use ConsoleOne.

X-REF

To stop and start the server, see the "Running NDS and LDAP" section in Chapter 2. To use ConsoleOne to refresh the server, refer to the "Editing the LDAP Server" in this chapter.

Setting the Refresh Interval

If you don't cause the server to refresh itself, it will automatically do so every 30 minutes. You can change the next date, time, and interval that the server will refresh itself by typing `LDAP Refresh <date> <time> <interval>`, replacing `<date>` with the next date to refresh the server, replacing `<time>` with the next time to refresh the server, and replacing `<interval>` to change the number of seconds between refresh cycles. If you set date and time to 00:00:00, the current date and time will be used.

You may also type `LDAP Refresh` to view the current settings.

Tuning the LDAP Server

In general, people tend to want two things out of a directory: fast search speed and high scalability. In general, two things get you there: lots of memory and lots of disk space. You can also realize performance gain by increasing the number of processors in your machine.

When talking about scalability, most people are referring to the number of objects that can reside in the directory. NDS has been populated with a billion users and has been able to maintain very good search response speeds at that number. The number of concurrent connections is another scalability concern — especially for those who want to run a high-traffic web site. NDS currently handles more than 1,500 simultaneous connections on NetWare, 300 on NT, and 700 on Solaris.

As far as speed goes, high search speed is generally sought after — and is generally obtained by creating the right indexes and using caches. People aren't usually too concerned about high performance when objects are being updated.

Speeding up Searches: Creating Indexes

When you perform an LDAP search, you specify, among other things, a search filter. This can be something simple like (cn=tom swift) or more complex like

(&(objectclass=person)(&(cn>=n)(cn<=o)(!(cn=o)))). In any case, the ldap server has to somehow find the directory entries that match that search filter. To quickly find the entries that match your search filter, Novell's LDAP server uses indexes.

What Is an Index?

An index is simply a way of grouping together all the entries that have something in common, in our case, the attribute you are searching for, and typically sorting the entries based on that attribute. When an index is built, you specify an attribute. Refer to Figure 10.11 for a visual representation of an index.

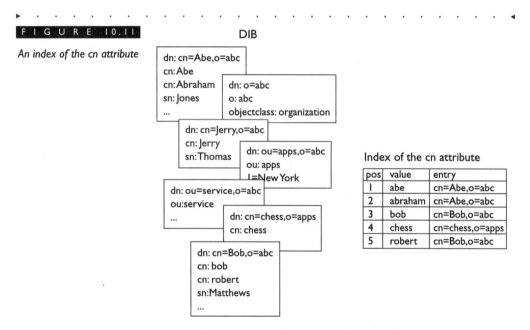

FIGURE 10.11

An index of the cn attribute

In Figure 10.11, the set of entries on the left represents all the entries in a directory. The set of entries on the right represents all the entries from the first set that are indexed when an index is created where the attribute used is cn.

When a search is performed, and the filter contains a cn attribute, the server uses this index to quickly find the matching entries. We won't go into the details of exactly how the server uses indexes to speed up the search operation, save to say that the index is ordered and is, in most cases, a smaller set than the entire set of directory entries. If we were to send a search to the server with a filter of (cn=a*), it could quickly discover, because the cn attribute is ordered, that cn=abe,o=abc is the only entry that needs to be returned.

Index Matching Rules When creating a new index, you must specify the attribute to be indexed, as well as a rule. The index rule determines what kinds of searches will use that index. In general, there are three types of searches: presence, value, or substring, and as such, these are the three types of index rules available. Here's a description of each type of index rule and the kind of searches that will use that index rule.

- ▸ **Presence:** This type of index is used when the search is a presence (or exists) type of search. An example is when you'd like to find all entries that have a cn attribute (the cn attribute has at least one value); the search filter is (cn=*).

- ▸ **Value:** This type of index is used when searching for an exact value. (cn=abe) is a good example of a search that would use a value index.

- ▸ **Substring:** Substring indexes are the most costly to create and maintain but are the most flexible. This index type is used when searching for a substring of an attribute value. Examples are (cn=*ini*), (cn=*ette), and (cn=will*). The first substring example is a query for entries that hold cn values that have the string ini anywhere in them. This is called an *any* substring filter and would match for cn values like finicky, initial, and milini. The second substring example is a query for entries whose cn value ends with the string ette. This is called an *ends with* substring filter and would match for cn values such as "Suzette" and "Minette." The third substring example is a query for entries that hold cn values that begin with the string will. This is called a *begins with* substring filter and would match for cn values such as "Will," "William," and "Willy."

TIP

A value index may be used for *begins with* searches such as (cn=will*). This is important to know because it's always better to create a value index as opposed to a substring index if you can. Begins with search filters are used much more often than the other two types of substring filters.

Why Create Indexes?

The most obvious answer is search performance. On a test server that holds two million objects, Novell finds that a search that normally takes 18 minutes to complete only takes 0.31 seconds after indexing the attribute being searched for.

Aside from the performance reason, an index must exist if you want to use the Server Side Sorting (SSS) control or the Virtual List View (VLV) control when performing LDAP searches on the Novell server. Both of these controls sort the result set that is returned from the search operation. You specify an attribute in the SSS control to be used as the sort key. The LDAP server uses the index for that attribute to return the sorted result set. This is possible because the index is already sorted — otherwise, the server would have to gather together the entire result set before returning entries to you and perform the sorting routines at that time. Currently, the LDAP server either ignores the request to sort the data, or fails the request (depending on the criticality flag in the control) if there is no index of the attribute to be sorted.

Creating an Index

The easiest way to create an index is by using the ConsoleOne management utility. The NDS Server object holds index definitions.

1. Using ConsoleOne, locate the NDS Server object. This is different from the LDAP Server object; it's typically in the same container and named `<Server>-NDS` (where `<Server>` is the name of your server).

2. Edit the properties of the NDS Server object by selecting it and choosing Properties from the File menu.

3. Switch to the Indexes tab. You should see a tab page similar to the one in Figure 10.12. Notice that there is already a set of predefined indexes. These are indexes that Novell has found to be commonly used.

4. Let's say your server receives many queries for e-mail addresses, so you want to create a new index on that attribute. Click Add to bring up the Create Index dialog box.

FIGURE 10.12

Index definitions in ConsoleOne

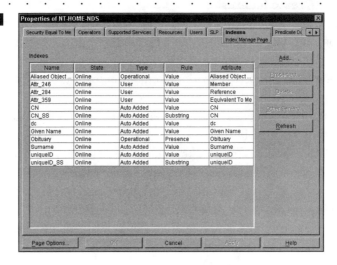

5. Enter a name such as **E-Mail value** for the Index Name.

6. Click Attributes to bring up a list of attributes from which to choose.

7. Select "Internet EMail Address" from the list of attributes and click the right arrow to move it to the list of selected attributes.

NOTE

The attribute names listed here are NDAP names. In our example, the LDAP name for the e-mail attribute is "mail," while the NDAP name is "Internet EMail Address." If you cannot find the attribute you're looking for here, it may be because there is an LDAP-to-NDAP name mapping. See Chapter 7 for more information on attribute name mappings.

8. Press OK to dismiss the Select Attributes dialog box.

NOTE

The only other option you can choose at this point is the matching rule with which this index coincides. For this example, we leave it as Value (equality), assuming that incoming searches are for the entire e-mail name (such as mail=jdoe@abc.com).

9. Press OK to dismiss this dialog box. You see the new index added to the bottom of the list.

At any time, you may click Properties to view the status of the index. It may take some time for the index to be completely built. While it's being built, the state remains at "Bringing Online." Once the index has been built, the state changes to "Online." At that point, the server uses the index and your search response time should increase.

Creating an Index with LDAP

If you'd rather create an index with LDAP, you need to know the following information:

▶ All indexes are stored in a multi-valued attribute called `indexDefinition` on the NDS server object.

▶ Each value of this attribute holds all the information for a single index. The string representation looks like: `<version>$<indexName>$<state>$<rule>$<type>$1$<attributeName>`.

  • `<version>` is a version value for indexes. This must be set to 0 for NDS 8.5.

  • `<indexName>` is the name you choose to name your index. We named our index "E-Mail value" in the preceding example.

  • `<state>` is a read-only value and may be one of the following:
    0 = suspended
    1 = bringing online
    2 = online
    3 = pending creation
    When creating a new index, set this to 1.

  • `<rule>` is the matching rule to be used by the index and may be:
    0 = value (equality or begins with substring)
    1 = presence
    2 = ends with substring or contains substring

- `<type>` shows how the index was created. It may be:

  0 = user defined

  1 = added when attribute was created

  2 = needed for operation of system (system created)

  3 = other system-created index

  When creating a new index, you must set this value to 0.

- `<attributeName>` is the name of the attribute to be indexed. This is the LDAP attribute name as opposed to the NDAP attribute name.

We added an e-mail index using ConsoleOne. If we were to add the same index using LDAP, we could use the following LDIF data to do so:

```
dn: cn=<myServer>-NDS,o=Novell
changetype: modify
add: indexDefinition
indexDefinition: 0$E-Mail value$1$0$0$1$mail
```

Note that any occurrence of the $ character in the name portion would need to be escaped using the \xx notation where xx is the hexadecimal equivalent of the character being replaced. In other words, to name an index $Money$ value, for the money attribute, you would specify `0$\24Money\24 value$1$0$0$1$money` for the indexDefinition value.

How Many Indexes Should I Create?

Though indexes are invaluable in increasing search performance, they come at a price. Every time you update an attribute value in the directory—whether you're adding, deleting, or replacing—that attribute value must also be updated in the corresponding index or indexes for the attribute. In other words, the more indexes you define, the slower updates will be for objects using those attributes you index. Luckily, there is a way to research those attributes that make more sense to index.

What Should I Index? Using Predicate Statistics

Predicate statistics is a fancy way of saying, "Show which search filters are most often used." Novell's LDAP server comes with a built-in mechanism that lets you track the types and frequency of search filters that are being sent to it. By examining this data, you are able to determine which attributes should be indexed on your server.

Enabling the Predicate Statistics Object

When you install NDS, a predicate statistics object is placed in the directory and associated with the NDS server. The predicate statistics object has a flag that enables or disables the tracking of search filters, which is off by default. You need to turn it on to start tracking search filter frequencies.

NOTE

Enabling the predicate statistics feature decreases performance. It should be used to gather data, and turned off in a production environment.

If you are experiencing a performance problem with a specific application, you should run that application with the predicate statistics feature enabled for some time — that way, you end up with a good representation of the types of queries that that application is sending to the server.

The easiest way to enable and track search filters is through the ConsoleOne management utility. From ConsoleOne, select the NDS server object and edit its properties by selecting Properties from the File menu. Select the Predicate Data tab to reveal the properties page. Click Properties to bring up the dialog box shown in Figure 10.13.

F I G U R E   10.13

Enabling Predicate Statistics in ConsoleOne

Change the State from Off to On and dismiss the dialog box by clicking OK. After completing this step, you must either wait up to 30 minutes for the background process that controls this feature to run, or you can stop and restart the NDS server. This can be done on NetWare by entering **unload ds** and then **load ds** at the command screen. On NT, you can use the NDS console to stop and start NDS. On Solaris, type **/etc/init.d/ndsd stop** then **/etc/init.d/ ndsd start**. On Linux, type **/etc/init.d/rc.d/ndsd stop** then **/etc/init. d/rc.d/ndsd start**.

Reading Predicate Statistics

After the server has been running for some time with search requests being sent to it, you can examine the statistics by clicking the View button on the Predicate Data properties tab of the NDS server object in ConsoleOne. You see a dialog box similar to the one in Figure 10.14, which shows the search filters that have been serviced on the right and their frequencies on the left.

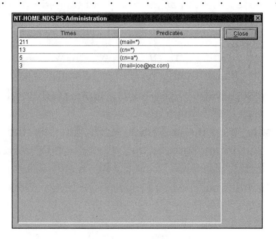

FIGURE 10.14

Viewing Predicate Statistics in ConsoleOne

If you find that a search filter is being used that contains attributes that haven't yet been indexed, you'll likely realize a performance gain by indexing those attributes. Notice that the search filters also show you which matching rule was used when attribute values are being searched. Sometimes, exact values are being searched for, while other times a substring or the simple presence of the attribute is being queried. In Figure 10.14, you can see that the filter mail=* is being searched for quite often. This tells you that you should create an index for mail using the presence rule.

The Database Cache

Though NDS employs many caches, only the underlying database cache is configurable. The server uses the database cache when you're searching or resolving DNs. The database cache is most effectively used when the same directory entries are being resolved, or when searches are being repeated. This is because the cache resides in memory, which is much faster to access than the hard drive. As you resolve names and perform searches, those entries are placed in the cache for quick subsequent retrievals.

How Big Should My Cache Be?

If you know that your server will be hit with many random requests, and your database cache is too small, not only will you see no benefit, but also you may see a decline in performance. This is because the server stays busy stuffing entries into the cache, but oftentimes the entries that it needs to retrieve have been pushed out of the cache by other entries being pushed into it.

If you have enough memory, Novell recommends that your database cache be twice the size of your DIB. You can calculate the size of your DIB by adding together the size of all the NDS* files in the directory that holds the database. On NetWare, this directory is hidden and is called _NETWARE on the SYS volume. On NT, the files are in a directory called DIBFiles in the NDS directory. The NDS directory resides in the directory that you installed NDS to. On Solaris, the directory is var/nds/dib/. The files are named NDS.DB, NDS00001.LOG, NDS.01, NDS.02, and so on.

TIP

> On NetWare, the _NETWARE directory is hidden. To view its contents, run the toolbox.nlm utility found on the CD-ROM in the utilities\netware\toolbox directory, then type `dir _netware`.

If the combined size of the NDS* files in the dib directory is larger than the available memory in your server, you may want to consider increasing your server's ram.

Older versions of NDS set the cache size to 8MB by default. If you wanted a larger cache, you had to manually set it. Current versions of NDS (NDS 8.5 and later) are a bit smarter about the way they allocate the cache size. When NDS 8.5 and later starts, it sets 70 percent of the total available memory aside for the database cache. Every 15 seconds, it reevaluates the total available memory and resizes the cache accordingly. This reduces the risk of NDS becoming a memory hog, while at the same time ensures that you have a reasonably large cache.

Configuring the Cache

If you want to adjust the percentage of free memory that NDS allocates for the cache, or if you want to force a specific limit, you can do so. Work is currently underway to enable you to easily configure the size settings. For now, you must either use a DSTrace option or edit a file in the database directory.

Using DSTrace to Set the Cache Size   On NetWare and Solaris, you can use DSTrace to examine the current cache size by performing the following steps (on Solaris, type `NDSTRACE` instead of `DSTRACE`):

1. Type `SET DSTRACE=ON`.

2. Type `SET DSTRACE=*P`.

3. Switch to the DSTrace window to view the current cache size. It's reported to the right of the string SMI Max Cache. The size is in bytes, so if it reads SMI Max Cache = 8192000, it means that the cache size is 8MB.

You can manually override this value with another DSTrace set option. Type `SET DSTRACE=!MBxxx`, where xxx is the number (in bytes). For example, `SET DSTRACE=!MB20000000` changes the database cache limit to 20MB. If you use this method of changing the cache size, remember that this sets a static cache limit that won't shrink or grow to accommodate other resources on your machine.

Using the Cache Configuration File   Another way to modify the cache size is by editing or creating a file called _NDSDB.INI in the DIB directory (see the "How Big Should My Cache Be" section to find the database directory). The _NDSDB.INI file can hold any of the following statements:

▶ `cache=<cacheBytes>`: Where `<cacheBytes>` is the limit (in bytes) of the cache. If this is set, the value does not change

- ► `cache=<options>`: Where `<options>` is a set of any of the following options:

  - • `%:<percentage>` represents a percentage of the available or physical memory.

  - • `AVAIL | TOTAL` determines whether the percentage of memory is based off the available memory or the total memory. Note: These are ignored if the DYN option is set.

  - • `MIN:<bytes>` causes the cache to be at least this large.

  - • `MAX:<bytes>` sets the maximum size that the cache may be.

  - • `LEAVE:<bytes>` specifies the amount of memory to leave (not allocate for the cache).

  - • `DYN | HARD` determines whether the limit is dynamic and may change as computer resources change, or is static and never changes.

- ► `cacheadjustinterval=<seconds>`: How often the cache size is reevaluated. This is ignored if the cache limit is HARD.

- ► `cachecleanupinterval=<seconds>`: How often the cache is purged.

Here are some examples of what you could place in the .INI file:

- ► `cache=DYN,%:75,MIN:16000000`: This specifies a dynamic limit of 75 percent of available memory, with a minimum of 16 megabytes.

- ► `cache=HARD,%:75,MIN:16000000,MAX: 80000000`: This specifies a hard limit of 75 percent total physical memory, with a minimum of 16 megabytes and a maximum of 80 megabytes.

- ► `cache=8000000`: This specifies a hard limit of 8 megabytes.

Once you've edited the _NDSDB.INI file, you must save it and restart NDS for the settings to take effect.

Summary

Though we had to use a configuration file for the last group of settings discussed in this chapter, you'll notice that most configurable LDAP server settings were made to the LDAP Server and LDAP Group objects in the directory. And the most convenient tool to make those changes is ConsoleOne. This is because ConsoleOne comes with special snap-ins that make a lot of the configuration tasks discussed here easier.

As NDS continues to evolve, watch for the set of configurable options on the LDAP Server, LDAP Group, and NDS Server objects to grow and to become increasingly easier to use.

CHAPTER 11

LDIF and Import/Export Utilities

The focus of the chapters in Part II of this book is on writing LDAP client applications. This chapter looks at a different side of LDAP: LDAP utilities. No matter how good your directory-enabled application is, you won't be able to test and deploy it unless you and your customers have a way to get data into their directory.

When you're testing your LDAP-enabled application, you'll need an easy way to load data into your test environment. Often, your customers will have data that they want to migrate from existing directories as they deploy your application. In both of these cases, the LDAP Data Interchange Format (LDIF) and utilities that produce and use it can make it a lot easier to solve these problems. This chapter explains the details of LDIF and shows you how to use LDIF to solve a number of common problems.

We also show you how to use the Novell Import/Export utility to quickly import data into LDAP directories, migrate data between LDAP directories, and export data from Novell's LDAP directory and other LDAP directories.

Since LDIF closely parallels the LDAP add, delete, modify, and modify DN (rename) operations, we recommend that you familiarize yourself with them before continuing in this chapter.

X-REF

You can get a quick introduction to these operations by reading the "LDAP Operations" section in Chapter 1. They are also covered in depth in Chapter 6.

▶ · ◀

An Introduction to LDIF

The roots of LDIF go back to the original reference implementation of LDAP written at the University of Michigan. The original designers of LDIF were Tim Howes, Mark Smith, and Gordon Good who were part of that project. The LDIF format developed at that time only allowed for the representation of directory data. (It could not explicitly represent modifications to be made to a directory.)

Since that time, LDIF has been progressing along the standards track in the IETF under the authorship of Gordon Good. Several successive Internet-Drafts have refined the file format and tightened the specification to ensure that it meets the author's intent. The most important changes made during this process were the addition of a new record type that extended LDIF to represent directory modifications as well as directory data along with the formal specification of how to represent internationalized values.

As of this writing, the Internet Engineering Steering Group (IESG) has just published "The LDAP Data Interchange Format (LDIF) — Technical Specification" as a Proposed Standard in RFC 2849.

What is LDIF?

LDIF is a widely used file format that describes directory information or modification operations that can be performed on a directory. LDIF is completely independent of the storage format used within any specific directory implementation and is therefore implementation-neutral. LDIF is typically used to export directory information from and import data to LDAP servers.

LDIF is designed to be human-consumable, meaning that the format can be easily read. The major exception to this rule is when the data is non-ASCII such as when a value is stored in binary format or is in a language other than English. In an effort to preserve readability, the LDIF specification even provides ways to somewhat mitigate this problem.

LDIF is designed to be easy to generate. This really simplifies things when you have to move data from some other proprietary format into an LDAP directory. Using tools like awk or Perl, you can often transform a file from some other format to LDIF with minimal effort. It's also easy to write scripts to generate test data in LDIF format.

LDIF intentionally mirrors many LDAP operations: a one-to-one correlation exists between LDIF changetypes (which we'll discuss shortly) and LDAP update operations. LDAP entries (like those returned from an LDAP search operation) can also be mapped directly to LDIF records.

LDIF File Format

The LDIF syntax is straightforward, and it's easy to write or generate files that conform to the syntax. Rather than bore you with a dramatic rendering of the formal syntax definition, we present the LDIF syntax through examples and discussion.

While we discuss every major feature of LDIF and what you need to know to generate conforming LDIF files, this informal approach may leave out some minor details that are spelled out precisely in the LDIF specification. If you are implementing an LDIF processor or simply want to know every nuance of LDIF, we encourage you to read the LDIF-related sections of this chapter to familiarize yourself with LDIF, and then read the LDIF specification, particularly the formal syntax definition with an eye toward these details. The LDIF specification is available at `http://www.ietf.org/rfc/rfc2849.txt`.

LDIF Version 0

Although not officially called version 0, the original LDIF file format developed as part of the University of Michigan LDAP implementation, and is often informally called version 0 to distinguish it from the IETF version 1 specification. We do not discuss this implementation of LDIF at any length in this book; however, in nearly all respects, LDIF version 1 is essentially a superset of version 0.

You can find additional information on LDIF version 0 at `http://www.umich.edu/~dirsvcs/ldap/doc/guides/slapd/toc.html`.

LDIF Version 1

Here are the basic rules for an LDIF version 1 file:

▸ The first non-comment line must be version: 1.

▸ A series of one or more records follows the version.

▸ Each record is composed of fields, one field per line.

▸ Lines are separated by either a new line or a carriage return/newline pair.

▸ Records are separated by one or more blank lines.

▸ Two distinct types of LDIF records exist: content records and change records. An LDIF file may contain an unlimited number of records, but they all have to be of the same type. You can't mix content records and change records in the same LDIF file.

TIP

Although you can't mix content and change records in the same LDIF file, LDIF change records that use the "add" changetype are roughly equivalent to content records. Since you can freely mix the various changetypes in an LDIF file, this enables you to have records that specify "content" (via the add changetype) and modifications (via the other LDIF changetypes) in a single LDIF file. We explain content and change records in detail in the next two sections of this chapter.

▶ Any line beginning with the hash character (#) is a comment and is ignored when processing the LDIF file.

LDIF Content Records

An LDIF content record represents the entire contents of a directory entry. Listing 11.1 is an example of an LDIF file with four content records:

LISTING 11.1

```
 1 version: 1

 2 dn: c=US
 3 objectClass: top
 4 objectClass: country
 5
 6 dn: l=San Francisco, c=US
 7 objectClass: top
 8 objectClass: locality
 9 st: San Francisco
10
11 dn: ou=Artists, l=San Francisco, c=US
12 objectClass: top
13 objectClass: organizationalUnit
14 telephoneNumber: +1 415 555 0000
15
```

Continued

(continued)

```
16 dn: cn=Peter Michaels, ou=Artists, l=San Francisco, c=US
17 sn: Michaels
18 givenname: Peter
19 objectClass: top
20 objectClass: person
21 objectClass: organizationalPerson
22 objectClass: iNetOrgPerson
23 telephonenumber: +1 415 555 0001
24 mail: Peter.Michaels@aaa.com
25 userpassword: Peter123
26
```

We now explain each part of this LDIF file.

Version Specifier

As required by the specification, the first line of the LDIF file contains the version. Zero or more spaces are allowed between the colon and the version number, which is currently defined to be 1 (one).

NOTE

> **Although a conforming LDIF file should always include a version specifier, Novell's utilities that process LDIF assume a file version of 1 when the version specifier is missing.**

Distinguished Name Specifier

The first line of every content record (lines 2, 6, 11, and 16 in our example) specifies the DN of the entry that it represents.

The DN specifier must take one of the following two forms:

```
dn: safe distinguished name
dn:: Base64 encoded distinguished name
```

Table 11.1 describes each of the distinguished name specifier elements.

TABLE 11.1	ELEMENT	DESCRIPTION
Distinguished Name Specifier Elements	dn	A keyword identifying this field as the DN portion of the content record.
	: (colon)	The separator used to indicate that this field contains a safe UTF-8 DN.
	:: (double colon)	The separator used to indicate that this field contains a Base64 encoded DN.
	safe distinguished name	A distinguished name (DN) as defined in RFC 2253 with certain restrictions to ensure that the string is a safe string. See the discussion below.
	Base64 encoded distingushed name	The Base64 encoding of the DN. Any distinguished name is allowed to be Base64 encoded, but some DNs must be Base64 encoded because they cannot otherwise be safely represented in an LDIF file. See the section on Base64 encoding later in this chapter.

Safe Strings

A safe string can begin with any character in the range 0x00 — 0x7F *except* the following:

- 0x00 (NUL)

- 0x0A (LF)

- 0x0D (CR)

- 0x20 (space " ")

- 0x3A (colon ":")

- 0x3C (less-than "<")

Subsequent characters in a safe string can be any character in the range 0x00 — 0x7F except the following:

- 0x00 (NUL)

- 0x0A (LF)

- 0x0D (CR)

IMPORTANT

Any distinguished name or attribute value that contains a prohibited character value must be Base64 encoded so that it can be safely represented in the LDIF file.

Line Delimiters

In LDIF files, the line separator can be either a newline or a carriage return/ newline pair. This resolves a common incompatibility between UNIX text files, which use a newline as the line separator and MS-DOS and Windows text files, which use a carriage return/newline pair as the line separator.

Record Delimiters

The blank lines (numbers 5, 10, 15, and 26) are record delimiters.

IMPORTANT

Note that every record of an LDIF file *including the last record* must be terminated with a record delimiter (one or blank lines). Although some implementations silently accept an LDIF file without a terminating record delimiter, the LDIF specification requires it.

TIP

A common error in LDIF files is to have stray white space (such as a leading space character) on the record separator line. When this happens, the LDIF parser doesn't recognize the record delimiter and two records are treated as a single record.

Attribute Value Specifier

The other lines in the content records are all value specifiers. Value specifiers must take on one of the following three forms:

```
attribute description: value
attribute description:: Base64 encoded value
attribute description:< url
```

Table 11.2 describes each of the attribute value specifier elements.

TABLE 11.2	ELEMENT	DESCRIPTION
Attribute Value Specifier Elements	attribute description	An attribute description as defined in Section 4.1.5 of RFC 2251. Note that an attribute description is an attribute type followed by zero or more options.
	: (colon)	The separator used to indicate that this field contains a string representation of the value.
	:: (double colon)	The separator used to indicate that this field contains a Base64 encoded representation of the value.
	:< (colon, less than)	The separator used to indicate that this field contains a URL.
	value	The string representation of the value.
	Base64 encoded value	The Base64 encoding of the string representation of a value. Any value is allowed to be Base64 encoded, but some values must be Base64 encoded because they cannot otherwise be safely represented in an LDIF file. See the previous discussion on safe strings.
	Url	A uniform resource locator as defined in RFC 1738. See the following "Using URLs in Attribute Value Specifiers" section for more details.

LDIF Change Records

LDIF change records contain modifications to be made to a directory. (Contrast this with LDIF content records that represent directory entries.) Any of the LDAP update operations: add, delete, modify, and modify DN can be represented in an LDIF change record.

NOTE

The Java LDAP SDK uses the rename method to issue the LDAP modify DN request. The LDIF format uses the term moddn to refer to the modify DN request.

LDIF change records use the very same format for distinguished name specifier, attribute value specifier and record delimiter as LDIF content records which we discussed in the previous section.

Changetype Specifier

A new keyword, changetype, is used in LDIF change records. The presence of the changetype field is what distinguishes an LDIF change record from an LDIF content record. The changetype field takes on one of the following five forms:

```
changetype: add
changetype: delete
changetype: moddn
changetype: modrdn
changetype: modify
```

Table 11.3 describes each of the elements of the changetype specifier.

TABLE 11.3 *Changetype Elements*	CHANGETYPE ELEMENT	DESCRIPTION
	changetype	A keyword identifying this record as a change record. The changetype field identifies the operation specified by the change record.

TABLE 11.3	CHANGETYPE ELEMENT	DESCRIPTION
Changetype Elements (continued)	: (colon)	Separates the changetype keyword from the rest of the field.
	add	A keyword indicating that the change record specifies an LDAP add operation.
	delete	A keyword indicating that the change record specifies an LDAP delete operation.
	moddn	A keyword indicating that the change record specifies an LDAP modify DN operation if the LDIF processor is bound to the LDAP server as a v3 client or a modify RDN operation if the LDIF processor is bound to the LDAP server as a v2 client.
	modrdn	A synonym for the moddn changetype. Even though the LDAPv2 modify RDN is a subset of the LDAPv3 modify DN operation, the modrdn and moddn keywords in LDIF are synonymous. The allowed behavior is determined by the protocol version being used by the client. (See the preceding description of the moddn keyword.)
	modify	A keyword indicating that the change record specifies an LDAP modify operation.

The Add Changetype

An add change record looks just like a content change record with the addition of the changetype: add field immediately before any attribute value fields. Here's the same LDIF file we showed previously, but we've changed all of the content records to change records with a changetype of add.

IMPORTANT

Remember: all records in an LDIF file have to be the same type. You can't mix content records and change records.

LISTING 11.2

```
 1 version: 1
 2 dn: c=US
 3 changetype: add
 4 objectClass: top
 5 objectClass: country
 6
 7 dn: l=San Francisco, c=US
 8 changetype: add
 9 objectClass: top
10 objectClass: locality
11 st: San Francisco
12
14 dn: ou=Artists, l=San Francisco, c=US
15 changetype: add
16 objectClass: top
17 objectClass: organizationalUnit
18 telephoneNumber: +1 415 555 0000
19
20 dn: cn=Peter Michaels, ou=Artists, l=San Francisco, c=US
21 changetype: add
22 sn: Michaels
23 givenname: Peter
24 objectClass: top
25 objectClass: person
26 objectClass: organizationalPerson
27 objectClass: inetOrgPerson
28 telephonenumber: +1 415 555 0001
29 mail: Peter.Michaels@aaa.com
30 userpassword: Peter123
31
```

The Delete Changetype

Because a delete change record specifies the deletion of an entry, the only fields required for a delete change record are the distinguished name specifier and a delete changetype. Here's the LDIF file you would use to delete the four entries created by the LDIF file just shown:

IMPORTANT

Note that we reversed the order of the entries. If we hadn't done so, the delete operations would fail since the container entries wouldn't be empty.

LISTING 11.3

```
1 version: 1
2 dn: cn=Peter Michaels, ou=Artists, l=San Francisco, c=US
3 changetype: delete
4
5 dn: ou=Artists, l=San Francisco, c=US
8 changetype: delete
9
10 dn: l=San Francisco, c=US
11 changetype: delete
12
13 dn: c=US
14 changetype: delete
15
```

The Modify Changetype

The modify changetype allows you to specify the addition, deletion, and replacement of attribute values for an entry that already exists. Modifications take one of the following three forms:

```
add: attribute type
delete: attribute type
replace: attribute type
```

Table 11.4 describes each of these modification specifiers.

TABLE 11.4 *Modification Specifier Elements*	MODIFICATION SPECIFIER ELEMENT	DESCRIPTION
	add	A keyword indicating that subsequent attribute value specifiers for the attribute type should be added to the entry.
	delete	A keyword indicating that values of the attribute type are to be deleted. If attribute value specifiers follow the delete field, the values given are deleted. If no attribute value specifiers follow the delete field, then all values are deleted. Note that if the attribute has no values, this operation fails, but the desired effect is still achieved because the attribute had no values to be deleted.
	replace	A keyword indicating that all the values of the attribute type are to be replaced. Any attribute value specifiers that follow the replace field become the new values for the attribute type. If no attribute value specifiers follow the replace field, then the current set of values is replaced with an empty set of values (which causes the attribute to be removed). Note that unlike the delete modification specifier, if the attribute has no values, the replace still succeeds.
	: (colon)	Separates the modification changetype from the attribute type.
	attribute type	An attribute type as defined in Section 4.1.4 of RFC 2251.

Example: Adding an Additional Telephone Number

Here's an example of a modify changetype that adds an additional telephone number to the cn=Peter Michaels entry:

```
1 version: 1
2 dn: cn=Peter Michaels, ou=Artists, l=San Francisco, c=US
3 changetype: modify
4 # add a telephone number to cn=Peter Michaels
4 add: telephonenumber
5 telephonenumber: +1 415 555 0002
6 -
7
```

Combining Modification Specifiers in a Single LDIF Record

Just as you can combine a mixture of modifications in a single LDAP modify request, you can specify multiple modifications in a single LDIF record. A line containing only the hyphen (-) character is used to mark the end of the attribute value specifications for each modification specifier.

Rather than show you examples of each modification specifier by itself, we now present an LDIF file containing a mixture of modifications. This LDIF file begins precisely as the previous example. The LDIF file documents itself via comments.

```
 1 version: 1
 2
 3 # An empty line to demonstrate that one or more
 4 # line separators between the version identifier
 5 # and the first record is legal.
 6
 7 dn: cn=Peter Michaels, ou=Artists, l=San Francisco, c=US
 8 changetype: modify
 9 # Add an additional telephone number value.
10 add: telephonenumber
11 telephonenumber: +1 415 555 0002
12 -
13 # Delete the entire fascimileTelephoneNumber attribute.
14 delete: facsimileTelephoneNumber
```

Continued

(continued)

```
15 -
16 # Replace the existing description (if any exists)
17 # with two new values.
18 replace: description
19 description: guitar player
20 description: solo performer
21 -
22 # Delete a specific value from the telephonenumber
23 # attribute.
24 delete: telephonenumber
25 telephonenumber: +1 415 555 0001
26 -
27 # Replace the existing title attribute with an empty
28 # set of values, thereby causing the title attribute
29 # to be removed.
30 replace: title
31 -
32
```

ModDN

The modify DN changetype enables you to rename an entry, move it, or both. When you use the modify DN changetype in an LDIF record three fields — two required and one optional — go along with it.

New RDN Specifier

The new RDN specifier gives the new name for the entry that will be assigned while processing this record. The new RDN specifier must take one of the following two forms:

```
newrdn: safe relative distinguished name
newrdn:: Base64 encoded relative distinguished name
```

Table 11.5 describes each of the new RDN specifier elements.

TABLE 11.5	ELEMENT	DESCRIPTION
New RDN Specifier Elements	newrdn	A keyword identifying this field as the desired new RDN for the entry.
	Safe relative distinguished name	The value of the new relative distinguished name (RDN) as defined in RFC 2253 with certain restrictions to ensure that the string is a safe string. See the discussion on safe strings in the previous "Distinguished Name Specifier" section for details.
	: (colon)	The separator used to indicate that this field contains a safe RDN.
	:: (double colon)	The separator used to indicate that this field contains a Base64 encoded RDN.
	Base64 encoded relative distingushed name	The Base64 encoding of the new RDN. Any RDN is allowed to be Base64 encoded, but some RDNs must be Base64 encoded because they cannot otherwise be safely represented in an LDIF file. See the discussion on safe strings in the "Distinguished Name Specifier" section and the section on Base64 encoding later in this chapter for details.

The new RDN specifier is required in all LDIF records with a modify DN changetype.

Delete Old RDN Specifier

The Delete Old RDN specifier is a flag that indicates whether the old RDN value should be replaced by the new RDN or if it should be kept. It takes one of the following two forms:

```
deleteoldrdn: 0
deleteoldrdn: 1
```

Table 11.6 describes each of the Delete Old RDN specifier elements.

T A B L E 11.6	ELEMENT	DESCRIPTION
Delete Old RDN Specifier Elements	deleteoldrdn: 0	Indicates that the old RDN value should be kept in the entry after it is renamed. Even so, this value is no longer a distinguished value that names the entry.
	deleteoldrdn: 1	Indicates that the old RDN value should be deleted when the entry is renamed.

New Superior Specifier

The new superior specifier gives the name of the new parent that will be assigned to the entry while processing the modify DN record. The new superior specifier must take one of the following two forms:

```
newsuperior: safe distinguished name
newsuperior:: Base64 encoded distinguished name
```

Table 11.7 describes each of the new superior specifier elements.

T A B L E 11.7	ELEMENT	DESCRIPTION
New Superior Specifier Elements	newsuperior	A keyword identifying this field as the desired new superior (parent) for the entry.
	: (colon)	The separator used to indicate that this field contains a safe DN.
	:: (double colon)	The separator used to indicate that this field contains a Base64 encoded DN.
	safe distinguished name	The distinguished name (DN), as defined in RFC 2253, of the entry's new superior with certain restrictions to ensure that the string is a safe string. See the discussion on safe strings in the "Distinguished Name Specifier" section for details.
	Base64 encoded distingushed name	The Base64 encoding of the new superior DN. Any DN is allowed to be Base64 encoded, but some DNs must be Base64 encoded because they cannot otherwise be safely represented in an LDIF file. See the discussion on safe strings in the "Distinguished Name Specifier" section for details.

NOTE

The new superior specifier is optional in LDIF records with a modify DN changetype. It is only given in cases where you want to move the entry.

Here's an example of a modify DN changetype that shows how to rename an entry:

LISTING 11.6

```
1 version: 1
2
3 # Rename ou=Artists to ou=West Coast Artists, and leave
4 # its old RDN value.
5 dn: ou=Artists,l=San Francisco,c=US
6 changetype: moddn
7 newrdn: ou=West Coast Artists
8 deleteoldrdn: 0
9
```

Here's an example of a modify DN changetype that shows how to move an entry:

LISTING 11.7

```
1 version: 1
2
3 # Move cn=Peter Michaels from
4 # ou=Artists,l=San Francisco,c=US to
5 # ou=Promotion,l=New York,c=US and delete the old RDN.
6 dn: cn=Peter Michaels,ou=Artists,l=San Francisco,c=US
7 changetype: moddn
8 newrdn: cn=Peter Michaels
9 deleteoldrdn: 1
10 newsuperior: ou=Promotion,l=New York,c=US
11
```

And finally, here's an example of a modify DN changetype that shows how to move an entry and rename it at the same time:

```
 1 version: 1
 2
 3 # Move ou=Promotion from l=New York,c=US to
 4 # l=San Francisco,c=US and rename it to
 5 # ou=National Promotion.
 6 dn: ou=Promotion,l=New York,c=US
 7 changetype: moddn
 8 newrdn: ou=National Promotion
 9 deleteoldrdn: 1
10 newsuperior: l=San Francisco,c=US
11
```

IMPORTANT

The LDAPv2 modify RDN operation doesn't support moving entries. If you try to move an entry using the LDIF newsuperior syntax with an LDAPv2 client, the request will fail.

Line Folding within LDIF Files

There are times when it is inconvenient to fit the data for an LDIF file on a single line. The LDIF syntax supports line folding to deal with this situation. To fold a line, simply insert a line separator (a newline or a carriage return/newline pair) followed by a space at the place you want the line folded. Whenever the LDIF parser encounters a space at the beginning of the line it knows to concatenate the rest of the data on the line with the previous line (the leading space is discarded).

Here's an example of an LDIF file with a folded line:

```
1 version: 1
2 dn: cn=Peter Michaels, ou=Artists, l=San Francisco, c=US
3 sn: Michaels
```

```
 4 givenname: Peter
 5 objectClass: top
 6 objectClass: person
 7 objectClass: organizationalPerson
 8 objectClass: inetOrgPerson
 9 telephonenumber: +1 415 555 0001
10 mail: Peter.Michaels@aaa.com
11 userpassword: Peter123
12 description: Peter is one of the most popular music
13  ians recording on our label. He's a big concert dr
14  aw, and his fans adore him.
15
```

TIP

If you need to fold a line at a space in an LDIF file, you fold it the same as you would any other character. It doesn't matter if you fold the line just before or just after the space. For instance, if you folded the string "... two words..." at the space between "two" and "words" you'd end up with "... two<line separator><space><space>words..." or "...two<space><line separator><space>words..." Either way is valid.

Base64 Encoding

Base64-encoded values can be used for any DN or attribute value in an LDIF file, but you have to use Base64-encoded values to represent binary values as we discussed in the previous "Distinguished Name Specifier" section.

A Primer on Base64 Encoding

Base64 encoding was designed to enable the representation of any arbitrary sequence of bytes within the confines of a text file. It was not designed to be human-readable. However, since its primary use in LDIF is to encode binary values, which are generally not human-readable anyway, this is an acceptable trade-off. Base64 encoding causes the data it represents to grow in size by approximately 33 percent, which is also a fairly efficient use of space.

Since you'll need to know how to encode Base64 to represent binary values in LDIF files, here's the algorithm. (Since decoding Base64 values is a simple and fairly obvious reversal of the encoding, we'll leave the decoding algorithm to you.) In order to encode a sequence of bytes into Base64, you do the following:

1. Break the input sequence into groups of three bytes. A couple of special rules exist for handling situations where the number of bytes is not evenly divisible by three. We discuss those in a moment.

2. Each group of three bytes has 24 bits. Divide each 24 bit group into four chunks, each with six bits.

3. Each six bit chunk has a decimal value in the range of 0 to 63. Use the decimal value of each six bit chunk as an index into the Base64 alphabet shown in Table 11.8. Place the corresponding element from the Base64 alphabet at the end of the output sequence.

4. At the end of the byte sequence one of these following three cases can occur:

a. Three bytes exist for the final input group. In this case, the 24 bits comprising the group are encoded precisely as in steps 2 and 3 above.

b. Two bytes comprise 16 bits in the final input group. In this case, two zero bits are added at the end to bring the number of bits to 18. The 18 bits are divided into three chunks of six bits, encoded, and added to the output sequence as described in step 3. A single equal sign (=) is added as padding at the end of the output sequence.

c. One byte comprises eight bits in the final input group. In this case, four zero bits are added at the end to bring the number of bits to 12. The 12 bits are divided into two chunks of six bits, encoded, and added to the output sequence as described in step 3. Two equal signs (=) are added as padding to the end of the output sequence.

5. Although the general Base64 encoding algorithm specifies a maximum line length of 76 characters for Base64 encoded values, this restriction is lifted for LDIF files. The length of Base64-encoded lines in LDIF files has no restriction, but line folding may still be done on Base64-encoded values. When line folding is used, it should be done as described in the previous "Line Folding within LDIF Files" section.

TIP
Even though there's no restriction on the length of Base64-encoded lines in LDIF files, you probably don't want to make lines extremely long because many text editors have limitations on the length of lines that they can edit.

6. Even though the general Base64 encoding algorithm allows extraneous characters in the encoded data, extraneous characters are not allowed in Base64 encoded values in an LDIF file.

T A B L E II.8

The Base64 Alphabet

VALUE	ENCODING	VALUE	ENCODING	VALUE	ENCODING
0	A	22	W	44	s
I	B	23	X	45	t
2	C	24	Y	46	u
3	D	25	Z	47	v
4	E	26	a	48	w
5	F	27	b	49	x
6	G	28	c	50	y
7	H	29	d	51	z
8	I	30	e	52	0
9	J	31	f	53	I
10	K	32	g	54	2
II	L	33	h	55	3
12	M	34	i	56	4
13	N	35	j	57	5
14	O	36	k	58	6
15	P	37	l	59	7
16	Q	38	m	60	8
17	R	39	n	61	9

Continued

T A B L E   11.8

The Base64 Alphabet
(continued)

VALUE	ENCODING	VALUE	ENCODING	VALUE	ENCODING
18	S	40	o	62	+
19	T	41	p	63	/
20	U	42	q		
21	V	43	r	(pad)	=

Using Base64-Encoded Values

Here's an example of an LDIF file that uses Base64-encoded values:

L I S T I N G   11.10

```
1 version: 1
2
2 dn: cn=Peter Michaels, ou=Artists, l=San Francisco, c=US
3 sn: Michaels
4 givenname: Peter
5 objectClass: top
6 objectClass: person
7 objectClass: organizationalPerson
8 objectClass: inetOrgPerson
9 telephonenumber: +1 415 555 0001
10 mail: Peter.Michaels@aaa.com
11 #
12 # userpassword value of Peter123 in Base64
13 userpassword:: UGV0ZXIxMjM=
14 #
15 # description value of "Peter is one of the most
16 # popular musicians recording on our label. He's
17 # a big concert draw, and his fans adore him." in
18 # Base64
19 description:: UGV0ZXIgaXMgb25lIG9mIHRoZSBtb3N0IHBv
```

```
20   cHVsYXIgbXVzaWNpYW5zIHJlY29yZGluZyBvbiBvdXIgbGFi
21   ZWwuICBIZSdzIGEgYmlnIGNvbmNlcnQgZHJhdywgYW5kIGhp
22   cyBmYW5zIGFkb3JlIGhpcy4=
23
```

Using URLs in Attribute Value Specifiers

Times exist when it is not very convenient to store all of the data for an attribute directly in the LDIF file. For instance, the attribute may contain a binary value, or be very long, or both. As we saw in the preceding section on Base64 encoding, this sort of data can greatly reduce the readability (and editability) of an LDIF file, especially when the data is very large. You can dramatically reduce these problems by using the `file://` URL to include an entire file verbatim as the value of an attribute value specifier.

Although the LDIF specification does not restrict the types of URLs that may be used in an attribute value specifier, the `file://` URL type is the only one defined by the LDIF spec and the only one we discuss in this book. The semantics of processing other URL formats are not part of the LDIF specification. The LDIF spec states, "The semantics associated with each supported URL [type] will be documented in an associated Applicability Statement." Novell's LDIF processors currently only support the `file://` URL construct.

You can read more on URLs and the file URL scheme in section 3.10 of RFC 1738 at `http://www.ietf.org/rfc/rfc1738.txt`.

Here's an example of an LDIF file that uses a URL in place of an attribute value specifier:

LISTING 11.11

```
1 version: 1
2 dn: cn=Peter Michaels, ou=Artists, l=San Francisco, c=US
3 changetype: modify
4 # add a photo to cn=Peter Michaels
4 add: jpegphoto
```

Continued

LISTING 11.11

(continued)

```
5 jpegphoto:< file:///c:/tmp/photos/peter_michaels.jpg
6 -
7
```

When you specify a URL in an LDIF file, the LDIF parser includes the contents of the URL verbatim in the interpreted output of the LDIF file. This means that the LDIF parser assumes the contents of the file are *not* Base64 encoded, and it sends the raw data from the file as the attribute value. This makes a lot of sense since one reason for allowing the use of URLs is to make data reusable. If you had to Base64 encode the jpeg photo in the example above before you could include it in an LDIF file, it would make your job a lot harder.

Control Specifier

You can specify one or more controls that you would like to be included as part of the update operation specified in a changetype record. A control specifier looks like this:

```
control: OID [criticality] [controlValue]
```

For more information on controls, see Chapter 9.

X-REF

As of this writing, Novell's Import/Export Utility does not yet support specifying controls in LDIF files. This feature will likely be added in NDS 8.5 service pack 1.

NOTE

Table 11.9 describes each of the control specifier elements.

TABLE 11.9	ELEMENT	DESCRIPTION
Control Specifier Elements	control	A keyword identifying this field as a control.
	:	Separates the control keyword and its value.
	OID	The ASN.1 object identifier for this control.

TABLE 11.9	ELEMENT	DESCRIPTION
Control Specifier Elements (continued)	criticality	Optional. Either the value true or the value false indicating the criticality of the control. If the criticality is not given, it defaults to false.
	controlValue	Optional. The controlValue, if any, required for this control. See Chapter 9 for more details on the control value.

Here's an LDIF file that uses a control in conjunction with a changetype record. This LDIF file uses the Forward References control to enable the creation of forward references for this entry.

TIP

If you choose, this same control can be automatically added to the LDAP request for every entry in an LDIF file by Novell's Import/ Export Utility to enable the creation of forward references. We discuss the forward references control at more length in the following "The Novell Import/Export Utility" section.

LISTING 11.12

```
1 version: 1
2 dn: cn=Peter Michaels, ou=Artists, l=San Francisco, c=US
3 # Attach the Forward References control to this
4 # record. The criticality is "true", and
5 # the controlValue is absent as defined for
6 # the control.
7 control: 2.16.840.1.113719.1.27.101.6 true
8 changetype: add
9 sn: Michaels
10 givenname: Peter
11 objectClass: top
12 objectClass: person
13 objectClass: organizationalPerson
14 objectClass: iNetOrgPerson
15 telephonenumber: +1 415 555 0001
16 mail: Peter.Michaels@aaa.com
17 userpassword: Peter123
18
```

▶ · ◀

Schema Extensions Using LDIF

You can use standard LDAP operations to modify schema. Since LDIF can represent LDAP update operations, it may be more convenient to use LDIF to make schema changes than to write a specialized application for that purpose. If you aren't already familiar with the format of information contained in the subschema subentry, you'll probably want to acquaint yourself with the information in Chapter 7 before proceeding with this section.

TIP

Most LDAP applications that you develop require schema additions. An LDIF file is a good way to deliver these schema changes to your customers. You can use the command line version of the Novell Import/Export Utility to apply the schema changes from an LDIF file to NDS as part of your application's installation.

Adding a New Attribute

Adding a new attribute to the schema is as simple as adding a single attribute value. To make reference easier, here's the NDSObjectClassDescription given in Chapter 7:

```
NDSAttributeTypeDescription = "(" whsp
    numericoid whsp                       ; AttributeType identifier
    [ "NAME" qdescrs ]                    ; name used in AttributeType
    [ "DESC" qdstring ]                   ; description
    [ "OBSOLETE" whsp ]
    [ "SUP" woid ]                        ; derived from this other
                                          ; AttributeType
    [ "EQUALITY" woid                     ; Matching Rule name
    [ "ORDERING" woid                     ; Matching Rule name
    [ "SUBSTR" woid ]                     ; Matching Rule name
    [ "SYNTAX" whsp noidlen whsp ]        ; Syntax OID
    [ "SINGLE-VALUE" whsp ]               ; default multi-valued
    [ "COLLECTIVE" whsp ]                 ; default not collective
    [ "NO-USER-MODIFICATION" whsp ];      default user modifiable
```

```
[ "USAGE" whsp AttributeUsage ]; default userApplications
[ "X-NDS_PUBLIC_READ" qdstrings ]
                         ; default not public read ('0')
[ "X-NDS_SERVER_READ" qdstrings ]
                         ; default not server read ('0')
[ "X-NDS_NEVER_SYNC" qdstrings ]
                         ; default not never sync ('0')
[ "X-NDS_NOT_SCHED_SYNC_IMMEDIATE" qdstrings ]
                         ; default sched sync immediate ('0')
[ "X-NDS_SCHED_SYNC_NEVER" qdstrings ]
                         ; default schedule sync ('0')
[ "X-NDS_LOWER_BOUND" qdstrings ]
                         ; default no lower bound('0')
                         ;(upper is specified in SYNTAX)
[ "X-NDS_NAME_VALUE_ACCESS" qdstrings ]
                         ; default not name value access ('0')
[ "X-NDS_NAME" qdstrings ]     ; legacy NDS name
whsp ")"
```

Attribute Values

To add an attribute, you have to add an attribute value that conforms to the specification for NDSObjectClassDescription to the attributes attribute of the subschemaSubentry. This example adds three attribute types—instruments, recordings, and bands—to the schema.

Because NDS has a global schema, cn=schema currently happens to be the one and only place where the subschemaSubentry exists in NDS. LDAP allows multiple subschemaSubentries to be placed at any location in the tree. In the future, it's possible that the location of the subschemaSubentry may change and/or that more than one subschemaSubentry may exist in NDS. Other LDAP implementations you encounter may already allow this.

See the "Finding and Reading the Schema" section in Chapter 7 for more information on locating subschemaSubentries.

X-REF

TIP

This example and several that follow it use line folding to make them easier to read. Because unfolding the lines removes the line separators, be sure to leave whitespace where it's needed. In the next example every line in the attributeTypes value, but the last one, begins with at least two spaces to meet this requirement.

L I S T I N G   11.13

```
 1 version: 1
 2 #
 3 # IMPORTANT NOTE: We've used bogus OIDs
 4 #    in this example. Be sure to get your
 5 #    own registered OIDs for schema
 6 #    elements you create.
 7 #
 8 dn: cn=schema
 9 changetype: modify
10 add: attributeTypes
11 attributeTypes: (
12    2.5.6.6.6.1.100
13    NAME 'instruments'
14    DESC 'instruments played by this musician'
15    SYNTAX 1.3.6.1.4.1.1466.115.121.1.44{64}
16    X-NDS_NOT_SCHED_SYNC_IMMEDIATE '1'
17    X-NDS_LOWER_BOUND '0'
18    )
19 attributeTypes: (
20    2.5.6.6.6.1.101
21    NAME 'recordings'
22    DESC 'recordings made by this musician'
23    SYNTAX 1.3.6.1.4.1.1466.115.121.1.44{64}
24    X-NDS_NOT_SCHED_SYNC_IMMEDIATE '1'
25    X-NDS_LOWER_BOUND '0'
26    )
27 attributeTypes: (
28    2.5.6.6.6.1.102
29    NAME 'bands'
```

```
30    DESC 'bands this musician has played in'
31    SYNTAX 1.3.6.1.4.1.1466.115.121.1.44{64}
32    X-NDS_NOT_SCHED_SYNC_IMMEDIATE '1'
33    X-NDS_LOWER_BOUND '0'34   )
35
```

TIP

You can look at attributeTypes values in the subschema subentry to see how to format attributeTypes. The Novell Import/Export Utility can be used to export the subschema subentry to an LDIF file. To export the subschema entry (assuming it's located at cn=schema), you can perform a search with a baseDN of cn=schema, a scope of base, and a search filter of objectclass=* to read the schema. See the following "The Novell Import/Export Utility" section for details on using the utility to export LDIF files.

Single-Valued versus Multi-Valued

As shown in the NDSAttributeTypeDescription definition above, an attribute defaults to multi-valued unless it is explicitly made single-valued. If you wanted to add a single-valued attribute type, you'd add the SINGLE-VALUE keyword after the SYNTAX section, like this:

LISTING 11.14

```
 1 version: 1
 2 #
 3 # IMPORTANT NOTE: We've used bogus OIDs
 4 #   in this example. Be sure to get your
 5 #   own registered OIDs for schema
 6 #   elements you create.
 7 #
 8 dn: cn=schema
 9 changetype: modify
10 add: attributeTypes
11 attributeTypes: (
12    2.5.6.6.6.1.104
13    NAME 'lastRecording'
14    DESC 'most recent recording by this musician'
```

Continued

(continued)

```
15    SYNTAX 1.3.6.1.4.1.1466.115.121.1.44{64}
16    SINGLE-VALUE
16    X-NDS_NOT_SCHED_SYNC_IMMEDIATE '1'
17    X-NDS_LOWER_BOUND '0'
18    )
19
```

Adding a New Object Class

Adding a new class to the schema is as simple as adding a single attribute value. To make reference easier, here's the NDSObjectClassDescription given in Chapter 7.

```
NDSObjectClassDescription = "(" whsp
    numericoid whsp
    [ "NAME" qdescrs ]
    [ "DESC" qdstring ]
    [ "OBSOLETE" whsp ]
    [ "SUP" oids ]
    [ ( "ABSTRACT" / "STRUCTURAL" / "AUXILIARY" ) whsp ]
    [ "MUST" oids ]
    [ "MAY" oids ]
    [ "X-NDS_NOT_CONTAINER" qdstrings ]
    [ "X-NDS_NONREMOVABLE" qdstrings ]
    [ "X-NDS_CONTAINMENT" qdstrings ]
    [ "X-NDS_NAMING" qdstrings ]
    [ "X-NDS_NAME" qdstrings ]
    whsp ")"
```

To add a class, you have to add an attribute value that conforms to the specification for NDSObjectClassDescription to the objectClasses attribute of the subschemaSubentry. Here's how you would add a new auxiliary class named musician to the schema using an LDIF file. Note that we use line folding to make the new objectClasses attribute value more readable.

```
 1 version: 1
 2 #
 3 # IMPORTANT NOTE: We've used bogus OIDs
 4 #   in this example. Be sure to get your
 5 #   own registered OIDs for schema
 6 #   elements you create.
 7 #
 8 dn: cn=schema
 9 changetype: modify
10 add: objectClasses
11 objectClasses: (
12   2.5.6.6.6.1.200
13   NAME 'musician'
14   SUP top
15   AUXILIARY
16   MUST (instruments)
17   MAY (recordings $ bands)
18   X-NDS_NOT_CONTAINER '1'
19 )
20
```

Mandatory Attributes

Mandatory attributes are listed in the MUST section of the object class description. In the case of the musician object class, the only mandatory attribute is instruments.

Optional Attributes

Optional attributes are listed in the MAY section of the object class description. The optional attributes in the musician object class are recordings, and bands.

Containment Rules

The object classes that can contain the object class being defined are given in the X-NDS_CONTAINMENT section of the object class description. Here's an

LDIF example that creates a new structural object class called band that can be contained by the organizationalUnit and domain object classes:

LISTING 11.16

```
 1 version: 1
 2 #
 3 # IMPORTANT NOTE: We've used bogus OIDs
 4 #    in this example. Be sure to get your
 5 #    own registered OIDs for schema
 6 #    elements you create.
 7 #
 8 dn: cn=schema
 9 changetype: modify
10 add: objectClasses
11 objectClasses: (
12    2.5.6.6.6.1.201
13    NAME 'band'
14    SUP top
15    STRUCTURAL
16    MUST (cn)
17    MAY (member)
18    X-NDS_NAMING ('cn')
19    X-NDS_CONTAINMENT ('organizationalUnit' 'domain')
20    X-NDS_NOT_CONTAINER '1'
21  )
```

Naming Rules

The X-NDS_NAMING section of the object class description defines the attribute or attributes that are used to name entries for this object class. In the example we just showed you, cn is the naming attribute for the band object class.

Adding an Optional Attribute to an Existing Object Class

You can also use LDIF to modify existing schema. The trick is to delete the schema attribute value you want to change and add it back in the same modify operation. Because the delete and add are part of the one operation, they are committed to the database together. Thus, the schema remains intact and the operation can complete successfully.

WARNING

While adding new schema elements is generally an acceptable practice, modifying or extending existing schema elements is usually a dangerous thing to do. Since every schema element is uniquely identified by an OID, when you extend a standard schema element, you have effectively created a second definition for the element even though it still uses the original OID. This can lead to incompatibility problems because there's no way to tell which of the definitions is the "true" definition since they are both using the same unique identifier.

Times exist when it is appropriate to change schema elements. For instance, you may need to extend or modify new schema elements as you refine them during development.

TIP

Generally, you'll want to use auxiliary classes to add new attributes to an existing object class or subclass an existing object class rather than adding new attributes directly to the class.

Suppose that you forgot to include the `lastRecording` attribute to the musician object class we defined earlier in this section. Here's an LDIF file that adds it:

LISTING 11.17

```
 1 version: 1
 2 #
 3 # IMPORTANT NOTE: We've used bogus OIDs
 4 #   in this example. Be sure to get your
 5 #   own registered OIDs for schema
 6 #   elements you create.
 7 #
 8 dn: cn=schema
 9 changetype: modify
10 delete: objectClasses
11 objectClasses: ( 2.5.6.6.6.1.200)
12 -
```

Continued

LISTING 11.17

(continued)

```
13 add: objectClasses
14 objectClasses: (
15   2.5.6.6.6.1.200
16   NAME 'musician'
17   SUP top
18   AUXILIARY
19   MUST (instruments)
20   MAY (recordings $ bands $ lastRecording)
21   X-NDS_NOT_CONTAINER '1'
22 )
23 -
24
```

TIP

In order to update an attribute value, you have to specify both its current value and the new value. Fortunately, since the OID uniquely identifies a schema element, you don't have to give the entire value; you can just supply the OID as shown in line 11 of Listing 11.17.

The Novell Import/Export Utility

To help you efficiently and easily load data, NDS eDirectory 8.5 includes a new utility called the Novell Import/Export Utility. The wizard enables you to easily perform LDIF imports, LDIF exports, and data migration between LDAP servers by presenting an intuitive user interface to an Import/Conversion/Export engine. A command line user interface is also included in the release which can be very useful for situations where you want to use scripts to do import and export operations.

The Import/Conversion/Export Engine

The Import/Conversion/Export engine manages a collection of handlers or drivers that know how to read or write data in a variety of formats. Handlers that know how to read data are called *source handlers*. Handlers that know how to write data are called *destination handlers*. The engine receives data from a source handler, optionally performs some processing or converting on the data then passes the data to a destination handler.

Four handlers are of interest in this discussion: the LDIF source handler, the LDIF destination handler, the LDAP directory source handler, and the LDAP directory destination handler. If you want to import LDIF data into your LDAP directory, you'd tell the engine to use the LDIF source handler to read an LDIF file and to use the LDAP destination handler to send the data to your LDAP directory server. Conversely, if you want to export data from your LDAP server to an LDIF file, you'd tell the engine to use the LDAP source handler to retrieve the data from an LDAP server and the LDIF destination handler to send the data to an LDIF file. You can also combine the LDAP source and LDAP destination handlers to do a migration of data between LDAP servers.

The Command Line Interface

Describing the command line interface is a good way to methodically describe each of the options available in the Import/Conversion/Export utility.

NOTE **The information in this section gives a lot of detail about the inner workings of the Novell Import/Export Utility, including descriptions for many options that are infrequently used. If you like, you can skip to the following "Wizard Interface" section. We refer back to parts of this section as we describe the dialog screens in the wizard, and you can jump back to the descriptions of the corresponding command line options in this section as needed.**

The name of the command line utility is ice, which is a lower-case acronym for Import/Conversion/Export. For Win32 and NetWare, the ice executable is installed as part of ConsoleOne and is located in the ConsoleOne/1.2/bin directory. On UNIX platforms, the ice executable is installed in the /usr/bin directory. The ice utility is invoked with these command line options:

```
ice <general options>
    -S<source handler> <source options>
    -D<destination handler> <destination options>
```

First, we explain the general options that affect the way the engine itself works. Next, we explain the options for the LDIF source and destination handlers and the LDAP source and destination handlers. We end by explaining the options for processing rules.

NOTE

**Options that may be omitted are enclosed in these square brackets: [ ].
Options that must be provided are not enclosed in square brackets.**

Some Basic Rules

A few basic rules exist regarding the structure of the ice command line that you'll want to know:

▸ All command line options are case sensitive.

▸ General options must come before any source or destination options (that is, all general options must be between "ice" and the first -S or -D option).

▸ The source and destination sections may come in any order, but the options for each section must be kept within that section to unambiguously identify them with the proper section. For example, these two command lines are equivalent (assuming that <gen opts>, <src opts>, and <dst opts> are constant):

```
ice <gen opts> -S <src opts> -D <dst opts>
ice <gen opts> -D <dst opts> -S <src opts>
```

▸ The options within a section — including general options — may be specified in any order as long as they are kept within that section (see rule 2).

General Options

General options affect the overall processing of the Import/Conversion/Export engine. Table 11.10 shows all of the general options for the engine along with their meanings.

TABLE 11.10	OPTION	DESCRIPTION
General Options for the Import/Conversion/ Export Utility	`[-1 < log file>]`	`< log file>` specifies a file name where output messages (including error messages) are logged. If this option is omitted, messages are sent to ice.log.
	`[-o]`	Overwrites the log file, if it exists. If this flag is not set, messages are appended to the log file.
	`[-e <error ldif log file>]`	`< error ldif log file>` specifies a file name where entries that fail are output in LDIF format. This file can be examined, modified to correct the errors, and then reapplied to the directory.
	`[-p <URL>]`	`<URL>` specifies the location of an XML placement rule to be used by the engine. See the following section on XML Rules Options for more detail.
	`[-c <URL>]`	`<URL>` specifies the location of an XML creation rule to be used by the engine. See the following section on XML Rules Options for more detail.
	`[-s <URL.>]`	`<URL>` specifies the location of an XML schema mapping rule to be used by the engine. See the following section on XML Rules Options for more detail.

LDIF Source Handler Options

The LDIF source handler reads data from an LDIF file and sends it to the Import/Conversion/Export engine. The LDIF source handler options are shown in Table 11.11.

LDIF Destination Handler Options

The LDIF destination handler receives data from the Import/Conversion/Export engine and writes it to an LDIF file. The LDIF destination handler options are shown in Table 11.12.

TABLE 11.11	OPTION	DESCRIPTION
LDIF Source Handler Options	-f <ldif file>	<ldif file> specifies a file name containing LDIF records that are to be read by the LDIF source handler and sent to the engine.
	[-a]	If the records in the LDIF file are content records (that is, they contain no changetypes), they are treated as records with a changetype of add. If this option is omitted, records are treated as having a changetype of modify with a modification specifier of add for all attribute values.
	[-c]	Prevents the LDIF source handler from stopping on errors. Instead, the handler continues processing even when errors are encountered. This includes errors on parsing LDIF and errors sent back from the destination handler. When this option is set and an error occurs, the LDIF source handler reports the error, finds the next record in the LDIF file, and goes on.
	[-n]	Does not perform update operations, just prints what would be done. When this option is set, the LDIF source handler parses the LDIF file but does not send any records to the ice engine (and hence the destination handler).
	[-v]	Enables the verbose mode of the handler.

TABLE 11.12	OPTION	DESCRIPTION
LDIF Destination Handler Options	-f <ldif file>	<ldif file> specifies a file name where LDIF records are to be written.
	[-v]	Enables the verbose mode of the handler.

LDAP Directory Source Handler Options

The LDAP directory source handler reads data from an LDAP server by sending a search request to the server. It sends the search entries it receives from the search operation to the Import/Conversion/Export engine. The LDAP directory source handler options are shown in Table 11.13.

T A B L E   11.13

LDAP Directory Source
Handler Options

OPTION	DESCRIPTION
[-s <server name>]	<server name> specifies the DNS name or IP address of the LDAP server to which the handler sends a search request. If this option is omitted, <server name> defaults to the local-host value of 127.0.0.1.
[-p <port>]	<port> is the integer port number of the LDAP server specified by <server name>. If this option is omitted, <port> defaults to 389.
[-d <DN>]	<DN> specifies the distinguished name of the entry that should be used when binding to the server specified in the bind operation. If this option is omitted, <DN> defaults to the empty string which means that an anonymous bind will be performed.
[-w <password>]	<password> specifies the password credentials for the entry specified by <DN>. If this option is omitted, <password> defaults to the empty string which means that an anonymous bind will be performed.
[-F <search filter>]	<search filter> is an RFC 2254 compliant search filter. If this option is omitted, the search filter defaults to objectclass=*.
[-n]	Specifies that the handler shouldn't actually perform a search, but just shows what search would be performed.
[-a <attribute list>]	<attribute list> is a comma-separated list of attributes to retrieve as part of the search. In addition to attribute names, three special values exist: 1) 1.1 means get no attributes 2) * is shorthand for all user (non-operational) attributes. It can be combined with other attribute names to get all user attributes plus the additional operational attributes that are explicitly listed. 3) an empty list gets all user (non-operational) attributes. If this option is omitted, the attribute list defaults to the empty list.

Continued

T A B L E   1 1 . 1 3

*LDAP Directory Source
Handler Options (continued)*

OPTION	DESCRIPTION
[-o <attribute list>]	<attribute list> is a comma-separated list of attributes to be omitted from the search results received from the LDAP server before they are sent to the engine. This option is very useful in cases where you want to use a wild card with the -a option to get all attributes of some class and then remove a few of them from the search results before passing the data on to the engine. Example: -a* -otelephoneNumber would retrieve all user-level attributes and filter the telephoneNumber from the results.
[-R]	Disables the utility from automatically following referrals. By default any referrals received by the utility are always followed using the DN and password value specified by the –d and –p options for the LDAP source handler..
[-e <value>]	<value> is an integer that specifies which debugging flags should be enabled in the LDAP client SDK. If the value is prefixed by 0x it is hexadecimal, otherwise it is decimal. See the following "Use LDAP SDK Debugging Flags" section for more details.
[-b <base DN>]	<base DN> contains the base DN for the search request. If this option is omitted, the base DN defaults to " " (empty string), and the tree root is then used as the base DN for the search.
[-c <search scope>]	<search scope> specifies the scope of the search request. It must be one of base, one, or sub. If this option is omitted, the search scope defaults to one.
[-r <deref aliases>]	<deref aliases> specifies the way that aliases should be dereferenced during the search operation. It must be one of never, always, search, or find. If this option is omitted, then the alias dereferencing behavior is never.
[-l <time limit>]	<time limit> specifies the maximum time in seconds allowed for the search to complete. If this option is omitted, the default is 0, which means unlimited.
[-z <size limit>]	<size limit> specifies the maximum number of entries to be returned by the search. If this option is omitted, the default is 0, which means unlimited.

T A B L E   11.13

LDAP Directory Source
Handler Options (continued)

OPTION	DESCRIPTION
[-V \<version\>]	\<version\> specifies the LDAP protocol version to be used for the connection. It must be 2 or 3. If this option is omitted, the default is 3.
[-v]	Enables the verbose mode of the handler.
[-L \<file name\>]	\<file name\> specifies a file in DER format containing a server key used for SSL authentication. If you use this option, you'll also need to use the -p option to specify the SSL port (usually port 636) for the LDAP server.
[-A]	Retrieves attribute names only; attribute values are not returned by the search operation.

LDAP Directory Destination Handler Options

The LDAP directory destination handler receives data from the Import/Conversion/Export engine and sends it to an LDAP server in the form of update operations to be performed by the server. The LDAP directory destination handler options are shown in Table 11.14.

T A B L E   11.14

LDAP Directory Destination
Handler Options

OPTION	DESCRIPTION
[-s \<server name\>]	\<server name\> specifies the DNS name or IP address of the LDAP server to which the handler sends a search request. If this option is omitted, \<server name\> defaults to the localhost value of 127.0.0.1.
[-p \<port\>]	\<port\> is the integer port number of the LDAP server specified by \<server name\>. If this option is omitted, \<port\> defaults to 389.
[-d \<DN\>]	\<DN\> specifies the distinguished name of the entry that should be used when binding to the server specified in the bind operation. If this option is omitted, \<DN\> defaults to the empty string which means that an anonymous bind will be performed.

Continued

TABLE 11.14

*LDAP Directory Destination
Handler Options (continued)*

OPTION	DESCRIPTION
[-w <password>]	<password> specifies the password attribute of the entry specified by <DN>. If this option is omitted, <password> defaults to the empty string which means that an anonymous bind will be performed.
[-B]	Do not use asynchronous LBURP requests for transferring update operations to the server; use standard synchronous LDAP update operation requests instead. See the following "LDAP Bulk Update/ Replication Protocol" section for more details.
[-F]	Allows the creation of forward references. See the following "Enable Forward References" section for details.
[-1]	Stores password values using the simple password method of Novell's Modular Authentication Service (NMAS). See the following "Use Simple Passwords" section for more information.
[-e <value>]	<value> is an integer that specifies which debugging flags should be enabled in the LDAP client SDK. If the value is prefixed by 0x it is hexadecimal, otherwise it is decimal. See the following "Use LDAP SDK Debugging Flags" section for more details.
[-V <version>]	<version> specifies the LDAP protocol version to be used for the connection. It must be 2 or 3. If this option is omitted, the default is 3.
[-v]	Enables the verbose mode of the handler.
[-L <file name>]	<file name> specifies a file in DER format containing a server key used for SSL authentication. If you use this option, you'll also need to use the -p option to specify the SSL port (usually port 636) for the LDAP server.

XML Rules Options

The Import/Conversion/Export engine allows you to specify a set of rules that describe processing actions to be taken on each record received from the source handler and before the record is sent on to the destination handler. These rules are specified in XML (either in the form of an XML file or XML data stored in the directory) using the same format as rules for Novell's DirXML product. This is the "Conversion" part of the Import/Conversion/Export engine.

You enable processing rules with the -p, -c, and -s general options on the ice executable. (See the preceding section on General Options.) For all three options, the URL must be one of the following:

▸ A URL of the form `file://` that specifies a file on the local file system that contains the appropriate set of conversion rules.

▸ An RFC 2255 compliant LDAP URL that specifies a base level search and an attribute list consisting of a single attribute description for a singled-valued attribute type. (As of this writing, the LDAP URL option is not supported, but it is anticipated that it will be in the first support pack for NDS eDirectory 8.5.)

There are three types of rules: placement rules, creation rules, and schema mapping rules.

Placement Rules   Placement rules allow you to change the placement of an entry. Imagine that you are importing a group of users from various containers but you want them to all end up in the l=Los Angeles, c=US container when the import is complete. You could use the following placement rule to do this:

```
<?xml version="1.0" encoding="ISO-8859-1" ?>
<placement-rules src-dn-format="ldap" dest-dn-format="ldap">
      <placement-rule>
            <match-class class-name="inetOrgPerson"></match-
class>
            <placement>l=Los Angeles,c=US<copy-
name/></placement>
      </placement-rule>
</placement-rules>
```

Creation Rules   Creation rules allow you to supply missing information that may be needed to allow an entry to be created successfully on import. For instance, imagine that you have exported LDIF data from a server whose schema requires only the cn (commonName) attribute for user entries but the server that you are importing the LDIF data to requires both the cn and sn (surname) attributes. You could use the creation rule to supply a default sn value, such as " ", for each entry as it is processed by the engine. When the entry is sent to the destination server, it would have the required sn attribute and the entry would be added successfully. The following creation rule does just this for inetOrgPerson entries:

```
<?xml version="1.0" encoding="ISO-8859-1" ?>
<create-rules>
        <create-rule class-name="inetOrgPerson">
                <required-attr attr-name="sn">
                        <value> </value>
                </required-attr>
        </create-rule>
</create-rules>
```

Another way that creation rules can be used is to ensure that certain attribute values are present before an entry can be created. The following creation rule ensures that every inetOrgEntry entry you add has a password attribute or the creation will fail:

```
<?xml version="1.0" encoding="ISO-8859-1" ?>
<create-rules>
        <create-rule class-name="inetOrgPerson">
                <required-attr attr-name="password"/>
        </create-rule>
```

Schema Rules   When you are transferring data between servers, either directly or via LDIF, it is very likely that there will be differences in the schema in the two servers. In some cases you may need to extend the schema on the destination server to accommodate all of the object classes and attribute types in entries coming from the source server. In other cases, all that may be needed is to map a schema element on the source to a different but equivalent schema element on the destination. Schema mapping rules allow you to do just this. The following schema rule changes attributes named lastName to be named sn (surname):

```
<?xml version="1.0" encoding="ISO-8859-1" ?>
<attr-name-map>
        <attr-name>
```

```
            <nds-name>lastName</nds-name>
            <app-name>sn</app-name>
        </attr-name>
    </attr-name-map>
```

So many things can be done with XML processing rules that we simply don't have the space to go into all of them in detail in this chapter. Instead, we've chosen to give you a sampling of ideas to help you see what's possible and get you thinking about how XML rules might be able to help you solve your problems. For more information on XML processing rules, please refer to the user guide and online help for the NDS Import/Export Utility.

Using the Novell Import/Export Utility with Other LDAP Directories

The Novell Import/Export Utility can be used with any LDAP Directory. When you use the utility to transfer data — either directly or via an intermediate LDIF file — between directories (even from the same vendor), you should ensure that the following conditions have been met:

▸ All object classes and attributes used in the data transferred between the two directories are defined in the schema of the destination directory, or appropriate XML schema mapping rules are used to map between the schemas of the two directories.

▸ Any proprietary attributes (such as ACLs or ACIs) that cannot be represented directly in the destination directory are either mapped to new values using XML rules or omitted from the source directory (by using the –o option of the LDAP Source Handler or by removing references to the attribute wherever they appear in the LDIF file.

Command Line Examples

There's no doubt that the Import/Conversion/Export engine and its associated handlers allow you to choose from a plethora of options. By now you may be wondering just how to put all of these options together into a command line that will do what you want. We present a few example command lines here to help you see how it all works.

To perform an LDIF import, you combine the LDIF source and LDAP destination handlers like this:

```
ice -SLDIF -fc:\temp\chapter2.ldif -DLDAP -sserver2.acme.com
   -p389 -dcn=admin,c=us -wsecret
```

This command line says: read LDIF data from c:\temp\chapter2.ldif, and send it to the LDAP server server2.acme.com at port 389 using the identity cn=admin,c=us and password "secret". No XML data conversion will be performed.

To perform an LDIF export, you combine the LDAP source and LDIF destination handlers like this:

```
ice -SLDAP -sserver1.acme.com -p389 -dcn=admin,c=us
   -wpassword -lobjectClass=* -csub -DLDIF
   -c:\temp\server1.ldif
```

This command line says: do a subtree search for all objects in the server server1.acme.com at port 389 using the identity cn=admin,c=us and password "password" and output the data in LDIF format to c:\tmp\server1.ldif.

To perform a data migration between LDAP servers, you combine the LDAP source and LDAP destination handlers like this:

```
ice -SLDAP -sserver1.acme.com -p389 -dcn=admin,c=us
   -wpassword -lobjectClass=* -csub -DLDAP
   -sserver2.acme.com -p389 -dcn=admin,c=us -wsecret
```

This command line says: do a subtree search for all objects in the server server1.acme.com at port 389 using the identity cn=admin,c=us with password "password" and send it to the LDAP server server2.acme.com at port 389 using the identity cn=admin,c=us and password "secret".

The Wizard Interface

The NDS Import/Export Wizard is a ConsoleOne snap-in designed to help you easily and quickly accomplish the import and export tasks that you most likely need to do with the Novell Import/Export Utility.

TIP

The NDS Import/Export Wizard is essentially self-documenting; however, if you have questions about a particular option, you can refer to the online help and the previous "The Command Line Interface" section for details. The controls on the wizard and their names correspond directly to the options available from the command line.

To start the wizard, you click Wizards, NDS Import/Export . . . on the ConsoleOne main window. The first screen of the wizard is shown in Figure 11.1. From this screen you can select one of three tasks: an LDIF import, an LDIF export, or a server-to-server data migration.

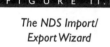

The NDS Import/Export Wizard

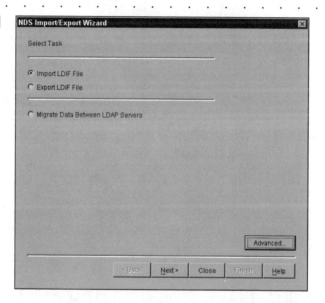

TIP

Required fields are on the main window of the wizard, and optional fields can be set on the Advanced options dialogs of each pane. For instance, your selection on the first screen of the NDS Import/Export Wizard is required to determine the source and destination handlers that are needed, and the advanced options dialog box for this screen allows you to specify the general options for the Novell Import/Export Utility as documented in the previous "General Options" section. As we discuss the rest of the wizard, we point out which handler (for example, LDIF source handler, LDAP directory destination handler, and so on) each wizard screen is for.

LDIF Import

When you select the Import LDIF File option on the Import/Export Wizard, the wizard steps you through the information required for the LDIF source handler and the LDAP destination handler in the following sequence:

▶ The second screen, as shown in Figure 11.2, asks you to select the LDIF file that contains the data you want to import. The advanced dialog box for this screen allows you to set the other LDIF source handler options.

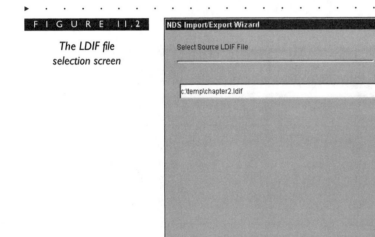

F I G U R E   11.2

*The LDIF file
selection screen*

▶ The third screen asks you to select the LDAP server where the data should be imported. To simplify the task of entering this data, the wizard allows you to store the information for several servers and name each set of information with a name you choose, as shown in Figure 11.3.

▶ By clicking New... you can add a new server using the dialog box shown in Figure 11.4.

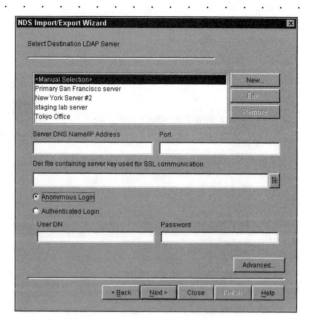

F I G U R E   11.3

The LDAP server
selection screen

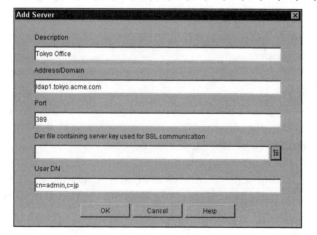

F I G U R E   11.4

Adding a new server to
the LDAP server list

▶ This server is then added to the server list for you to use, as shown in
   Figure 11.5. The advanced dialog box for this screen allows you to set
   the other options for the LDAP destination handler.

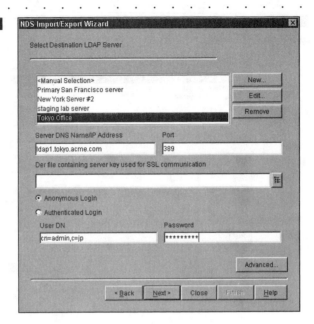

F I G U R E 11.5

*Using the new server
in the LDAP server list*

▸ The final screen, shown in Figure 11.6, summarizes the selections you have made. When you click Finish on this screen, the LDIF import operation begins, and a progress dialog box pops up to display the status of your import operation.

LDIF Export

When you select the Export LDIF option on the first screen of the Import/Export Wizard, the wizard collects the information needed for the LDAP source handler and the LDIF destination handler.

▸ The second screen (similar to Figure 11.4) asks you to select the LDAP server holding the entries you want to export. The advanced dialog box for this screen allows you to set most of the options for the LDAP source handler. (The rest of the options for the LDAP source handler are on the next wizard screen.)

FIGURE 11.6

The LDIF Import summary screen

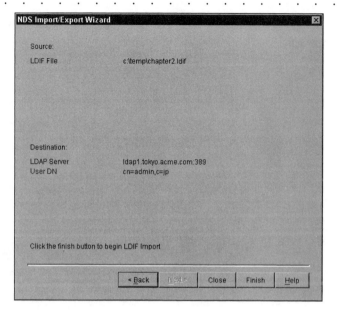

▶ The third screen asks you to select the search criteria for the entries you want to export. Three tabs on this screen allow you to specify the Base DN and scope of the search, the filter used for the search, and the attributes to be returned for each search entry. This screen is shown in Figure 11.7.

▶ The fourth screen (similar to Figure 11.2) prompts you for the name of the LDIF file where you want the exported information stored. The advanced dialog box for this screen allows you to set the other options for the LDIF destination handler.

▶ The final screen summarizes the selections you have made. When you click Finish on this screen, the LDIF export operation begins, and a progress dialog pops up to display the status of your import operation.

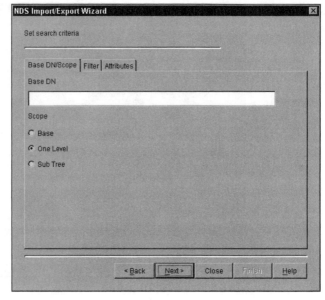

FIGURE 11.7

*The LDAP search
criteria screen*

Server-to-Server Data Migration

When you select the Migrate Data Between LDAP Servers option on the Import/
Export Wizard, the wizard steps you through the screens for the LDAP source handler (where you select the source server and set search criteria) followed by screens
for the LDAP destination handlers (where you select the destination server). As
with other operations, the final screen summarizes your selections, and a progress
dialog box pops up when you click Finish.

The Novell Import/Export Utility versus LDAPModify

You may have heard of or used a command line utility called LDAPModify
which reads LDIF files and applies the records in them to an LDAP server. In this
regard, LDAPModify is functionally similar to the Novell Import/Export Utility;
however, it may be useful for you to understand the differences between these two
utilities to see how they work.

The Problem: Operation Ordering

The records in an LDIF file imply a sequential ordering of a set of changes to be
applied to a DIT (Directory Information Tree) . When an LDIF file is processed,

the order of these changes must be preserved or unexpected results might occur. For instance if the records in an LDIF file that deleted an entry then added a new entry with the same DN were switched, the add would fail because the entry already existed, and the entry would be deleted. Instead of having a new version of the entry, you'd have no entry at all!

To ensure that the changes in an LDIF file are applied to the DIT in the proper order, LDAPModify sends a request for one record in the LDIF file and waits for a response before sending the request for the next record. While this guarantees that the operations are applied to the DIT in the same order that they appear in the LDIF file, it also means that the LDAP server sits idle from the time it sends one response until the time it receives the next request. The use of synchronous requests in this fashion is a performance bottleneck. LDAPModify could eliminate this bottleneck by sending the requests from the LDIF file asynchronously, but then the order for processing the requests wouldn't be guaranteed. If you only have a few records in your LDIF file, it's probably not a big deal if the processing isn't very fast. But if you have a million records in your LDIF file, you'll probably want to squeeze every bit of performance possible out of NDS while you're processing the file.

LDAP Bulk Update/Replication Protocol

The Novell Import/Export Utility uses the LDAP Bulk Update/Replication Protocol (LBURP) to allow it to send asynchronous requests to an LDAP server; meanwhile it still guarantees that the requests are processed in the order specified by the protocol, and not in an arbitrary order influenced by things such as multiprocessor interactions, the operating system's scheduler, and so on. LBURP also allows the Novell Import/Export Utility to send several update operations in a single request and receive the response for all of those update operations in a single response, which adds to the network efficiency of the protocol. Here's how the protocol works:

- The client (Import/Export Utility) binds to an LDAP server.

- The server sends a bind response to the client.

- The client sends a Start LBURP extended request to the server.

- The server sends a Start LBURP extended response to the client.

▸ The client sends zero or more LBURP Operation extended requests to the server. These requests may be sent asynchronously. Each request contains a sequence number identifying the order of the request relative to other requests sent by the client over the same connection. Each request also contains one or more LDAP update operations.

▸ The server processes each of the LBURP Operation extended requests in the order specified by the sequence number and sends an LBURP Operation extended response for each request.

▸ After all of the updates have been sent to the server, the client sends an End LBURP extended request to the server to mark the end of the LBURP session.

▸ The server sends an End LBURP extended response to the client.

 The entire LBURP specification is available at `http://www.ietf.org/ internet-drafts/draft-rharrison-lburp-02.txt.`

Essentially, the LBURP protocol enables the client to present data to the server as fast as the network connection between the two will allow. Generally this allows the server to stay busy processing update operations 100 percent of the time because it never has to wait for the client to give it more work to do. The LBURP processor in NDS also commits update operations to the database in groups to gain further efficiency in processing the update operations. In our lab tests, the Novell Import/Export Utility using LBURP has demonstrated performance up to ten times faster than synchronous LDAP update operations via LDAPModify. As you can see, LBURP can greatly improve the efficiency of your LDIF imports over a traditional synchronous approach.

The Novell Import/Export Utility versus LDAPSearch

The LDAPSearch utility is commonly used to retrieve information from an LDAP server and output the data in LDIF format. When you use the Novell Import/Export

Utility to export LDIF files, you get essentially the same functionality as LDAPSearch with some additional features.

Rules Processing

With the Novell Import/Export Utility, you can apply XML rules to modify the data as it passes through the ICE engine so that the resulting LDIF output file contents are customized for your needs. See the previous "XML Rules Options" section for more information.

Other Destination Handlers

With the Novell Import/Export Utility, you can choose to send the data from an LDAP server to a different destination handler. Currently, the only other supported handler is the LDAP destination handler, which enables you migrate data directly between two LDAP servers without having to store the data in an LDIF file as an intermediate step.

We expect additional destination servers to be written by Novell over time, and also expect to see Novell provide an SDK for developers to use to develop their own custom ICE source and destination handlers for special needs.

Improving the Speed of LDIF Imports

Although processing speed may not matter much in cases where you have only a few LDIF records to be imported, often you'll have thousands or possibly even millions of records in a single LDIF file. In these cases, you'll want to squeeze every bit of performance you can from the NDS Import/Export Wizard and the server to which it is sending updates. In this section we describe some steps you can take to get the best performance possible.

Import Directly to a Server with a Writeable Replica

If it's possible to do so, select a destination server for your LDIF import that has writeable replicas for all of the entries represented in the LDIF file. This maximizes network efficiency. You can get more information on creating and managing partitions and replicas in Chapter 8.

If at all possible, you want to avoid having the destination server chain to other NDS servers to do updates as this dramatically reduces performance. However, if some entries to be updated are only on NDS servers not running LDAP servers, you may have to allow chaining to occur to import the LDIF file.

TIP

Use LBURP

The Novell Import/Export Utility was designed to maximize network and NDS server processing efficiency by using LBURP to transfer data between the wizard and the server. LBURP is enabled by default in the Import/Export Utility for this reason. Unless you have a reason for not using LBURP, using this protocol greatly improves the speed of your LDIF import.

Since LBURP is a relatively new protocol, NDS servers before version 8.5 and most non-NDS servers do not yet support it. If you're using the NDS Import/Export Wizard to import an LDIF file to a server that doesn't support LBURP, the Novell Import/Export Utility detects this and automatically shifts over to using synchronous LDAP update operations to allow the import to succeed. When the utility shifts, it prints a message indicating that it has changed modes so that you'll know it is no longer using LBURP.

TIP

Configure the Database Cache

The amount of database cache available for use by NDS has a direct bearing on the speed of LDIF imports, especially as the total number of entries on the server increases. When you're doing an LDIF import, you may want to consider allocating the maximum memory possible to NDS during the import then lowering the cache size somewhat after the import is completed and the server is handling an average load. This is especially true if the LDIF import is the only activity taking place on the NDS server.

See the "Configuring the Database Cache" section in Chapter 10 for details on how to configure the NDS database cache.

X-REF

Use Simple Passwords

NDS traditionally uses public and private key pairs for authentication. Generating these keys is a very CPU-intensive process. Beginning with NDS eDirectory 8.5, you can choose to store passwords using the simple password method of the Novell Modular Authentication Service (NMAS). When you do this, passwords are kept in a secure location in the directory, but key pairs are not generated until they are actually needed for authentication between servers. This greatly improves the speed with which an object that has password information can be loaded.

You should be aware that if you choose to store passwords using simple passwords, you need to use an NMAS-aware version of the Novell (NetWare) Client software to log in to access traditional file and print services from NDS and NetWare. LDAP applications work seamlessly with the simple password method and do not require anything special.

When you're using the NMAS simple passwords method to store password values, NDS automatically detects whether each the password value is clear text or hashed by looking for a prefix string of {*<hash algorithm>*} in the password value, which *<hash algorithm>* specifies the algorithm used to hash the value. This allows you to store both clear text and hashed password values using the simple passwords method.

When you are migrating data from other vendors' directories, you may have hashed password values that you want to migrate into NDS. You can store passwords hashed with the SHA-1, UNIX Crypt, and MD5 algorithms when you enable the use of the simple password method.

To enable the use of simple passwords you must first install NMAS and configure the NMAS simple passwords method on the NDS server where you will be storing simple passwords. Although the simple passwords method is supported by the NMAS Enterprise Edition, which you must pay for, you also can get full support for the simple passwords method used by the Novell Import/Export Utility using the NMAS Starter Pack, which is free.

Lots of information about **NMAS**, including full product documentation, is available at `http://www.novell.com/products/nmas`. **You can download the NMAS Starter Pack and NMAS-aware versions of the Novell Client by following links on this page.**

Once NMAS is installed and configured for the simple passwords method, you can import LDIF files using the simple passwords method to store password values. To tell the LDAP server to use the simple passwords method, you must also check the "Store NMAS Simple passwords/Hashed passwords" option on the advanced options dialog box for the Destination LDAP Server page of the wizard or specify the -l option for the LDAP destination handler.

Use Indexes Appropriately

Having unnecessary indexes can slow down your LDIF import because each index that is defined requires additional processing for each entry that has attribute values stored in that index. Be sure that you don't have unnecessary indexes before you do an LDIF import, and you may even want to consider creating some indexes after you've completed loading the data and have had time to review predicate statistics to see where they're really needed.

See the "Speeding Up Searches: Creating Indexes" section in Chapter 10 for more information on tuning indexes.

X-REF

Debugging Your LDIF Files

Sooner or later you'll probably run into problems with an LDIF file. Whether it's a problem caused by minor differences between two directory implementations or a syntax error of your own making, the need to debug LDIF files is a virtual certainty. The following sections offer a few tips you can use to solve the most common problems we see in LDIF files.

Use SSL or Allow Clear Text Passwords

The most common problem we hear about from people trying to do LDIF imports has nothing to do with their LDIF file! It actually is caused by the fact that Novell ships its LDAP server with clear text password support disabled. If you get an error saying that the import/export utility cannot bind to the LDAP server, either use SSL (Secure Sockets Layer) for your connection, or configure LDAP to allow clear text passwords (via the LDAP Group object).

Disabling the use of clear text passwords by default is done to ensure that you won't unwittingly put your password or other sensitive LDAP information onto the Net in the clear, which is a security problem. When you enable the clear text password option, you are actually saying that all the data sent over connections made to the clear text LDAP port (usually port 389) will be sent in clear text form. Don't enable the use of clear text passwords unless you are working in an environment where it won't be a problem for all of your LDAP data (including password values) to be transmitted in the clear!

The "Editing the LDAP Group" section in Chapter 10 discusses this option in detail. Chapter 4, especially the "Secure Sockets Layer" section, discusses using SSL.

X-REF

If you know you want to use clear text passwords with an LDAP server, beginning with NDS eDirectory 8.5, you can choose to enable clear text passwords during the installation of NDS.

TIP

Enable Forward References

From time to time you may encounter LDIF files where the record to add an entry includes an LDAP DN that refers to another entry that doesn't yet exist.

The Problem: Referential Integrity

For example, imagine the case where you attempt to create an entry before you create its parent like this:

```
version: 1

dn: cn=Kevin Johnson,o=Acme
```

```
      changetype: add
      objectClass: inetOrgPerson
      sn: Johnson

      dn: o=Acme
      changetype: add
      objectClass: organization
```

When this situation occurs, an error is generated because the new entry's parent does not exist when the LDAP server attempts to add the entry. We know that you usually wouldn't intentionally create an LDIF file like this, but sometimes it happens inadvertently or when an LDIF file is machine-generated.

A more common case is when you create an LDAP groupOfNames entry that has a group member that doesn't yet exist because it will be added later in the file:

```
      version: 1

      dn: cn=Administrators,o=Acme
      changetype: add
      objectClass: groupOfNames
      uniqueMember: cn=Kevin Johnson,o=Acme

      dn: cn=Kevin Johnson,o=Acme
      changetype: add
      objectClass: inetOrgPerson
      sn: Johnson
```

Because NDS enforces *referential integrity*, it won't let the groupOfNames be created until the group member it references exists. This means that your request to add the groupOfUniqueNames will fail.

One way of solving this problem is to edit the LDIF file so that the inetOrgPerson record comes before the groupOfNames record like this:

```
      version: 1

      dn: cn=Kevin Johnson,o=Acme
```

```
changetype: add
objectClass: inetOrgPerson
sn: Johnson

dn: cn=Administrators,o=Acme
changetype: add
objectClass: groupOfNames
uniqueMember: cn=Kevin Johnson,o=Acme
```

But this won't always solve the problem. Sometimes, you may have a two way link between the inetOrgPerson and the to which group it belongs.

```
version: 1

dn: cn=Kevin Johnson,o=Acme
changetype: add
objectClass: inetOrgPerson
sn: Johnson
groupMembership: cn=Administrators,o=Acme

dn: cn=Administrators,o=Acme
changetype: add
objectClass: groupOfNames
uniqueMember: cn=Kevin Johnson,o=Acme
```

To solve this problem, you'd have to break the file up like this:

```
version: 1

dn: cn=Kevin Johnson,o=Acme
changetype: add
objectClass: inetOrgPerson
sn: Johnson

dn: cn=Administrators,o=Acme
changetype: add
```

```
objectClass: groupOfNames
uniqueMember: cn=Kevin Johnson,o=Acme

dn: cn=Kevin Johnson,o=Acme
changetype: modify
add: groupMembership
groupMembership: cn=Administrators,o=Acme
-
```

Now imagine having to do this for an LDIF file with 70,000 users! (We did this — once . . .)

The Solution: Forward References

An easy way to automatically solve all of these problems is to enable the use of forward references in the Novell Import/Export Utility (from the advanced options dialog box for the Destination LDAP Server page of the wizard or via the -F option for the LDAP destination handler).

When you attempt to create an entry that references another non-existent entry and forward references are enabled, NDS first creates a placeholder called a forward reference for the non-existent entry so that the create operation will succeed. Later, if an operation to attempts to create an entry that already exists as a forward reference, then the forward reference is changed into a normal entry.

Changing Forward References into Normal Entries

Normally when you attempt to create an entry that already exists, the attempt will fail with a result code of `entryAlreadyExists`. This is a perfectly sensible thing to do, because allowing multiple entries with the same name would make it impossible to uniquely identify entries in the directory.

In this respect, forward references are treated differently from other directory entries. When you attempt to add an entry that already exists as a forward reference, NDS simply replaces the forward reference with the entry you asked it to create and returns a result code of success.

It's possible that one or more forward references will be left in the DIT once your LDIF import is complete (if, for instance, NDS created a forward reference for an entry's parent but the LDIF file never created the parent to change forward reference into a normal entry). Forward reference entries show as "unknown" objects in ConsoleOne and have round yellow icons with question marks in the center. You won't be able to read values from the forward reference entry (because it doesn't have any attributes or attribute values), but all LDAP operations will work normally on the "real" object entries located below the forward reference.

Check the Syntax of Your LDIF File

If you think you might have a syntax error in your LDIF file, you can check its syntax before you try processing the records in it by selecting the "Display operations but do not perform" option from the Advanced Options dialog box for the Select LDIF Source File in the wizard. Or if you're using the command line utility, you use the -n option for the LDIF source handler. The LDIF source handler always checks the syntax of the records in an LDIF file as it processes them. Using this option just disables the processing of the records and lets you verify the syntax

Operation failed: 65(Object class violation), dn:

A common syntax error in LDIF files is to have stray white space (such as a leading space character) on the record separator line. When this happens, you can't see the problem because the line looks empty, but the stray white space means that the LDIF parser doesn't recognize the line as a record delimiter. When this happens, two records are treated as a single record. It then thinks that dn: is an attribute name isn't allowed in the object class of the first record and reports an object class violation error.

To solve this problem, make sure the record separator for the LDIF record reported in the error message is completely empty, including spaces and tabs.

Use the LDIF Error File

The import/export utility automatically creates an LDIF file containing each of the records that failed processing by the destination handler. You enable this function by giving the name of the LDIF error file you want the utility to use on the advanced options dialog for the first screen in the wizard. Or if you're using the command line utility, you use the -l option in the general options section.

You can take the LDIF error file generated by the import/export utility, edit it to fix the errors, then reapply it to the server using the import/export utility to finish an import or data migration that had failed records.

Set the Server Search Entry and Search Time Limits

If you're doing an LDIF export and you're not getting all of the records you expect, it may be because there's a hard limit set on the server that limits the number of search entries you can get back in a single search operation or the amount of time that can be spent by the server executing a single search operation. You can temporarily adjust these values to allow you to get all of the entries you need.

See the "Editing the LDAP Server Settings" section in Chapter 10 for details on adjusting these settings.

X-REF

Use LDAP SDK Debugging Flags

Although this is a fairly low-level technique, times exist when you may need to see how the LDAP client SDK is functioning to understand a problem. You can set LDAP SDK debugging flags for the LDAP source handler, the LDAP destination handler, or both. This functionality is currently only available in the command line interface for the import/export utility. You use the -e option for the LDAP Source and LDAP Destination handlers to enable it. The integer value you give for the -e option is a bitmask that enables various types of debugging information in the LDAP SDK. Table 11.15 shows each of the values and their associated meaning.

VALUE	DESCRIPTION
0 x 0001	Trace LDAP function calls.
0 x 0002	Print information on packets.
0 x 0004	Print information on arguments.
0 x 0008	Print connections information.
0 x 0010	Print BER encoding and decoding information.

TABLE 11.15

LDAP SDK Debugging Flags

Continued

TABLE 11.15	VALUE	DESCRIPTION
LDAP SDK Debugging Flags	0 x 0020	Print search filter information.
	0 x 0040	Print configuration information.
	0 x 0080	Print ACL information.
	0 x 0100	Print statistical information.
	0 x 0200	Print additional statistical information.
	0 x 0400	Print shell information.
	0 x 0800	Print parsing information.
	0 x FFFF (-1 Decimal)	Enable all debugging options.

Summary

The LDAP Data Interchange Format is a very useful tool in your LDAP development toolbox. It provides you with a standard, vendor-neutral way to exchange LDAP information as well as a convenient form for representing the content of an LDAP directory or a set of changes to be applied to an LDAP directory. This chapter explained the LDIF syntax in its entirety and gave you examples of every feature of LDIF. It also showed you how to perform schema modifications using LDIF.

The Novell Import/Export Utility is an efficient way to import LDIF files, export LDIF files, and do data migration between LDAP servers. This chapter discussed the command line and wizard interfaces to the import/export utility and explained the theory behind its operation. Finally, it presented some tips on maximizing the performance of data imports using the import/export utility and how you can diagnose and solve problems in your LDIF files.

What's on the CD-ROM

In this book we referenced many documents, utilities, and software development kits (SDKs). We also showed you sample source code that demonstrates how to perform the LDAP operations we discussed. For your convenience, we included as many of these materials as possible on the CD-ROM located on the inside back cover of this book, including a working evaluation copy of the Novell Directory Services (NDS) eDirectory. The section headings in this appendix correspond with the directories on the CD-ROM.

Examples

This directory holds source code listings from the book as well as an LDAP client application.

Listings

All of the source code and LDIF examples that are identified with a listing number are included as listings on the CD-ROM. Except for a couple of instances where we felt that a lengthy source code fragment warranted inclusion on the CD-ROM, all of the source code listings are complete programs that can be compiled and run. The listings that are fragments are identified as such by comments in the source code that show where additional code would be needed to make them fully-working examples.

The listings can be found under the \Examples\Listings directory. There is a directory for each chapter that has a listing, and the listings are located under subdirectories of the chapter directories. We have included both C and Java versions when possible.

When building the C examples, you must have first installed the Novell LDAP Libraries for C. This is located in the \SDKs\C\ Novell LDAP Libraries for C directory. You must also point to the proper "include" and "lib" paths, which are found in the ndk\cldapsdk directory where the SDK was installed. The appropriate .DLLs and .NLMs are located in the ndk\cldapsdk\bin directory where the SDK was installed.

When building the Java examples, you must include LDAPJDK.JAR in your classpath. This Java Archive (JAR) file is located on the CD-ROM in the \SDKs\Java\Netscape Directory SDK for Java directory.

Application

We've also included a working example in Java that shows how to build an LDAP client application. It is a schema browser and manager tool called SchemaManager and it's located in the \Examples\Application\SchemaManager directory. To run the example, include SCHEMAMANAGER.JAR, LDAPJDK.JAR, and SWING.JAR in your classpath, and run javaSchemaManager. The source files for this application are in the \Examples\Application\SchemaManager\src directory.

IETF Documents

The Internet Engineering Task Force (IETF) defines and controls LDAP through a series of engineering documents that either define proposed standards or give useful information related to LDAP. The two types of documents used are Requests for Comments (RFCs) and Internet-Drafts.

We have gathered together most of the IETF documents that are related to LDAP and put them on the CD-ROM.

NOTE

IETF documents use the newline character to mark the end of lines. Because the Notepad utility on Windows platforms expects a carriage return/newline pair to mark the end of lines, IETF documents do not display properly in Notepad; however, Wordpad utility displays them properly.

RFCs

RFCs fall into one of several categories, which include proposed standard, informational, and experimental. For details about the standards process and different RFC categories, refer to RFC 2026 — The Internet Standards Process, which is also included on the CD-ROM.

Most of the LDAP-related RFCs contain proposed standards. If these proposed standards become official standards, each will be reissued as an STD, which is an abbreviation for Standard. It is usually quite a lengthy process for an RFC to become an STD, and, as of yet, there are no LDAP-related STDs.

An RFC may eventually be obsoleted by a new RFC. We included the current version of the RFCs listed in Table A.1 on the CD-ROM for your convenience. They are in the \IETF Documents\RFCs directory.

 To make sure that you are reading the most current version, you can do a search for the RFC title at http://www.rfc-editor.org/rfc.html. **The direct URL to these documents is** http://www.ietf.org/rfc/rfcxxxx.txt, **where** *xxxx* **is the number of the RFC.**

FILE NAME	DOCUMENT TITLE
rfc1777.txt	Lightweight Directory Access Protocol (LDAPv2)
rfc1778.txt	The String Representation of Standard Attribute Syntaxes
rfc1779.txt	A String Representation of Distinguished Names
rfc1781.txt	Using the OSI Directory to Achieve User Friendly Naming
rfc1804.txt	Schema Publishing in X.500 Directory
rfc1823.txt	The LDAP Application Program Interface
rfc1959.txt	An LDAP URL Format
rfc1960.txt	A String Representation of LDAP Search Filters
rfc2026.txt	The Internet Standards Process – Revision 3
rfc2079.txt	Definition of an X.500 Attribute Type and an Object Class to Hold Uniform Resource Identifiers (URIs)
rfc2164.txt	Use of an X.500/LDAP directory to support MIXER address mapping
rfc2222.txt	Simple Authentication and Security Layer (SASL)
rfc2247.txt	Using Domains in LDAP/X.500 Distinguished Names
rfc2251.txt	Lightweight Directory Access Protocol (v3)
rfc2252.txt	Lightweight Directory Access Protocol (v3): Attribute Syntax Definitions

T A B L E A.1

LDAP-Related RFCs

	FILE NAME	DOCUMENT TITLE
TABLE A.1 *LDAP-Related RFCs* *(continued)*	rfc2253.txt	Lightweight Directory Access Protocol (v3): UTF-8 String Representation of Distinguished Names
	rfc2254.txt	The String Representation of LDAP Search Filters
	rfc2255.txt	The LDAP URL Format
	rfc2256.txt	A Summary of the X.500(96) User Schema for use with LDAPv3
	rfc2307.txt	An Approach for Using LDAP as a Network Information Service
	rfc2425.txt	A MIME Content-Type for Directory Information
	rfc2426.txt	vCard MIME Directory Profile
	rfc2559.txt	Internet X.509 Public Key Infrastructure: Operational Protocols – LDAPv2
	rfc2587.txt	Internet X.509 Public Key Infrastructure: LDAPv2 Schema
	rfc2589.txt	Lightweight Directory Access Protocol (v3): Extensions for Dynamic Directory Services
	rfc2596.txt	Use of Language Codes in LDAP
	rfc2649.txt	An LDAP Control and Schema for Holding Operation Signatures
	rfc2657.txt	LDAPv2 Client vs. the Index Mesh
	rfc2696.txt	LDAP Control Extension for Simple Paged Results Manipulation
	rfc2713.txt	Schema for Representing Java(tm) Objects in an LDAP Directory
	rfc2714.txt	Schema for Representing CORBA Object References in an LDAP Directory
	rfc2739.txt	Calendar Attributes for vCard and LDAP
	rfc2798.txt	Definition of the inetOrgPerson LDAP Object Class
	rfc2820.txt	Access Control Requirements for LDAP
	rfc2849.txt	The LDAP Data Interchange Format (LDIF) – Technical Specification

Internet-Drafts

The Internet-Drafts included on the CD-ROM contain engineering designs that have not yet become RFCs, as well as useful information provided by independent parties involved in LDAP development. Internet-Drafts are works in progress; they typically expire after six months. Internet-Draft documents have file names that indicate they are in draft status. The draft names typically include the word draft, the name of the principal author or IETF working group that is responsible for the Internet-Draft, the topic, and the draft number. For example, the Internet-Draft regarding the LDAP Bulk Update/Replication Protocol is named draft-rharrison-lburp-02.txt, which indicates that it was written by Roger Harrison and is the second version of the draft, because first version drafts end with 00.

The Internet-Drafts that are related to LDAP and are current as of the time this book goes to press are listed in Table A.2. They can be found on the CD-ROM in the \IETF Documents\Internet-Drafts directory.

To check for updated versions of these documents, look on the index page for the LDAP Extensions working group of the IETF at `http://www.etf.org/ids.by.wg/ldapext.html`.**The direct URL to these documents is** `http://www.ietf.org/internet-drafts/filename.txt`, **where filename.txt stands for the current file name.**

Remember that the version number gets updated at least once every six months, so you may need to try draft names with version numbers higher than the one listed. For example, if you were looking for the latest version of the LDAP Bulk Update/Replication Protocol draft, you might need to replace the -02 with a higher number like this: draft-rharrison-lburp-02.txt or draft-rharrison-lburp-04.txt. Also, keep in mind the Internet-Drafts may eventually become RFCs.

TABLE A.2	FILE NAME	DOCUMENT TITLE
LDAP-Related Internet-Drafts	draft-armijo-ldap-dirsync-01.txt	Microsoft LDAP Control for Directory Synchronization
	draft-armijo-ldap-treedelete-02.txt	Tree Delete Control
	draft-behera-ldap-password-policy-02.txt	Password Policy for LDAP Directories

TABLE A.2	FILE NAME	DOCUMENT TITLE
LDAP-Related Internet-Drafts (continued)	draft-ietf-ldapext-acl-model-05.txt	Access Control Model for LDAP
	draft-ietf-ldapext-authmeth-04.txt	Authentication Methods for LDAP
	draft-ietf-ldapext-ldap-c-api-04.txt Program Interface	The C LDAP Application
	draft-ietf-ldapext-ldap-java-api-10.txt	The Java LDAP Application Program Interface
	draft-ietf-ldapext-ldap-java-api-asynch-ext-05.txt	The Java LDAP Application Program Interface Asynchronous Extension
	draft-ietf-ldapext-ldap-taxonomy-02.txt	A Taxonomy of Methods for LDAP Clients Finding Servers
	draft-ietf-ldapext-ldapv3-dupent-04.txt	LDAP Control for a Duplicate Entry Representation of Search Results
	draft-ietf-ldapext-ldapv3-tls-06.txt	Lightweight Directory Access Protocol (v3): Extension for Transport Layer Security
	draft-ietf-ldapext-ldapv3-vlv-04.txt	LDAP Extensions for Scrolling View Browsing of Search Results
	draft-ietf-ldapext-locate-02.txt	Discovering LDAP Services with DNS
	draft-ietf-ldapext-matchedval-01.txt	Returning Matched Values with LDAPv3
	draft-ietf-ldapext-psearch-02.txt	Persistent Search: A Simple LDAP Change Notification Mechanism

Continued

TABLE A.2	FILE NAME	DOCUMENT TITLE
LDAP-Related Internet-Drafts (continued)	draft-ietf-ldapext-sorting-03.txt	LDAP Control Extension for Server Side Sorting of Search Results
	draft-ietf-ldapext-x509-sasl-03.txt	X.509 Authentication SASL Mechanism
	draft-ietf-ldup-framing-00.txt	Extended Operations for Framing LDAP Operations
	draft-ietf-ldup-infomod-01.txt	LDUP Replication Information Model
	draft-ietf-ldup-model-04.txt	LDAP Replication Architecture
	draft-ietf-ldup-protocol-01.txt	LDUP Replication Update Protocol
	draft-ietf-ldup-replica-req-02.txt	LDAP V3 Replication Requirements
	draft-ietf-ldup-subentry-03.txt	LDAP Subentry Schema
	draft-just-ldapv3-rescodes-02.txt	LDAPv3 Result Codes: Definitions and Appropriate Use
	draft-langer-ldup-mdcr-00.txt	LDUP Multiple Draft Conflict Resolution (MDCR)
	draft-leach-digest-sasl-05.txt	Using Digest Authentication as a SASL Mechanism
	draft-mmeredith-rootdse-vendor-info-02.txt	Storing Vendor Information in the LDAP root DSE
	draft-moats-ldap-dereference-match-02.txt	Extensible Match Rule to Dereference Pointers
	draft-nadas-diffserv-experience-01.txt	IBM Diffserv Implementation Experiments
	draft-natkovich-ldap-lcup-01.txt	LDAP Client Update Protocol

TABLE A.2	FILE NAME	DOCUMENT TITLE
LDAP-Related Internet-Drafts (continued)	draft-rharrison-lburp-02.txt	LDAP Bulk Update/ Replication Protocol
	draft-rharrison-ldap-extpartresp-02.txt	Extended Partial Response Protocol Enhancement to LDAPv3
	draft-salzr-ldap-repsig-00.txt	LDAP Controls for Reply Signatures
	draft-sermersheim-nds-ldap-schema00.txt	LDAP Schema for NDS
	draft-smith-ldap-c-api-ext-lderrno-00.txt	C LDAP API LDERRNO Extension
	draft-smith-ldap-c-api-ext-vlv-00.txt	LDAP C API Virtual List View Extension
	draft-vmodi-ldapext-compound-attr-00.txt	Compound Attribute Support in LDAP
	draft-wahl-ldap-digest-example-00.txt	An Example of DIGEST-MD5 Authentication within an LDAP server
	draft-weltman-ldap-java-controls-04.txt	Java LDAP Controls
	draft-weltman-ldapv3-auth-response-01.txt	LDAP Authentication Response Control
	draft-weltman-ldapv3-proxy-04.txt	LDAP Proxied Authorization Control
	draft-zeilenga-ldap-authpasswd-02.txt	LDAP Authentication Password Attribute
	draft-zeilenga-ldap-c-api-concurrency-00.txt	LDAP C API Concurrency Extensions
	draft-zeilenga-ldap-c-api-errno-00.txt	LDAP C API Error Reporting Extension
	draft-zeilenga-ldap-passwd-exop-04.txt	LDAP Password Modify Extended Operation

LDIF

Most of the examples we use in the book can be understood by simply reading them. However, we have included an LDIF file on the CD-ROM that will add entries to an LDAP server so that you can follow along by trying the examples on your own server. (See the next section on NDS eDirectory, for information about the evaluation version of NDS eDirectory that you can install.) The LDIF file is in the \LDIF directory on the CD-ROM.

See Chapter 11 for details about loading an LDIF file into your directory.

X-REF

NDS

As of press time, the NDS eDirectory 8.5 is almost ready to ship. We included evaluation copies of the beta 5 version of NDS for Windows NT, NetWare, Solaris, and Linux on the CD-ROM in the NDS directory.

To find updated versions of NDS, check the Web at http://www.novell.com/products/nds/promotions.html. **If you register as a developer (which is free) you can get a free license for the NDS eDirectory. Get details at** http://developer.novell.com/nds/edirectory/

Refer to Chapter 2 for instructions on installing NDS.

X-REF

SDKs

For your convenience, we included several LDAP client SDKs on the CD-ROM. In the \SDKs\C directory, you'll find the Novell LDAP Libraries for C SDK. In the \SDKs\Java directory, we've placed two different LDAP SDKs for Java; one is the

Netscape Directory SDK for Java and the other is Novell LDAP Service Provider for JNDI.

To install the Novell LDAP Libraries for C SDK or LDAP SDKs for Java, run the setup.exe program from the appropriate directory. The Netscape Directory SDK for Java requires no installation, simply include LDAPJDK.JAR in your classpath.

Refer to Chapter 3 for information on additional SDKs that may be available from Novell or third parties.

X-REF

We also included the Novell SSL for Java SDK in the \SDKs\Java\Novell SSL for Java directory, which can be used to establish an SSL connection to Novell's LDAP server.

See Chapter 4 for more information about how to use the Novell SSL for Java SDK.

X-REF

Utilities

We included two useful utilities on the CD-ROM in the \Utilities directory.

Toolbox (for NetWare)

Toolbox is a utility that allows access to the NetWare file system from the server console.

In Chapter 10 we tell you how to set the size of the database cache. We also mention that on NetWare this can be done by using a tool called toolbox.nlm.

X-REF

Novell Import/Export Utility

NDS eDirectory 8.5 includes a new utility called the Novell Import/Export Utility. Among other things, it can be used to import LDIF data into your LDAP server. The Novell Import/Export Utility includes two user interfaces: a

ConsoleOne snap-in and a command line utilty. Both interfaces are installed when you install ConsoleOne, and the command line version is included in the Novell LDAP Libraries for C SDK so that developers can use it when installing their LDAP applications. We've also provided the command-line version of the utility from the latest Novell LDAP Libraries for C SDK on the CD-ROM so you can run the Novell Import/Export Utility directly from the CD-ROM. This utility works best when you add the directory where the ICE executable is located to your PATH environment variable.

See Chapter 11 for information on the LDIF specification, including numerous LDIF examples and details on using the Novell Import/Export Utility.

X-REF

Understanding LDAP Error Codes and Solving Common Problems

Though we tried to call out potential pitfalls throughout the book, there is always a set of problems that you, the reader, will commonly encounter. Here, we try to pull together, from our experiences of working with the directory and helping others, a list of the most common problems and their solutions. Instead of just "giving you a fish," we're going to first teach you *how* to fish. We are going to show you how you can become an expert at understanding and solving problems you encounter, by making use of the LDAP error codes and messages, and tracing the messages produced as the result of problems. After that we go over some common problems and their solutions.

Though a few common problems are discussed here, your attention to the following "General Debugging Techniques" section will prove to be most helpful in the long run.

TIP

General Debugging Techniques

Before jumping into the list of problems, we want to stress the value of learning how to quickly identify the type of problem you're having and being able to narrow the problem down. The first resource you have is the LDAP error message that is returned when a failure occurs. The second is the use of the DSTrace utility on the server.

Understanding LDAP Errors

When something goes wrong with your LDAP application, an erroneous LDAP result code is typically returned to the client from the server. There may be some cases where no error is sent to the client and things go awry anyway — but this is the exception, not the rule. All LDAPResult messages have a result code. When things flow smoothly, the result code is either `success`, or one of the other non-erroneous result codes (such as `compareFalse` or `referral`). The LDAPResult message may also contain a human-readable error message that points you closer to the root of the problem.

Getting the Error Code

The first step in resolving a problem is finding out what that error code is — and what the client was trying to do when the code was returned.

If you're writing an application, you'll have direct access to the LDAP error code that is returned as a result of whatever problem you're dealing with. If you're using the Java LDAP SDK and an error is encountered, the SDK throws an LDAPException. You can use the getLDAPResultCode method to get the error code. If you're using the C LDAP SDK, you simply evaluate the return value of the function called, or if you're using asynchronous functions, you can use ldap_result() to obtain the error code.

Decoding the Error Code

The LDAP specification (RFC 2251) defines a set of result codes that are returned by the server in the LDAPResult message and numbers them from 0 to 80. Some are error codes, some are reserved, and others are non-erroneous result codes. The C and Java APIs define other error codes that are generated by the client — these are numbered from 81 to 97.

As of this writing, you can find the draft at `http://www.ietf.org/ internet-drafts/ draft-just-ldapv3-rescodes-02.txt`.

The following is a listing of each error code by value (we skip the non-erroneous result codes). We discuss what each error code means, what operations might cause them under which scenarios, and what can be done to remedy the problem that may have caused the error.

For an even more complete discussion of what causes these errors, you should read through the Internet-Draft "LDAPv3 Result Codes: Definitions and Appropriate Use."

X-REF

Each of the following errors is represented in the Java LDAP SDK as data members of the LDAPException class, using the name of the error in all caps with the words separated by underscores, so operationsError is represented by LDAPException.OPERATIONS_ERROR. In the C LDAP SDK, each error value is #defined in a similar manner — except that the word LDAP_ is prepended to them, so operationsError is #defined as LDAP_OPERATIONS_ERROR.

In this appendix, we also typically look at the return codes from the perspective of the server. So, if we say, "operationsError is *returned*," you should read it to mean that, if you are using the Java LDAP SDK, an LDAPException is *thrown*, and it will have the value LDAPException.OPERATIONS_ERROR.

operationsError (1)   At one time this error was returned where other (80) should have been. The version of NDS that is included with this book fixes that problem and returns other. Currently, the server only returns this error when an internal error occurs on the server (like the server runs out of memory).

protocolError (2)   This indicates that the client sent a bad request, meaning that the message sent to the server was either malformed or there was missing information. This error is returned in the following circumstances:

▸ Either the client SDK used to write the application had a problem (bug) encoding the LDAP request, or the server has a bug and can't decode it properly.

▸ The client presents itself as an LDAPv2 client during the bind operation and later requests an LDAPv3 operation.

▸ An extended operation was requested but the server does not support that operation.

timeLimitExceeded (3)   To date, Novell's LDAP server only returns this error when, while processing a search operation, the time limit elapses before the search is complete. This could be due to an extremely large set of results to be returned, due to the absence of an index on the attributes you're searching for, or due to the server chaining (contacting other servers to service the request). Be aware that the server evaluates the time limit set on the LDAP Server object as well as the time limit sent as part as the search request. The smaller of the time limit on the LDAP Server object and the time limit you specify in your search request will be used.

To remedy this problem, make sure that the time limit set on the LDAP Server object is sufficiently large (setting it to 0 allows a search to take an unlimited amount of time to complete). If that doesn't fix the problem, your application is probably sending a time limit in the search request. This can be verified by looking at the request in the DSTrace screen. See if there's a way to configure search time limits in your application. If you are developing the application, use the LDAPContraints class to modify the time limit.

NOTE **In the future, this may be returned if the server takes an excessive amount of time to chain any request to other servers (not just search requests). You probably won't be able to specify a "chaining timeout" as part of an LDAP request; rather it would most likely be a configurable setting on the server.**

sizeLimitExceeded (4) This is returned if the search entry limit is reached before the search is done. Like with the timeLimitExceeded error, the server evaluates both the size limit sent with the search request and the size limit set on the LDAP Server object. If two size limits exist (one on the LDAP Server object and one specified in the search request), the smaller one is used.

To remedy this problem, make sure that the size limit set on the LDAP Server object is sufficiently large (setting it to 0 allows a search to return an unlimited number of search results). If that doesn't fix the problem, the application you are using is probably sending a size limit in the search request. This can be verified by looking at the request in the DSTrace screen. See if there's a way to configure search size limits in your application. If you are developing the application, use the LDAPContraints class to modify the time limit.

authMethodNotSupported (7) If this is returned, it means that you tried to use an SASL mechanism that isn't supported by the server as part of the bind request. As of this writing, only the "EXTERNAL" SASL mechanism is supported when performing an SASL bind.

X-REF **See Chapter 4 for more information on SASL authentication and how to use the "EXTERNAL" mechanism.**

strongAuthRequired (8) This is one of the first errors that most people encounter after installing the LDAP server. It is returned after the client connects to the clear text (non-SSL) port, sends a bind request and specifies a username and password, and the server is configured to not accept clear text binds.

There are a number of ways to remedy this problem. You can bind anonymously by not specifying a username or password, you can configure the server to accept clear text passwords, or you can configure the server and client to establish an SSL connection prior to sending the bind request.

X-REF **Anonymous binds and SSL connections are covered in Chapter 4. See Chapter 2 or Chapter 10 for instructions on allowing clear text passwords.**

adminLimitExceeded (11)   As of this writing, this error is never returned by Novell's LDAP server. In the future, it may be returned due to some administrative limit being reached while servicing a request. An example might be the server not being able to process a Server Side Sorting control because there are too many search results to sort.

unavailableCriticalExtension (12)   If you send a control with an LDAP request, and mark that control as critical (see Chapter 9), this error could be returned as a result of that control not being available or being disabled. This could also be returned if you try to use a critical control with an operation that the control was not intended for. For example, if you mark a Server Side Sorting control as critical and then send it with a modify operation, this error is returned. This is also returned if you request an extended operation that the server is unable to service for some reason. This is different from the case where the server does not support an extended request. In that case, protocolError is returned.

confidentialityRequired (13)   This error is not currently returned from Novell's LDAP server.

noSuchAttribute (16)   This may be returned from a modify operation if you attempt to delete an attribute that doesn't exist on the entry. It may be returned from a compare operation if the attribute you're comparing doesn't exist on the entry.

In both of these cases, the error is benign and only notifies you that the operation couldn't be completed as intended.

undefinedAttributeType (17)   This is returned from an add or modify operation if you specify an attribute that is not part of the server's schema.

Try to find out which attribute is causing the error and make sure it's defined in the schema (See Chapter 7). Currently, the only way to discover the erroneous attribute is by trial and error.

inappropriateMatching (18)   This is returned from a search when you attempt to use a matching rule that is not supported by the attribute you're searching for. For example, if you use the filter (flag=tru*) where flag is an attribute that uses Boolean syntax (which doesn't allow substring matching), this error is returned.

Make sure that the search being sent to the server isn't attempting to do something more fancy than the server can handle. If a complex search filter is being sent, try breaking it down and using smaller pieces of it in separate requests to narrow the problem down to a specific portion.

constraintViolation (19)   This can be returned by the modify, add, or modifyDN operations. It's returned if an attribute value is specified that is either too long or too short (or in the case of numerical attributes, too high or too low). It may also be returned if you attempt to add multiple values to a single-value attribute.

Check the minimum and maximum limits set in the schema for the attribute that is causing this problem and make sure you're not exceeding a limitation.

attributeOrValueExists (20)   During a modify or add operation, this error is returned if you try to add an attribute value that already exists.

invalidAttributeSyntax (21)   This error is returned from a modify or add operation if an attribute value specified is malformed, invalid, or doesn't adhere to the syntax for that attribute.

Determine which attribute value is causing the problem by breaking the add or modify into smaller operations, each holding a single value, then look up the syntax in effect for that attribute by checking the schema (see Chapter 7). Find the syntax definition (most likely in RFC 2252 or the Internet-Draft "LDAP Schema for NDS" and make sure the value you've provided is correct.

RFC 2252 or the Internet-Draft "LDAP Schema for NDS" can be found at http://www.ietf.org/internet-drafts/ draft-sermersheim-nds-ldap-schema-00.txt.

noSuchObject (32)   This can be returned as a result of any operation that takes a DN. It signifies that the DN passed to the operation cannot be found in the directory.

aliasProblem (33)   This is returned from a search operation if the server attempted to dereference an alias object but the object that the alias references does not exist.

This indicates a database inconsistency; you should run DSRepair to fix the problem.

Documentation for the DSRepair utility can be found online at
`http://www.novell.com/documentation/lg/nds8/usnds/usrefenu/data/hv7lr8sz.html.`

invalidDNSyntax (34)   This is returned by any operation that takes a DN argument. This is sent if the DN doesn't adhere to the syntax set forth in RFC 2253 (or RFC 1779 if you're using an LDAP v2 client).

Make sure that the DN isn't malformed.

aliasDereferencingProblem (36)   This can be returned from a search operation if the referenced object can't be dereferenced due to access control restrictions. It can also be returned if you attempt to create an alias object that references another alias object.

Make sure you have sufficient rights to read the `aliasedObjectName` attribute on the alias object being dereferenced.

inappropriateAuthentication (48)   Novell's LDAP server never returns this error message.

invalidCredentials (49)   This is only returned from a bind operation. It signifies that the password supplied is either incorrect, or it has expired.

insufficientAccessRights (50)   The client doesn't have the rights needed to perform the operation. This can be returned from any operation response other than bind.

Make sure that you have the necessary permissions to perform the operation. Most likely you need to look at the access control list (ACL) attribute on the entry that you're trying to modify. NDS allows ACLs to be inherited from container objects. You may also need to check the ACL on each container object up to the root of the tree. In the future, LDAP will allow you to ask for the effective privileges that a subject has to an object.

busy (51)   As of this writing, Novell's LDAP server doesn't return this error. It could be returned in the future to signify that the server is currently busy and the client should retry the request later.

unavailable (52)   This is returned if the server is currently in the process of shutting down or when an idle connection is being dropped.

unwillingToPerform (53)   This is returned in the following scenarios:

▶ A control can't be serviced as it is specified. If this error is returned as a result of a control, check the accompanying error message for further help.

▶ You've attempted to modify your password without supplying the old one and you don't have administrator rights. See "How Do I Change My Password" in the "Frequently Encountered Problems" section later in this appendix.

▶ While mapping a schema element (object class or attribute type), you specified an NDS name that clashes with an existing LDAP element.

▶ You're attempting to update the schema while it's being replicated or updated by another process. Retry the operation later.

loopDetect (54)   As of this writing, the server doesn't return this error. It could be returned in the future to signify that the server encountered an error while chaining or dereferencing an alias. This would probably signify either a database problem or a replica management problem, in which case you would run DSRepair to fix the database and/or the replica ring.

namingViolation (64)   This is returned from the add or modifyDN operations when you attempt any of the following:

▶ Name an entry using an attribute that is not a naming attribute (see Chapter 7)

▶ Add or move an entry to a place in the tree that it isn't allowed by the containment rules (for example, trying to place an organization below an organizational unit)

Make sure that the attribute used to name the object is a valid naming attribute and that the structure rules for the object class that you're using are being followed.

objectClassViolation (65)   This is returned from an add or modify operation (modifyDN could also return it) when you've asked to create or modify an object in such a way that is not allowed by the object class definition for that object. For example, if you try to add an object, but forget to populate one of the mandatory attributes, this error is returned. Other scenarios include

▶ Deleting all the values of a mandatory attribute or deleting the attribute itself

▶ Adding an attribute that is neither an optional nor a mandatory attribute

▶ Renaming an entry and, in the process, deleting the last value of a naming attribute which also happens to be a mandatory attribute

Look carefully at what attributes are being updated and make sure that all modifications and additions jibe with the requirements of the object class(es) being used for the entry.

See Chapter 7 for a discussion of naming, mandatory and optional attributes.

X-REF

notAllowedOnNonLeaf (66)   The server returns this error if you attempt to delete an entry that has subordinate entries below it. You also receive this error if you try to move an entry (using modifyDN) and the entry has subordinate entries. Novell's LDAP server doesn't currently support moving a subtree.

notAllowedOnRDN (67)   You may only change the naming attribute value using the modifyDN operation. This error is returned when you try to use the modify operation to change the distinguished value of the naming attribute.

entryAlreadyExists (68)   This is returned from add or modifyDN if you try to create an entry or rename an entry and the new name is already used in the directory.

objectClassModsProhibited (69)   This is returned if you attempt to change the structural object class value of an entry. For example, if you try to change a person into a printer, you get this error.

affectsMultipleDSAs (71)   So far, the LDAP server doesn't return this error. In the future it could be used to signify that you tried to move an object from one replica to another, and the LDAP server doesn't allow that.

other (80)   Novell's LDAP server returns this error when it can't come up with anything better to return. Typically, the error is accompanied by a more descriptive error message.

Client Error Codes

The following error codes are generated by the client side SDK rather than by the server.

serverDown (81)   The server has gone down or could not be contacted. Make sure that the server is running and responding to requests. Possible problems include the following:

- The server is in a bad state and must be restarted.

- The server is misconfigured. Check that the server is configured to listen on the same port that your client application is sending on.

- Trying to connect to the wrong address. Make sure the address is correct and that DNS is working by pinging the address and the DNS name.

localError (82)   Some general error has occurred on the client.

encodingError (83)   The client SDK has encountered an error while encoding a request to be sent to the server.

decodingError (84)   The client SDK has encountered an error while decoding a request that was received by the server.

timeout (85)   When you set a timeout constraint, the client SDK employs a built-in timer to cause a timeout to happen in the event that the server's timeout mechanism isn't sufficient. If the client timer expires, an abandon operation is sent to the server, and a timeout error is returned from the SDK operation.

authUnknown (86)   This signifies that you've specified an authentication method for the bind operation that is currently unsupported by the SDK.

filterError (87)   The search methods return this if they encountered a problem while encoding the search filter. Essentially this means that there is a syntax error in the construction of the search filter. Make sure that the search filter is constructed correctly.

userCancelled (88) This error is not yet returned.

paramError (89) This error may be returned if you've specified a parameter that is invalid. For example, it is returned if you specify null for a String parameter that is required for the method to successfully complete.

noMemory (90) The client couldn't allocate memory when it attempted to do so.

connectError (91) You typically see this error during a bind if the client is able to connect to the specified port, but then doesn't hear anything back from the server, or gets a message from the server that it doesn't recognize. Possible reasons that this might happen include:

▶ Some other service is listening on the port you specified in the bind request.

▶ You established an initial connection to the LDAP server, but it is too busy to respond to your bind request.

notSupported (92) The client SDK attempts to ensure that you don't send LDAPv3 operations after performing an LDAPv2 bind. If you get this error, try binding as an LDAPv3 client.

X-REF

Refer to Chapter 4 for more information on the bind operation.

controlNotFound (93) This is returned if you've asked for a particular response control and none came back with the response from the server.

noResultsReturned (94) This signifies that no results have been returned. This may be returned in an exception from the getResponse method of the LDAPResponseListener class. With the C SDK it is returned from the ldap_parse_ result function.

moreResultsToReturn (95) This is not returned by the Java SDK. It is returned from ldap_parse_result in the C SDK to signify that there are more results.

clientLoop (96) If the client is following referrals and a loop is detected, this error is returned.

referralLimitExceeded (97) This signifies that the referral hop limit has been exceeded.

See Chapters 5 and 8 for more information about setting the number of allowed referral hops.

X-REF

Getting and Using the Error Message

In some cases, the error code itself doesn't provide enough information about a problem to help you understand what caused it. This is especially true in the case of ambiguous errors such as other. The LDAPMessage also allows for a human-readable error message to be included when there is an error condition that can aid you in narrowing the root of the problem.

If you're using the Java SDK, you can use the getLDAPErrorMessage method of the LDAPException to examine the error message. With the C SDK, you can use the function ldap_parse_result(), and examine the errmsgp parameter.

As of NDS 8.5, the error message includes an internal NDS error number. You can get more information about the meanings of these numbers by referring to the Web page http://developer.novell.com/ndk/doc/docui/index.htm#../ndslib/dsov_enu/data/hcvwzt90.htm.

TIP

Making Use of the Matched DN

When certain errors are returned — namely noSuchObject, aliasProblem, invalidDNSyntax, and aliasDereferencingProblem — the matchedDN field of the LDAPMessage is populated with the part of the DN that the server was able to match when resolving (or parsing) the DN passed in an operation. For example, let's say you try to add an object and you named it cn=fred, ou=bakers, ou=employees, o=caterer corner, but the organizationalUnit named ou=bakers doesn't exist under ou=employees, o=caterer corner. You would receive a noSuchObject error code, and the matched DN would be set to ou=employees, o=caterer corner, because that object does exist.

The matched DN helps you quickly locate the point in the directory that name resolution failed, or the point in the DN you specified that caused an invalidDNSyntax error. To get the matched DN using the Java SDK, you can use the getMatchedDN method of LDAPException. Alternately, use ldap_parse_result() with the C SDK and look at the matcheddnp variable.

Using DSTrace

If you haven't yet, it's a good idea to familiarize yourself with DSTrace by running it and watching what happens when you change the LDAP Server object's screen options and then send LDAP requests to the server.

X-REF **Setting up and running the DSTrace debugging utility is covered in Chapter 2. Chapter 10 shows how to configure your LDAP Server object to allow certain messages to be sent to the DSTrace screen.**

At first, some of the messages may seem cryptic and not of much help, but as you become more familiar with LDAP, you'll find that the information in the messages will begin to make more sense. If nothing else, LDAP trace messages are helpful if you need to draw on the help of others to assist you in resolving the problem.

Frequently Encountered Problems

Here, we cover some of the more common problems that users and developers run into when using Novell's LDAP server. We group the problems into five major areas: Installation problems, connection and authentication problems, problems encountered while searching, update problems, and miscellaneous problems.

Installation Problems

This set of problems consists of things that go wrong during an install.

My installation failed partway through — what can I do to fix it?

When NDS is installed, the installation program first loads all the files necessary to run NDS (without LDAP support). It may happen that this portion of the install succeeds but the LDAP installation fails. If this happens, you need to reinstall NDS. NDS 8.5 allows you to use the NDS Install utility, which is accessible through the NDS Service program (NDSCONS.EXE), to do this. If you have a prior version, you must fully uninstall NDS and reinstall it.

Connection and Authentication Problems

These problems occur when you're trying to establish a connection to the LDAP server or issue a bind request and it fails for some reason.

I just installed my server, and I can't bind to it

If you get an error code of `confidentialityRequired`, or in the case of older versions of NDS, `strongAuthenticationRequired`, and a message that states: `Server does not accept clear text passwords`, you've come up against one of the most commonly encountered problems. Luckily, it's one of the easiest to remedy. The problem is that Novell's LDAP server wants you to make a secure connection before you send your password over the wire. There are two ways to remedy this.

▸ Use an SSL connection. This is described in Chapter 4.

▸ Mark the "Allow Clear Text Passwords" option in the LDAP Group object. This is described in Chapters 2 and 10.

I just installed my LDAP server, and I can't connect to it

If you have other software installed on your server that is listening on the default LDAP ports (389 and 636), that application may block the LDAP server from receiving your LDAP messages. To test and remedy this problem, change the TCP and SSL ports to different port numbers in the LDAP Server object. If you do this, make sure you configure your client software to make LDAP connections to the new ports you specify.

I could bind fine previously; now I get an invalidCredentials error

If you were able to bind for some time and suddenly can't, you may have an expired password. A common problem when using Novell's LDAP server is that it doesn't expose the grace login feature that is used by legacy NDAP applications. What this means is that your password may expire without you being aware of it. Because you're not warned about the situation, you end up using all your grace logins until you're no longer able to connect. If this happens, the administrator must reset your password using the ConsoleOne utility.

I can't connect with the Netscape or Exchange Address Book using SSL

You may have followed all the directions in Chapters 4 and 10 to create a certificate authority and server certificate, exported it, and successfully imported into your browser or into Windows, but you still have problems getting the connection to work. This may be due to a key size mismatch. When you created the server certificate (key material), you probably chose the standard creation method. This creates a certificate with the strongest key size available. If you have a domestic strength version of NDS and your address book is an export strength version, the address book will not work correctly with the larger certificate key size that was exported from NDS. To fix this, reinstall your Certificate Authority and Key Material object. While installing these objects, choose the custom option to allow you to set the key size to something small (like 512).

Problems while Searching

This section is devoted to problems commonly encountered while using LDAP to search for entries or using the search operation to read an entry.

I don't get all the entries that I should

If you know there are entries in the tree that match your search filter, but they aren't returned while searching, it may be a rights issue. Beginning with NDS 8.35, a restrictive check is performed on the attributes in the search filter. After an entry is found that matches the search filter, your rights are calculated and compared for that entry. For the server to return the entry to you, you must have browse rights to the entry, and you must have compare rights to all the attributes listed in the search filter. It is the second restriction (compare rights to all attributes listed in the search filter) that bites most people.

When NDS is installed, it automatically gives all users browse rights to all objects in the tree, but it doesn't give ordinary users the ability to perform compares against all attributes. To remedy this problem, you can grant all users the right to perform compares on all attributes by doing the following in ConsoleOne:

1. Right-click on the tree object for your server, and then choose Trustees of this Object . . . .

2. Select the trustee named [Public], and press the Assigned Rights button.

3. Press Add Property, select [All Attributes Rights], and press OK.

4. Uncheck the Read rights if you do not want to allow everyone to read every attribute.

5. Press OK to dismiss these two dialog boxes and retry your search.

My search returns entries but some attributes are missing

If you know that an entry has attributes that aren't being returned by a search operation, it's likely that one of the following problems exist:

▸ You don't have sufficient rights to read the attribute. Check your rights on the object in question to make sure you have read access to the attributes that aren't being returned.

▸ The attribute has an invalid LDAP name. NDS is less restrictive in regards to the allowable character set that you can use to name an attribute. If your attribute contains spaces, colons, or dashes, you need to make an LDAP mapping before you can see them with LDAP. Refer to Chapters 7 and 10 for instructions on how to do this. Beginning with NDS version 8.5, this is no longer a problem because nonstandard attribute names are automatically mapped to valid LDAP attribute names on the fly.

▸ You didn't ask for the attributes to be returned. Remember that if you ask for certain attributes to be returned, only those attributes are returned. Chapter 5 discusses the various ways in which you can specify the attributes to be returned.

Netscape's Address Book won't perform the search

Two common symptoms present themselves when using Netscape's Address Book to query Novell's LDAP server. If you configure the Address Book to prompt for name and password, you'll occasionally witness a situation where the Address Book appears to be hung. If this is happening, reconfigure the Address Book to not require a username and password. The problem is with Netscape's Address Book implementation. In this case, the Address Book is sending an asynchronous bind followed by a search. If the bind operation happens to be serviced by the server after the search (which does happen sometimes), the search is abandoned. This is normal behavior on the server's part and a bug with the Address Book. Netscape is working to remedy this problem.

NOTE **You should never send an asynchronous bind because you may encounter problems like the one mentioned in the preceding example.**

The other symptom often encountered is a message that states that a bind hop limit has been exceeded. This only happens when you try to establish an SSL connection with the server. Again, this is a Netscape Address Book problem. Actually it's a problem with the 3.1 version of Netscape's C LDAP SDK, which is used by the Address Book application in version 4.7 of Netscape's Communicator. This problem has been fixed with subsequent versions of the Netscape C SDK. Try upgrading to version 4 or later of Netscape's C SDK if you experience this problem.

The Server Side Sorting control or Virtual List View control won't work for me

You should be aware of some limitations with Novell's implementation of the Server Side Sorting control. These limitations also affect the Virtual List View control because it depends on the Server Side Sorting control to operate. You get an error code of `unwillingToPerform` if any of the following cases cause a failure:

- You are limited to a single sort key. The sort control takes a list of keys (attributes) to sort on. Novell's LDAP server currently only supports a single key.

- The sort key attribute must be indexed. If the sort key is not indexed, you must index it. Chapter 10 talks about indexing attributes.

- The orderingRule field is not supported. If you specify an orderingRule, the control fails to operate.

- Reverse order searches are not yet supported.

- If you wish to use the typedown feature of the Virtual List View control, the search filter specified must contain only the sort key attribute. If your sort key is cn, the search filter must be something like (cn=*) or (cn=abe).

If you just need your results sorted and can't work around the problem, consider using the sort method or LDAPSearchResults. This causes the client to sort the results instead of the server.

Update Problems

This section deals with problems that are encountered when using LDAP update operations like modify, add, delete, and modifyDN.

How do I change my password?

With many LDAP servers, you can change your user password by modifying the userPassword attribute and replacing it with a new value. Novell's LDAP server requires a bit more in order to do this if you do not have administrative rights. To change your password, you must use a single modify operation that specifies the old password in a delete action, and the new password in an add action. In LDIF terms, the operation looks like this:

```
dn: cn=myObject,o=myOrg
changetype: modify
delete: userPassword
userPassword: myOldPassword
-
add: userPassword
userPassword: myNewPassword
```

This is required to ensure that it's really you who are changing your password and not someone else. Imagine logging in to your directory, leaving your computer for a moment, and someone else changing your password while you're away! This is what other LDAP servers have opened themselves up to by allowing you to change your password without providing proof of your old password.

NOTE

If you are the directory administrator, you are not bound by this restriction; you may send a modify operation that simply replaces the userPassword with a new value without specifying the old one.

Miscellaneous Problems

This section lists problems that aren't directly tied to a specific LDAP operation.

I don't see any LDAP messages on the DSTrace screen

The following three steps are required to view LDAP messages in the DSTrace screen:

1. DSTrace must be running.

2. The DSTrace LDAP option must be enabled.

3. The appropriate screen options on the LDAP Server object must be enabled.

If any one of these steps has not been taken, you won't see the messages you are looking for.

See Chapters 1 and 10 for instructions on running DSTrace, setting the DSTrace LDAP option, and setting the screen options for the LDAP Server object.

X-REF

LDAP applications work with Netscape and Active Directory but not NDS

The following are a few common problems that sometimes prevent applications which run fine with Netscape or Active Directory from running with NDS.

▶ **NDS employs structure rules.** This means that NDS won't allow any old object to be created in any arbitrary place in the tree. It uses structure rules to limit which objects can be contained by other objects. For instance, an organization may reside under a country, but a country may not reside under a person. If you have an application that creates objects in the tree, make sure that the object it attempts to create can be placed in the locations that the application is attempting to place them.

Chapters 6 and 7 talk more about structure rules and how you can modify the allowable structure of your tree.

X-REF

▶ **NDS checks the schema to ensure data integrity.** Some directories allow you to "turn off schema checking". This allows you to create objects with attributes that aren't part of the object class for that object. While this makes it very easy to write applications, because you don't have to worry about extending the schema, it makes for a sloppy application and a sloppier directory. The manufacturers of these directories warn against using the "turn off schema checking" flag. If you have an application that works with other directories only because you've disabled schema checking, you need to find out why and amend the schema appropriately. Then the application should work with NDS.

Getting Help and More Information

There are a number of resources available for you when you need help, support, or just a bit more information about a particular aspect of Novell's LDAP server or LDAP in general. This appendix lists what's currently out there.

Getting Help

If you find yourself in a bind, you can turn to any one of the support options detailed in the following sections.

Novell Web Resources

You'll find a host of information dealing with NDS and LDAP at these Novell Web sites.

- ▸ `http://www.novell.com/products/nds/`. This site is the springboard for product information relating to the NDS and LDAP product. From here you can jump to `http://www.novell.com/products/nds/services.html` where you'll find a number of support options.

- ▸ `http://support.novell.com/`. From here you can explore support's knowledge base as well as read support forums, file electronic incident reports, and learn about a variety of Novell's support programs.

- ▸ `http://developer.novell.com/`. This site is geared more towards developers. It contains all the documentation for Novell's SDKs, example code, support forums, and so on. You'll need to register in order to access many of the areas. Registration is free.

Public Novell LDAP and NDS Newsgroups

These newsgroups are devoted to NDS, either set up as peer support or supported by Novell itself.

▸ `news://devforums.novell.com/novell.devsup.ldap_j`. This newsgroup is supported by Novell and is where most people go to ask developer questions relating to the LDAP server and JNDI as well as the Java SDK.

▸ `news://devforums.novell.com/novell.devsup.njcl`. This is another Novell-supported newsgroup that deals with Novell Java Class Libraries (NJCL). NJCL incorporates the JNDI service providers that Novell ships, which include a JNDI provider for LDAP. Note that Novell's JNDI provider for LDAP is being phased out in favor of the one that ships with the Java 2 SDK 1.3.

▸ `news://forums.novell.com/novell.directoryservices.ldap`. This is a peer-support newsgroup hosted by Novell. This is probably where most Novell LDAP questions are asked and answered.

▸ `news://forums.novell.com/novell.directoryservices.nds` This newsgroup deals with NDS problems. Remember that the LDAP server relies on NDS; this means that the LDAP server automatically inherits any NDS problems.

LDAP-Related Mailing Lists

Though not hosted by Novell, these mailing lists are monitored by Novell employees as well as dozens of other LDAP experts from around the world.

▸ `ldap@umich.edu`. The original LDAP reference implementation was created at the University of Michigan. This mailing list remains as a vital support and discussion venue for LDAP servers, clients, and deployments. You can subscribe to this newsgroup by sending mail to `ldap-request@umich.edu` with the message body "subscribe ldap".

▶ ietf-ldapext@netscape.com. Most of the LDAP-related work currently being done through the IETF is being done in the LDAP Extensions Working Group. This mailing list is used for all the topics being discussed in that working group. Some questions are asked and answered, but only questions concerning the protocol itself are appropriate — not questions about a particular vendor's implementation. You can subscribe to this newsgroup by sending mail to ietf-ldapext-request@netscape.com with the message body "subscribe".

More Information

You can use the following list of resources to answer LDAP-related questions ranging from "What's being done to ensure interoperability among LDAP servers?" to "How is access control handled in the X.500 specification?"

Standards

LDAP is an open standard protocol defined by the IETF. The LDAP definition is held in a series of RFCs and is based on the ITU's X.500 set of recommendations. RFCs start out as Internet-Drafts. Here, we've compiled a list of those RFCs, Internet-Drafts and X.500 recommendations.

RFCs

As of this printing, these are the RFCs used to specify LDAP. They can be found at http://ietf.org/rfc.html. It is anticipated that some of these RFCs will be revised and updated by new ones before LDAP becomes a Standard (STD).

The Core LDAPv3 RFCs   The core set of LDAPv3 RFCs are listed here. Many of these RFCs have made older RFCs obsolete. The older RFCs represent LDAPv2.

▶ **RFC 2251 – Lightweight Directory Access Protocol (v3):** This contains the formal definition of the LDAPv3 protocol as well as elements of the data model. This document describes all of the LDAP operations. Available at http://ietf.org/rfc/rfc2251.txt.

▶ **RFC 2252 – LDAPv3 Attribute Syntax Definitions:** This document defines the core set of syntax definitions as well as a few attribute types, object classes, and matching rules. Values of most syntax definitions are defined here, to be transmitted as human-readable strings. Available at `http://ietf.org/rfc/rfc2252.txt`.

▶ **RFC 2253 – LDAPv3 UTF-8 String Representation of Distinguished Names:** This contains the rules used to transmit DNs as strings. Available at `http://ietf.org/rfc/rfc2253.txt`.

▶ **RFC 2254 – The String Representation of LDAP Search Filters:** This RFC is one of the more useful RFCs for LDAP client writers and consumers. It describes what a search filter can look like. Some applications allow the user to enter a formal search filter, while others take some kind of user input and concoct a search filter from it. These applications pass that search filter to the SDK, which in turn decodes the search filter and sends an LDAP search request to the LDAP server. Available at `http://ietf.org/rfc/rfc2254.txt`.

▶ **RFC 2255 – The LDAP URL Format:** Another useful RFC for client and application writers and LDAP consumers. This describes the format of the LDAP URL. It shows how to create an LDAP URL and describes all the fields. Available at `http://ietf.org/rfc/rfc2255.txt`.

▶ **RFC 2256 – A Summary of the X.500(96) User Schema for Use with LDAPv3:** This gathers various syntaxes, attribute types, object classes, and matching rules from the X.500 series of recommendations and defines them in terms of LDAP. The schema elements defined by this RFC represent the most popular schema elements at the time it was published. Available at `http://ietf.org/rfc/rfc2256.txt`.

Related LDAPv3 RFCs   These remaining RFCs supplement the core set of RFCs.

▶ **RFC 2247 – Using Domains in LDAP/X.500 Distinguished Names:** This defines the attribute type and object classes needed to represent domains in an LDAP directory.

Using the schema described here you can represent DNS names in your directory. For example: the DNS name bilbo.novell.com can be represented as dc=bilbo,dc=novell,dc=com. The growing trend is to use NDS as a DNS repository and to use DNS naming conventions to build directories. This is because DNS is a global namespace. Available at `http://ietf.org/rfc/rfc2247.txt`.

▸ **RFC 2307 – An Approach for Using LDAP as a Network Information Service:** This is an experimental RFC that shows how to map UNIX NIS entities into an LDAP directory. It defines the syntaxes, attribute types, object classes, and implementation details needed to use your LDAP directory as a Network Information Service. Available at `http://ietf.org/rfc/rfc2307.txt`.

NOTE

If you use RFC 2307, you will notice that it specifies an attribute called `homeDirectory`. **Novell's LDAP server already has an attribute map by this name that serves a different purpose. To work around this problem, remove the mapping and replace it with one named** `ndsHomeDirectory`. **Attribute mappings are discussed in Chapter 7.**

▸ **RFC 2559 – Internet X.509 Public Key Infrastructure Operational Protocols:** This shows how LDAP can be used as a repository for Public Key Infrastructure (PKI) information. Available at `http://ietf.org/rfc/rfc2559.txt`.

▸ **RFC 2587 – Internet X.509 Public Key Infrastructure LDAPv2 Schema:** This is used with 2559 to store PKI information in the directory. Available at `http://ietf.org/rfc/rfc2587.txt`.

▸ **RFC 2589 – LDAPv3 Extensions for Dynamic Directory Services:** This describes how an LDAP directory can be used to store dynamic data — that is, data that only hangs around as long as you keep refreshing it. It does this by attaching Time to Live (TTL) data to objects in the directory. Available at `http://ietf.org/rfc/rfc2589.txt`.

▶ **RFC 2596 – Use of Language Codes in LDAP:** This shows how to use attribute descriptions to transmit and request attributes using language tags. Available at `http://ietf.org/rfc/rfc2596.txt`.

▶ **RFC 2649 – An LDAP Control and Schema for Holding Operation Signatures:** This experimental RFC describes a way to digitally sign LDAP operations in such a way that the sender and receiver can be verified and an audit trail can be kept to track operations. Available at `http://ietf.org/rfc/rfc2649.txt`.

▶ **RFC 2696 – LDAP Control Extension for Simple Paged Results Manipulation:** This is an informational RFC that shows how to get search results back one page at a time. The more flexible Virtual List View control replaces this control (see Chapter 9). Available at `http://ietf.org/rfc/rfc2696.txt`.

▶ **RFC 2713 – Schema for Representing Java(tm) Objects in an LDAP Directory:** This informational RFC describes a schema that allows Java objects to be stored in the directory. The JNDI LDAP service provider has the capability to store Java objects. Available at `http://ietf.org/rfc/rfc2713.txt`.

▶ **RFC 2714 – Schema for Representing CORBA Object References in an LDAP Directory:** This informational RFC describes a schema that allows Common Object Request Broker Architecture (CORBA) object references to be stored in the directory. The JNDI LDAP service provider has the capability to store CORBA object references. Available at `http://ietf.org/rfc/rfc2714.txt`.

▶ **RFC 2739 – Calendar Attributes for vCard and LDAP:** This describes a schema that allows user calendar data (such as busy times) to be stored in and retrieved from the directory for use by scheduling programs. Available at `http://ietf.org/rfc/rfc2739.txt`.

▸ **RFC 2798 – Definition of the inetOrgPerson LDAP Object Class:** This describes the schema elements commonly in use that represent user data in today's LDAP directories. Available at `http://ietf.org/rfc/rfc2798.txt`.

Internet-Drafts

An Internet-Draft is a document that is written as a precursor to an RFC. Internet-Drafts usually start out as very volatile documents and are categorized as "works in progress." Unless another Internet-Draft or an RFC updates them, they expire six months from the time they are written. After the details of the draft are solidified, it is reviewed by the Internet Engineering Steering Group (IESG) and converted into an RFC. The following Internet-Drafts are those that have to do with LDAP and its use.

Internet-Drafts of the LDAP Extensions Working Group The LDAP Extensions working group is responsible for addressing any outstanding issues that prevent LDAP from being deployed as an interoperable directory. It does this by coming up with new LDAPv3 controls, extensions, and in rare cases, new LDAP functionality. These drafts are those that the working group is currently chartered to work on. It is compiled from the IETF's Web page at `http://ietf.org/ids.by.wg/ldapext.html`.

▸ **draft-ietf-ldapext-ldap-java-api – "The Java LDAP Application Program Interface":** This document defines a Java API for LDAP in the form of a class library. It complements but does not replace RFC 1823, which describes a C language API. The companion document draft-ietf-ldapext-ldap-java-api-asynch defines the mandatory to implement asynchronous layer of the API. These are the APIs that we have used in the code examples of this book. Available at `http://ietf.org/internet-drafts/draft-ietf-ldapext-ldap-java-api-10.txt`.

▸ **draft-ietf-ldapext-ldap-java-api-asynch-ext – "The Java LDAP Application Program Interface Asynchronous Extension":** This document defines asynchronous extensions to the preceding Java LDAP API document. Available at `http://ietf.org/internet-drafts/draft-ietf-ldapext-ldap-java-api-asynch-ext-05.txt`.

As of this writing, work is underway to update draft-ietf-ldapext-ldap-java-api-10.txt to include the APIs in draft-ietf-ldapext-ldap-java-api-asynch-ext-05.txt. The resulting document will be named draft-ietf-ldapext-ldap-java-api-11.txt.

▸ **draft-ietf-ldapext-ldap-c-api** – "The C LDAP Application Program Interface": This document defines a C language API for LDAP. This document replaces the previous definition of this API, defined in RFC 1823, updating it to include support for features found in version 3 of the LDAP protocol. Available at `http://ietf.org/internet-drafts/ draft-ietf-ldapext-ldap-c-api-04.txt`.

▸ **draft-ietf-ldapext-acl-reqts** – "Access Control Requirements for LDAP": This document describes the requirements of an access control list (ACL) model for the LDAP directory service. It is intended to be a gathering place for access control requirements needed to provide authorized access to directories, as well as interoperability between directories. Available at `http://ietf.org/internet-drafts/draft-ietf-ldapext-acl- reqts-03.txt`.

▸ **draft-ietf-ldapext-acl-model** – "Access Control Model for LDAP": This document describes the access control model for LDAP. It includes a description of the model and the LDAP controls and extended operations used to expose various parts of the model. Available at `http://ietf. org/internet-drafts/draft-ietf-ldapext-acl-model-05.txt`.

▸ **draft-ietf-ldapext-authmeth-04.txt** – "Authentication Methods for LDAP": This document specifies particular combinations of security mechanisms, which are required and recommended in LDAP implementations. Available at `http://ietf.org/internet-drafts/ draft-ietf-ldapext-authmeth-04.txt`.

▸ **draft-ietf-ldapext-ldapv3-tls** – "LDAPv3 Extension for Transport Layer Security": This document defines an LDAP extended request used to support the Start Transport Layer Security (TLS) Operation for LDAPv3.

This allows you to turn SSL encryption on and off during an LDAP session. Available at `http://ietf.org/internet-drafts/draft-ietf-ldapext-ldapv3-tls-06.txt`.

▸ **draft-ietf-ldapext-x509-sasl – "X.509 Authentication SASL Mechanism":** This document defines a SASL authentication mechanism based on X.509 strong authentication, providing two-way authentication. Available at `http://ietf.org/internet-drafts/draft-ietf-ldapext-x509-sasl-03.txt`.

▸ **draft-ietf-ldapext-ldapv3 – "LDAP Extensions for Scrolling View Browsing of Search Results":** This document describes a Virtual List View control extension for the LDAP Search operation. See Chapter 9 for more information about this control. Available at `http://ietf.org/internet-drafts/draft-ietf-ldapext-ldapv3-vlv-04.txt`.

▸ **draft-ietf-ldapext-sorting – "LDAP Control Extension for Server Side Sorting of Search Results":** This document describes two LDAPv3 control extensions for server side sorting of search results. See Chapter 9 for more information about this control. Available at `http://ietf.org/internet-drafts/draft-ietf-ldapext-sorting-02.txt`.

▸ **draft-ietf-ldapext-ldapv3-dupent – "LDAP Control for a Duplicate Entry Representation of Search Results":** This document describes a Duplicate Entry Representation control extension for the LDAP Search operation. By using the control with an LDAP search, a client requests that the server return separate entries for each value held in the specified attributes. If a specified attribute of an entry holds multiple values, the search operation returns multiple instances of that entry, with each instance holding a separate single value in that attribute. Available at `http://ietf.org/internet-drafts/draft-ietf-ldapext-ldapv3-dupent-03.txt`.

▸ **draft-ietf-ldapext-psearch – "Persistent Search: A Simple LDAP Change Notification Mechanism":** This document defines two controls that extend the LDAPv3 search operation to provide a simple mechanism by which an LDAP client can receive notification of changes that occur in an LDAP server. The mechanism is designed to be very flexible and easy for clients and servers to implement. Because the IETF is likely to pursue a different, more comprehensive solution in this area, this document will eventually be published with informational status to document an existing practice. Available at `http://ietf.org/internet-drafts/draft-ietf-ldapext-psearch-02.txt`.

▸ **draft-ietf-ldapext-matchedval – "Returning Matched Values with LDAPv3"**: This document describes an LDAPv3 control that is used to return a subset of attribute values from an entry, specifically, only those values that contributed to the search filter evaluating to true. Available at `http://ietf.org/internet-drafts/draft-ietf-ldapext-matchedval-01.txt`.

▸ **draft-ietf-ldapext-ldap-taxonomy – "A Taxonomy of Methods for LDAP Clients Finding Servers"**: There are several different methods by which an LDAP client can find an LDAP server. This draft discusses these methods and provides pointers for interested parties wanting to learn more about implementing a particular method. Available at `http://ietf.org/internet-drafts/draft-ietf-ldapext-ldap-taxonomy-02.txt`.

▸ **draft-ietf-ldapext-locate – "Discovering LDAP Services with DNS"**: This document specifies a method for discovering LDAP servers using information in the Domain Name System (DNS). Available at `http://ietf.org/internet-drafts/draft-ietf-ldapext-locate-02.txt`.

Internet-Drafts of the LDUP Working Group   The LDUP working group is defining the protocols, data models, and algorithms needed to replicate between two LDAP servers over the Internet. This set of drafts is compiled from the IETF's Web page at `http://ietf.org/ids.by.wg/ldup.html`.

▸ **draft-ietf-ldup-replica-req-02.txt – "LDAP V3 Replication Requirements"**: This document covers the fundamental requirements for replication of data accessible via the LDAPv3 protocol. It is intended to be a gathering place for general replication requirements that are needed in order to provide interoperability between LDAP directories.

Available at `http://ietf.org/internet-drafts/draft-ietf-ldup-replica-req-02.txt`.

▸ **draft-ietf-ldup-model-03.txt – "LDAP Replication Architecture"**: This architectural document gives a high level view of the schema and protocol extensions to LDAPv3 that may be used to enable LDAP servers to exchange directory content and updates. Available at `http://ietf.org/internet-drafts/draft-ietf-ldup-model-03.txt`.

▸ **draft-ietf-ldup-infomod-01.txt – "LDUP Replication Information Model"**: This document picks up where the LDAP Replication Architecture document leaves off. It details the information model and schema elements that are described in the architecture document. Available at `http://ietf.org/internet-drafts/draft-ietf-ldup-model-03.txt`.

▸ **draft-ietf-ldup-subentry-02.txt – "LDAP Subentry Schema"**: This document describes an object class that is used to construct and represent LDAP subentries. This long-needed object class is now being defined in the LDUP working group because the information model document requires it. Available at `http://ietf.org/internet-drafts/draft-ietf-ldup-subentry-02.txt`.

▸ **draft-ietf-ldup-urp-02.txt – "LDUP Update Reconciliation Procedures"**: This document covers the various collisions that can happen when servers in a replicated environment replicate. It also describes the procedures used to reconcile the updates. Available at `http://ietf.org/internet-drafts/draft-ietf-ldup-urp-02.txt`.

▸ **draft-ietf-ldup-protocol-01.txt – "The LDUP Replication Update Protocol"**: The protocol described in this document allows one LDAP server to replicate its directory content to another LDAP server. Available at `http://ietf.org/internet-drafts/draft-ietf-ldup-protocol-01.txt`.

▸ **draft-ietf-ldup-framing-00.txt – "Extended Operations for Framing LDAP Operations":** This describes a portion of the protocol used in the Update Protocol document. This portion of the protocol was abstracted to make its usefulness available to other LDAP mechanisms that can take advantage of its capability to frame and order requests. Available at `http://ietf.org/internet-drafts/draft-ietf-ldup-framing-00.txt`.

Other Pertinent LDAP-Related Internet-Drafts   These drafts are individual submissions. Though they are not officially part of the LDAP Extensions working group charter, the working group reviews most of them before they are sent to the IESG for review. Some are documents that eventually affect the next revision of the LDAP documents, some augment LDAP by providing special security-related features, and others define various and sundry features and useful mechanisms by virtue of LDAP's extension mechanisms.

▸ **draft-weltman-ldap-java-controls – "Java LDAP Controls":** This defines how one would write Java classes that can be used by the Java LDAP API to work with the Server Side Sorting control, Virtual List View control, Persistent Search control, and the Proxied Authentication control. Available at `http://ietf.org/internet-drafts/draft-weltman-ldap-java-controls-04.txt`.

▸ **draft-smith-ldap-c-api-ext-vlv – "LDAP C API Virtual List View Extension":** This describes functionality and interfaces to be added to the C Language API for LDAP to service the Virtual List View control. Available at `http://ietf.org/internet-drafts/draft-smith-ldap-c-api-ext-vlv-00.txt`.

▸ **draft-zeilenga-ldap-c-api-concurrency – "LDAP C API Concurrency Extensions":** This document defines extensions to the LDAP C API to support use in concurrent execution environments. It defines requirements for multiple concurrency levels: thread safe, session thread safe, and operation thread safe. Available at `http://ietf.org/internet-drafts/draft-zeilenga-ldap-c-api-concurrency-00.txt`.

▸ **draft-zeilenga-ldap-c-api-errno – "LDAP C API Error Reporting Extension":** This defines a consistent, easy-to-use error reporting mechanism that is to be implemented when implementing the C Language API for LDAP. Available at `http://ietf.org/internet-drafts/draft-zeilenga-ldap-c-api-errno-00.txt`

▸ **draft-smith-ldap-c-api-ext-lderrno – "C LDAP API LDERRNO Extension":** This provides an alternate solution to the problem addressed by the preceding LDAP C API Error Reporting Extension draft. Ultimately, one of these drafts will be chosen as the preferred way to report errors for those functions that don't currently return errors in the C Language API. Available at `http://ietf.org/internet-drafts/draft-smith-ldap-c-api-ext-lderrno-00.txt`.

▸ **draft-good-ldap-ldif – "The LDAP Data Interchange Format (LDIF) – Technical Specification":** See Chapter 11 for a full description of this draft. Available at `http://ietf.org/internet-drafts/draft-good-ldap-ldif-06.txt`.

▸ **draft-just-ldapv3-rescodes – "LDAPv3 Result Codes: Definitions and Appropriate Use":** This formally defines the proper uses of the LDAPv3 result codes that are defined in RFC 2251. Available at `http://ietf.org/internet-drafts/draft-just-ldapv3-rescodes-02.txt`.

▸ **draft-rharrison-ldap-extpartresp – "Extended Partial Response Protocol Enhancement to LDAP v3":** This adds another operation to the LDAPv3 set of operations that is used to send multiple extended partial responses to the client before sending the final extended response. See Chapter 9 for more on this draft. Available at `http://ietf.org/internet-drafts/draft-rharrison-ldap-extpartresp-00.txt`.

▸ **draft-leach-digest-sasl – "Using Digest Authentication as a SASL Mechanism":** This describes an SASL authentication mechanism that uses DIGEST-MD5. Available at `http://ietf.org/internet-drafts/draft-leach-digest-sasl-05.txt`.

▶ **draft-wahl-ldap-digest-example – "An Example of DIGEST-MD5 Authentication within an LDAP server":** This shows how one can implement the DIGEST-MD5 SASL mechanism for binding. Available at `http://ietf.org/internet-drafts/draft-wahl-ldap-digest-example-00.txt`.

▶ **draft-zeilenga-ldap-authpasswd – "LDAP Authentication Password Attribute":** This describes a new attribute that can be used to store hashed passwords. Available at `http://ietf.org/internet-drafts/draft-zeilenga-ldap-authpasswd-02.txt`.

▶ **draft-zeilenga-ldap-passwd-exop "LDAP Password Modify Extended Operation":** this describes a control that can be used to change passwords. Available at `http://ietf.org/internet-drafts/draft-zeilenga-ldap-passwd-exop-01.txt`.

▶ **draft-behera-ldap-password-policy – "Password Policy for LDAP Directories":** This contains the LDAP schema, an LDAP control, and the algorithms that are used to enforce password-related policies such as intruder detection, password histories, and so on. Available at `http://ietf.org/internet-drafts/draft-behera-ldap-password-policy-01.txt`.

▶ **draft-weltman-ldapv3-proxy – "LDAP Proxied Authentication Control":** This describes a control that can be used to act as if you are another entity for the duration of an operation. Available at `http://ietf.org/internet-drafts/draft-weltman-ldapv3-proxy-04.txt`.

▶ **draft-weltman-ldapv3-auth-response – "LDAP Authentication Response Control":** This control returns the DN of the authenticated user. This is analogous to a whoami operation. Available at `http://ietf.org/internet-drafts/draft-weltman-ldapv3-auth-response-01.txt`.

▸ **draft-salzr-ldap-repsig – "LDAP Controls for Reply Signatures"**: This can be used by a client acting as a Certification Authority (CA) to verify whether a certificate that it deposited in an LDAP directory was actually deposited without any compromise. Available at `http://ietf.org/ internet-drafts/draft-salzr-ldap-repsig-00.txt`.

▸ **draft-natkovich-ldap-lcup – "LDAP Client Update Protocol"**: This consolidates the controls defined in the Persistent Search, Triggered Search, and Microsoft Directory Synchronization drafts into a single control. Available at `http://ietf.org/internet-drafts/draft-salzr- ldap-repsig-00.txt`.

▸ **draft-ietf-ldapext-psearch – "Persistent Search: A Simple LDAP Change Notification Mechanism"**: Like the Triggered Search draft, this allows a client to receive changes as they happen. Available at `http://ietf. org/internet-drafts/draft-ietf-ldapext-psearch-02.txt`.

▸ **draft-armijo-ldap-dirsync – "Microsoft LDAP Control for Directory Synchronization"**: This is another stab at allowing a client to receive updates from the directory. Available at `http://ietf.org/internet- drafts/draft-armijo-ldap-dirsync-01.txt`.

▸ **draft-good-ldap-changelog – "Definition of an Object Class to Hold LDAP Change Records"**: This is used by Netscape's directory to track updates to the directory. Available at `http://ietf.org/internet- drafts/draft-good-ldap-changelog-01.txt`.

▸ **draft-rharrison-lburp – "LDAP Bulk Update/Replication Protocol"**: This describes how to send many update operations to the server in an efficient manner. Refer to Chapters 9 and 11 for more information. Available at `http://ietf.org/internet-drafts/draft-rharrison-lburp- 01.txt`.

▸ **draft-sermersheim-nds-ldap-schema – "LDAP Schema for NDS"**: This describes the schema elements found in Novell's LDAP server that are not otherwise defined in standard LDAP documents. Available at `http://ietf.org/internet-drafts/draft-sermersheim-nds-ldap-schema-00.txt`.

- **draft-wahl-ldap-adminaddr – "Administrator Address Attribute"**: This describes how an LDAP server can advertise the contact information for the administrator of that server. Available at `http://ietf.org/internet-drafts/draft-wahl-ldap-adminaddr-00.txt`.

- **draft-greenblatt-ldap-certinfo-schema – "LDAP Object Class for Holding Certificate Information"**: This describes how many X.509 certificates may be stored in the directory for a user, and at the same time be easily retrievable. Available at `http://ietf.org/internet-drafts/draft-greenblatt-ldap-certinfo-schema-02.txt`.

- **draft-wood-ldapext-float – "Directory string representation for floating point values"**: This defines the encoding rules needed to represent floating point numbers as strings in an LDAP directory. Available at `http://ietf.org/internet-drafts/draft-wood-ldapext-float-00.txt`.

- **draft-mmeredith-rootdse-vendor-info – "Storing Vendor Information in the LDAP root DSE"**: This shows how the vendor name and release tag of the LDAP server being talked to is advertised. Available at `http://ietf.org/internet-drafts/draft-mmeredith-rootdse-vendor-info-02.txt`.

- **draft-armijo-ldap-treedelete – "Tree Delete Control"**: This describes a control that can be used with the LDAP delete operation to delete an entire subtree. Available at `http://ietf.org/internet-drafts/draft-armijo-ldap-treedelete-02.txt`.

- **draft-moats-ldap-dereference-match – "Extensible Match Rule to Dereference Pointers"**: This attempts to use a special matching rule that instructs the LDAP server to examine the DN in an attribute, dereference that object, and continue the search from that object. Available at `http://ietf.org/internet-drafts/draft-moats-ldap-dereference-match-02.txt`.

▸ **draft-vmodi-ldapext-compound-attr – "Compound Attribute Support in LDAP":** This describes how LDAP can be changed to handle compound attributes. Using this technology, you can nest one or more attributes within another. In this way, you can build your own structured data. Available at `http://ietf.org/internet-drafts/draft-vmodi-ldapext-compound-attr-00.txt`.

The X.500 Directory Specification

The following is a list of RFCs that make up the X.500 Directory Specification. These RFCs are available from the International Telecommunications Union (ITU) at `http://www.itu.int/POD/how-to-buy.html`.

▸ **X.500 – "The Directory: Overview of concepts, models and services":** This is a simple introduction to the X.500 directory that includes a high-level view of what the directory is all about — much like the introduction from Chapter 1 of this book.

▸ **X.501 – "The Directory: Models":** This document describes the different ways the directory can be viewed and the models that make up the directory. It goes into detail describing the Directory Information Tree (DIT), what a Directory Server Agent (DSA) is, and so on.

▸ **X.509 – "The Directory: Authentication framework":** This deals with those things needed to authenticate to the directory. You may recognize the term "X.509 certificate" or even just "certificate" or "user certificate." This document defines what that certificate is and how it is used.

▸ **X.511 – "The Directory: Abstract service definition":** This document contains definitions of all the directory operations: bind, unbind, search, modify, and so forth. It also describes the error codes that are sent from the server to the client.

▸ **X.518 – "The Directory: Procedures for distributed operation":** This details the processing of operations. It contains flowcharts and algorithms used by directory servers while processing requests.

▶ **X.519 – "The Directory: Protocol specifications":** This simply describes how the directory operations (which were defined in X.511) are to be encoded and transferred over the wire. This is one place where LDAP and the X.500 specifications diverge.

▶ **X.520 – "The Directory: Selected attribute types":** This defines a few attribute types. These are redefined in LDAP terms by RFC 2256.

▶ **X.521 – "The Directory: Selected object classes":** This is similar to X.520. It defines some object classes. They, too, are redefined in RFC 2256.

▶ **X.525 – "The Directory: Replication":** This shows how the directory is replicated. The IETF LDUP working group uses some of the information described here to define how LDAP is replicated.

LDAP-Related Web Sites

This section contains pointers to web pages that are not hosted by Novell, but that provide useful information regarding X.500 and LDAP.

Understanding X.500 — The Directory
http://www.salford.ac.uk/its024/X500.htm
This is an online version of a very informative and helpful book by David Chadwick on the X.500 directory.

The X.500 Directory Standards Home Page at Nexor
http://www.nexor.com/info/directory.htm
This page contains many pointers to online X.500 resources.

University of Michigan Information Technology Division Distributed Directory Services
http://www.umich.edu/~dirsvcs/
The University of Michigan, the birthplace of LDAP, hosts this Web page.

Innosoft's LDAP World
http://www.innosoft.com/ldapworld/
This Web page contains useful pointers as well as an LDAP FAQ.

An LDAP Roadmap & FAQ

`http://www.kingsmountain.com/ldapRoadmap.shtml`

This is a tutorial aid to navigating various LDAP and X.500 Directory Services resources on the Internet.

LDAP Extension Charter

`http://www.ietf.org/html.charters/ldapext-charter.html`

This is the IETF LDAP extensions working group charter page. It links to all the working group documents and the listserver.

The Open Group Directory Program

`http://www.opengroup.org/directory/`

The Open Group hosts DirConnect, an annual LDAP interoperability get-together where LDAP directories from different vendors are tested using the Basic LDAP Interoperability Test Suite (BLITS). They also plan to come up with standardized criteria in order to be branded as LDAP-interoperable.

The Directory Interoperability Forum

`http://www.directoryforum.org/`

This forum represents a group of open directory providers, working through standards bodies to accelerate the evolution and adoption of open directory-based applications.

Other Books

Understanding and Deploying LDAP Directory Services by Tim Howes, Mark C. Smith, Gordon S. Good.

This book is sometimes referred to as the LDAP Bible. It's certainly big enough and full of enough information to warrant that moniker. This book provides some insight into LDAP, but, more importantly, helps answer the types of questions an IS department might have when deploying an LDAP directory in their corporation.

Understanding X.500 – The Directory by David Chadwick

Though this book is out of print, you can get an online version at `http://www.salford.ac.uk/its024/X500.htm`. This book goes through the X.500 specifications in a very easy to understand way.

Differences Between NDAP and LDAP

If you have had experience using or writing applications that work with NDS in the past, you've probably been exposed to NDAP in one form or another. This appendix covers what kinds of differences you may encounter as you move to LDAP. In this appendix, we do the following:

▸ Introduce NDAP

▸ Discuss the differences between NDAP and LDAP

▸ Talk about the various APIs that speak NDAP

▸ Show how the functionality provided by NDAP maps to LDAP

▸ Provide detailed information on how the functionality provided by Novell's most popular and complete NDS NDAP SDK — the NDS Libraries for C — maps to LDAP operations

What Is NDAP?

NDAP stands for Novell Directory Access Protocol. The term is useful to set it apart from LDAP. If you think of what the term LDAP implies, you can think of NDAP as being the set of those things as Novell saw them before the advent of LDAP. In this book, we've applied NDAP to the naming and data models of NDS as well as the wire protocol used by the client and server to communicate.

The NDAP Protocol

The protocol used by legacy NDS applications and SDKs is a set of NDS verbs. These NDS verbs are packaged inside NetWare Core Protocol (NCP) packets, which we refer to as NCPs. Each NDS verb represents instructions sent between the client and server, which in turn affect the directory. In this way, NDS verbs are much like the LDAP Protocol Data Units (PDUs) that LDAP uses to communicate.

Rather than use the term LDAP PDU, this book uses the more generic term "LDAP operation." To date, there are 120 NDS verbs where each verb defines its own response, compared to the 20 that make up LDAP.

NOTE We won't go into detail about each specific **NDS** verb or how **NCPs** are used to deliver them between the client and server. Instead, we talk in general terms about the functionality that is available through **NDAP**, and how you can use **LDAP** operations to achieve that same functionality.

The NDAP Data Model

The terms LDAP data model and NDAP data model are really misnomers, but are used to tie the data model of the directory to the protocol being used to access that directory. Since both NDS and LDAP have common roots in X.500, their data models are so similar that most differences are negligible. Each consists of one or more servers that hold parts of a hierarchical directory tree. Each holds entries made up of attributes. Each uses Distinguished Names to name the entries.

Who Uses NDAP?

You've probably been using the ConsoleOne management utility while reading this book. That utility uses NDAP to speak to NDS. In the future, ConsoleOne will probably be rewritten to use LDAP. Once ConsoleOne is rewritten to use LDAP, it will no longer be dependent on the Novell client libraries being installed on your machine. It will also be able to manage LDAP servers from other vendors that you may have deployed.

If you use NetWare and log in so that you can share network resources, you are using technology that speaks NDAP. Work is underway to move these technologies to LDAP, but because LDAP is so new, it hasn't been done yet.

Most developers that have written directory-enabled applications for NDS in the past have used SDKs that speak NDAP. The most popular SDKs are the NDS Libraries for C and the Novell Java Class Libraries.

What Differences Will I Notice between NDAP and LDAP?

If you've used NDS applications, you've already been exposed to some of the peculiarities of NDAP. We discussed one of these in Chapter 2; that is, the DNs in an NDS directory differ slightly in composition from those in an LDAP directory. We cover this and other peculiarities here.

The Data Model

Though there are few differences between the LDAP data model and the NDS data model, those that do exist should be called out.

While other X.500 and LDAP directories have the notion of a tree, only NDS chooses to name them. When you install NDS, you're asked to provide a tree name. Other LDAP servers typically assume that there's a global tree, or that there is no overriding tree and they require one or more "suffixes" at the root of the DIT when installing. The term suffix simply means the name of the entry at the top of your subtree. Some LDAP servers require that you include at least a suffix as the base name of your LDAP operations whereas Novell's LDAP server allows you to root operations, such as search, at the empty name. Because NDS allows a tree name, you can easily deploy and manage many NDS trees at once. NDS advertises the names of its trees and servers in a proprietary way. Novell is looking into LDAP server advertisement, but hasn't begun doing this yet.

NDS has a physical, shared object at the root of the tree. LDAP prescribes a special, per-server object at the root called the "root DSE". NDS uses the root object for some of its partition and replication management mechanisms. It also enables you to place access control information on the root object and specify that the access control information inherits down the tree. Because LDAP places a server-specific root DSE object at the root of the tree, you can't read the values of NDS's root object via LDAP.

The Naming Model

As was mentioned in Chapter 2, the name of an entry is made up of RDNs. One difference between NDS names and LDAP names is that the RDNs are separated by commas in LDAP, while they're separated by periods in NDS. Another difference is that LDAP requires each RDN to contain an attribute value assertion (AVA), while NDS allows you to specify a name without the attributes. This is termed "typeless names" in NDS. For example, the LDAP name cn=admin,o=administration, could be represented in NDS as either cn=admin.o=administration or simply admin. administration.

The Access Control Model

As of this writing, there is no standard way to represent Access Control Information (ACI) in an LDAP directory. ACI is the information that specifies who has rights to examine and manipulate what data. Most LDAP servers (including Novell's) include a way to specify ACI, but in a proprietary way. The IETF Extensions working group is working on an RFC that will standardize on a single ACI model in the future. For now, users of Novell's LDAP server can use the ACL attribute that NDS employs to represent ACI.

The format of the ACL attribute is described in Section 5.7 of draft-sermersheim-nds-ldap-schema-00.txt available at http://search.ietf.org/internet-drafts/draft-sermersheim-nds-ldap-schema-00.txt.

The Schema

Two differences exist between LDAP schema and NDS schema. The first is the data held in the schema. The other is in the way you read and update the schema. NDAP provides specialized functionality that allows you to read and modify schema elements while LDAP allows you to use existing LDAP operations to do this.

Refer to Chapter 7 for details on the differences between LDAP and NDS schema. The chapter also gives examples of how to read and modify the schema.

X-REF

Authentication

One of the benefits of NDAP is that by using Novell's client libraries for NDAP, you only need to authenticate to the directory once. After that, any NDS-aware application running on your computer can take advantage of the authenticated connection. With LDAP, each application must bind separately. The only problem with this benefit of NDAP is that you must install the proprietary libraries on your computer. Work is being done to extend this functionality to LDAP, but it isn't available yet.

Mapping NDAP Functionality onto LDAP

The bulk of directory operations that are available through NDAP are also available through LDAP, and the mapping between them needs no explanation. These operations include authentication (binding), searching and comparing, as well as adding, deleting, renaming, and modifying entries.

There are some NDAP operations, however, whose LDAP counterparts aren't readily apparent. We talk about those operations here.

Password Verification and Maintenance

NDAP provides a way to verify a user's password without actually logging in to the directory. Novell's LDAP server allows you to achieve this same functionality by using the compare operation. When you send a compare request to the server and ask to compare a value against the userPassword value, the server verifies whether that is the correct password by returning either compareTrue or compareFalse.

NDS allows a password administrator to reset or change a user's password without restriction and the LDAP server follows this behavior. If a user wants to change his own password, he must supply the old password when doing so. NDAP has a special change password verb that allows you to specify the old and the new passwords. The LDAP server achieves this by using the LDAP modify operation and requiring a user to specify both the old and new passwords. Here's how it works: LDAP allows you to delete and add multiple values in a single modify operation. To change your own password, Novell's LDAP server requires that you send a modify operation that contains both a delete and an add action. The delete action specifies to delete the old value from the `userPassword` attribute while the add action specifies to add the new value to the `userPassword` attribute. Note that the delete must occur before the add. Here's how a change password operation would look in LDIF:

```
dn:cn=myName,o=myOrg
changetype: modify
delete: userPassword
userPassword: oldsecret
-
add: userPassword
userPassword: newsecret
```

Partitioning and Replication

In the "Creating and Managing Partitions and Replicas" section of Chapter 8, we talked about using ConsoleOne to manage your partitions and replicas. ConsoleOne does this by using NDAP to issue the operations to NDS. We didn't talk about how this is done through LDAP because the ability to do that has only recently been added. NDS 8.5 adds a set of LDAP extended requests that may be used to perform partition and replica management. Novell has not published the partition extensions, but there are functions in the LDAP Libraries for C that you can use to access this functionality.

The functions in the LDAP Libaries for C can be found at `http://developer.novell.com/ndk/cldap.htm`. **These functions are described in the documentation, which can be viewed at** `http://developer.novell.com/ndk/doc/cldap/ldaplibc/data/a2et2co.htm`.

The underlying implementation (the extension information) to these functions may change in the future; therefore, Novell has not released the functional specifications yet. When Novell releases its LDAP Libraries for Java, that SDK should also include the same functionality.

Iterating

NDAP includes methods for reading indexed data by using an iterator. If you know of an index, you can request an iterator and use that iterator to perform operations such as next, previous, jump, and so on. This lets you view a small portion of the larger result set. LDAP provides mechanisms that produce the same kinds of results but in a slightly different manner. The Server Side Sorting (SSS) control allows you to get data back in a sorted manner—something the iterator does as a side effect, and the Virtual List View (VLV) control lets you look at a specific set of indexed data. If you've used the NDS iterator functions in the past, it might seem like a leap to use the SSS and VLV control to achieve the same functionality, but it can be done.

X-REF

Chapter 9 covers the SSS and VLV controls.

Schema Maintenance

As we mentioned earlier, the NDAP data model separates schema functions from normal directory functions. When using LDAP, rather than use functions such as readClassDef, modifyClassDef, and removeClassDef, you would use normal LDAP operations such as search, modify, and delete. If you were working with objectclasses (class definitions in NDAP speak) you would perform operations on the objectClasses attribute of the schema entry cn=schema.

X-REF

Chapter 7 covers the schema operations that can be performed through LDAP.

Though the schema is read and modified through normal LDAP operations, some LDAP client SDKs provide convenience methods for accessing and updating the schema. For example, the Netscape Directory SDK for Java has two classes — LDAPSchema and LDAPSchemaElement that make it easier to read and update schema. We talk about these classes later in this appendix.

Reading DSI Object Flags

NDAP provides the ability to read certain flags from an object that aren't stored in the object's attributes. Most NDAP SDKs refer to these as Entry Information Flags or Directory Services Information (DSI) flags. The LDAP server exposes some of these as operational attributes that you can request to be returned from a search operation. Table D.1 lists all the NDAP Entry Information Flags along with the name of the LDAP operational attribute that is used to read that value.

TABLE D.1	NDAP ENTRY INFORMATION FLAG	LDAP OPERATIONAL ATTRIBUTE
Entry Information Flags versus Operational Attributes	DSI_ENTRY_ID	`localEntryID` Returns an integer that represents the entry's back-end database ID; this localEntryID is only valid when talking to a single LDAP server.
	DSI_ENTRY_FLAGS	`entryFlags` Returns an integer of the same value returned by NDAP SDKs. Refer to your legacy NDAP SDK documentation for the meaning of this integer.
	DSI_SUBORDINATE_ COUNT	`subordinateCount` Returns the number of entries that are directly subordinate to this entry.
	DSI_MODIFICATION_ TIME	`modifyTimeStamp` Returns the last time this entry was modified.
	DSI_CREATION_ TIMESTAMP	`createTimeStamp` Returns the time that this entry was created.
	DSI_PARTITION_ ROOT_ID	Not yet supported.

Continued

TABLE D.I Entry Information Flags versus Operational Attributes (continued)	NDAP ENTRY INFORMATION FLAG	LDAP OPERATIONAL ATTRIBUTE
	DSI_PARENT_ID (continued)	Not yet supported.
	DSI_REVISION_ COUNT	`revision` The number of times the entry has been modified.
	DSI_REPLICA_TYPE	Not yet supported.
	DSI_BASE_CLASS	`structuralObjectClass` Returns the name of the object class that is the bottommost object class in the structural object class chain.
	DSI_ENTRY_RDN	Not supported or needed as the DN is returned as part of the search result.
	DSI_ENTRY_DN	Not supported or needed as the DN is returned as part of the search result.
	DSI_PARTITION_ ROOT_DN	Not yet supported.
	DSI_PARENT_DN	Not supported or needed as the DN is returned as part of the search result.
	DSI_PURGE_TIME	Not yet supported.
	DSI_DEREFERENCED_ BASE_CLASS	Not yet supported.
	DSI_REPLICA_ NUMBER	Not yet supported.
	DSI_REPLICA_STATE	Not yet supported.

Complete Mapping of the NDS Libraries for C to LDAP

The following sections compare the functions that exist in the NDS Libraries for C to the LDAP operations that are used to achieve the same functionality. We split these into functional groups in the same way the NDS Libraries for C documentation does. This is because some functional groups (like backup services and event services) have no equivalent mapping in LDAP. It is also helpful to note that many of the functions from the NDS Libraries for C listed below don't actually converse with the server; they are merely helper functions. Some of these convenience functions are not applicable because they aid in a peculiarity of the NDS C SDK. These are marked "Not applicable".

NDS Backup Services

This group of functions contains those that can be used to back up and restore NDS information that is server-specific. None of this functionality exists yet via LDAP, so we won't bother to show a map. These functions are NDSBackup ServerData, NDSFreeNameList, NDSGetReplicaPartitionNames, NDSIsOnlyServer InTree, NDSSYSVolumeRecovery, and NDSVerifyServerInfo.

NDS Core Services

Table D.2 lists the group of NDS C functions that make up the core of those used to work. They are listed in alphabetical order for easy reference.

TABLE D.2	C API	LDAP OPERATION
NDS C Library Core Services versus LDAP Operations	NWDSAbbreviateName	None. This is simply a client-side convenience function.
	NWDSAbortPartition Operation	There is no standard LDAP operation for this, but there is a function available in the C LDAP SDK called ldap_abort_naming_ context_operation. This functionality is not yet available through the Java SDK.
	NWDSAddFilterToken	Not applicable. Search filters are constructed using the grammar specified in RFC2254. The entire filter is presented to the API as a string; therefore, filter-building APIs are not necessary.
	NWDSAddObject	Use the add operation.

Continued

T A B L E D.2	C API	LDAP OPERATION
NDS C Library Core Services versus LDAP Operations (continued)	NWDSAddReplica	There is no standard LDAP operation for this, but there is a function available in the C LDAP SDK called ldap_add_replica. This functionality is not yet available through the Java SDK.
	NWDSAdd SecurityEquiv	This is a convenience function. It adds the equalsTo DN to the `securityEquals` attribute of the equalsFrom object and adds the equalsFrom DN to the `equalToMe` attribute of the equalTo object. You can use the modify operation to achieve the same results.
	NWDSAllocBuf	Not applicable.
	NWDSAllocFilter	Not applicable.
	NWDSAuditGet ObjectID	Read the `localEntryID` operational attribute of the object using a base scope search. See "Reading DSI Object Flags".
	NWDSAuthenticate NWDSAuthenticate Conn NWDSAuthenticate ConnEx	Use the bind operation.
	NWDSBackupObject	Not available. You could use the search operation to get the values of the entry's attributes and later use those values to restore the object. See Chapter 11 for related information about exporting and importing.
	NWDSBeginClassItem	Not applicable.
	NWDSCanDS Authenticate	Not applicable.
	NWDSCanonicalize Name	None. This is simply a client-side convenience function.

T A B L E D.2	C API	LDAP OPERATION
NDS C Library Core Services versus LDAP Operations (continued)	NWDSChange ObjectPassword	Use the modify operation to change the userPassword value. See the "Password Verification and Maintenance" section for more information.
	NWDSChange ReplicaType	There is no standard LDAP operation for this, but there is a function available in the C LDAP SDK called ldap_change_replica_ type. This functionality is not yet available through the Java SDK.
	NWDSCIStringsMatch	None. This is simply a client-side convenience function.
	NWDSCloseIteration	Not applicable. LDAP operations don't require you to notify the server if you prematurely stop processing responses. The closest thing to this in LDAP is the abort operation.
	NWDSCompare	Use the compare operation.
	NWDSCompute AttrValSize	Not applicable.
	NWDSCreate ContextHandle	Not applicable.
	NWDSDefineAttr	Use the modify operation to modify the `attributeTypes` attribute in the cn=schema object. Refer to Chapter 7.
	NWDSDefineClass	Use the modify operation to modify the `objectClasses` attribute in the cn=schema object. Refer to Chapter 7.
	NWDSDelFilterToken	Not applicable.
	NWDSDuplicate ContextHandle	Not applicable, though the Java SDK provides a clone method for the LDAPConnection class.

Continued

T A B L E   D.2

*NDS C Library
Core Services versus
LDAP Operations
(continued)*

C API	LDAP OPERATION
NWDSExtSyncList NWDSExtSyncRead NWDSExtSyncSearch	This functionality is not available yet.
NWDSFreeBuf	Not applicable.
NWDSFreeContext	Not applicable.
NWDSFreeFilter	Not applicable.
NWDSGenerate ObjectKeyPair	This creates a new password. Use the modify operation on the userPassword attribute to delete the old password and add a new password. See the previous "Password Verification and Maintenance" section for more information.
NWDSGetAttrCount	Not applicable. See LDAPAttribute.size() in the Java SDK.
NWDSGetAttrDef	Not applicable, though the Java LDAP SDK allows you to get an attribute definition from the LDAPSchema class using the getAttribute() method.
NWDSGetAttrName	Not applicable. See LDAPAttribute.getName() in the Java SDK or ldap_first_attribute() and ldap_next_attribute() in the C SDK.
NWDSGetAttrVal	Not applicable. See the LDAP Attribute.get*Value*() methods in the Java SDK or the ldap_get_values() function in the C SDK.
NWDSGetAttrValFlags	Not directly available. Most of the information is available by querying the schema.
NWDSGetAttrVal ModTime	Not yet available.
NWDSGetBindery Context	Not applicable.

C API	**LDAP OPERATION**
NWDSGetClassDef	Not applicable, though the Java LDAP SDK allows you to get an object class definition from the LDAPSchema class using the getObjectClass() method.
NWDSGetClass DefCount	Not applicable, though the Java LDAP SDK allows you to get an enumeration of object class definitions from the LDAPSchema class using the getObjectClasses() method.
NWDSGetClassItem	Not applicable, though the Java LDAP SDK allows you to get specific information about object classes by using the get*() methods of the LDAPObjectClassSchema class.
NWDSGet ClassItemCount	Not applicable. See NWDSGetClassItem.
NWDSGetContext	Not applicable.
NWDSGetCount ByClassAndName	Performing a one-level search and specifying the appropriate search filter produces the same results.
NWDSGet CurrentUser	Not applicable.
NWDSGetDef NameContext	Not applicable.
NWDSGetDSIInfo	Use the search operation and specify the appropriate operational attribute to be returned. See discussion in the "Reading DSI Object Flags" section.
NWDSGetDSVerInfo	Some functionality is available by reading the root DSE and examining the `vendorVersion` and `directoryTreeName` attributes.

T A B L E   D.2

*NDS C Library
Core Services versus
LDAP Operations
(continued)*

Continued

T A B L E D . 2	C API	LDAP OPERATION
NDS C Library Core Services versus LDAP Operations (continued)	NWDSGet EffectiveRights	Not yet available through the Java SDK but available using the ldap_get_effective_privileges() function in the C SDK.
	NWDSGetMonitored ConnRef	Not applicable.
	NWDSGetNDSInfo	Some functionality is available by reading the root DSE and examining the `vendorVersion` and `directoryTreeName` attributes.
	NWDSGetObjectCount	Not applicable.
	NWDSGetObject HostServerAddress	Use the search operation to read the entry and examine its `hostServer` attribute. The `hostServer` attribute holds the DN of the server. Using the server's DN, read the `networkAddress` attribute from the server object.
	NWDSGetObjectName	Not applicable. See Chapter 3 for an example of getting the name from an entry.
	NWDSGetObject NameAndInfo	Not applicable. See NWDSGetObjectName.
	NWDSGet PartitionExtInfo NWDSGetPartition ExtInfoPtr NWDSGetPartitionInfo	Not applicable.
	NWDSGetPartitionRoot	Not yet available.
	NWDSGetServer Addresses2	This is the address of the server you're talking to. You specified the server address when connecting; you can just keep track of it.
	NWDSGetServerDN NWDSGetServerName	Not yet available.

TABLE D.2	C API	LDAP OPERATION
NDS C Library Core Services versus LDAP Operations (continued)	NWDSGetSyntaxCount	Not applicable. See the LDAPSchema class in the Java SDK.
	NWDSGetSyntaxDef	Not applicable. See the LDAPSyntax Schema class in the Java SDK.
	NWDSGetSyntaxID	Not applicable.
	NWDSInitBuf	Not applicable.
	NWDSInspectEntry	Not yet available.
	NWDSJoinPartitions	Available from the ldap_merge_ naming_contexts() function in the C SDK; not yet available from the Java SDK.
	NWDSList	Use the search operation and specify a one-level search scope.
	NWDSListAttrs EffectiveRights	This functionality is available by calling the ldap_get_effective_ privileges() function in the C SDK once for each attribute. This is not yet available from the Java SDK.
	NWDSListByClass AndName	See NWDSGetCountByClass AndName.
	NWDSListContainable Classes	Not directly available. You can discover this by examining the object classes of the entry, then looking at the X-NDS_CONTAINMENT field of those object classes in the schema.
	NWDSListContainers	Not directly available. You could arrive at this list by listing all subordinate objects (perform a one-level search using a filter of objectclass=*) and asking for each object's structuralObjectclass operational attribute. Then, look at the schema definition of each object class to see if it either doesn't have an X-NDS_CONTAINER field or that it is set to "0". If so, that entry is a container.

Continued

. . . .

TABLE D.2	C API	LDAP OPERATION
NDS C Library Core Services versus LDAP Operations (continued)	NWDSListPartitions	Read the root DSE and look at the `namingContexts` attribute.
	NWDSListPartitions ExtInfo	See NWDSListPartitions and use the ldap_get_replica_info() function from the C SDK. This is not yet available from the Java SDK.
	NWDSLogin	Use the bind operation.
	NWDSLoginAsServer	Not yet available.
	NWDSLogout	Use the unbind operation.
	NWDSMapIDToName	Not applicable.
	NWDSMapNameToID	Not applicable.
	NWDSModifyClassDef	Use the modify operation to modify the `objectclasses` attribute of the cn=schema object. See LDAPS chemaElement.modify() in the Java SDK. See Chapter 7.
	NWDSModifyDN	Use the modify DN operation.
	NWDSModifyObject	Use the modify operation.
	NWDSModifyRDN NWDSMoveObject	Use the modify DN operation.
	NWDSMutateObject	Not available.
	NWDSOpenConn ToNDSServer	Not applicable. The LDAP SDKs have similar notions.
	NWDSOpen MonitoredConn	Not applicable.
	NWDSOpenStream	Not available. Attributes that are of stream syntax are readable and writable via the normal LDAP search and modify operations, but you cannot use random I/O functions on them.
	NWDSPartition ReceiveAllUpdates	Available as ldap_receive_all_ updates() from the C SDK. Not yet available from the Java SDK.

TABLE D.2	C API	LDAP OPERATION
NDS C Library Core Services versus LDAP Operations (continued)	NWDSPartition SendAllUpdates	Available as ldap_send_all_updates() from the C SDK. Not yet available from the Java SDK.
	NWDSPutAttrName NWDSPutAttr NameAndVal NWDSPutAttrVal	Not applicable. See the LDAP Attribute class in the Java SDK or the LDAPMod structure in the C SDK.
	NWDSPutChange NWDSPutChange AndVal NWDSPutClassItem NWDSPutFilter NWDSPutSyntaxName	Not applicable.
	NWDSRead	Use the search operation and specify a search scope of base.
	NWDSReadAttrDef	Read the `attributeTypes` attribute in the cn=schema object. See LDAPSchema in the Java SDK as well as Chapter 7.
	NWDSReadClassDef	Read the `objectClasses` attribute in the cn=schema object. See LDAPSchema in the Java SDK as well as Chapter 7.
	NWDSReadNDSInfo	See NWDSGetNDSInfo.
	NWDSReadObject DSIInfo	See NWDSGetDSIInfo.
	NWDSReadReferences	Not yet available.
	NWDSReadSyntaxDef	Read the `ldapSyntaxes` attribute in the cn=schema object. See LDAPSchema in the Java SDK as well as Chapter 7.

Continued

T A B L E D.2	C API	LDAP OPERATION
NDS C Library Core Services versus LDAP Operations (continued)	NWDSReloadDS	Not yet available.
	NWDSRemove AllTypes	Not applicable.
	NWDSRemoveAttrDef	Use the modify operation to delete the attribute definition from the `attributeTypes` attribute in the cn=schema object. See LDAP SchemaElement.remove() in the Java SDK and refer to Chapter 7.
	NWDSRemove ClassDef	Use the modify operation to delete the object class from the `objectClasses` attribute in the cn=schema object. See LDAPSchemaElement.remove() in the Java SDK and refer to Chapter 7.
	NWDSRemoveObject	Use the delete operation.
	NWDSRemovePartition	Use the delete operation to first delete any subordinate objects under the partition root then delete the partition root object.
	NWDSRemoveReplica	Available as ldap_remove_replica () from the C SDK. Not yet available from the Java SDK.
	NWDSRem SecurityEquiv	See NWDSAddSecurityEquiv and reverse the steps.
	NWDSRepair TimeStamps	Not yet available.
	NWDSReplace AttrNameAbbrev	Not applicable.
	NWDSResolveName	Use the search operation with a search scope of base. See Chapter 8 for more information on name resolution in LDAP.
	NWDSRestoreObject	Not available. See NWDSBackupObject.

TABLE D.2	C API	LDAP OPERATION
NDS C Library Core Services versus LDAP Operations (continued)	NWDSReturnBlock OfAvailableTrees NWDSScanConns ForTrees NWDSScanFor AvailableTrees	Not available.
	NWDSSearch	Use the search operation.
	NWDSSetContext	Not applicable.
	NWDSSet CurrentUser	Not applicable.
	NWDSSetDef NameContext	Not applicable.
	NWDSSetMonitored Connection	Not applicable.
	NWDSSplitPartition	Available as ldap_create_naming_ context() from the C SDK. Not yet available from the Java SDK.
	NWDSSyncPartition	Available as ldap_request_naming_ context_sync() from the C SDK. Not yet available from the Java SDK.
	NWDSSyncReplica ToServer	Not yet available.
	NWDSSyncSchema	Available as ldap_request_schema_ sync() from the C SDK. Not yet available from the Java SDK.
	NWDSUnlock Connection	Not applicable.
	NWDSVerify ObjectPassword	See the previous "Password Verification and Maintenance" section.
	NWDSWhoAmI	You can keep track of the DN used during the bind operation to get this functionality.

Continued

	C API	LDAP OPERATION
TABLE D.2 *NDS C Library* *Core Services versus* *LDAP Operations* *(continued)*	NWGetDefault NameContext	Not applicable.
	NWGetFileServer UTCTime	Not applicable.
	NWGetNum Connections NWGetNW NetVersion NWGetPreferred ConnName NWIsDS Authenticated NWNetInit NWNetTerm NWSetDefault NameContext NWSetPreferred DSTree	Not applicable.

NDS Event Services

This group of functions is used to subscribe to events generated by NDS. Currently, none of these are available through LDAP. The functions include NWDSE ConvertEntryName, NWDSEGetLocalAttrID, NWDSEGetLocalAttrName, NWDSE GetLocalClassID, NWDSEGetLocalClassName, NWDSEGetLocalEntryID, NWDSE GetLocalEntryName, NWDSERegisterForEvent, NWDSERegisterForEventWith Result, and NWDSEUnRegisterForEvent.

NDS Iterator Services

These functions are used for searching and retrieving object information from NDS containers that have thousands or hundreds of thousands of objects. All of the functionality provided here is attainable through the LDAP search operation by using the SSS and VLV controls. Table D.3 lists each function along with a description of how to use the VLV control to get the same information.

NOTE

To keep the descriptions concise, we assume you've performed or are performing a search with a VLV control rather than state that each time. We also refer to the elements of the VLV control rather than to the accessor methods for those fields.

T A B L E D.3	C API	LDAP OPERATION
NDS Iterator Services versus LDAP VLV Control	NWDSItrAtEOF	Examine the VLV response. If the targetPosition equals the content Count, you are at the end of the list.
	NWDSItrAtFirst	Examine the VLV response. If the targetPosition equals one, you are at the beginning of the list.
	NWDSItrClone	Perform another search with a new VLV control (don't specify a contextID).
	NWDSItrCount	Examine the VLV response. Subtract the targetPosition from the contentCount.
	NWDSItrCreateList	Not applicable.
	NWDSItrCreateSearch	Not applicable.
	NWDSItrDestroy	Not applicable.
	NWDSItrGetCurrent	Send a VLV search request with the offset and contentCount set to the last received targetPosition and contentCount respectively. Set beforeCount and afterCount to zero.
	NWDSItrGetInfo	Not available. This information is handled opaquely as part of the contextID.
	NWDSItrGetNext	Send a VLV search request with the appropriate offset, the contentCount set to the last received targetPosition and contentCount respectively. Set beforeCount to zero and afterCount to the number of entries you want.

Continued

T A B L E D.3	C API	LDAP OPERATION
NDS Iterator Services versus LDAP VLV Control (continued)	NWDSItrGetPosition	Read the targetPosition value in the VLV response and divide it by the contentCount.
	NWDSItrGetPrev	See NWDSItrGetNext and set afterCount to zero, and beforeCount to the number of entries you want.
	NWDSItrSetPosition	Send a VLV search request with the appropriate offset.
	NWDSItrSetPosition FromIterator	Not applicable.
	NWDSItrSkip	This will happen if you send subsequent VLV requests and you specify a new offset that is in close proximity with the set of entries returned. In other words, if you ask for offset 100, before = 9 and after = 9, then ask for offset 111, the iterator will skip 10 entries.
	NWDSItrTypeDown	Use the greaterThanOrEqual field of the VLV control.

Glossary

A

abstract class: An object class that is used as a superclass for other object classes. Directory entries cannot be created with an abstract object class. A synonym for the NDS term *noneffective class*. See *auxiliary class* and *structural class*.

alias: A directory entry that represents or acts as an additional name (alias) for another directory entry. See *entry* and *object*.

anonymous bind: An LDAP authentication that uses no name or password. Since no credentials are used when binding anonymously, the rights granted to an anonymously bound client are generally quite restrictive. See *bind* and *implied anonymous bind*.

API: The acronym for *Application Programming Interface*, a collection of data types and associated methods or functions used to provide a set of functionality to application developers.

ASN.1: An abbreviation for Abstract Syntax Notation One. ASN.1 is a notation for describing abstract data types and values. You can use ASN.1 to describe complex data types by combining simpler types. (This is much like defining a data structure in a programming language using integers, strings, arrays, other data structures, and so on.) When combined with an encoding rule (such as BER), ASN.1 also describes the actual format of data represented by an ASN.1 data type. This data format is machine-independent and is used as the data format for networking protocols, file formats, and so forth. See *BER* and *DER*.

asynchronous request: An LDAP message that is sent by a client, over its connection to the server, before the response for one or more previous requests sent by that client have been received. This implies that there is no guaranteed relationship between the processing order of that request and one or more other outstanding requests on the same connection. See *synchronous request*.

attribute: One of the pieces of data associated with an entry. An attribute is composed of a type and one or more values. See *attribute type*, *attribute value*, and *entry*.

attribute description: A superset of the attribute type that enables the addition of options to the attribute's type. See *attribute type*.

attribute type: An attribute's name or OID. Also, the entire formal definition of an attribute's properties including its name, OID, syntax, matching rules, and so forth. See *schema*.

attribute value: One of the values contained in an attribute. See *single-valued attribute* and *multi-valued attribute*.

attribute value assertion: An expression containing an attribute description and a value (applied according to a matching rule) that is appropriate for the attribute's type. For example: cn=jerry.

authentication: The process of verifying the identity of a system entity. Authentication usually involves two parts: First, the system entity asserts its identity (typically, a DN) and provides credentials to back up its claim, and second, the system verifies that the credentials provided belong to that asserted identity. See *credentials*.

AVA: The acronym for *attribute value assertion*.

auxiliary class: An object class that can be added to a specific entry. When an auxiliary class is added to an entry, additional attributes can then be added to the entry. See *abstract class* and *structural class*.

B

base object: A DN identifying the entry used as the starting point for an LDAP search operation. All entries returned from an LDAP search operation are either the base object entry or its subordinate entries. See *search scope, object, entry,* and *subordinate entry*.

Base64 encoding: An encoding that allows arbitrary binary values to be represented by using a defined set of 65 printable ASCII characters. It increases the size of the binary value by approximately 33 percent.

BER: The acronym for Basic Encoding Rules, a set of rules for encoding data — especially the data for an ASN.1 data type — into an array of bytes. Data items encoded via BER are marked with a identifying tag followed by the length of the data item and the actual value of the data item. In general, the Basic Encoding Rules allow more than one valid encoding for an ASN.1 data type. See *ASN.1* and *DER*.

bind: The LDAP operation used to authenticate (log in) a client connection. When the operation completes successfully, the connection is bound to the identity specified in the bind operation. See *anonymous bind*.

C

CA: The acronym for *certification authority*.

cache: A secondary storage location where copies of frequently used data values can be stored for faster retrieval than would otherwise be possible if they were retrieved from their primary storage location.

certificate: (Also user certificate, server certificate) A digital document that certifies the identity or the truth of something. To prevent tampering with its contents, a certificate is signed by a digital value that is based on the value of the data stored within it.

certificate authority: A term used in some Novell products as a synonym for *certification authority*.

certification authority: An entity that issues digital certificates and vouches for the validity of the information contained within the certificate. See *certificate*.

certification path: An ordered sequence of public-key certificates that allows a certificate user to obtain a verifiable public key for the entity that is the subject of the last certificate. Also an ordered sequence of public-key certificates followed by a single attribute certificate that allows a certificate user to obtain certified attributes for the entity that is the subject of the last certificate. See *certificate*.

chaining: A form of name resolution where a server, acting as a proxy for a client, locates an entry within the DIT when the entry is not stored locally. Chaining can occur when a server is performing name resolution on the base object of an LDAP operation; it can also occur when the server is performing name resolution to locate an entry that is both subordinate to the base object of a search operation and within the scope of that search operation. See *name resolution* and *referral*.

connection option: In the Java LDAP SDK, an option set on an LDAP connection object that modifies the behavior of all LDAP operations performed using that connection object. For instance, a connection option can be used to set the default referral processing behavior for all LDAP operations made using the same connection object. See *constraint*.

ConsoleOne: The Novell utility used to perform NDS administration.

constraint: In the Java LDAP SDK, an object passed as a parameter to an LDAP connection method that modifies the behavior of that method. For instance, a constraint can be used to add a control to an LDAP operation request or to set the Java SDK's referral processing behavior for a search operation. See *connection option*.

container: An entry whose object class is allowed to contain other entries, usually an entry that actually has subordinate entries. See *containment*.

containment: A schema rule that specifies the object classes that can contain objects of another object class. For instance, the containment rule for an organization container says that it can only exist at the root of the tree, or within a country or locality. See *structure rules, schema,* and *container.*

continuation reference: An intermediate message sent from an LDAP server to an LDAP client as part of processing a search request that contains referrals for one or more servers, one of which must be contacted to complete the search request. See *referral.*

control: An element of the LDAPv3 protocol that allows an operation to be extended by providing additional information with the request specifying that the normal behavior of the operation should be modified or extended in some pre-defined way. See *critical control.*

credentials: Data that is transferred or presented to establish the claimed identity or the authorizations of a system entity. See *authentication.*

critical control: A control that must be processed for an LDAP operation to be successful. The LDAP client specifies if a control is critical as one of the parameters to the control. If the control is marked critical and the server cannot fulfill the operation with the control, then the operation will not be performed. If the control is not marked critical and the server cannot fulfill the operation with the control, the server ignores the control and processes the request as if no control had been sent. See *control.*

cryptography: The mathematical science dealing with methods of transforming data in a manner that makes its meaning unintelligible, makes it impossible to be changed without detection, and protects it from unauthorized use. If the transformation method can be reversed, cryptography also deals with the process of restoring the data to a state where its meaning is once again intelligible.

NOTE

One branch of cryptography, asymmetric cryptography (more commonly know as "public-key" cryptography), uses algorithms that employ a pair of keys, referred to as the public and private keys. An advantage of asymmetric cryptography algorithms is that one key, the "private key," does not need to be known by anyone except its owner. The other key, the "public key," can be shared freely among all entities that need to use it. Additionally, the public key does not need to be kept secret from other non-using entities to maintain integrity of the algorithm.

D

DAP: The acronym for Directory Access Protocol, the X.500 directory access protocol. See *LDAP* and *NDAP*.

DER: The acronym for Distinguished Encoding Rules, a subset of BER used for encoding the data for an ASN.1 data type into an array of bytes. The Distinguished Encoding Rules restrict the encoding options provided by BER to guarantee a single valid encoding for each ASN.1 data type. See *ASN.1* and *BER*.

DIB: The acronym for the Directory Information Base where directory data is stored. The data in the DIB only represents the data held in a single server and is typically stored in a proprietary format. Contrast with *DIT*.

directory: Sometimes used as a synonym for *DIT*.

distinguished name: The full name of an entry that uniquely identifies it within the DIT, for example, cn=Peter Michaels,ou=Artists,l=San Francisco,c=US. A distinguished name is composed of one or more relative distinguished names for the entry and each of its superior entries back to the root of the directory tree. See *relative distinguished name* and *distinguished values*.

distinguished value(s): The attribute value(s) used to name an entry.

DIT: The acronym for Directory Information Tree. The entire collection of directory entries with a common root. See *tree*.

DN: The acronym for *distinguished name*.

DSA: The acronym for Directory Server Agent. The X.500 name for a directory server.

E

effective class: See *structural class*.

entry: The basic unit of storage within a directory. An entry has a distinguished name and one or more attributes that contain data values for the entry. See *distinguished name*, *distinguished values*, and *attributes*.

extended operation: An operation added to the LDAPv3 protocol using the framework provided for by the extended request, extended response, and extended partial response messages. See *extended request*, *extended response*, and *extended partial response*.

extended partial response: An LDAPv3 message that provides a framework for an LDAPv3 server to send intermediate responses to an extended request received by a client. See *extended request*, *extended response*, and *extended partial response*.

extended request: An LDAPv3 message that provides a framework for new operation requests to be added to the protocol. See *extended response, extended partial response,* and *extended operation.*

extended response: An LDAPv3 message that provides a framework for a LDAPv3 server to send a response to an extended request received by a client. See *extended request, extended partial response,* and *extended operation.*

extension: A term used to describe an LDAPv3 extended operation and its associated semantics. It may also refer to the server implementation of the processing logic for an LDAPv3 extended operation. See *extended operation.*

external reference: A permanent placeholder entry used in NDS name resolution. External references represent each of the directory entries between the partition roots and the tree root on a server.

F

filtered replica: A replica that contains a subset of the entries and/or attributes for a partition. Two independent filters are used to determine the object classes allowed in the filtered replica and which attributes from those object classes will be included. See *master replica, read/write replica,* and *read-only replica.*

forward reference: An NDS directory entry that acts as a semi-permanent superior entry placeholder for an object to allow it to be created when its superior entry does not yet exist. If an object is created for an entry that already exists as a forward reference, the forward reference is morphed into a regular directory object. See *entry* and *object.*

H

hash: (or more properly, *hash result*) The output from a *hash function.*

hash function: An algorithm used to map a large, usually variable-length data value (such as a file or message) onto a smaller, usually fixed-length data value called a hash result. Because of the way that the data value is mapped, the results from most hash functions appear to be random, thus obscuring the original value used as input to the hash function. See *hash.*

I

implied anonymous bind: An anonymous bind that occurs when an LDAPv3 operation is requested by a client that has not yet performed a bind operation. Because it has not yet explicitly bound the connection, the client implies that it wishes to be bound anonymously by issuing an LDAP operation request on its unbound connection. See *anonymous bind*.

immediate subordinate object (or entry): An entry located one level below another entry in the DIT — that is, a "child" of the entry. See *subordinate object (or entry)* and *immediate superior object (or entry)*.

immediate superior object (or entry): The entry located one level above another entry in the DIT — that is, the "parent" of the entry. See *superior object (or entry)* and *immediate subordinate object (or entry)*.

Internet-Draft: A document submitted to the IETF containing engineering designs or other information regarding an Internet protocol. Internet-Drafts expire after a period of six months from the date they are issued. An Internet-Draft may become an RFC, which makes it a permanent document. See *RFC*.

IESG: The Internet Engineering Steering Group, a body that maintains and promotes the set of Internet standards contained in RFCs. See *RFC* and *IETF*.

IETF: The Internet Engineering Task Force, a body that engineers new protocols and practices for the Internet. See *Internet-Draft* and *IESG*.

K

key: An input parameter that varies the transformation performed by a cryptographic algorithm. See *public key* and *private key*

knowledge reference: A general term applying to information regarding the server or servers containing a specific directory entry. See *referral*, *subordinate reference*, and *external reference*.

L

LBURP: The acronym for *LDAP Bulk Update/Replication Protocol*.

LDAP: The acronym for Lightweight Directory Access Protocol

LDAP Bulk Update/Replication Protocol: An LDAP protocol that utilizes LDAP extended operations to efficiently transfer large quantities of asynchronous LDAP update operations from an LDAP client to an LDAP server while enabling the server to know the order in which they were sent from the client.

LDAP Group object: An object in NDS used to store administrative information shared among a set of one or more NDS LDAP servers. See *LDAP Server object.*

LDAP Server object: An object in NDS used to store administrative information specific to a single NDS LDAP server. See *LDAP Group object.*

LDIF: The acronym for LDAP Data Interchange Format. An implementation-neutral, text-based format for representing the content of LDAP directory entries or a set of LDAP update operations to be performed on a directory.

leaf entry: Any directory entry, either a container or a noncontainer, that has no subordinate entries.

locality of reference: The principle that the closer something is to the entity referencing it, the easier or less expensive it is to access it.

M

mandatory attribute: An attribute that must have a value in order for a directory entry to exist.

master replica: A read/write replica of a partition that also coordinates changes in state to the partition with all other replicas of the same partition. See *read/write replica, read-only replica,* and *filtered replica.*

matching rule: A way of expressing how a server should compare an assertion value for an attribute with a data value. For instance, two types of matching rules that could be used with an attribute with a string syntax are case-sensitive matching and case-insensitive matching. See *attribute value assertion.*

multi-threaded: A process that can have more than one thread of execution simultaneously active. On a single processor machine, processor time is allotted to threads of execution according to a scheduling algorithm, and only one thread is actually executing on the processor at any given time. In this scenario, it's possible that the scheduling algorithm could interrupt the execution of a thread at any time. On a multiple processor machine, threads are still subject to the dictates of whatever scheduling algorithm is in effect, but multiple threads from the same process may be executing on multiple processors simultaneously.

multi-valued attribute: An attribute that may contain more than one value. See *single-valued attribute.*

N

name: Sometimes used as a synonym for *distinguished name*.

name resolution: The process of finding a specific entry within the DIT, especially when the entries for the DIT are distributed among more than one server. See *chaining* and *referrals*.

naming attribute(s): The attribute or attributes that contain distinguished values for an entry. See *distinguished values*.

naming context: The set of entries beginning at an entry mastered by a particular server and including all of that entry's subordinate entries, and their subordinate entries, down to leaf entries or entries that are mastered by other servers. Contrast with *partition*.

NDAP: The acronym for Novell Directory Access Protocol, a proprietary directory access protocol based on X.500. See *DAP* and *LDAP*.

non-effective class: See *abstract class*.

O

object: A directory entry that is not an alias or a reference. See *entry, alias, external reference, forward reference*, and *subordinate reference*.

object class: The formal definition of a class of directory objects including the name of the class, an OID, a type (either structural, abstract, or auxiliary), a set of mandatory attribute types, and a set of optional attribute types. Also, the value of the `objectClass` attribute of an entry. See *abstract class, structural class, auxiliary class*.

object identifier: A string in dotted decimal form (for example 1.2.3.55.834.7) that uniquely identifies something.

OID: A commonly-used acronym for *object identifier*.

operational attribute: An attribute used by the DSA. The values of an operational attribute are usually generated either directly or indirectly by the DSA and therefore cannot be modified by users. Operational attributes are not returned in search results unless explicitly requested by name. See *user attribute*.

optional attribute: An attribute that is allowed to be contained by an entry but not required to have any values for an entry to exist. See *mandatory attribute*.

P

partition: A subset of the entries of the DIT composed of a partition root and all of its subordinate entries down to the partition roots of subordinate partitions or leaf entries. See *partition root* and *leaf entry*.

partition root: A single entry that is a direct superior to all other entries in a partition. See *partition*.

password: A secret data value, usually a character string, that is used for authentication. See *authentication* and *credentials*.

private key: One of a pair of keys used in asymmetric or "public-key" cryptography whose value is a secret known only by its owner. See *cryptography* and *public key*.

public key: One of a pair of keys used in asymmetric or "public-key" cryptography whose value can be known by any entity that needs to use it. See *cryptography* and *private key*.

R

RDN: The acronym for *relative distinguished name*.

RFC: Request For Comments, an engineering document produced by the IESG for which comments are solicited from the Internet community at large. Based on response from the Internet community, an RFC may be classified as experimental, proposed standard, standard, informational, or current best practice. See *IESG*, *IETF*, and *Internet-Draft*.

read-only replica: A replica of a partition whose entries cannot be modified. See *master replica*, *read/write replica*, *filtered replica*, *partition*, and *replica*.

read/write replica: A replica of a partition whose entries can be modified according to any access control restrictions that are in effect for the partition. See *master replica*, *read-only replica*, *filtered replica*, *partition*, and *replica*.

referral: An LDAP URL that specifies a server that can be contacted to progress an operation. Also, a form of name resolution where a server sends referrals to a client to help it locate an entry within the DIT when the entry is not stored locally. See *referral result*.

referral hops: The count of connections made to follow consecutive referrals received in trying to process a single operation. See *referral result* and *continuation reference*.

referral result: An LDAP response indicating that the entry for an operation does not exist on the server to which the client is connected. The referral result contains referrals that identify one or more servers that can be contacted to progress the operation. See *referral* and *continuation reference*.

relative distinguished name: The name of an entry that uniquely identifies it with respect to other entries with the same superior entry, for example cn=Peter Michaels. See *distinguished name* and *distinguished values*.

replica: A copy of the entries for a partition that is stored on a particular server. See *master replica, read/write replica, read-only replica, filtered replica,* and *partition*.

replica ring: An attribute of an NDS partition root entry that contains the addresses of all of the servers that hold the partition root object or a subordinate reference entry for the partition root. See *partition, replica, partition root,* and *subordinate reference*.

replication: The process of sending the updates made to one replica of a partition to all other replicas of the same partition. See *replica* and *partition*.

root DSE: The DSA Specific Entry located at the root of the DIT. It contains information about the DSA (directory server) including the location of the subschema subentry, a list of supported controls, and a list of supported extensions for the server. The root DSE is not part of any naming context nor is it returned from a normal search operation. See *subschema subentry, naming context, DSA,* and *DIT*.

root: An imaginary entry that is superior to all other entries in the DIT. See *entry, superior entry, DIT*.

S

SASL: The acronym for Simple Authentication and Security Layer, an Internet specification for adding an authentication service to connection based protocols. The protocol to which SASL is added must include a command used to authenticate users to the service. The command may optionally be used to negotiate the protection of subsequent protocol interactions between client and server. The authentication command names a registered security mechanism such as Kerberos, GSSAPI, S/Key, and so forth. See *authentication*.

schema: The set of rules that govern the types of data that can be stored in a directory and the hierarchical structure that the data must adhere to. The schema is the collection of object classes, attribute types, matching rules, syntaxes, and other information that controls the way data is stored within the directory. See *attribute types, object classes, matching rule,* and *syntax*.

search base: A synonym for *base object*.

search constraint: In the Java LDAP SDK, an object class used to place a constraint on an LDAP search operation. See *constraint*.

search filter: A Boolean expression that identifies the criteria used in determining which entries should be returned from a search operation. Entries whose attribute values cause the value of the search filter to be true are returned, and entries whose attribute values cause the value of the search filter to be false or undefined are not returned.

search (result) reference: A synonym for *continuation reference*.

Secure Sockets Layer: (Often abbreviated as SSL.) An Internet protocol that uses end-to-end connection-oriented data encryption to provide confidentiality and integrity for the data sent between a client and server. SSL can also optionally provide peer-to-peer authentication between the client and server. SSL is independent of the application it encapsulates which enables other high level protocols (such as LDAP) to be transparently layered on top of SSL.

Server Side Sorting control: An LDAPv3 control that enables a client to request that entries be returned in sorted order based on sort keys for one or more attributes.

search scope: A parameter to a search request that specifies the scope of the entries to be considered for return to the client. A search scope of base indicates that only the search base entry will be returned. A search scope of onelevel indicates that only immediate subordinate entries of the search base entry will be returned. A search scope of subtree indicates that the search base entry and its entire set of subordinate entries will be returned. See *search base* and *search filter*.

Service Location Protocol: An Internet protocol that provides a scalable framework for the discovery and selection of network services. The service location protocol enables computers using the Internet to have little or no static configuration of network services for network-based applications, thus greatly reducing the need for administration of this information.

single-valued attribute: An attribute type that can contain no more than one value.

simple authentication: An authentication method that uses a static (that is, repetitively used) password as the authentication credentials. See *authentication* and *credentials*.

SLP: The acronym for *Service Location Protocol*.

SSL: The acronym for *Secure Sockets Layer*.

SSS control: A synonym for the *Server Side Sorting control.*

stacking: Combining two or more controls in a single LDAP message. See *control.*

structural class: An object class that can be used to instantiate directory entries. A synonym for the NDS term *effective class.* See *abstract class* and *auxiliary class.*

structure rules: A set of schema rules used to mandate the way the hierarchy of a tree is laid out. For example, structure rules could be used to make it impossible to allow a country object to exist under a printer object. NDS uses containment rules instead of structure rules to specify the hierarchical structure. See *schema, containment.*

subclass: The act of deriving a new object class from another object class. Also, an object class that has been subclassed (that is, derived) from another object class. When an object class is subclassed, the new object class inherits all of the optional and mandatory attributes of the class from its superclass. See *object class* and *superclass.*

subentry: A special type of entry, usually located immediately below an administrative point or a naming context in the LDAP directory that contains administrative or configuration information for the DSA. Subentries are not returned from normal search operations. To read the attributes of a subentry, you must do a search with a scope of base on the subentry's DN as the base object of the search. See *subschema subentry, search scope,* and *base object.*

subordinate object (or entry): An entry located below another entry in the DIT along a direct line of descent — that is, a "descendant" of the entry. See *superior object (or entry)* and *immediate subordinate object (or entry).*

subordinate reference: A copy of the partition root kept on servers that holds the partition immediately superior to the partition root's partition. The subordinate reference contains a replica ring attribute that is used to find the servers that hold an actual copy of the partition during name resolution. See *name resolution, replica ring, partition,* and *partition root.*

subschema subentry: A subentry containing the schema in effect for the DIT or a particular naming context. See *subentry.*

superclass: The object class from which a new object class was derived. See *subclass.*

superior object (or entry): An entry located above another entry in the DIT along a direct line of ascent — that is, an "ancestor" of the entry. See *subordinate object (or entry)* and *immediate superior object (or entry)*.

synchronous request: An LDAP message that is sent by a client over its connection to the server after the response for the previous request sent by that client has been received. This implies that there is a guaranteed relationship between the order of processing requests on the same connection because the client knows that the previous request has completed before it issues the next request. See *asynchronous request*.

syntax: A property of an attribute type that determines the format that data must conform to when stored in attributes of that type. See *attribute type*.

T

tree: A commonly-used synonym for the term *DIT*.

typedown: A method employed by the VLV control that allows a user to type one or more alphanumeric characters used to position the list at the first item matching them.

U

unsolicited notification: An LDAPv3 extended response message sent by a server to a client without first receiving a corresponding request from the client. It is generally used to notify the client of an abnormal condition on the server or in the connection between the client and server. See *extended request*.

UTF-8: An encoding of the unicode character set that allows every unicode character to be represented as a string of one or more consecutive 8-bit values. It has the property that all characters between 0 and 127 decimal are identically represented in ASCII and UTF-8.

user attribute: An attribute that can be stored and modified by a directory client (subject to access control). Any attribute that is not an operational attribute. User attributes are returned in search results that use the empty list or "*" wildcard as a shorthand for all attributes. See *operational attribute*.

V

Virtual List View control: An LDAPv3 control that enables a client to request a subset of entries matching a search criteria centered around a target entry. The target entry may be specified as an index into the sorted list of entries that match the search filter or as the first entry with a value greater than or equal to an attribute value assertion.

VLV control: A synonym for the *Virtual List View control*.

X

X.500: The OSI directory service. Also, the family of OSI directory standards based on X.500.

Index

Continued

Continued

F

Continued

NDS Services program, 52

stopping and starting LDAP on,
  51–52

IDG Books Worldwide, Inc.
End-User License Agreement

READ THIS. You should carefully read these terms and conditions before opening the software packet(s) included with this book ("Book"). This is a license agreement ("Agreement") between you and IDG Books Worldwide, Inc. ("IDGB"). By opening the accompanying software packet(s), you acknowledge that you have read and accept the following terms and conditions. If you do not agree and do not want to be bound by such terms and conditions, promptly return the Book and the unopened software packet(s) to the place you obtained them for a full refund.

1. **License Grant.** IDGB grants to you (either an individual or entity) a nonexclusive license to use one copy of the enclosed software program(s) (collectively, the "Software") solely for your own personal or business purposes on a single computer (whether a standard computer or a workstation component of a multiuser network). The Software is in use on a computer when it is loaded into temporary memory (RAM) or installed into permanent memory (hard disk, CD-ROM, or other storage device). IDGB reserves all rights not expressly granted herein.

2. **Ownership.** IDGB is the owner of all right, title, and interest, including copyright, in and to the compilation of the Software recorded on the disk(s) or CD-ROM ("Software Media"). Copyright to the individual programs recorded on the Software Media is owned by the author or other authorized copyright owner of each program. Ownership of the Software and all proprietary rights relating thereto remain with IDGB and its licensers.

3. **Restrictions On Use and Transfer.**

   (a) You may only (i) make one copy of the Software for backup or archival purposes, or (ii) transfer the Software to a single hard disk, provided that you keep the original for backup or archival purposes. You may not (i) rent or lease the Software, (ii) copy or reproduce the Software through a LAN or other network system or through any computer subscriber system or bulletin-board system, or (iii) modify, adapt, or create derivative works based on the Software.

(b) You may not reverse engineer, decompile, or disassemble the Software. You may transfer the Software and user documentation on a permanent basis, provided that the transferee agrees to accept the terms and conditions of this Agreement and you retain no copies. If the Software is an update or has been updated, any transfer must include the most recent update and all prior versions.

4. Restrictions on Use of Individual Programs. You must follow the individual requirements and restrictions detailed for each individual program in Appendix A of this Book. These limitations are also contained in the individual license agreements recorded on the Software Media. These limitations may include a requirement that after using the program fora specified period of time, the user must pay a registration fee or discontinue use. By opening the Software packet(s), you will be agreeing to abide by the licenses and restrictions for these individual programs that aredetailed in Appendix A and on the Software Media. None of the material on this Software Media or listed in this Book may ever beredistributed, in original or modified form, for commercial purposes.

5. Limited Warranty.

(a) IDGB warrants that the Software and Software Media are free from defects in materials and workmanship under normal use for a period of sixty (60) days from the date of purchase of this Book. If IDGB receives notification within the warranty period of defects in materials or workmanship, IDGB will replace the defective Software Media.

(b) IDGB AND THE AUTHORS OF THE BOOK DISCLAIM ALL OTHER WARRANTIES, EXPRESS OR IMPLIED, INCLUDING WITHOUT LIMITATION IMPLIED WARRANTIES OF MERCHANTABILITY AND FITNESS FOR A PARTICULAR PURPOSE, WITH RESPECT TO THE SOFTWARE, THE PROGRAMS, THE SOURCE CODE CONTAINED THEREIN, AND/OR THE TECHNIQUES DESCRIBED IN THIS BOOK. IDGB DOES NOT WARRANT THAT THE FUNCTIONS CONTAINED IN THE SOFTWARE WILL MEET YOUR REQUIREMENTS OR THAT THE OPERATION OF THE SOFTWARE WILL BE ERROR FREE.

(c) This limited warranty gives you specific legal rights, and you may have other rights that vary from jurisdiction to jurisdiction.

6. Remedies.

(a) IDGB's entire liability and your exclusive remedy for defects in materials and workmanship shall be limited to replacement of the Software Media, which may be returned to IDGB with a copy of your receipt at the following address: Software Media Fulfillment Department, Attn.: *Novell's LDAP Developer's Guide*, IDG Books Worldwide, Inc., 10475 Crosspoint Blvd., Indianapolis, IN 46256, or call 1-800-762-2974. Please allow three to four weeks for delivery. This Limited Warranty is void if failure of the Software Media has resulted from accident, abuse, or misapplication. Any replacement Software Media will be warranted for the remainder of the original warranty period or thirty (30) days, whichever is longer.

(b) In no event shall IDGB or the authors be liable for any damages whatsoever (including without limitation damages for loss of business profits, business interruption, loss of business information, or any other pecuniary loss) arising from the use of or inability to use the Book or the Software, even if IDGB has been advised of the possibility of such damages.

(c) Because some jurisdictions do not allow the exclusion or limitation of liability for consequential or incidental damages, the above limitation or exclusion may not apply to you.

7. U.S. Government Restricted Rights. Use, duplication, or disclosure of the Software by the U.S. Government is subject to restrictions stated in para-graph (c)(1)(ii) of the Rights in Technical Data and Computer Software clause of DFARS 252.227-7013, and in subparagraphs (a) through (d) of the Commercial Computer — Restricted Rights clause at FAR 52.227-19, and in similar clauses in the NASA FAR supplement, when applicable.

8. General. This Agreement constitutes the entire understanding of the parties and revokes and supersedes all prior agreements, oral or written, between them and may not be modified or amended except in a writing signed by both parties hereto that specifically refers to this Agreement. This Agreement shall take precedence over any other documents that may be in conflict herewith. If any one or more provisions contained in this Agreement are held by any court or tribunal to be invalid, illegal, or otherwise unenforceable, each and every other provision shall remain in full force and effect.

MORE BOOKS FROM NOVELL PRESS™

Certification:

Novell's CNE® Study Set for NetWare® 5	0-7645-4554-X	US $174.99 / CAN $262.99
Novell's CNE® Study Guide for NetWare® 5	0-7645-4543-4	US $ 99.99 / CAN $139.99
Novell's CNE® Update to NetWare® 5 Study Guide	0-7645-4559-0	US $ 49.99 / CAN $ 69.99
Novell's CNE® Clarke Notes™ for NetWare® 5 Administration: Course 560	0-7645-4577-9	US $ 24.99 / CAN $ 37.99
Novell's CNE® Clarke Notes™ Update to NetWare® 5: Course 529	0-7645-4575-2	US $ 24.99 / CAN $ 37.99
Novell's CNA℠ Study Guide for NetWare® 5	0-7645-4542-6	US $ 74.99 / CAN $105.99
Novell's CNE® Study Set for IntranetWare/NetWare® 4.11	0-7645-4533-7	US $148.99 / CAN $208.99
Novell's CNE® Study Guide for IntranetWare/NetWare® 4.11	0-7645-4512-4	US $ 89.99 / CAN $124.99
Novell's CNA℠ Study Guide for IntranetWare/NetWare® 4.11	0-7645-4513-2	US $ 69.99 / CAN $ 96.99
Novell's CNE® Study Guide for Core Technologies	0-7645-4501-9	US $ 74.99 / CAN $104.99
Novell's Certified Internet Business Strategist℠ Study Guide	0-7645-4549-3	US $ 39.99 / CAN $ 56.99
Novell's Certified Web Designer℠ Study Guide	0-7645-4548-5	US $ 49.99 / CAN $ 69.99

NetWare:

Novell's NetWare® 5 Resource Kit	0-7645-4545-0	US $ 99.99 / CAN $149.99
Novell's Guide to NetWare® 5 Networks	0-7645-4544-2	US $ 74.99 / CAN $105.99
Novell's NetWare® 5 Administrator's Handbook	0-7645-4546-9	US $ 39.99 / CAN $ 56.99
Novell's Guide to Troubleshooting NetWare® 5	0-7645-4558-2	US $ 49.99 / CAN $ 69.99
Novell's NetWare® 5 Basics	0-7645-4563-9	US $ 29.99 / CAN $ 44.99
Novell's Guide to Integrating NetWare® 5 and NT	0-7645-4580-9	US $ 44.99 / CAN $ 67.99
Novell's Guide to NetWare® 5 and TCP/IP	0-7645-4564-7	US $ 49.99 / CAN $ 69.99
Novell's Guide to IntranetWare Networks	0-7645-4516-7	US $ 59.99 / CAN $ 84.99
Novell's IntranetWare Administrator's Handbook	0-7645-4517-5	US $ 39.99 / CAN $ 54.99
Novell's Introduction to intraNetWare	0-7645-4530-2	US $ 39.99 / CAN $ 56.99
Novell's Guide to Integrating intraNetWare and NT	0-7645-4523-X	US $ 44.99 / CAN $ 67.99
Novell's Guide to TCP/IP and IntranetWare	0-7645-4532-9	US $ 49.99 / CAN $ 69.99
Novell's Guide to NetWare® for Small Business 4.11	0-7645-4504-3	US $ 34.99 / CAN $ 49.99
Novell's Guide to NetWare® 4.1 Networks	1-56884-736-X	US $ 59.99 / CAN $ 84.99
Novell's NetWare® 4.1 Administrator's Handbook	1-56884-737-8	US $ 29.99 / CAN $ 42.99
Novell's Guide to Integrating NetWare® and TCP/IP	1-56884-818-8	US $ 44.99 / CAN $ 62.99
Novell's Guide to NetWare® Printing	0-7645-4514-0	US $ 44.99 / CAN $ 62.99

Novell Directory Services™ (NDS):

Novell's Guide to Troubleshooting NDS™	0-7645-4579-5	US $ 44.99 / CAN $ 67.99
Novell's NDS™ Developer's Guide	0-7645-4557-4	US $ 59.99 / CAN $ 84.99
NDS™ for NT	0-7645-4551-5	US $ 39.99 / CAN $ 56.99

Available wherever books are sold or call 1-800-762-2974 to order today.
Outside the U.S. call 1-317-572-3993.

ManageWise:

Novell's ManageWise® Administrator's Handbook	1-56884-817-X	US $ 29.99	/ CAN $ 42.99

GroupWise:

Novell's GroupWise® 5.5 Administrator's Guide	0-7645-4556-6	US $ 44.99	/ CAN $ 63.99
Novell's GroupWise® 5.5 User's Handbook	0-7645-4552-3	US $ 24.99	/ CAN $ 35.99
Novell's GroupWise® 5 Administrator's Guide	0-7645-4521-3	US $ 44.99	/ CAN $ 62.99
Novell's GroupWise® 5 User's Handbook	0-7645-4509-4	US $ 24.99	/ CAN $ 34.99
Novell's GroupWise® 4 User's Guide	0-7645-4502-7	US $ 19.99	/ CAN $ 27.99

Border Manager:

Novell's BorderManager™ Administrator's Handbook	0-7645-4565-5	US $ 34.99	/ CAN $ 52.99
Novell's Guide to BorderManager™	0-7645-4540-X	US $ 49.99	/ CAN $ 69.99

ZENworks:

Novell's ZENworks™ Administrator's Handbook	0-7645-4561-2	US $ 39.99	/ CAN $ 59.99

Internet/Intranets:

Novell's Internet Plumbing Handbook	0-7645-4537-X	US $ 34.99	/ CAN $ 48.99
Novell's Guide to Web Site Management 0-7645-4529-9	US	$ 59.99	/ CAN $ 84.99
Novell's Guide to Internet Access Solutions	0-7645-4515-9	US $ 39.99	/ CAN $ 56.99
Novell's Guide to Creating IntranetWare Intranets	0-7645-4531-0	US $ 39.99	/ CAN $ 54.99
Novell's The Web at Work: Publishing Within and Beyond the Corporation	0-7645-4519-1	US $ 29.99	/ CAN $ 42.99

Networking Connections/Network Management:

Novell's Guide to Troubleshooting TCP/IP	0-7645-4562-0	US $ 59.99	/ CAN $ 89.99
Novell's Guide to LAN/WAN Analysis: IPX/SPX™	0-7645-4508-6	US $ 59.99	/ CAN $ 84.99
Novell's Guide to Resolving Critical Server Issues	0-7645-4550-7	US $ 59.99	/ CAN $ 84.99

General Reference:

Novell's Guide to Networking Hardware	0-7645-4553-1	US $ 69.99	/ CAN $ 98.99
Novell's Encyclopedia of Networking	0-7645-4511-6	US $ 69.99	/ CAN $ 96.99
Novell's Dictionary of Networking	0-7645-4528-0	US $ 24.99	/ CAN $ 34.99
Novell's Introduction to Networking	0-7645-4525-6	US $ 19.99	/ CAN $ 27.99

Available wherever books are sold or call 1-800-762-2974 to order today.
Outside the U.S. call 1-317-572-3993.

Novell, NetWare, GroupWise, ManageWise, Novell Directory Services and NDPS are registered trademarks; Novell Press, the Novell Press logo, NDS, Novell BorderManager, ZENworks, IPX/SPX, Clarke Notes and Novell Distributed Print Services are trademarks; CNE is a registered service mark; and CNI, CNA, Certified Internet Business Strategist, and Certified Web Designer are service marks of Novell, Inc. in the United States and other countries. All other registered trademarks and trademarks are the property of their respective owners. The IDG Books Worldwide logo is a registered trademark under exclusive license to IDG Books Worldwide, Inc., from International Data Group, Inc.

my2cents.idgbooks.com

Register This Book — And Win!

Visit **http://my2cents.idgbooks.com** to register this book and we'll automatically enter you in our fantastic monthly prize giveaway. It's also your opportunity to give us feedback: let us know what you thought of this book and how you would like to see other topics covered.

Discover IDG Books Online!

The IDG Books Online Web site is your online resource for tackling technology — at home and at the office. Frequently updated, the IDG Books Online Web site features exclusive software, insider information, online books, and live events!

10 Productive & Career-Enhancing Things You Can Do at www.idgbooks.com

- Nab source code for your own programming projects.

- Download software.

- Read Web exclusives: special articles and book excerpts by IDG Books Worldwide authors.

- Take advantage of resources to help you advance your career as a Novell or Microsoft professional.

- Buy IDG Books Worldwide titles or find a convenient bookstore that carries them.

- Register your book and win a prize.

- Chat live online with authors.

- Sign up for regular e-mail updates about our latest books.

- Suggest a book you'd like to read or write.

- Give us your 2¢ about our books and about our Web site.

You say you're not on the Web yet? It's easy to get started with IDG Books' *Discover the Internet,* available at local retailers everywhere.

CD-ROM Installation Instructions

The CD-ROM included with this book contains source code for many examples in the book as well as LDAP-related IETF documents, a working trial version each of NDS eDirectory for NetWare, Windows NT/2000, Solaris and Linux, several LDAP client SDKs, and useful utilities.

Checking the System Requirements

To use the software on the CD-ROM, you'll need Windows 95/NT and at least one of the following systems:

- Novell NetWare 5.0 or later

- Microsoft Windows NT 4.0 or later

- Solaris 2.6 with patch 105591-07

- Solaris 7 (32-bit) with patch 106327-06

- Solaris 7 (64-bit) with patch 106300-07

- Solaris 8 (no patch is required)

- Linux 2.2, glibc 2.1.3, and RPM 3.0. (Successfully tested and recommended: Red Hat 6.2)

Solaris and Linux require a minimum of 128 MB of RAM and 56 MB of disk space to install the NDS Server. Add 35 KB of disk space per 100 certificates in the replica.

NOTE

The Solaris OS patches are available at SunSolve Online (www.sunsolve.com). **Make sure that the Solaris systems used are SPARC V9 compliant.**

Accessing the Contents of the CD-ROM

To access the contents of this disk, insert it into your CD-ROM drive and use your favorite shell or file system explorer to browse the contents of the CD-ROM. Most of the directories contain files that you can simply copy or view. Instructions for installing NDS eDirectory and the SDKs are given:

▸ Examples: This directory holds source code listings from the book as well as an LDAP client application.

    • *Listings:* All of the source code and LDIF examples that are identified with a listing number are included as listings on the CD-ROM. The listings can be found under the \Examples\Listings directory. There is a directory for each chapter that has a listing, and the listings are located under subdirectories of the chapter directories. We have included both C and Java versions when possible.

    When building the C examples, you must have first installed the Novell LDAP Libraries for C. This is located in the \SDKs\C\ Novell LDAP Libraries for C directory. You must also point to the proper "include" and "lib" paths (found in the ndk\cldapsdk directory where the SDK was installed). The appropriate .DLLs and .NLMs are located in the ndk\cldapsdk\bin directory where the SDK was installed.

    When building the Java examples, you must include LDAPJDK.JAR in your classpath. This JAR file is located on the CD-ROM in the \SDKs\Java\Netscape Directory SDK for Java directory.

    • *Application:* We also included a working example in Java that shows how to build an LDAP client application. It is a schema browser and manager tool called SchemaManager and is located in the \Examples\ Application\SchemaManager directory. To run the example, include SCHEMAMANAGER.JAR, LDAPJDK.JAR, and SWING.JAR in your classpath and run javaSchemaManager. The source files for this application are in the \Examples\Application\SchemaManager\src directory.

▸ IETF Documents: We have gathered together most of the IETF documents that are related to LDAP and put them on the CD-ROM.

IETF documents use the newline character to mark the end of lines. Because the Notepad utility on Windows platforms expects a carriage return/newline pair to mark the end of lines, IETF documents do not display properly in Notepad; however, Wordpad displays them properly.

- *RFCs:* An RFC may eventually be made obsolete by a new RFC. We included the current version of the RFCs listed in Table A.1 on the CD-ROM for your convenience. They are in the \IETF Documents\ RFCs directory.

- *Internet-Drafts:* The Internet-Drafts that are related to LDAP and are current as of the time this book goes to press are listed in Table A.2 and can be found on the CD-ROM in the \IETF Documents\Internet-Drafts directory.

▸ LDIF: The LDIF file is in the \LDIF directory on the CD-ROM.

▸ NDS: As of press time, NDS eDirectory 8.5 is almost ready to ship. We included evaluation copies of the beta 5 version of NDS for Windows NT/2000, NetWare, Solaris, and Linux on the CD-ROM in the NDS directory.

Refer to Chapter 2 of the book for instructions on installing NDS. You may also find the following files helpful in getting NDS installed:

- \NDS\DOCUMENTATION\ENGLISH\NDSEDIR\ PDFDOC\QCSTAO.PDF (NetWare and Windows NT/2000)

- \NDS\SOLARIS\QUICK_START.HTM (Solaris)

- NDS\LINUX\QUICK_START.HTM (Linux)

▸ SDKs: For your convenience, we included several LDAP client SDKs on the CD-ROM. In the \SDKs\C directory, you'll find the Novell LDAP Libraries for C SDK and in the \SDKs\Java directory, we've placed two different LDAP SDKs for Java, one is the Netscape Directory SDK for Java and the other is Novell LDAP Service Provider for JNDI.

To install the Novell LDAP Libraries for C SDK or LDAP SDKs for Java, run the SETUP.EXE program from the appropriate directory. The Netscape Directory SDK for Java requires no installation; simply include LDAPJDK.JAR in your classpath.

We also included the Novell SSL for Java SDK in the \SDKs\Java\Novell SSL for Java directory that can be used to establish an SSL connection to Novell's LDAP server.

▶ Utilities: We included two useful utilities on the CD-ROM in the \Utilities directory.

- *Toolbox (for NetWare):* The Toolbox utility is a command line shell for NetWare. You can use it to perform common tasks such as listing the contents of a directory, making and removing directories, and copying, renaming, and deleting files. The toolbox utility is referenced in the "Configuring the Database Cache" section of Chapter 10.

- *Novell Import/Export Utility:* The Novell Import/Export Utility includes two user interfaces: a ConsoleOne snap-in and a command line utility. Both interfaces are installed when you install ConsoleOne, and the command line version is included in the Novell LDAP Libraries for C SDK so that developers can use it when installing their LDAP applications. We've also provided the command-line version of the utility from the latest Novell LDAP Libraries for C SDK directly on the CD-ROM so you can run the Novell Import/Export Utility directly from the CD-ROM. The utility works best when you add the directory where the ICE executable is located to your PATH environment variable.